Maximizing Your SAP® CRM Interaction Center

 **PRESS**

SAP PRESS is a joint initiative of SAP and Galileo Press. The know-how offered by SAP specialists combined with the expertise of the Galileo Press publishing house offers the reader expert books in the field. SAP PRESS features first-hand information and expert advice, and provides useful skills for professional decision-making.

SAP PRESS offers a variety of books on technical and business related topics for the SAP user. For further information, please visit our website: *www.sap-press.com*.

Srini Katta
Discover SAP CRM
2008, 406 pp.
978-1-59229-173-1

George Fratian
Planning Your SAP CRM Implementation
2008, 276 pp.
978-1-59229-096-0

Markus Kirchler and Dirk Manhart
Service with SAP CRM
2009, ~400 pp.
978-1-59229-206-6

John Burton

Maximizing Your SAP® CRM
Interaction Center

Galileo Press

Bonn • Boston

ISBN 978-1-59229-197-7

© 2009 by Galileo Press Inc., Boston (MA)

1st Edition 2009

Galileo Press is named after the Italian physicist, mathematician and philosopher Galileo Galilei (1564–1642). He is known as one of the founders of modern science and an advocate of our contemporary, heliocentric worldview. His words *Eppur si muove* (And yet it moves) have become legendary. The Galileo Press logo depicts Jupiter orbited by the four Galilean moons, which were discovered by Galileo in 1610.

Editor Meg Dunkerley
Copyeditor Lori Newhouse
Cover Design Jill Winitzer
Photo Credit photos.com
Layout Design Vera Brauner
Production Iris Warkus
Typesetting Publishers' Design and Production Services, Inc.
Printed and bound in Canada

Dedication

This book is dedicated to the Development team from SAP, who put hours of hard work, thought, and love into the SAP CRM Interaction Center product.

I would especially like to thank several individuals who put 10 years (or more) of their lives into this product:

— Michael Kuehn

— Johnnie Wilkenschildt

— Markus Wieser

Contents at a Glance

1 Introduction 21

2 Computer Telephony Integration (CTI) and Multi-Channel
   Integration 49

3 IC User Interface and Technology 81

4 IC Marketing 115

5 IC Sales 153

6 IC Service 183

7 IC Management and Analytics 221

8 Interactive Scripting 263

9 Rule Modeler and Category Modeler 295

10 Back-Office Interaction Centers for Industries and
   Shared Services 337

11 Partnerships and Certifications 367

12 Frequently Asked Questions 385

13 Conclusion 413

A SAP Partners 437

B The Author 453

Contents & Charts

Contents

Dedication 5
Acknowledgments 19

1 Introduction 21

1.1 Terminology 22
    1.1.1 Call Center, Contact Center, Interaction Center 22
    1.1.2 Interaction Center Employees – Agents, CSRs, TSRs 24
1.2 Functions of an Interaction Center 24
    1.2.1 The Interaction Center is the Front Door 24
    1.2.2 The Interaction Center is the Emergency Room 25
1.3 History and Evolution of Interaction Centers 26
    1.3.1 History of the Call Center 26
    1.3.2 From "Call Center" to "Interaction Center" 27
    1.3.3 Evolving Metrics and Mindsets 28
    1.3.4 Modern Metrics 29
    1.3.5 Leveraging Economies of Scale via Consolidated Call
          Centers 31
    1.3.6 Leveraging Efficiency via Shared Service Centers 32
    1.3.7 Outsourcing and Homesourcing 34
    1.3.8 The Typical Interaction Center 36
1.4 The SAP CRM Interaction Center 39
    1.4.1 The History of the Interaction Center 40
    1.4.2 The Interaction Center Moves from SAP GUI to the
          Web Browser 41
    1.4.3 Capabilities of the SAP CRM Interaction Center 44
1.5 Summary 48

2 Computer Telephony Integration (CTI) and Multi-Channel Integration 49

2.1 Telephony 50
    2.1.1 Queuing 51
    2.1.2 Call Treatment 51
    2.1.3 Routing 51

2.2	Computer Telephony Integration (CTI)	52
	2.2.1 Automatic Number Identification (ANI) Lookup	52
	2.2.2 Dialed Number Identification Service (DNIS)	53
	2.2.3 Interactive Voice Response (IVR) and Voice Portals	54
	2.2.4 Screen Pop	55
	2.2.5 Call-Attached Data (CAD)	57
	2.2.6 Softphone Control	57
	2.2.7 Screen Transfer	59
	2.2.8 Outbound Dialing Integration (Preview, Progressive, and Predictive/Power Dialing)	60
2.3	Multi-Channel Integration	60
	2.3.1 Email	61
	2.3.2 E-Mail Response Management System (ERMS) & Web Forms	63
	2.3.3 Fax, Letter, and SMS	64
	2.3.4 Web Chat	66
2.4	SAP's Multi-Channel Integration Strategy	69
	2.4.1 SAP's Certified Multi-Channel Interfaces	69
2.5	SAP's Multi-Channel Partners	71
	2.5.1 PBX/ACD Switches	72
	2.5.2 Communication Management Software (CMS) Products ...	74
2.6	SAP Business Communications Management (BCM)	76
2.7	Adding CTI or Multi-Channel Integration to an Existing Project ...	77
	2.7.1 Building a Business Case for CTI/Multi-Channel Integration	77
	2.7.2 Implementing CTI or Multi-Channel Integration	78
2.8	Summary	79

3	**IC User Interface and Technology**	**81**

3.1	Browser Versions and Settings	82
3.2	Interaction Center User Interface	83
	3.2.1 Title Bar	84
	3.2.2 Context Area	84
	3.2.3 Communication Toolbar	86
	3.2.4 Scratch Pad	87
	3.2.5 System Messages	88
	3.2.6 Navigation Bar & Index Page	89
	3.2.7 Breadcrumbs	92

3.2.8 Agent Dashboard 92
3.2.9 Broadcast Messaging 93
3.3 Interaction Record 94
3.4 Getting the Interaction Center Up and Running 97
3.4.1 CRM Business Role/IC WebClient Profile 98
3.4.2 Navigation Bar 100
3.4.3 Transaction Launcher 103
3.4.4 HR Organizational Model 107
3.5 Architecture and Technology 108
3.5.1 BOL/GenIL 108
3.5.2 BSP Applications 109
3.6 Summary 112

4 IC Marketing 115

4.1 Campaigns 116
4.2 Call Lists and Planned Activities 120
4.2.1 Call List Creation 121
4.2.2 Planned Activities Creation 124
4.2.3 Processing Call Lists from the Interaction Center 126
4.2.4 Do Not Call List Integration 129
4.3 Outbound Dialing 131
4.3.1 Manual Outbound Dialing 133
4.3.2 Preview Dialing/Auto Dialing 133
4.3.3 Power Dialing/Progressive Dialing 134
4.3.4 Predictive Dialing 134
4.4 Interactive Scripting 135
4.5 Questionnaire/Survey and Lead Integration 136
4.5.1 Survey Integration 137
4.5.2 Lead Integration 138
4.6 Marketing-Based Product Proposals 142
4.6.1 Maintaining Accessories and Spare Parts (Service Parts) 143
4.6.2 Maintaining Cross-Sellers, Up-Sellers, and Down-Sellers ... 145
4.6.3 Using Product Proposals in the Interaction Center 148
4.7 SAP Real-Time Offer Management (RTOM) 149
4.8 Summary 150

5	IC Sales	153

5.1	Leads and Opportunities	155
5.2	Searching for Products	157
	5.2.1 Standard Product Search	158
	5.2.2 Product Catalog	161
	5.2.3 Add-to-Cart Button and Product List Preview	165
5.3	IC Sales Transactions	166
	5.3.1 Sales Order for Interaction Center	166
	5.3.2 Sales Ticket for Interaction Center	168
	5.3.3 PC-UI Sales Order	170
	5.3.4 R/3 Sales Order for Interaction Center	171
	5.3.5 ERP Sales Order for Interaction Center	172
	5.3.6 CRM WebClient ERP Sales Order	173
	5.3.7 CRM WebClient Sales Order	175
5.4	Configurable Products	176
5.5	Product Proposals	178
5.6	Available-to-Promise (ATP) and Pricing	180
5.7	Summary	181

6	IC Service	183

6.1	About Help Desks	184
6.2	Information Help Desk	184
	6.2.1 Customer Identification and Registration	186
	6.2.2 Product Identification and Registration	189
	6.2.3 Customer Overview and Details	193
	6.2.4 Knowledge Search	197
6.3	Service Order Management	204
	6.3.1 IC Service Order	205
6.4	Service Desk (for External Customers)	208
6.5	Complaint Management	212
6.6	Case Management	216
6.7	A Few Words About Self Service	219
6.8	Summary	220

7   IC Management and Analytics **221**

7.1   Monitoring Operations 224
    7.1.1   Business Transaction Assignment 224
    7.1.2   IC Manager Dashboard 226
    7.1.3   E-Mail Status Overview & E-Mail Volume 229
7.2   Managing Operations 233
    7.2.1   Business Transaction Assignment 233
    7.2.2   E-Mail Workbench 234
    7.2.3   ERMS Simulator 236
    7.2.4   Business Role Assignment 239
    7.2.5   E-Mail Status Overview 239
    7.2.6   Broadcast Messaging 240
    7.2.7   Call List Generation 241
7.3   Knowledge Management 242
    7.3.1   Categorization Schemas 243
    7.3.2   Document Templates 244
    7.3.3   Mail Forms 244
    7.3.4   SDB Detailed Feedback 246
    7.3.5   SDB Usage Report 248
    7.3.6   SAF Compilation Administration 248
7.4   Process Modeling 250
    7.4.1   Alerts 250
    7.4.2   Rule Policies 252
    7.4.3   Interactive Script Editor 252
    7.4.4   Scripting Evaluation 252
7.5   Reports 254
    7.5.1   Service Ticket Reports 255
    7.5.2   Live Interaction Reports 257
    7.5.3   E-Mail Reports 258
    7.5.4   Blended Analytics 259
    7.5.5   Intent-Driven Interaction 259
7.6   Dashboards 259
7.7   Summary 260

8   Interactive Scripting **263**

8.1   Interactive Script Editor 264
    8.1.1   Accessing the Interactive Script Editor 265

8.1.2   Working with the Interactive Script Editor 265

8.1.3   Creating Scripts 270

8.1.4   Creating Objection Scripts 273

8.1.5   Transporting Scripts 274

8.2   Launching Interactive Scripts in the Interaction Center 275

8.2.1   Manual Selection of Scripts 276

8.2.2   Automatically Launching Scripts 277

8.3   Using Interactive Scripts in the Interaction Center 285

8.3.1   Questions and Answers 286

8.3.2   Objection Scripts 287

8.3.3   Updating Master Data and Marketing Attributes 288

8.3.4   Survey Integration 289

8.3.5   Creating and Qualifying Leads 290

8.3.6   Chat Integration 292

8.3.7   Transferring Scripts 292

8.4   Summary 293

9   Rule Modeler and Category Modeler 295

9.1   Rule Modeler 296

9.2   E-Mail Response Management System (ERMS) 299

9.2.1   Send Auto Acknowledgement 300

9.2.2   Auto Respond 301

9.2.3   Auto Prepare 303

9.2.4   Routing Actions 304

9.2.5   Integrating ERMS with Web Forms 310

9.3   Order Routing (Ticket Dispatching/Escalation) 312

9.4   Intent-Driven Interaction (IDI) 315

9.4.1   Triggering and Terminating Alerts 319

9.4.2   Launching Scripts 320

9.4.3   Navigation 321

9.4.4   Additional Actions 323

9.5   Category Modeler 324

9.5.1   Multi-Level Categorization of Business Transactions 328

9.5.2   Interaction Center Automation Using Categorization
        Schemas 331

9.6   Summary 334

10 Back-Office Interaction Centers for Industries and Shared Services **337**

10.1 Shared Service Centers 338
    10.1.1 IT Help Desk 339
    10.1.2 Employee Interaction Center 346
    10.1.3 Accounting Interaction Center (Consulting Solution) 351
10.2 Industry Solutions 354
    10.2.1 Interaction Center for Utilities 354
    10.2.2 Telco Interaction Center 358
    10.2.3 Insurance Interaction Center (Consulting Solution) 361
    10.2.4 Automotive Interaction Center 361
10.3 Summary 364

11 Partnerships and Certifications **367**

11.1 Types of SAP Partnerships and Certifications 368
    11.1.1 SAP Software Solution Partners 368
    11.1.2 SAP Service Partners 371
11.2 Contact Center Infrastructure Partners 373
    11.2.1 Genesys Telecommunications Laboratories 374
    11.2.2 Avaya Inc. 374
    11.2.3 SAP Business Communications Management (BCM) Software 375
11.3 Workforce Optimization Partners 376
    11.3.1 Verint Systems 377
11.4 Systems Integration/Consulting Partners 378
    11.4.1 ecenta 378
    11.4.2 Axon Consulting 379
    11.4.3 The Principal Consulting (TPC) 379
    11.4.4 Sparta Consulting 380
    11.4.5 iServiceGlobe 380
    11.4.6 MindTree Consulting 380
    11.4.7 EoZen 381
    11.4.8 enapsys 381
    11.4.9 SAP Consulting 382
    11.4.10 The "Big 5" 382
11.5 Summary 383

12 Frequently Asked Questions 385

12.1 User Interface and Framework Questions 385
    12.1.1 Browsers That are Supported 386
    12.1.2 Windows Vista Support 386
    12.1.3 Interaction Center Requirement for a J2EE Server 386
    12.1.4 JRE Requirements 387
    12.1.5 ActiveX Browser Plug-Ins 387
    12.1.6 Extranets, VPNs, and Firewalls 387
    12.1.7 WinClient or WebClient 388
    12.1.8 WebDynpro Usage or Future Plans 388
    12.1.9 Spell-Check Integration 388
12.2 Migration/Upgrade Questions 389
    12.2.1 Effort Required to Migrate from WinClient to WebClient 389
    12.2.2 WinClient Availability in CRM 2006s/CRM 2007 390
    12.2.3 PC-UI Availability in CRM 2006s/CRM 2007 390
    12.2.4 Effort Required to Upgrade from CRM 2005 to CRM
             2006s/CRM 2007 390
    12.2.5 Automated Tool for Converting PC-UI Screens to BSP 391
    12.2.6 Problem/Solution Maintenance in WebClient 392
    12.2.7 Call List Maintenance in WebClient 392
12.3 Performance and Benchmarking Questions 392
    12.3.1 High-Volume IC Customers 393
    12.3.2 System Performance of IC WebClient Compared to IC
             WinClient 394
    12.3.3 Performance Benchmark Tests 394
12.4 CTI Questions 394
    12.4.1 Certified CTI Hardware (PBX/ACD) and Software 395
    12.4.2 How to Configure CTI 395
    12.4.3 How to Identify Account via Call Attached Data (CAD) ... 396
    12.4.4 How to Configure the CCSUI Tool 397
    12.4.5 SAPphone or ICI 397
12.5 ITIL and IT Service Desk Questions 398
    12.5.1 ITIL Certification 398
    12.5.2 Interaction Center or Solution Manager 398
    12.5.3 Business Process Outsourcing 399
12.6 Workforce Management (WFM) Questions 399
    12.6.1 SAP and Workforce Management (WFM) Functionality .. 400

12.6.2 The Size of an Interaction Center That Needs WFM 400

12.6.3 Call/Screen Recording or Quality Monitoring
Functionality 400

12.7 "Which One Should We Choose" Questions 401

12.7.1 Employee Interaction Center: CRM or HCM 401

12.7.2 CRM Billing or ERP Billing 402

12.7.3 Interaction Record, Service Ticket, Service Order,
Complaint, Case 403

12.7.4 Creation or Suppression of the Interaction Record 404

12.7.5 Sales Order, Sales Ticket, ERP Sales Order, R/3 Sales
Order 405

12.7.6 Alerts, System Messages, Broadcast Messages 407

12.7.7 JavaScript or ABAP for Multi-Level Categorization 408

12.7.8 IC Knowledge Search or SAP NetWeaver Knowledge
Management 408

12.8 Bonus: Top 20 SAP Notes for the Interaction Center 409

12.9 Summary 410

13 Conclusion 413

13.1 Real Customers, Real (Short) Stories 413

13.1.1 ICICI Prudential AMC, Presented by MindTree 414

13.1.2 Sloan Valve Company, presented by Sloan Valve
Company 416

13.1.3 "CAD-CAM Systems," Presented by ecenta 417

13.1.4 Data Domain Presented by ecenta 419

13.1.5 Eclipse Aviation, Presented by Eclipse Aviation 420

13.2 A Case Study: Portugal Telecom 421

13.2.1 Service Ticket Processing 422

13.3 SAP Future Roadmap and Strategy 428

13.3.1 Upgrade Strategy 429

13.3.2 CRM 2007 Interaction Center New Features 431

13.3.3 SAP Roadmap for the Interaction Center 433

13.3.4 SAP Long-Term Future Strategy of the
Interaction Center 435

13.4 Thank You! 436

Appendices 437

A   SAP Partners 439
     A.1   Avaya 439
         A.1.1   Company Overview 439
         A.1.2   Value Proposition 440
         A.1.3   Core Areas of Expertise 440
     A.2   Axon Consulting 442
         A.2.1   Company Overview 442
         A.2.2   Value Proposition 442
     A.3   ecenta 443
         A.3.1   Company Overview 443
         A.3.2   Value Proposition 443
         A.3.3   Core Areas of Expertise 444
         A.3.4   Core Industries 445
     A.4   enapsys 445
         A.4.1   Company Overview 445
         A.4.2   Value Proposition 446
         A.4.3   Core Industries 446
     A.5   EoZen 447
         A.5.1   Company Overview 447
         A.5.2   Value Proposition 447
         A.5.3   Core Areas of Expertise 448
     A.6   Genesys 448
         A.6.1   Company Overview 448
         A.6.2   Core Areas of Expertise 448
     A.7   MindTree 449
         A.7.1   Company Overview 449
         A.7.2   Value Proposition 449
         A.7.3   Core Areas of Expertise 449
         A.7.4   Core Industries 451
B   The Author 453

Index 455

Acknowledgments

I would like to thank the following experts who directly contributed to the book by providing content or sharing their industry knowledge and insights:

- Tim Bolte
- Mike Burianek
- Donghua Chen
- Shridhar Deshpande
- Henning Duerholt
- Bruno Garcia
- Juergen Kuhmann
- Frederic Laruelle
- Glenn Michaels
- Kevin Munkres
- Satit Nuchitsiripattara
- Mike Petrosh
- Rohit Raturi
- Gert Tackaert
- Micha Van Nijen
- Amit Venugopal
- Thorsten Wewers
- Renee Wilhelm

And, of course, I want to provide super-extra-special thanks to my wife, Amy (and my one-year old son, John Paul), for tolerating the fact that daddy spent every free minute during the past months sitting at his desk typing away at the computer — while living off jelly beans and Diet Mountain Dew.

This chapter will introduce you to the concept of interaction centers – explaining what they are, what they do, and how they can support your overall CRM strategy.

1 Introduction

You can think of the interaction center as the *virtual* front door of any company or organization — inviting customers to come in and do business. Obviously, if the front door is closed or if there is a long line (or *queue*, as we say in the interaction center world) customers are likely to go someplace else to do business. Hence, the interaction center is of critical importance in maintaining healthy customer relationships. Companies rely on interaction centers to facilitate meaningful *business transactions* with customers, such as resolving customer service issues, generating sales leads, processing sales orders, handling complaints and returns, and so on.

This chapter introduces you to the basic concepts of interaction centers, including common usages, technologies, metrics, and trends. We'll discuss the role of the interaction center in providing employees with access to the tools and functionality they need to deliver world-class customer service. And while service is understandably the most frequent focus of interaction center projects, we'll also examine how the interaction center supports marketing and sales projects. We'll introduce you to some of the most common usages of the interaction center including help desk, service desk, IT help desk, telemarketing, telesales, employee interaction center, accounting interaction center, and so on.

Chapter 2 will discuss computer telephony integration (CTI) in great depth. However, in Chapter 1 we'll introduce basic telephony technologies such as the PBX and ACD, and touch on the historical (and continuing) importance of telephony in the interaction center — while also covering more contemporary technologies such as email and Web chat. We'll discuss historic and contemporary metrics for evaluating and running interaction centers, and go over the important trends that are making news in the interaction center world today, including consolidation, outsourcing, homesourcing, VoIP, virtual agents, shared service centers, business process outsourcing, and so on. Finally, we'll introduce the SAP CRM Interaction

Center and briefly discuss its history and current capabilities. In sum, we'll explain what the interaction center is, what it does, and how the SAP CRM Interaction Center can be used to support your end-to-end CRM strategy.

1.1 Terminology

Before we proceed, it will be helpful to first discuss some terminology. Many readers are understandably confused by all the different terms that seem to describe the same thing: call center, contact center, e-contact center, interaction center, customer interaction center, customer interaction hub, customer care center, and so on. In addition, the employees who work in these organizations are often referred to by different terms: agents, reps, TSRs, CSRs, and so on. So let's take a minute to agree on some terminology.

1.1.1 Call Center, Contact Center, Interaction Center

Although almost every software vendor and analyst has their own preferred terminology, the three most widely used terms to describe software that allows customers to interact with companies are: *call center, contact center,* and *interaction center*. In theory, each of these three terms has its own subtle connotation and nuance, as explained below.

The term *Call Center* usually has a very specific connotation, implying that an organization handles only telephone calls, as opposed to other forms of multimedia communication such as email or Web chat (we'll refer to this simply as "chat" from here on). Sometimes when used in a more classical vernacular, the term "call center" denotes an organization that only handles inbound telephone calls — typically in a very high-volume, short-call duration setting often associated with industries such as airline reservations, retail catalog sales, magazine subscriptions, and Telecommunications (abbreviated simply as Telco) services.

For example, some old-school call-center purists might suggest that the term "call center" should only apply to organizations that have over 10,000 concurrent telephone agents, spending less than three minutes per call, processing over 100,000 calls per hour (25 calls per second). In general, call centers (as opposed to interaction centers) typically have limited or no integration to front-office Customer Relationship Management (CRM) and back-office Enterprise Resource Planning (ERP) business applications, with the exception of standalone contact management, calendar management, account management, or order entry applications.

The term *Contact Center* is a more modern term that refers to a department within an organization that communicates with customers (and other business partners) via multimedia communications channels beyond simple telephony including — for example — email, chat, or Voice over Internet Protocol (VoIP). This is currently the preferred term by industry vendors and analysts. It has been adopted more than the similar terms e-contact center, customer care center, or customer interaction hub. In general, contact centers usually have at least some integration to other standalone business applications, including contact management, calendar management, account management, trouble-ticketing, and knowledge management — although the integration is not as robust as with an interaction center.

The term *Interaction Center* is used by CRM and customer service software vendors to refer to customer-facing business applications that enable companies to interact with customers to resolve business issues such as providing product information, creating sales orders, generating service requests, handling complaints and returns, and so on. The term "interaction center" implies that the organization is doing more than just taking telephone calls or contacting customers. In general, interaction centers provide full integration to all front-office CRM and back-office ERP applications, including full customer service and order management.

The above terms are often used interchangeably and indiscriminately, causing confusion for those who recognize the subtle nuances. For example, when someone uses the term "call center," you can never be sure whether they are using the classical definition and referring to an organization that deals specifically with *telephone calls only*, or whether they are referring generically to any kind of organization that communicates with customers *regardless of the channel*.

In this book, we'll use the SAP-preferred term "interaction center" and avoid the terms "contact center" and "call center," except when referring specifically to telecommunications systems that don't have CRM capabilities. We'll use the lowercase spelling (i.e., interaction center) when referring to interaction centers generically, while we'll use capitalization (i.e., Interaction Center) when referring to the capabilities of the SAP CRM Interaction Center specifically.

1.1.2 Interaction Center Employees – Agents, CSRs, TSRs

The employees who work in interaction centers answering telephone calls, emails, and chat messages are commonly referred to as *interaction center agents*, or "agents" for short. In the interaction center agents are also sometimes referred to as Customer Service Representatives (CSRs) or Telephone Sales Representatives (TSRs) depending on the job function they perform. In this book, we will use the term "interaction center agent," or sometimes just "agent" for brevity.

1.2 Functions of an Interaction Center

As mentioned earlier, an interaction center is the *virtual* front door of a company. Interaction centers are typically departments within companies that handle inbound and/or outbound communications with customers, channel partners, and employees. This communication can occur via various communication channels including telephone, email, chat, Voice over Internet Protocol (VoIP), fax, postal letter, and so on. Most communication has occurred traditionally primarily via telephone. While telephone is still the dominate means of communication today, usage of other channels such as email, chat, and VoIP is steadily increasing.

> **Note**
>
> Recent studies have shown that the majority of interaction centers accept email in addition to telephone calls, but that telephone is still used as the primary communication channel. For example, the 2007 Aspect Software Contact Center Satisfaction Index (North America) found that 73% of customer interactions still take place via telephone rather than email or chat. Chat in particular is still not widely used. Historically, less than 10% of interaction centers utilize chat.

1.2.1 The Interaction Center is the Front Door

Companies use interaction centers for a variety of communication and business needs, such as:

- Answering questions
- Taking orders
- Providing customer service and support

An interaction center is typically included as part of a larger CRM program at a company, designed to help the company better understand and manage its customer relationships in order to increase customer satisfaction, loyalty, and profitability. Although there are other business channels that customers can use to interact with a company outside of the interaction center (e.g., retail store, stand-alone kiosk, self-service website, automated telephone system, and so on), the interaction center is the most powerful business channel for delivering and supporting a company's integrated marketing, sales, and service efforts. It is the only business channel that provides a full-service customer experience based on a 360-degree complete overview of the customer's information and history, combining the warmth, decision-making capability, and sales skills of properly trained and empowered human beings.

Companies use the interaction center not just to acquire new customers, but also to grow those newly acquired customers into life-long profitable customers, and protect long-term profitable customers from defecting to lower-priced competitors. Companies also sometimes use the interaction center to deal with other types of channel partners as well, including suppliers, distributors, value-added resellers (VARs), and other third-party vendors. Companies even use the interaction center *internally* to provide consistent, personalized communications with their own employees for a variety of topics including human resources (HR), information technology (IT) and accounting issues. For example, an employee who has a question about their paycheck, medical benefits, or vacation requests can contact a human resources person via an HR employee interaction center (EIC). Similarly, an employee having a technical problem with their computer could call the internal IT help desk for support.

1.2.2   The Interaction Center is the Emergency Room

In addition to serving as the virtual front door of a company, in many respects the interaction center is also like a hospital emergency room (ER). Similar to a hospital ER, the interaction center is a fast-paced, unpredictable environment where customers can come in at any second screaming for immediate attention. In fact, customer service — or call triage — is one of the primary uses of interaction centers.

To better understand the critical role that the interaction center plays within a company's customer service organization, continue to think of the customer-service organization as a hospital, and the interaction center as the ER. For example, a customer contacts a company when he has a question or a problem with a product, much like a patient visits a hospital for a check-up or treatment. The interaction center agents are similar to the ER doctors, standing by to triage patients.

While interaction center agents obviously don't wear hospital scrubs or perform actual life-saving operations, they do often work in very traumatic, fast-paced environments where every second counts. Impatient customers want issues resolved immediately, and cost-focused companies (like cost-focused insurance companies and hospitals) want agents to process as many customer issues as possible, and to resolve every issue as fast as possible to minimize service-related costs.

1.3 History and Evolution of Interaction Centers

One could argue that early call centers were enabled (and perhaps also defined) by technological innovation, specifically by a specific product known as the automatic call distributor (ACD). An ACD is a device that is capable of queuing incoming telephone calls (when no agent is immediately available to answer the call), playing announcements and on-hold music (also known as "call treatment"), and routing calls to the agents who have been idle the longest (or to the first agent who becomes available in case all agents are currently busy). Basically, an ACD is a *workflow engine* for telephone calls. Before the advent of the ACD, companies had to rely on in-house telephone switchboards known as private branch exchanges (PBXs) that were connected to an external network of telephone lines and central offices known as the public switched telephone network (PSTN). The PBX allowed incoming telephone calls from customers to be manually routed to specific telephone lines, staffed, of course, by agents. According to call-center historians, Continental Airlines initially asked AT&T to develop a device that could be used to automatically route calls to available agents. Reportedly, AT&T wasn't confident that there was a big enough market for such a product at the time and declined; instead, a company named Rockwell International (who had recently merged with another company named Collins Radio) developed the first digital ACD — the Rockwell Galaxy — in 1973.

1.3.1 History of the Call Center

Where did call centers — the early-day predecessor to contact centers and interaction centers — come from? Like many unsolved mysteries of the world (Atlantis, Stonehenge, pyramids, crop circles) no one knows for certain where the first call centers originated. Industry experts agree that modern-day interaction centers probably evolved from airline flight-reservation systems and telephone operator switchboards used in the 1960s and 1970s.

One technological innovation that played a major role in the use of call centers for outbound telemarketing and telesales was the invention of the *automated dialer*. Automated dialers, as their name suggests, help automate the process of placing outbound telephone calls to customers or prospects. Automated dialers are also referred to sometimes as predictive dialers, although technically predictive dialing is only one type of automated dialing. In general, automated dialing can be done in one of three modes, including preview dialing, progressive/power dialing, or predictive dialing. These modes are explained in detail in Chapter 2. Automated dialers were first used by banks for telemarketing and collections purposes. By automating the process of dialing outbound calls and by screening out busy signals, unanswered calls, and answering machines, the automated dialer greatly increased the efficiency of outbound telesales and telemarketing agents within the call center.

The first use of call centers for inbound *customer service* processes probably began in the United States in the 1970s and 1980s with telephone companies (AT&T and Bell), airlines, and insurance agencies. Clearly, customers needed a way to check and change airline reservations, dispute phone bills, and file insurance claims. While these activities could of course also be done in person, for example at a branch office, there are benefits to both the customer and the company of enabling these customer service activities via telephone. For customers, it is faster and more convenient to pick up the telephone than to drive to the nearest service center; for companies, it can be much cheaper to provide customer service via telephone than in person, thanks to outsourcing of call center jobs to locations where worker salaries are cheaper. While the above examples involved the first use of call centers for customer service, they did not yet qualify however as true *interaction centers*.

1.3.2   From "Call Center" to "Interaction Center"

There are a number of distinctions between call centers, contact centers, and interaction centers. Cleary, one obvious distinction is that call centers, by definition, only handle one type of communication (telephone calls), while contact centers and interaction centers can handle multimedia communication including telephony, email, chat, and so on. Another distinction is that call centers and contact centers typically have very limited (if any) integration with business software applications — with contact centers typically having more integration than call centers, though usually only to a few front-office programs such as contact management, calendar/appointment management, or trouble-ticketing applications. Interaction centers, on the other hand, usually provide full integration to front-end CRM applications (marketing campaign management, sales force automation, trouble-ticketing, case management, complaint management, and so on) as well as to back-end ERP applications (order management, accounting and finance, service and asset management, and so on).

1.3.3 Evolving Metrics and Mindsets

Now that you are familiar with the history of interaction centers, let's move forward and discuss recent trends in the evolution of the contemporary, modern-day interaction center. Companies have historically viewed customer service and interaction centers as a necessary cost of doing business, because customer service departments acted as *cost centers* — incurring costs without directly contributing to bottom-line revenue and profits. Companies understandably then wanted to keep customer service costs as low as possible, in order to maximize profits and shareholder value. With the majority (60% or more) of costs associated with running an interaction tied directly to agent salaries, companies have historically instructed agents to work as fast as possible, spending as little time on the necessary in order to keep costs down. As will be explained in Chapter 2, this is where many classic — though increasingly antiquated — interaction center metrics (such as average handling time) originated.

Even today, companies of course still recognize the need to control costs and maximize profits. However, the attitudes that companies express toward customer service and interaction centers have started to change. Ironically, as organizations face continual pressure to come up with new ways to increase revenues, reduce costs, and deliver larger profits, companies have started to realize that interaction centers can in fact help contribute to revenue and profits — via up-selling, cross-selling, and customer retention — rather than acting as mere cost centers.

The basic concept is that after the agent satisfactorily answers the customer's question or resolves the customer's service-related issue, the agent can offer the customer additional, related products and services such as accessories or extended service contracts. In theory, a customer is much more likely to accept these well-timed and relevant offers than if a sales person were to cold call, email, or send postal mail to a customer with an unsolicited offer. Additionally, by spending a little more time with each customer to ensure the customer is happy rather than rushing to get the customer off the phone, companies are more likely to retain or save unhappy customers who would otherwise churn and defect to a competitor. Thus, the company protects a source of future revenue stream.

Not only have companies changed their interaction-center focus from cost-savings to revenue-generation and customer retention, but they have also changed the metrics by which they evaluate interaction centers and agents. Rather than focusing on operational metrics that measure, for example, how quickly the agent answers the phone and then gets customer off the phone — today's interaction centers are switching their focus to performance metrics.

▸ How efficiently the agent resolves customer issues on the first interaction, known *first contact resolution (FCR)* rate

▸ How effectively the agent up-sells and cross-sells, as measured by *sales revenue*

▸ How proficiently the agent is at persuading unhappy customers to stay with the company, known as *save/retention rate*

▸ The value of any particular customer or prospect to the company, known as *customer lifetime value (CLV)*

1.3.4 Modern Metrics

Let's look at some of these more modern metrics in detail. One increasingly commonly used metric is the concept of *First Call Resolution* or *First Contact Resolution* (FCR). This metric measures the percentage of customer issues where the company is able to successfully resolve the customer's issue via the first telephone call, email, or chat. Studies have shown that a customer would much rather contact a company once for any given issue than call back or email repeatedly for the same issue; this is true even if the company needs to transfer the customer to another queue, or even (surprisingly) if the company needs to put the customer on hold until the appropriate expert is available to resolve the issue. Customers would rather wait a few minutes and get the right answer the first time than to have to contact the company multiple times to get an issue resolved.

Another new metric that interaction centers are utilizing is the concept of *cross-sell revenue* within customer service interactions. The idea is that after successfully answering the customer's question or resolving their service issue, the agent has an ideal opportunity to extend the company's relationship with the customer by offering additional related products or services such as accessories, replacements items, or extended service contracts. Even though such efforts require additional time and extend the duration — and therefore also the cost — of an interaction, the incremental sales revenue usually exceeds the incremental costs of the extended interaction and often even turns a costly service interaction into a profitable sales interaction.

An additional metric that interaction centers have started to adopt is the concept of *customer save/retention rate*. This metric is often measured as the percentage of customers who expressed some indication that they wanted to end their business relationship with the company, but who were ultimately convinced to continue doing business with the company. In some companies, there is a special group of agents often known as "retention agents," who specialize in resolving customer issues and complaints, overcoming customer objections, and otherwise convincing customers to give the company another chance. In theory this is a very useful process — both to the customer and the company. The company gets a second chance to retain an unhappy customer who would otherwise defect to a competitor. An unhappy customer receives the attention of an empowered customer advocate who has the authority to rectify the mistakes the company has made and offer the customer an apology as well as an appropriate retention offer (such as discounted service, free upgrade, free product, and so on). However, in actual practice, many companies have been accused of going too far with their retention efforts. Customers have complained that retention agents refuse to take "no" for an answer and use intimidation or abusive language to prevent customers from trying to end their business relationship with the company. Several high-profile cases became public after understandably upset customers recorded their conversations with abusive agents and then posted the transcripts and recordings on the Internet.

Another new metric that interaction centers are embracing is the concept of Customer Lifetime Value (CLV) — a metric that attempts to measure the value of a customer or prospect over their entire lifetime with the company, including a prediction of future potential sales revenue. The concept of Customer Lifetime Value originated in the magazine subscription industry and spread to most other industries. In theory, this metric calculates how much money an existing customer or prospect is worth (in today's dollars), allowing marketing and customer service departments to decide how much money and effort should be spent to acquire or retain a customer or prospect. This metric underscores the fact that new customers are both more expensive to acquire than existing customers and less profitable than existing customers.

The driving force behind these new metrics is the high costs of sales required to capture new customers in tough, competitive markets. Because it is generally five to ten times cheaper to sell to an existing customer than to acquire a new customer, companies are focusing their efforts on retaining their most valuable customers. Additionally, companies have also started increasing their efforts to sell incremental products and services to existing customers, such as accessories, extended service contracts, product or service bundles, or upgraded services and packages.

1.3.5 Leveraging Economies of Scale via Consolidated Call Centers

Historically, companies with telephony-only call centers have tended to create very large call centers in a single location to leverage economies of scale in order to improve their ability to forecast telephone call volumes and schedule agents. One of the challenges of operating a call center is that it is never possible to perfectly predict when customers are going to call. There are of course general guidelines depending on the industry and other factors like hours of operation, geographic location, and so on. For example, in general, across all industries and geographic locations, mornings and lunch time tend to be the busiest periods with call volume falling off in the late afternoon. Similarly, more calls tend to arrive at the beginning of the week on Monday morning than at the end of the week on late Friday afternoon. (Figure 1.1).

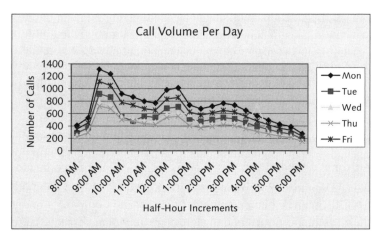

Figure 1.1 Call Volumes Per Day, Per Half-Hour Increments

In addition to these general guidelines, there are also various mathematical models and sophisticated computer software packages that can attempt to predict call volumes. In the past, Erlang Traffic Model equations (of which *Erlang C* is the most famous) worked quite well in traditional inbound telephony-only call centers. However, Erlang has lost relevance in today's interaction centers, which blend inbound and outbound dialing, support multiple communication channels, and leverage skills-based routing. Today, powerful computer software packages called workforce management (WFM) applications are used to more accurately forecast inbound call volumes down to half-hour increments.

Despite powerful tools such as Erlang equations and WFM applications, it is never possible to predict *exactly* when customers are going to contact you. Although Erlang equations and WFM applications do a very good job of predicting call volume down to increments of time as short as a half hour, calls tend to arrive somewhat randomly within those half half-hour blocks — often in clusters or bunches, rather than in a smooth evenly distributed flow. In order to answer each call within a desired amount of time (e.g., within 20 seconds), interaction centers would need to staff more agents than would be otherwise required to handle the calls if the calls arrived in a smooth, evenly-spaced fashion.

Companies realized that they could mitigate the effects of this randomization by taking advantage of economies of scale, as mathematically, larger call centers are less susceptible to small variations in incoming call volume because there are more agents handling calls, and thus a greater chance that at least one agent will be free and available to take an incoming call. Hence, one large call center is more effective than several smaller call centers.

> **Note**
>
> If you are deeply interested in understanding the mathematics behind inbound call distribution and Erlang equations, you might enjoy the book, *Call Center Mathematics: A scientific method for understanding and improving contact centers* (Ger Koole, 2007), which can be downloaded for free from *http://www.math.vu.nl/~koole/ccmath/*.

1.3.6   Leveraging Efficiency via Shared Service Centers

While consolidation for the sake of efficiency gains was a driving force in old-fashioned single-channel (telephony-only) call centers, a newer trend has emerged in today's modern multi-channel, blended interaction centers. Companies today are consolidating their interaction centers in order to create global shared service centers — globally centralized interaction centers that perform back-office functions such as IT help desk, HR help desk, accounting/finance help desk, facilities management help desk, or travel help desk. For example, rather than maintaining several physical IT help desks locations (e.g., one in North America, one in Europe, and one in Asia) companies are consolidating to single, centralized technologies and (often "low cost") locations.

While shared service centers are definitely about reducing redundancy and costs, there is more involved than just outsourcing to low-cost locations. While the previous move by call centers toward consolidation was driven by efforts to level out incoming call-volume fluctuation, the shared services center trend is being driven by the desire to not only reduce redundancy but to also harness synergies and collective expertise. Companies have discovered that they can use today's modern technologies like the Internet, VoIP, and IP-based telephony and video streaming to facilitate information sharing across the globe. It is no longer necessary to have a separate interaction center location serving each geographic region. Companies have realized that they can consolidate disparate regional operations into a single centralized (or virtually centralized) interaction center.

An interesting difference between globally consolidated shared service centers and regionally dedicated interaction centers involves how the interaction center is funded and how services are billed. In a shared service center, variable costs are often charged directly to the internal departments or organization within the company that consume the services (while the fixed costs are shared by everyone). Whereas in non-shared service interaction centers, all costs (both fixed and variable) are typically charged to a fixed budget allocated directly to the interaction center. Thus, one of the advantages of shared service centers over regional interaction centers is that the costs of services can be more accurately charged to the groups who actually consume the services.

Additionally, companies can even extend this cost-allocation model outside the company, offering services to other companies via business process outsourcing (BPO). For example, the German chemical company, BASF, runs a shared service center that offers IT, HR, and accounting services both internally to users of BASF as well as externally to users of other companies. Companies often will spin these shared service centers off as separate corporate entities, offering services to other companies, sometimes even including competitors. Such was the case, for example, when American Airlines spun off their SABER passenger-reservations operations, which now provide reservations for various airlines as well as railways, hotels, and travel agents.

1.3.7 Outsourcing and Homesourcing

In addition to changing the way that companies consolidate and organize their interaction centers, companies are also changing their strategies around where they locate their interaction centers and how they structure their employee workforce. Over the past 30 years, there was a consistent trend toward outsourcing and relocating interaction centers to areas with low-cost labor. For example, many North American companies moved their interaction centers overseas to places in Asia such as India or the Philippines that had a large pool of highly educated English-speaking labor, at a comparatively lower cost.

Challenges with Outsourcing

In recent years however, the cost-differential has eroded in these locations as the supply of skilled labor in such countries has decreased while salaries have increased. European companies have also historically taken advantage of outsourcing, setting up interaction centers in lower-cost countries outside the European Union such as Morocco, Kenya, South Africa, China, Romania (who joined the EU in January 2007), and so on. Other companies chose not to outsource but rather elected to move their interaction center locations to lower-cost, sometimes rural, areas within their own countries or regions. In the United States, for example, many interaction centers are located in areas outside of high-cost markets like Silicon Valley or New York City, such as Tucson and Phoenix (Arizona), Albuquerque (New Mexico), Boise (Idaho), and Omaha (Nebraska).

Despite the cost-savings opportunities provided by outsourcing and off-shoring, many companies are actually moving their interaction centers back to the geographic areas where their customers are located. This trend has been driven by a number of factors, one of which is customer backlash. For example, many US customers have complained about the difficulty of communicating with offshore agents who are not familiar with American culture and who speak British English rather than American English. A March 2006 study by GMI/NetReflector found that the top complaint US customers have about interaction centers is bad foreign accents, placing substantially ahead of other complaints such as receiving rude service or having to wait too long on hold. Similarly, a 2007 report released by the CFI Group from Ann Arbor, Michigan, found that customers who believed they interacted with agents located outside the United States rated their overall satisfaction much lower than customers who believed they interacted with US agents and were almost twice as likely to discontinue business relations with the company.

Even though offshore agents may speak the same language as the customer base that they are serving, customers are sensitive to subtle differences in foreign accents, dialects, and figures of speech. Though the majority of interaction center agents in India have university degrees and speak superb British English, non-Indian customers sometimes have trouble communicating with these agents. For example, unless agents have watched a lot of Western cowboy movies they probably have little idea what is meant by regional North American phrases such as "all hat and no cattle," "riding the gravy train with biscuit wheels," or "happy as a hog in the slops."

Other factors besides language and cultural differences are also driving organizations to reclaim their off-shored interaction center operations including rising costs of outsourcing due to wage increases and labor supply decreases, quality issues with outsourced interaction centers, and general lack of oversight and control over outsourced operations based overseas in other time zones. Many companies are rethinking their use of outsourcing, deciding to bring some or all of their outsourced interaction center positions back to their home markets.

In the United States, several well-known companies such as Apple, AT&T, Coca-Cola, and Dell have either cancelled plans to outsource, set up new interaction centers in the US, or brought formerly outsourced operations back to the US. For example, in 2006 AT&T shut down an interaction center in India and brought 2,000 interaction center tech-support positions back to the US. Similarly, Dell decided to stop routing tech-support calls to India for certain product lines after some US business customers complained about the level of support they were receiving; the calls are now routed to locations in Texas, Idaho, and Tennessee. In 2006, Apple announced plans to set up an offshore interaction center in Bangalore, India, but months later cancelled the plans. In November 2007, Coca-Cola Enterprises announced that it was setting up a $16 million interaction center in East Tulsa, Oklahoma, rather than outsourcing the operations overseas.

Homesourcing and Home-Based Agents

Another factor that is contributing to the decline of outsourcing is the increased use of home-based agents — sometimes referred to as "homesourcing." With the mainstream adoption of Voice over Internet Protocol (VoIP) and Session Initiation Protocol (SIP) — which we will discuss in detail in Chapter 2 — companies are increasingly making use of agents who work from their own homes rather than from the office. Homesourcing provides benefits for both the employers and the agents. Agents enjoy the flexibility and freedom of working from home and setting their own schedules. Companies are often able to save money on a variety of costs including real estate, health insurance, office equipment, supplies, and even toilet paper. Companies are also able to better schedule workers for periods of peak volume as well as more efficiently handle unexpected spikes in volume by taking advantage of the flexible nature of home workers. For example, it would be impractical to ask an employee to drive all the way into work during rush-hour morning traffic to work a 30-minute shift and then go home — only to return again for another 30-minute shift around lunchtime. However, this is no problem for home-based agents who don't mind scheduling short 30-minute shifts that conveniently fit their schedule.

Companies find this an excellent way to schedule additional personnel for increased seasonal activity, or to instantly add more capacity in response to sudden spikes in call volume due to unforeseen events such as service outages, storms, natural disasters, or perhaps just to greater than expected customer response to a new marketing promotion. Employees enjoy the flexibility of being able to work from home and to schedule their own hours. One segment of workers who have really embraced the home-based-agent model is work-at-home mothers (also known as WAHMs).

Well-known companies who have started to adopt the home-based-agent model include AAA roadside assistance, 1-800-Flowers, Office Depot, Jet Blue Airways, Verizon, Walgreens, Citibank, GE, AIG, US Internal Revenue Service, UnitedHealth Group, Sears Holding, Wyndham Hotels, J. Crew, and Vermont Teddy Bear Co. Various software and staffing companies have rushed to support this emerging market including Working Solutions, West at Home, Alpine Access, LiveOps, and of course SAP.

1.3.8   The Typical Interaction Center

The typical interaction center involves a group of agents sitting together in rows or clusters in a large open building, with each agent located at a workstation with a computer as well as a telephone and high-quality (usually wireless) headset. Although the use of homesourcing and virtual agents is on the rise with an estimated over 100,000 home-based agents in the US alone, the majority of interaction center agents (about 97%) still work in centralized brick-and-mortar locations. Although some companies rely exclusively on home-based agents, the majority of companies use home-based agents for supplemental purposes, typically for high seasonal demand or to handle call-volume overflow during peak hours.

Average Size of Typical Interaction Center

Despite the fact that large high-volume interaction centers tend to get much more press and publicity than small two-person help desks, the typical interaction center is usually quite small and often consists of between 30 to 40 agents. Reports and studies usually mention that the average interaction center size (based on calculated average) is around 250 to 300 agents. For example, the 2007 Dimension Data "Global Contact Centre Benchmarking Report" puts the average number of interaction center seats at 301 while the 2007 Genesys "Executive Survey Report: Insights Into Optimizing Contact Center Performance" suggests that 230 seats is the average size.

However, these numbers usually represent a calculated average (or median for those readers who remember their university statistics courses) rather than the number of agents that occurs most often (or mode). Small interaction centers of 30 to 40 agents are probably still much more common than larger 200 to 300 seat interaction centers. Large interaction centers do exists, with some having more than 10,000 users. However, the typical "large" interaction center is more likely to have 300 to 400 agents rather than 3,000 to 4,000. According to the 2007 Genesys report, only 14% of interaction centers have 1,500 or more seats, whereas 77% of interaction centers have less than 500 seats.

Physical Layout of Typical Interaction Center

Regardless of the size, the physical layout of most interaction centers is typically very similar. Interaction centers tend to utilize large open floors (rather than enclosed offices) with agents sitting at open workstations or low-walled cubicles. For each cluster of around 15 to 20 agents, a supervisor is assigned on the floor to coach agents, answer questions, and provide other immediate support. Most interaction centers have on-site analysts, schedulers, and quality assurance monitors — depending on the size of the interaction center. Conference rooms are generally available for one-on-one performance reviews and coaching, and separate facilities are usually available for group trainings and team meetings.

CTI Usage in a Typical Interaction Center

Despite the fact that almost every interaction center deals with telephony and uses special hardware and software for receiving and making telephone calls and routing calls to the appropriate agents, many interaction centers today still do not utilize computer telephony integration (CTI). While the advantages of CTI are well known and documented, the majority of interaction centers today still do not fully leverage the capabilities of CTI and multi-channel integration. Rather, many interaction centers tend to use standalone telephone systems where the agent receives a telephone call and then manually searches for the customer data and history in the business software application.

Only about half of companies use some form of CTI or multi-channel integration with their interaction center. The 2007 Dimension Data report indicates that only 53.4% of companies currently have CTI. Similarly, most companies do not take full advantage of the possibility to integrate additional channels such as email and chat in order to do automated skills-based routing, customer identification, and retrieval of customer data and history based on incoming email address or other criteria. For example, the Aspect 2007 Contact Center Satisfaction Index North America reports that only 24% of interaction centers utilize email and that only 4% utilize chat.

VoIP Usage in a Typical Interaction Center

Obviously, if a majority of interaction centers don't yet even have computer telephony integration, you would assume that VoIP is even further behind. However, Internet Protocol (IP)–based communications such as Voice over Internet Protocol (VoIP) are being adopted by the leading-edge companies. IP-based communications enable companies to enhance how they structure and organize their interaction centers by allowing some (or all) agents to work remotely from home, full time or (more likely) part time. Even though these agents don't physically sit in the same office where the interaction center is located, the agents are utilized in exactly the same as their in-office counterparts. When a new telephone call arrives at the interaction center, the call can be routed to the home agent who is equipped with a laptop computer and a USB headset. This allows companies to be more flexible in their shift planning in order to better compensate for fluctuations in call volumes.

Summary of Typical Interaction Center

Table 1.1 describes a "typical" interaction center in terms of number of agent seats, usage of outsourcing and home-based agents, support of CTI and multi-channel integration, and agent-to-supervisor ratio. While this characterization is certainly not representative of every interaction center, it does help you envision the most common type of interaction center — similar to the type of interaction center you might be involved with. It is important to realize that not every interaction center is a 10,000-plus-seat, high-performance, multi-channel, blended, outsourced, global interaction center. Many interaction centers are 10 user help desks without CTI, email, or chat.

Number of agents	40
Use of outsourcing	None
Use of home-based agents	Some use home-based agents, typically just for seasonal use or overflow call volume
Telephony integration	No current integration, but with plans for future integration
Communication channels supported	Telephony only (no email or chat) with plans for future email integration
Agent to supervisor ratio	20:1

Table 1.1 "Typical" Interaction Center

1.4 The SAP CRM Interaction Center

The SAP CRM Interaction Center provides direct integration to SAP CRM Marketing, Sales, Order Management, Service, and Analytics including:

▶ Contact management
▶ Activity management
▶ Lead qualification
▶ Sales order entry
▶ Help desk and trouble ticketing
▶ Service request management
▶ Case management

▶ Complaint management

▶ Reporting and analytics

Nearly half of all SAP CRM customer projects involve the SAP CRM Interaction Center. Additionally, thousands of consultants, developers, and project managers have received training and/or certification on the SAP CRM Interaction Center.

1.4.1 The History of the Interaction Center

SAP's first interaction center product was actually delivered with *SAP R/3* (the predecessor to SAP ERP) before SAP ever offered a CRM solution. The R/3 Customer Interaction Center (CIC) was first provided to customers with SAP R/3 4.5B. The R/3 CIC was a SAP GUI for a Microsoft® Windows™ application that could be accessed via transaction code CIC0 in the R/3 system (Figure 1.2).

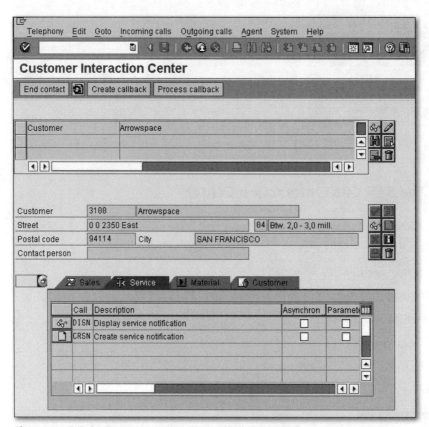

Figure 1.2 R/3 Customer Interaction Center (CIC) Circa 1999

Later that same year in 1999, SAP also made the interaction center available in SAP's debut CRM product, SAP CRM 1.2A (later renamed SAP CRM 2.0A). The CRM-based interaction center, introduced as the Service Interaction Center (SIC) scenario, was also a SAP GUI for Windows application based on the same framework and coding of the R/3 Customer Interaction Center and was also accessed via transaction code CIC0 — from the CRM system. This product was later renamed to IC WinClient (Figure 1.3).

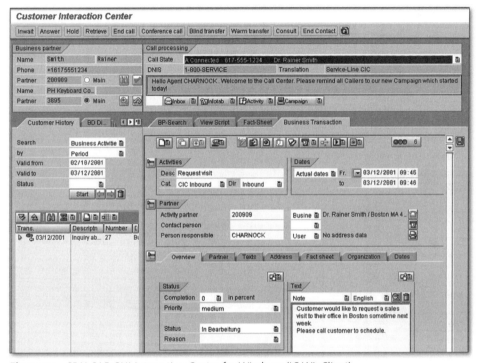

Figure 1.3 CRM SAP GUI Interaction Center for Windows (IC WinClient)

1.4.2 The Interaction Center Moves from SAP GUI to the Web Browser

In 2002, SAP introduced a thin-client web browser–based version of the Interaction Center called the Interaction Center (IC) WebClient (Figure 1.4). The IC WebClient was first released with SAP CRM 3.1 only for select customers on a project basis, and then later officially released in 2003 as part of CRM 4.0. In order to avoid confusion and to adopt a consistent naming strategy, SAP renamed the older

SAP GUI-based CRM Service Interaction Center (SIC) to Interaction Center (IC) WinClient, a reference to the "SAP GUI for Windows" user interface.

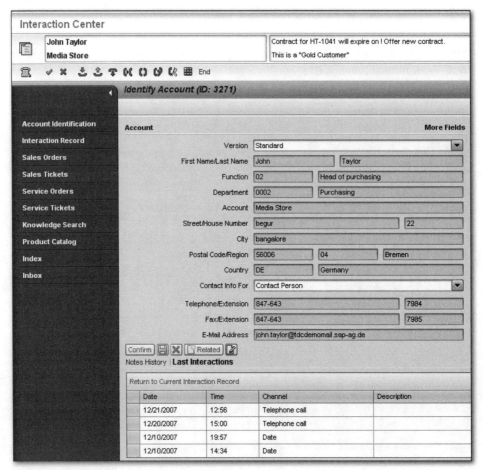

Figure 1.4 CRM Interaction Center (IC) WebClient

The IC WebClient user interface was designed with the help of award-winning San Francisco design firm. And, like many web-based applications of the time, the CRM 4.0 IC WebClient heavily leveraged popular programming techniques such as Java 2 Enterprise Edition (J2EE) server applications and Web-browser based Java applets. In later years, however, due to customer demand for lower Total Cost of Ownership (TCO) and a more homogenous SAP architecture, the J2EE functionality along with most of the Java applets were replaced with standard ABAP coding.

SAP delivered both a J2EE server version and an ABAP version of the IC WebClient in CRM 4.0 Add-on for Service Industries, allowing customers to choose between the J2EE and ABAP configuration. In CRM 2005, SAP only delivered the ABAP version, eliminating the need for a separate J2EE server to run core Interaction Center functionality, the Software Agent Framework (SAF), and Interaction Center Broadcast Messaging.

> **Note**
>
> Although a J2EE server is no longer required in CRM 4.0 Add-on for Service Industries or CRM 2005 for core IC WebClient functionality, a J2EE server is still required to run the TREX search engine used by the IC WebClient Knowledge Search as well as by ERMS for language detection and categorization of incoming emails. Additionally, other CRM applications outside of the Interaction Center such as Internet Sales may still also require separate J2EE servers.

Please see the matrix in Table 1.2 for an overview of the various SAP Interaction Center releases by product, release, and year.

Application name	Product	User Interface	Release	Release year
Customer Interaction Center (CIC)	R/3	SAP GUI for Windows	4.5B	1998 – 1999
Service Interaction Center (SIC) *Later renamed Interaction Center (IC) WinClient*	CRM	SAP GUI for Windows	CRM 1.2A *(Later renamed CRM 2.0A)*	1998 – 1999
Interaction Center (IC) WebClient	CRM	Web browser	CRM 4.0	2002 – 2003
Interaction Center for CRM WebClient	CRM	Web browser	CRM 2006s/ CRM 2007	2006 – 2007

Table 1.2 SAP Interaction Center Release Matrix

SAP continued to offer (and enhance) both versions of its CRM Interaction Center product — IC WinClient and IC WebClient — until the release of SAP CRM 2006s/CRM 2007, at which point the entire SAP CRM product migrated from SAP GUI to the new *CRM WebClient* user interface (based on the underlying technical framework of the IC WebClient). With CRM 2006s/CRM 2007 and beyond, IC WinClient is longer available.

> **Note**
>
> As of CRM 2006s/CRM 2007, all SAP CRM business-user applications are accessible via the new WebClient user interface only. SAP GUI is now only used for administrative tasks applications such as configuration. PC-UI is no longer supported. The Enterprise Portal (EP) is still available, but is no longer required. All functionality previously accessible only from the Enterprise Portal is now available in the new CRM WebClient user interface. For example, the IC Manager functionality is available via the CRM business role "IC_Manager."

The R/3 SAP GUI for Windows-based CIC application is available with all versions of SAP R/3. The CIC is also available with SAP's new *ERP* product, including the most current version SAP ERP 2007. However, *SAP stopped all development and enhancement of the CIC with R/3 and has not added any new capabilities or features for the CIC in ERP.* While quite a few SAP R/3 customers are still (very happily) running the R/3 Customer Interaction Center, SAP recommends that new customers implement the interaction center in CRM rather than ERP for the following two reasons. First, customer-facing operations like the interaction center are now best leveraged as part of the front-office CRM program, rather than a back-office ERP implementation. Second, the IC WebClient framework and architecture of the CRM Interaction Center is vastly more flexible and powerful than the framework and architecture of the SAP GUI for Windows-based R/3 Customer Interaction Center.

When SAP introduced the IC WebClient user interface on a project basis in 2002 with CRM 3.1 and then later for general availability with CRM 4.0, SAP also continued to offer the IC WinClient interface in parallel. SAP continued to offer both CRM Interaction Center interfaces through CRM release 2005. However, after CRM 2005, SAP no longer delivered the IC WinClient and only offers the IC WebClient. CRM 2005 customers can of course continue using the IC WinClient with CRM 2005 until the end of normal maintenance in 2011 or until the end of extended maintenance in 2013 or 2014. However, IC WinClient customers who upgrade from CRM 2005 to CRM 2006s/CRM 2007 or above must migrate to the IC WebClient; IC WinClient is not available in these releases.

1.4.3 Capabilities of the SAP CRM Interaction Center

Customer Relationship Management, as its name implies, is all about front-office customer-facing activities. The three pillars of CRM are marketing, sales, and service. These activities are all focused around the customer — getting the customer interested in a product or service, convincing the customer to actually purchase the product or service, and making sure the customer is happy with the purchased product or service. It seems simple enough — three easy steps. Alas, if everything was simple and easy you wouldn't need to buy software, hire consultants and systems integrators, or even read this book. Luckily for book authors, things are seldom easy and they rarely go exactly as planned. This book assumes that you are already familiar with the concept of CRM and that you have a basic understanding of marketing, sales, and service. In this book, we will discuss how the Interaction Center integrates with SAP CRM Marketing, Sales, and Service functionality to give interaction center agents and managers the information and tools they need to drive customer profitability, customer retention, and customer satisfaction.

Marketing

CRM starts with Marketing: segmenting customers via marketing attributes and analytics (e.g., income, interests, churn risk, life-time profitability), generating campaigns (e.g., new product launch, product bundles, high-churn-risk retention effort), assigning desired customer segments to the campaigns, and generating call lists and email lists of customers who should be contacted as part of each campaign. The SAP CRM Interaction Center is used, together with core CRM Marketing to target particular customer segments with special offers or promotions. For example, a company might create a marketing campaign to generate interest for a new product that is being launched.

Using the SAP CRM Interaction Center, agents can review campaign details, process call-lists, and generate and qualify leads. At the start of their shift, the interaction center agent may take a few minutes to familiarize themselves with the details of any new campaigns, such as the campaign description, priority, and tactics, along with a linked interactive script (if provided). If an agent is assigned to an outbound call list, the agent will begin processing the calls and dialing the respective customers — either manually, or else via automated outbound dialing such as preview dialing, progressive dialing, or predictive dialing.

If a customer expresses interest in the campaign or product, the agent can create and qualify a lead using built-in marketing survey integration. If the customer is ready to buy, the agent can of course directly take an order. However, in a business-to-business software sales model, an inside-sales rep would most likely set an appointment for the prospective customer with a regional field-sales rep. In the consumer magazine subscription industry on the other hand, there would be little need to create an actual lead document; rather, the agent would simply process the customer's order.

Sales

CRM sales takes over where marketing leaves off. When a customer is ready to buy something, they have a number of options available for placing the order including (e.g., an Internet web shop or the company's interaction center). In some industries, such as specialty chemicals, a sales representative would probably call on a professional buyer each week or month using a call list or scheduled activity via the interaction center. The same could be true of the direct-store delivery (DSD) model in the food and beverage industry where a truck makes weekly deliveries to a retail location. And in certain industries, such as banking, insurance and, financial services, a consumer would often initiate the contact, by calling into the interaction center periodically to speak with an expert regarding a particular issue.

Similarly, a customer who has already placed an order through another channel — such as the Internet — may call in to the interaction center to change the order, or to check the status. While not every sales transaction is initiated via the interaction center, the interaction center often becomes involved in the process at some point — such as when the customer wants to check an order status or delivery date, or make changes to an existing order.

Service

Once a sales order has been placed or a sales contract has been signed, a prospect becomes a customer and CRM Service becomes important. Most often, when a customer needs help, if they don't find the answer on the first page of a Google Internet search result, they will contact the company's interaction center to seek help. Some tech-savvy customers, especially the younger generation who grew up with computers, may also take a quick look at the company's corporate website to search for a frequently asked question (FAQ) or knowledge-base article. But these tech-savvy customers will also usually turn to the interaction center if they can't find the answers they are looking for.

Customers contact the interaction center for a variety of issues, such as to request product support, seek answers to questions, to file a complaint, or to return or exchange a product. For example, a customer may call to ask about the shipping status of an item they have ordered. Sometimes, the customer might have a technical question about how to assemble or configure an item. Or, a customer might want to exchange a product for another size or color, or even return a defective item. SAP CRM Interaction Center agents have access to tools to handle all of these types of service-related issues.

Using a knowledge search application, agents can search for answers to customer questions and then either provide the answer over the telephone or send the answer via email, fax, chat, or other means. If an agent doesn't know how to proceed or needs help answering a customer's question, the agent can access interactive scripts that adeptly guide the agent through the correct steps (including questions and answers) to resolve the customer's issue. An agent can also log a service request on behalf of a customer and schedule appointments for a service technician to visit the customer for an installation or repair.

Reporting and Analytics

In addition to providing access to marketing, sales order management and customer service functionality the interaction center also provides real-time monitoring, daily reporting, and historic analytics. The Interaction Center Manager Dashboard is available that interfaces with CTI software to provide a real-time snapshot of current telephone, email, and chat queue volumes as well as agent activity. The E-Mail Status Overview report provides a summary of daily incoming email volume (including escalated emails) by organization and queue. Historic analysis of communication channels is available via standard SAP BI reports that can display data imported from CMS systems via the SAP Statistics Interface, including service level, connection volume, average handling time, average speed of answer, and abandonment rate (these will be discussed in more detail in Chapter 2).

Out-of-the-box SAP NetWeaver BI reports are provided for email processing that display historic email volume, average handling time, average response time, and service level. Reports are also available for service tickets, including service ticket overview, volume, history, and lead time. In addition, as of CRM 2006s/CRM 2007 out-of-the-box OLTP reports are also available for service tickets that provide BI-type reporting without requiring an actual SAP BI installation; it is also possible to create your own ad hoc service ticket reports on the fly. BI reports are also available for so-called "blended analytics" that combine computer telephony integration (CTI) reports with business transaction reports to provide managers with deeper insight into their interaction center operations.

1.5   Summary

This chapter has been a general introduction to the interaction center. The interaction center has evolved from the 1960s into one of the most important tools for customer management. The following are key points to remember from this chapter.

- The interaction center is the virtual front door to your company, allowing customers to come in to do business. If the door is closed, or if the line is too long, customers will take their business elsewhere.

- Although interaction centers support a variety of communication channels, telephone is still the method that customers prefer most with over 70% of customer interactions taking place via telephone.

- The most common use of the interaction center is still for customer service. Around 50% of companies use the interaction center exclusively for service (with no marketing or Sales functionality) while 80% of companies use the interaction center for service and other tasks.

- The typical interaction center consists of about 30 to 40 agents. Large interaction centers consist of around 300 to 400 agents. Very large interaction centers may have 10,000 or more agents.

- In the 1980s and 1990s, many companies outsourced their interaction centers to low-cost locations. Today, companies are "homesourcing" their interaction centers using virtual home-based agents.

- Due to the fact that 60% to 70% of the costs associated with running an interaction center are directly related to agent salaries, companies have traditionally tried to reduce costs by focusing on keeping customer interactions as short as possible.

- Recently, as interaction centers are now focusing more on customer retention and profitability, new customer-based performance metrics have emerged, such as first-call resolution (FCR), customer retention rate, and customer lifetime value (CLV).

- The SAP CRM Interaction Center provides direct integration to SAP CRM Marketing, Sales, Order Management, Service, and Analytics functionality.

Now that we understand what the interaction center is and what it can do, in the next chapter we will look at how to extend the capabilities of the interaction center using computer telephony integration (CTI) and multi-channel integration.

Computer telephony integration (CTI) and multi-channel integration allow you to integrate real-time telephone calls, emails, Web chats, and other modes of communication into your SAP CRM Interaction Center.

2 Computer Telephony Integration (CTI) and Multi-Channel Integration

Suppose that your company recently put *you* in charge of setting up an interaction center to handle incoming customer-service telephone calls for a new product line that has some known quality issues. Assuming that your company is an existing SAP Business Suite customer, perhaps you happily discover that you already own several CRM user licenses. You quickly run out to Wal-Mart and get a great deal on a shopping cart full of laptop computers and telephones. You even hire your nephew and his friends to answer calls. You read somewhere that on average it costs a company about $5.00 to handle each customer telephone call. Unfortunately, you are expecting lots of calls from unhappy customers and your company already spent most of its annual budget on a viral marketing campaign. How are you going to pay for this new customer service initiative?

Somehow you need to keep the costs of each call to a minimum while ideally also generating incremental sales revenue per call. You initially consider a four-part strategy: 1) put each caller on hold at least an hour to decrease the number of callers who remain on the line and reach a live agent, 2) outsource callers to agents in remote locations to reduce salary costs, 3) institute a 30-second maximum talk time to keep call duration short and keep costs down, and 4) force agents to attempt at least five different cross-sell offers to each caller. Luckily, you quickly regain your sanity and realize that driving all of your customers away (and into the arms of competitors) is probably not the best way to reduce your customer service costs. So instead you look to technology for ways to reduce costs while also increasing customer satisfaction and lifetime profitability. For example, what was this computer telephony integration (CTI) stuff you read about a while back — and could it help?

This chapter will introduce you to the basics of CTI as well as other types of multi-channel integration including the integration of email, Web chat, fax, and postal letter with your SAP CRM Interaction Center. The difference will be explained between pure telephone-system functionality (such as call queuing, routing, and call treatment) and computer telephony integration, which involves capabilities such as:

▶ Searching for customer records based on data collected from the telephone system

▶ Providing customer information to agents via automatic screen population (screen pop)

▶ Using software-based telephone controls that allow the agent to control the telephone system from the computer

▶ Transfering the telephone call and computer screen from one agent to another

▶ Integrating automated outbound dialing which involves automatically dialing telephone calls from computer call lists via the telephone system

We will discuss SAP's strategy for enabling CTI and multi-channel integration including the various SAP interfaces: SAPphone, SAPconnect, and the Integrated Communication Interface (ICI). We will also look at the multi-channel and telephony capabilities provided by optional, additional software available from SAP (i.e., SAP BCM) or SAP's certified partners including Genesys, Avaya, and others.

2.1 Telephony

Computer telephony integration, as its name suggests, refers to the *integration* of computer software applications and telephone systems. For example, some common uses of CTI include letting a computer software application answer an incoming telephone call, or allowing the telephone system to collect data from the caller and pass the data to a computer software application. However, before we start talking about computer telephony integration, let's first discuss *telephony* itself.

Telephony basically refers to the equipment and process used to connect telephones so that one person can talk to another. The following are core telephony functions that are useful in an interaction center, but generally not considered part of computer telephony integration. This functionality is not provided by the SAP CRM Interaction Center but can be enabled for the SAP CRM Interaction Center via other products, including SAP Business Communications Management (BCM) as well as third-party products from SAP partners.

2.1.1 Queuing

As was discussed in Chapter 1, due to the random and unpredictable nature of which inbound telephone calls arrive from customers, it is necessary to either over-staff the interaction center with agents (which is usually cost prohibitive) or to require callers to wait on hold for a period of time whenever there are more callers than available agents.

The process of waiting in line to speak with an agent is referred to as "queuing" and the line itself is referred to as the "queue." The queue is managed by the telephone system, typically by a device known as an automated call dispatcher (ACD), which is responsible for connecting inbound telephone calls from customers to the telephone extension of an appropriate agent based on defined rules and algorithms.

2.1.2 Call Treatment

When a telephone call arrives, the telephone system — typically the ACD — is responsible for deciding what to do with the call. Should the caller be routed to a live agent, and if so, to which agent? Should the caller be sent to an interactive voice response (IVR) menu? Should the caller be put on hold, and if so, should the caller hear a recorded message, on-hold music, or silence? The automated call-handling procedure is known as "call treatment" and is typically defined in scripts, which are executed by the ACD.

2.1.3 Routing

After an incoming telephone call has gone through call treatment (e.g., IVR menu, recoded messages, on-hold music, etc.) and the telephone system is ready to connect the caller with a live agent, the call is routed to the most suitable agent based on rules maintained in the ACD. The basic process of connecting a caller to an agent is known as call routing. There are various advanced forms of call routing such as skill-based routing, multi-channel routing, and so on.

2.2   Computer Telephony Integration (CTI)

The technology that allows a computer to access functionality of a telephone or telephone system (such as a PBX or ACD switch) is known as *Computer Telephony Integration* (CTI). For example, one very common use of CTI is to enable a *screen pop (population)* — the ability to automatically populate a computer screen with the identity, details, and customer history of an incoming caller before the agent even answers the telephone call. Another common use of CTI is to allow computer applications to perform typical telephony functions such as answering incoming calls, placing callers on hold, initiating conference calls, and so on; when a toolbar or other buttons are made available in a computer software application for this purpose, it is typically referred to as a *softphone* (*soft*ware + tele*phone*) control.

Let's take a detailed look at some of the various uses of CTI.

2.2.1   Automatic Number Identification (ANI) Lookup

In North America, telephone companies provide services such as *Automatic Number Identification* (invented by AT&T) that digitally identify the telephone number of the incoming caller. Similar services also exist in Europe and the U.K. such as Calling Line Identification (CLI) and Caller Line Identification (CLID). These services are different from consumer-oriented telephone services like caller-ID that display the name of the incoming caller. For example, the benefit of ANI to a business, such as an interaction center, is that the ANI data can be used to cross-reference the telephone number of an incoming call against the company's existing customer database in order to look up the customer details and history (assuming that the caller is already a customer and that the caller's telephone number is already on file in the database).

However, ANI *lookup* does not work 100% of the time. In fact, in many industries, the success rate of ANI lookup is be quite low — typically between 20% and 40%. This relatively low success rate is due to a number of factors, including the proliferation of various mobile telephone devices as well as increased concerns about consumer privacy. For example, especially in business-to-consumer industries, customers may register their home telephone number with the company but then call from another device such as mobile phone, IP phone, office work phone, car phone, airplane phone, or payphone (for example, in rural areas not yet served by cell phone coverage). ANI lookup rates are slightly higher in business-to-business scenarios and in situations where a caller is likely to call from their home telephone for security purposes (such as when activating a new credit card). However, due to the low success rate of ANI lookups, many companies have supplemented or replaced ANI with other, more successful technologies for identifying inbound callers such as Interactive Voice Response (IVR) systems. See Section 2.2.3 for more information about IVRs.

In the SAP CRM Interaction Center, the SAP Business Address Service (BAS) can be used to locate and retrieve a customer record based on the ANI. The Interaction Center agent will see the name of the caller (and also the name of the company the caller represents in a business-to-business scenario) as well as the caller's telephone number in the upper-most portions of the screen known collectively as the "context area." The context area contains three sub-areas, including the account info (far left), alerts (middle), and communication information (far right). See Figure 2.1.

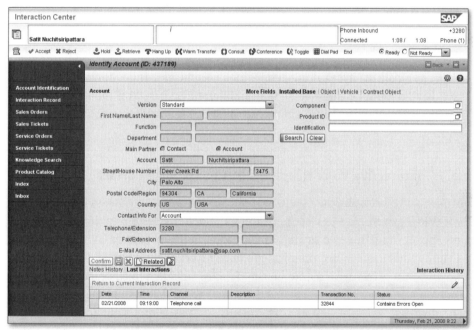

Figure 2.1 Customer Information Automatically Retrieved in SAP CRM Interaction Center Based on ANI Lookup

2.2.2 Dialed Number Identification Service (DNIS)

While ANI service identifies the telephone number of the person making the telephone call, another service called *Dialed Number Identification Service* (DNIS) digitally identifies the telephone number that the caller has dialed. This information can be useful to a large company who may have dozens (or even hundreds) of 1-800 numbers for various lines of business, products, customers, and marketing promotions. For example, by assigning a unique 1-800 to each promotion or campaign, a company is able to use the DNIS information to automatically determine (based on the dialed number) which campaign, promotion, or offer a customer is calling about. This allows the company to automatically route the caller to the correct queue or agent and to automatically populate the computer screen with the correct campaign details, product information, or agent call script.

Similarly, a dedicated telephone number can be assigned to a particular high-value customer (or customer group), allowing the system to use the DNIS information to identify the customer or customer group and route the call to the correct queue or agent. For example, United Airlines provides a dedicated customer-service telephone number to its Premier customers, while eBay similarly provides a special customer service number to its Power Sellers and other most valued members.

In the SAP CRM Interaction Center, the DNIS information is displayed in the right side of the context area, along with other communication information such as the caller's telephone number, as seen in Figure 2.1. Based on the DNIS information, the agent might pull up a particular marketing promotion or interactive call script.

2.2.3 Interactive Voice Response (IVR) and Voice Portals

An *Interactive Voice Response* (IVR) system, sometimes also called a *Voice Response Unit* (VRU) system, is a device that allows a telephone system to detect and interpret spoken human voice as well as dual-tone multi-frequency (DTMF) signaling — the sounds made when pressing the buttons on a telephone — perhaps better known by the AT&T trademarked term "Touch-Tone." When customers call a company, the company often first sends the callers to an IVR system that prompts the callers with a series of nested voice menus such as "Enter your unique 16-digit account ID," "Press 1 for sales, press 2 for service, press 3 to use our automated system," and so on. IVR systems provide a number of benefits — both to the company as well as to the callers (although perhaps to a lesser extent).

One of the main benefits of an IVR is to gather information about the caller in order to help route the caller to the best-suited queue or agent. This saves the company time and reduces costs; customers also benefit by being transferred directly to the correct company resource without being transferred numerous times between agents. Another benefit of IVR is to deflect calls from the interaction center and re-direct them to an automated voice self-service system or voice portal. For example, customers who only need to perform basic transactions or inquiries such as check-ing an account balance, activating a credit card, paying a bill, or inquiring about an order or delivery status are very well suited for automated voice self-service systems.

Re-directing customers to voice self-service for these types of simple transactions saves the company money because voice self-service is significantly cheaper than agent-assisted phone interactions. Some customers may also prefer voice self-ser-vice since self-service is often quicker than waiting for an agent. Additionally, many customers feel safer conducting financial transaction via self-service because they don't need to read their credit card number and other personal information out loud to another person.

A *voice portal* is different than an IVR or VRU. Whereas an IVR is designed to prompt the user for various pieces of information by following a pre-configured menu tree, a voice portal is not structured with nested menus. Rather, voice portals take advantage of speech-recognition technology to allow users to ask questions or give commands using natural spoken language. Based on the commands, the voice portal can access data and applications that reside on the Internet (or Intranet). Basically, you can think of a voice portal as a voice-enabled web browser — with-out the actual web browser. Using natural spoken language, a customer can inquire about store locations, hours or operation, or return policies; check on the status of an order or delivery; or ask to speak with a specific employee.

The SAP CRM Interaction Center does not provide IVR capabilities itself; however, the Interaction Center can receive and process data provided by IVR systems — including SAP BCM and products from other SAP partners. Data collected in the IVR, VRU, or voice portal can be passed along to the SAP CRM Interaction Center as call-attached data/contact-attached data (CAD).

2.2.4   Screen Pop

Another advantage that CTI provides is so-called "screen pop," or the ability to pre-populate the computer screen with the customer's information and history based on identification of the caller via IVR (Interactive Voice Response) data or ANI (Automatic Number Identification). When an incoming telephone call is routed to an agent, the agent can view the caller's account data and other information while the phone is still ringing before the agent even answers the call.

The primary benefit of a screen pop is to save the agent time by eliminating the need to do a manual search for the customer's account information. While it is nice that the agent also knows who is calling before answering the telephone, this provides little actual business value. For example, most companies refrain from answering the telephone with "Hello, Mr. John" because real-life experience has shown that this increases the average call duration as the customer often demands to know how the agent knew the customer's name.

In the SAP CRM Interaction Center, the screen pop consists of various information displayed in the Context Area of the Interaction Center including account information such as the name of the account and contact person (in a business-to-business scenario), as well as communication information such as the ANI and DNIS. In addition, the system can be configured to either automatically accept the incoming telephone call, or to prompt the agent with blinking accept and reject buttons, allowing the agent to choose whether to accept the call or to send the caller back to the queue. See Figure 2.2.

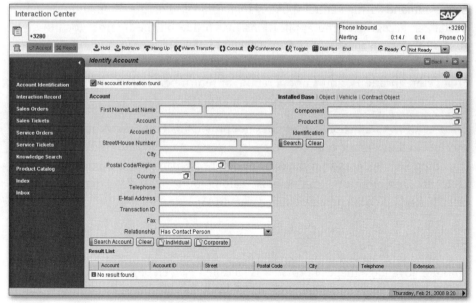

Figure 2.2 Incoming Telephone Call "Screen Pop" in SAP CRM Interaction Center with Blinking Accept/Reject Icons

2.2.5 Call-Attached Data (CAD)

CTI also enables companies to attach data — such as ANI, DNIS, IVR data, and other information — to a telephone call when routing the call from the telephone system to an agent. By capturing and transferring important data that has already been collected by the telephone system, this information is also available in the computer system without the agent having to ask the customer to re-enter the information. Few things are more annoying to a caller than being asked to provide information (such as an account number) to an agent that the customer just provided seconds ago to the telephone system.

Information such as ANI, DNIS, and other data collected in the IVR, VRU, or voice portal can be passed along to the SAP CRM Interaction Center as call-attached data (CAD). For example, the IVR system could collect the customer's account number and then pass that data along to the SAP CRM Interaction Center, which would use the data to identify the account. See OSS note *707104* for full details on how this process works.

> **Note**
>
> See SAP note *707104* "Account identification from attached data" for full details on you can perform automatic account identification based on call-attached data collected via an external source such as an interactive voice response (IVR) system.

2.2.6 Softphone Control

A softphone is a computer application that allows users to control their telephone (or telephone system) via computer. For example, a user could answer an incoming call, place the caller on hold, consult with another colleague, transfer the caller to another department, and so on — all without ever touching an actual telephone. The SAP CRM Interaction Center, for example, contains a toolbar embedded in the application that provides interaction center agents with full access to telephone functions such as answer, hold, retrieve, consult, warm transfer, blind/cold transfer, and so on, directly from the softphone control without the need for an actual physical phone on the desk.

The SAP CRM Interaction Center contains an embedded multi-channel communication toolbar that can be connected with other products including SAP BCM as well as products from SAP partners in order to enable CTI integration. The toolbar allows agents to access standard functionality provided by the telephone system, including the ability to answer, hold, retrieve, consult, transfer, hang up, and so on (see Figure 2.2).

The following telephony features are supported by SAP in the Interaction Center toolbar. It is important to note that the SAP CRM Interaction Center does not actually provide the following telephony capabilities but rather only integrates these capabilities, which are provided by the underlying communication management software such as Genesys, Avaya, or SAP BCM. In some cases, vendors may not support all features. The following telephony toolbar buttons are available out of the box from SAP:

► Accept — Accepts the telephone call, similar to manually picking up the telephone receiver.

► Reject — Sends the telephone call back to the queue for re-routing by the telephone switch (ACD) or communication management software.

► Hold — Places the active call on hold.

► Retrieve — Retrieves a held call and makes it active again.

► Transfer (*blind transfer*, *cold transfer*) — Puts the caller on hold while the agent transfers the call to another agent's extension without first consulting with that agent.

► Warm transfer — Puts the caller on hold while the agent consults with another agent and then transfers the call to that agent's extension.

► Consult — Places a caller on hold while an agent initiaties a call to a second agent to ask for advice or help. After the agent is done consulting with the second agent, the caller is retieved from being on hold.

► Conference — Places the caller on hold while the agent calls another agent. Once the second agent is connected, the caller is also connected at the same time so that all three parties can participate in a discussion.

► Toggle — Switches between a caller on hold and an active consultation call, automatically placing the active call on hold and vice versa.

► Dial pad — Opens a dial pad that looks like the numbers on a telephone, which the agent can use to make a telephone call.

► Hang up — Terminates a telephone call, similar to hanging up the telephone receiver manually.

The Interaction Center toolbar also provides an area for agents to set their agent work mode. When the agent sets their work mode to "ready," this indicates to the underlying communication management software that the agent is ready to accept a telephone call. However, the agent may also set their work mode to "not ready" and provide additional data to indicate whether they are wrapping up another call, taking a lunch break, participating in training, and so on.

The underlying communication management software (CMS) is responsible for correctly setting and managing the work mode when the agent receives a call. For example, the CMS should set the agent's work mode to "not ready" after the agent has received a call. After the current call has ended, the CMS can decide whether the agent is immediately ready for the next call, or whether the agent needs a certain period of time (for example, 30 seconds) to wrap up the previous call and prepare for the next call.

2.2.7 Screen Transfer

Sometimes it is necessary for one agent to transfer a caller to another agent. For example, if the first agent is not able to fully resolve the caller's issue, the agent may need to transfer the caller to a specialist in customer service, sales, accounting/billing, or information technology (IT). When transferring the caller, it is desirable to also be able to transfer all of the customer data and information currently shown on the computer screen, so that the agent who receives the transfer can immediately continue from where the first agent left off, instead of asking the customer to start over and provide all of the customer's information again.

In the SAP CRM Interaction Center, it is possible to transfer a telephone call — as well as the related customer data — from one agent to another. It is important to note that only the actual business objects involved in the interaction will be transferred. This includes items such as the customer and contact person, interaction record, business transactions, knowledgebase solutions, sent and received emails, and so on. Technically, these items are all stored in a container called the activity clipboard (part of the interaction record) that stores all objects involved in the current customer interaction.

The activity clipboard and the interaction record will be explained in detail in later chapters. Any other information on the screen that is not included in the activity clipboard will not be transferred. This includes all free text that has been typed in the scratchpad area, as well as unsaved emails, and so on.

2.2.8 Outbound Dialing Integration (Preview, Progressive, and Predictive/Power Dialing)

Many companies — and not just telemarketing companies — utilize automated outbound dialing to automatically dial customers from a list of scheduled calls. Using automated dialing with call lists saves time (and hence money) because the agent does not need to manually dial any calls. Additionally, using advanced dialing techniques such as progressive and predictive dialing, the agent is only connected once an actual person is reached, filtering out answering machines, busy signals, and unanswered calls. Outbound dialing integration allows call lists generated by the computer system (i.e., CRM system) to be processed automatically by the telephone system (i.e., outbound dialer).

The SAP CRM Interaction Center does not include out of the box automated outbound dialing capabilities. However, both progressive dialing and predictive dialing modes can be integrated through the SAP ICI or SAP phone interfaces using communication management software products. Preview dialing is not currently supported in the Interaction Center, although call lists can be used instead of preview dialing to allow the agent to view the details of each call before placing the actual call. For more information about outbound dialing integration, please see the section on automated outbound dialing in Chapter 4, "IC Marketing."

2.3 Multi-Channel Integration

So far in this chapter we have talked only about computer *telephony* integration. However, in today's modern interaction centers, customers demand that companies also integrate additional ways to communicate in addition to telephony, including email, chat, fax, postal letter, and so on. In particular the use of email has grown dramatically over the past years — and continues to grow. Although the telephone is still the most common method of interaction between customers and companies, email usage is catching up.

Other methods like Web chat and Short Message Service (SMS) are also growing, although they are not growing as fast as email and are still not as widely used or supported. In addition, older communication channels like fax and postal letter are also still supported, especially in certain industries such as manufacturing where noise makes telephones difficult to use, or in public service agencies where signatures are required on documents and where documents cannot be sent over the Internet due to security and legal concerns.

The SAP CRM Interaction Center supports numerous channels including telephone, email, Web chat, SMS, fax, postal letter, and so on. Although the SAP CRM Interaction Center itself does not provide out of the box telephony or multi-channel functionality, SAP does provide interfaces against which certified products can be integrated. These products — often referred to in the industry as "contact-center infrastructure software" and referred to by SAP as "Communication Management Software" — are available from SAP (via SAP Business Communications Management) as well as from SAP's partners including Genesys, Avaya, and others.

2.3.1 Email

The usage of email is growing rapidly. Today, most companies today allow their customers to contact the company via email. An October 2007 report by Radicati Group, an independent market research firm, estimates that are 1.2 billion active email users. Companies have recognized the growing importance of email and have responded by integrating support for email into their interaction centers. A September 2006 study by the International Customer Management Institute (ICMI) found that 85.6% of interaction centers now support email. SAP provides two options for handling email in the SAP CRM Interaction Center. Emails can either be pushed directly to agents via a screen pop in so-called *push mode*, or emails can be routed to an inbox where agents process the emails — when time permits — via so-called *pull mode*.

Real-time "Push Mode" Email with Screen Pop

The push mode email option requires multi-channel integration via a communication management software package such as SAP BCM, Genesys, Avaya, or other certified SAP partner. Companies who utilize the push method for emails usually do so in conjunction with other communication channels (such as telephony) as part of a larger business strategy to route all customer communications directly to a live agent — regardless of channel. These companies want to provide customers with the same level of service regardless of whether the customer sends an email or places a telephone call. In this case, all communications — including telephone calls and emails — are routed real time to an agent using routing rules (such as skills-based routing) via the communication management software. The agent receives the email or telephone call via a screen pop in the SAP CRM Interaction Center.

Agent Inbox "Pull Mode" Email

Other companies, however, prefer to give priority to real-time communication channels like the telephone, while routing emails to a queue where they can be processed via pull mode as time permits, for example, during slow periods or lulls where the rate of inbound calls drops off. The pull mode option does not require additional communication management software and relies on the SAPconnect interface to route incoming emails to a shared queue — the Interaction Center Agent Inbox — to which a group of agents are assigned. Agents process emails from the Agent Inbox, one email at a time, working through the list of emails. The emails in the Agent Inbox can be sorted as desired to suit the company's business process using sorting criteria such as due date, status, priority, creation date, responsible employee, and so on. See Figure 2.3.

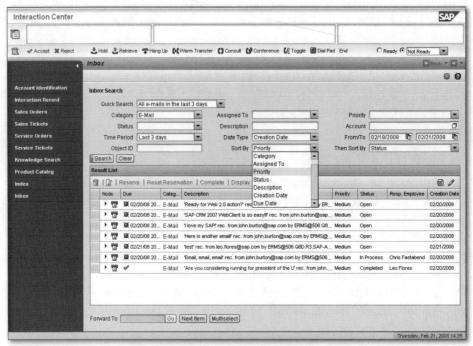

Figure 2.3 Email in the Agent Inbox Sorted by Priority and Status

The Agent Inbox is used for processing emails (including ERMS emails) in situations where emails do not need to be routed in real time to one particular agent. Rather, emails are routed to a shared inbox where a group of agents collectively process the emails, each agent working on one email at a time. Of course, the Agent Inbox is used for more than just emails.

The Agent Inbox can also be used for faxes, letters, service tickets, cases, SAP workflow items, and other transactions. The Agent Inbox is ideal for back-office, second and third-level support, or other offline scenarios where real-time communication with the customer is not required. We will discuss the Agent Inbox in more detail in Chapter 6 as part of the Interaction Center Service discussion.

▶ For a detailed explanation of how the Agent Inbox works, please see the 82-page FAQ document attached to SAP note *882653* "Frequently Asked Questions (FAQs) about the Agent Inbox."

▶ For general information on configuring the CRM system to accept email, fax, or SMS messages in the Agent Inbox, please see SAP note *455140* "Configuration of email, fax, paging or SMS using SMTP."

2.3.2 E-Mail Response Management System (ERMS) & Web Forms

SAP introduced E-Mail Response Management System (ERMS) in the CRM 4.0 Add-on for Service Industries. ERMS helps companies to better manage high volumes of inbound emails by automating much of the email handling process. Instead of just blindly routing all incoming emails to the same group of users in the Agent Inbox, ERMS allows you to route emails to different CRM organizational units, positions, or users based on attributes of the email such as content, subject, language, sender address, and so on. ERMS also provides advanced capabilities for sending auto-acknowledgements, auto-responses, and auto-preparing reply emails on behalf of an agent. ERMS can be used both for emails and Web forms.

A Web form is very similar to an email, except that instead of sending a message from an email client application like Microsoft® Outlook™ or IBM® Lotus Notes™, the user creates a message on the company's website using a form-based tool that controls the type of information and values that the user is allowed to enter. For example, a Web form will often have mandatory fields for customer name, account number, and email address. The user may be prompted to enter a problem description via free text, or the user might be asked to select an issue from a list of predefined options. Based on the values entered into the form — such as the user's email address and the problem category — ERMS is able to either auto-respond with a solution, or to route the email to the appropriate person or group for resolution.

> **Note**
>
> ERMS will be discussed in more detail in Chapter 9 during the discussion of the Rule Modeler.
>
> ▶ See SAP note *940882* "ERMS FAQ Note" that contains two attachments: "ERMS Overview" and "ERMS How-to-Guide." The note also contains links to other important ERMS related notes.

2.3.3 Fax, Letter, and SMS

While many industries and companies have embraced newer technologies such as email, Web chat, SMS text messaging, and Web services, some industries and companies continue to rely on time-proven communication channels of fax and postal letters. Fax, for example is often used in noisy manufacturing environments such as the shop floor where communication via telephone would be difficult. Fax and postal letters are also still used for legal documents where signatures are required and where security is a concern.

The SAP CRM Interaction Center can receive, process, print, create, and send fax and letter documents. SAPconnect provides a fax server interface. Faxes are received via SAPconnect and routed to the IC Agent Inbox using SAP workflow in a process similar to emails. Optionally, on a project basis, faxes could also be received via ICI by re-using the email handling capabilities for faxes. In this manner, faxes would be pushed to agents in real time via a screen pop.

Letter processing works slightly differently than email and fax handling, in that letter processing additionally relies by default on SAP ArchiveLink functionality. Letters are first manually scanned into digital format (such as a JPG image file). Typically, a mailroom clerk scans an incoming letter and then stores the corresponding file locally as a JPG file. The clerk then runs SAP GUI transaction OAWD to start the ArchiveLink scenario, which uses SAP workflow integration to create work items that appear in the Interaction Center Agent Inbox as category type "Letter."

When selected, a preview of the scanned fax or letter will appear alongside the customer's information (see Figure 2.4). Alternatively, on a project basis, it would also be possible to re-use the email handling capabilities of the ICI to push scanned letters to agents in real time via a screen pop.

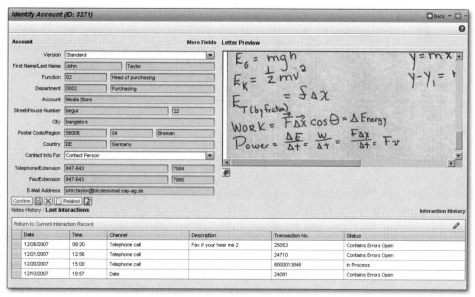

Figure 2.4 Scanned Letters Available in SAP CRM Interaction Center

SMS can be integrated into the Interaction Center on a project basis. SMS messages can be received via SAPconnect, either using the out of the box email processing capabilities (if the messages are treated as regular emails, which most communication management software vendors do by default) or via the SAPconnect Pager interface. If you want to handle SMS messages separately from emails, a small amount of project-based work would be required to customize the Agent Inbox to show "SMS" as a separate channel. It would also be possible to receive SMS messages via ICI, by re-using the email handling capabilities of ICI to push SMS messages to agents in real time via a screen pops. However, regardless of which option is selected for accepting inbound SMS messages, an additional project-based enhancements would be required to create an SMS Editor — or more typically, to enhance the existing IC E-Mail Editor to compose and send SMS messages.

> **Note**
> ▶ For full details on fax and letter integration with the Interaction Center Agent Inbox, please see the 43 page FAQ document attached to SAP note *894493* "Frequently Asked Questions for Fax and Letter."
> ▶ For a detailed explanation of how the Agent Inbox works, please see the 82-page FAQ document attached to SAP note *882653* "Frequently Asked Questions (FAQs) about the Agent Inbox."
> ▶ For general information on configuring the CRM system to accept email, fax, or SMS messages in the Agent Inbox, please see SAP note *455140* "Configuration of e-mail, fax, paging or SMS using SMTP."

2.3.4 Web Chat

Many companies today are encouraging their customers to use the Internet for Web-based self service in order to reduce service costs. While this strategy obviously does not make sense in *every* situation, Web-based self service can definitely complement your interaction center — perhaps for low-value customers, low-margin products, or simple easy-to-solve service requests (like account balance inquiries, requests for store hours or locations, online payments, address updates, and so on). However, when a Web self-service customer is not able to successfully resolve their issue on their own, the customer needs to be able to reach an interaction center agent. Web-based text chat is an ideal solution because it allows the customer to easily and immediately request assistance without leaving the Web.

The SAP CRM Interaction Center provides an agent-facing tool that allows agents to accept chat requests from customers and to reply using an integrated chat editor. See Figure 2.5. The chat editor is integrated with a number of tools to increase agent productivity including access to standard responses and interactive scripts. Agents can select commonly used phrases and standard responses from a drop-down list box and insert them into the chat message with the click of a button.

You can leverage interactive scripts to automatically insert text into the chat editor based on customer response. See Figure 2.6. Additionally, it is possible to save chat transcripts as part of the Interaction Record with the customer — either automatically or manually — based on configuration settings.

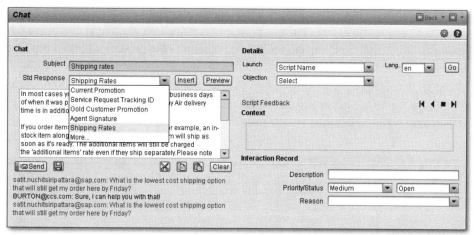

Figure 2.5 Agent-Facing Chat Editor in the SAP CRM Interaction Center with Standard Response Integration

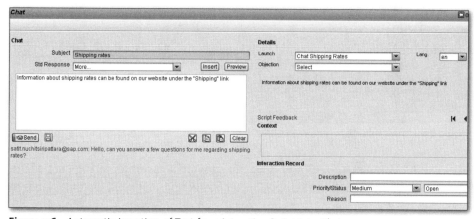

Figure 2.6 Automatic Insertion of Text from Interative Script into Chat

As of CRM 2007 (SP02), SAP offers a new multi-chat feature in the Interaction Center that allows one agent to chat with several different customers in parallel from the same Interaction Center session. Prior to CRM 2007, each agent can only chat with one customer at a time for a given Interaction Center session; in order to chat with multiple customers in parallel an agent would need to use a workaround solution such as logging on with multiple different user IDs and sessions. With the new multi-chat feature an agent can chat with up to six different customers from the same Interaction Center session. Each new customer chat request will open a new "tab" inside the agent's current web browser. Whenever a new chat message arrives from a customer, the tab for that customer's chat session will turn orange, letting the agent know that they need to click over and respond to the customer. When a customer's chat session has ended and the agent wraps up the interaction and clicks the End button on the toolbar, the tab will disappear. See Figure 2.7, which shows the new multi-chat feature.

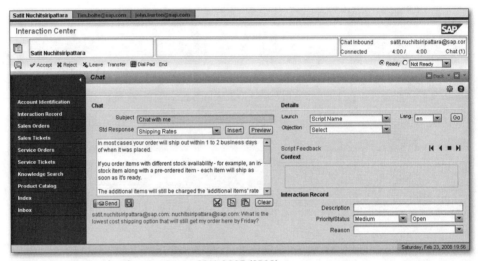

Figure 2.7   New Multi-Chat Feature in CRM 2007 (SP02)

The SAP CRM Interaction Center does not provide a customer-facing chat client. However, the SAP CRM Interaction Center has accept and send chat messages to any Web-based chat client that uses standard XML messaging as defined in the SAP Integrated Communication Interface (ICI) specification available for download from the SAP Community Network.

Note
To download the ICI specification that describes the requirements for integrating a customer-facing Web chat client, go to *http://www.sdn.sap.com* and follow the menu path: "Partners and ISVs" — "Integration and Certification". Then click the link "overview of all integration scenarios". Choose the interface "CA-ICI-CTI." Then click on the link, "Integrated Communication Interface."

2.4 SAP's Multi-Channel Integration Strategy

Now that we have explained the concepts of telephony, computer telephony integration, and multi-channel integration, let's talk about SAP's strategy around integrating these technologies into the SAP CRM Interaction Center. As mentioned already, SAP works with a number of partners who provide CTI and Multi-Channel Integration — more commonly known as Contact Center software. SAP refers to these partners and their technology using the term Communication Management Software (CMS).

Until recently SAP has never directly provided communication management software itself. Rather, SAP's strategy was — and still is — to provide certifiable interfaces against which third-party vendors can obtain certification from SAP. However, with the release of SAP Business Communication Management (BCM) software SAP now also offers its own CMS product — in addition to the CMS products available from SAP certified partners.

SAP does not intend to discontinue any partner relationships; rather, SAP BCM is offered as an *additional* option to the existing partner solutions. SAP BCM integrates to the SAP CRM Interaction Center via the ICI — the same way that other CMS partner solutions do — and works with all CRM releases that support the ICI, beginning with the CRM 4.0 Add-on for Service Industries. SAP BCM will be discussed in more detail later in this chapter, along with other CMS products.

2.4.1 SAP's Certified Multi-Channel Interfaces

There are many rivalries in the world that divide families, friends, and nations: Mac versus PC, PlayStation versus Wii, Ohio State versus Michigan. But perhaps no rivalry stirs up more animosity than the SAP ICI versus SAPphone Interface rivalry.

ICI and SAPphone are two SAP certifiable interfaces that both support integration of (typically third-party) multi-channel communication products into the SAP CRM Interaction Center. SAPphone is an older interface that uses a very unglamorous Remote Function Call (RFC) technology, and only supports one communication channel — telephony. ICI, on the other hand, is newer, utilizes more versatile SOAP/XML web service technology, and supports a variety of communication channels, including telephony, email, and chat. Additionally, SAPphone only works in a "pull mode" requiring agent-initiated screen refreshes, while ICI provides real-time screen pops (automatic population of customer data onto the screen) via so-called "push mode."

Supporters of SAPphone like the fact that SAPphone is low cost, simple to use, and Microsoft TAPI compliant; SAPphone supporters attack ICI as being complex and less-widely implemented in the current customer base. Proponents of ICI praise the fact the ICI is web-service XML/SOAP-based and that ICI supports real-time chat, email, and telephony; ICI proponents dismiss SAPphone as outdated and one-dimensional (telephony only).

SAPphone has historically been the only official option available for IC WinClient customers who want server-side telephony integration. IC WinClient customers who wanted email or chat integration could use a special client-side (web browser Active X control) solution from Genesys, leveraging the Genesys Suite and the Genesys G+ Adapter inside the IC WinClient. While SAPphone had historically been the only official solution for IC WinClient customers, some IC WinClient customers had actually implemented the newer ICI interface on a custom project basis. Today, SAP officially supports the use of ICI for multi-channel interaction for the IC WinClient, including telephony, email, and chat. ICI for IC WinClient is available with CRM 2005 (SP08 and beyond) and CRM 4.0 Add-on for Service Industries (SP07 and beyond).

The ability to use ICI with IC WinClient provides IC WinClient customers with a greater choice of multi-channel options, and offers reduced total cost of ownership (TCO) and increased flexibility to eventually migrate from IC WinClient to IC Web-Client. To implement ICI for IC WinClient, customers must perform some manual steps; they must also apply prerequisite SAP note *1038519*. For more information please see SAP note *1001703* written by SAP developer Satit Nuchitsiripattara.

SAP recommends the ICI for IC WebClient customers who need multi-channel integration of telephony, email, and/or chat. Although as of CRM 2005, SAP now also supports use of the older, RFC-based SAPphone interface (for telephony only) for IC WebClient customers — this option is targeted primarily at existing SAPphone customers who migrate from IC WinClient to IC WebClient and need to buy some time before switching to the newer, more powerful ICI interface. For all other IC WebClient customers, SAP exclusively recommends ICI.

	ICI	SAPphone
Technology	SOAP/XML	RFC
Channels Supported	Telephone, Email, Chat	Telephone
Push/Pull Model	Real-time "push"	Manual "pull"
Interaction Center User Interface Supported	WebClient WinClient (with OSS note *1001703* as of CRM 2005 SP08 and beyond or CRM 4.0 Add-on for Service Industries SP07 and beyond)	WinClient WebClient (as of CRM 2005, but not recommended for new implementations)

Table 2.1 ICI Versus SAPphone Interface for Interaction Center Multi-Channel and CTI Integration

2.5 SAP's Multi-Channel Partners

Some explanation of SAP's partner program and certification process is required. First, it is important to note that SAP does not directly certify telephone switch hardware (or software) such as PBX/ACD systems. Next, it is also important to note that SAP does not directly certify the vendors of communication management software (CMS) — the layer that sits on top of the PBX/ACD and handles the queuing and routing of the telephone calls, emails, chats, and other types of communication channels. What SAP actually certifies is the *adapter* that connects the CMS to one of the SAP interfaces such as the Integrated Communication Interface or the older SAPphone interface. Some CMS vendors including Genesys, Avaya, Cisco and even SAP's own SAP Business Communications Management provide their own certified adapters. In other cases, in order to use software from your chosen CMS vendor, you will need to purchase an adapter from another third-party company whose adapters are certified for your chosen CMS product.

A partial list of some of the vendors for which certified adapters are available includes: SAP Business Communication Management (BCM), Genesys, Avaya, Cisco, Siemens, Ericsson, Cycos, Alcatel, Altitude, Aspect, Interactive Intelligence, Nortel, and so on. For a full list of certified adapters per communication channel for ICI and SAPphone, you can visit the SAP partner section of the SAP website at *http://www.sap.com/partners/directories/SearchSolution.epx.*

▶ For *SAPphone Telephony*-certified products and connectors choose: BC-CTI 4.5 - Computer Telephony Integration (SAPphone) 4.5

▶ For *ICI Telephony*-certified products and connectors choose: CA-ICI-CTI 6.2 - Integrated Communication Interface - CTI 6.20

▶ For *ICI E-Mail*-certified products and connectors choose: CA-ICI-MAIL 6.2 - Integrated Communication Interface - Mail Add-On 6.20

▶ For *ICI Chat*-certified products and connectors choose: CA-ICI-CHAT 6.2 - Integrated Communication Interface - Chat Add-On 6.20

> **Note**
>
> It is important to note that in some cases, your chosen CMS vendor may additionally require an SAP-specific adapter to connect the CMS system to SAP's interface. These third-party adapters are certified by SAP, but the adapters are not sold by SAP. To inquire about availability and pricing of such third-party adapters you should of course contact the vendor who offers the adapter. SAP is not able to answer such inquiries.
>
> Additionally, in order to find out which underlying PBX/ACD switches your chosen CMS vendor supports, you should, of course, directly consult your CMS vendor. SAP cannot provide such information.

2.5.1 PBX/ACD Switches

Every organization that wants to receive telephone calls and other types of communications from customers (such as emails, chats, and so on) needs to have the proper technology infrastructure in place. This typically includes a device called a PBX and a sometimes-separate device known as an ACD — or more commonly a single hybrid device known as PBX/ACD. Traditionally these devices — known generically as *switches* — were hardware based, meaning that customers bought a particular piece of hardware consisting of a large computer server loaded with some proprietary software. However, today these devices are increasingly becoming software based, thanks to the mainstream acceptance of Internet technologies like Internet Protocol and Session Initiation Protocol (SIP).

At present, while the majority of existing PBX switches being used are still hardware based, most new switches being sold today are software based.

Note

Hardware-based PBX switches are sometimes also referred to as TDM-based switches. TDM stands for *time-division multiplexing*, which is the practice of sending different signals (each signal perhaps representing one telephone conversation) over the same digital data stream by transmitting each signal in short micro-second bursts of time — and then *demultiplexing* the signal when it arrives on the other end.

A PBX system is essentially responsible for connecting incoming telephone calls to the correct telephone extension — a process that is technically referred to as *circuit switching*. You can think of a PBX as a modern, computerized equivalent of the old-fashioned telephone switchboard operators of the 1930s to 1950s. However, while the PBX can connect incoming telephone calls to a particular telephone extension, a PBX usually has very limited logic for matching incoming calls with the appropriate agents/telephone extensions. For example, many PBXs use relatively unsophisticated logic such as a *hunt group*, which is basically just a list of telephone extensions (with an agent assigned to each extension). For each inbound call, the system tries to send the call to the first extension on the list; if the extension is currently busy the system tries the next extension on the list, and so on. Obviously, under such an arrangement the agents assigned to the telephone extensions on the top of the list receive many calls (and hence lots of work) while the agents assigned to extensions on the bottom of the list might never receive a call all day (and sit around doing nothing).

An ACD provides more powerful and elegant call routing options. Typically, the ACD functionality sits on top of the PBX, or is included as part of the hybrid PBX/ACD. For example, instead of using simple hunt group routing, an ACD might use *longest idle* routing where the system routes an incoming caller to the telephone extension of the agent who has been idle longest (i.e., has not received a telephone call). ACDs also often provide features like *look-ahead routing* that allows one ACD, which might be getting near maximum capacity during a busy period of peak inbound calls, to look into the queues of other ACDs in the same network to see which other ACD it might be able to deflect calls to. Another advantage of ACDs is that an ACD can also work with other technology like ANI or an IVR to enable *skills-based routing* — the matching of an incoming call to an appropriate agent based on the needs of the caller and the skills of the agent.

Up until several years ago, most PBX/ACD systems were hardware based, using something known as Time-Division Multiplexing (TDM) for *circuit-switching*–based telephony. The market is increasingly shifting to software-based PBX/ACD that rely on Internet Protocol (IP) for *packet-switching*-based telephony — as well as multi-channel integration.

As mentioned earlier in this chapter, SAP does not directly certify any particular switch vendor or product and you should contact your chosen communication management software vendor to find out which switches they support. However, below are a list of some of the most commonly used switches that are generally supported by most large vendors.

Commonly used hardware/TDM-based PBX/ACD switches

▸ Avaya Definity G3

▸ Nortel Meridian 1 (Option 11C, Option 61C, Option 81C, etc.)

▸ Siemens Hicom (150, 300, etc.)

▸ Ericsson MD110 PBX

Commonly used software/IP-based PBX/ACD switches

▸ Avaya S8000 Media Server

▸ Cisco IPCC

▸ Nortel Symposium

▸ Siemens Hipath (4000, 8000, etc.)

2.5.2 Communication Management Software (CMS) Products

As mentioned, CMS products provide the layer of intelligence that sits on top of the telephone switch (PBX, ACD, or hybrid PBX/ACD) and email server in order to facilitate optimized queuing, call treatment, and multi-channel routing (including skill-based routing) of incoming customer telephone calls and other communication channels such as email, SMS, chat, and so on. In addition, CMS products generally provide much more robust monitoring and reporting capabilities than the telephone switch provides.

Each CMS vendor has their own strengths and the list of features and functions vary across CMS products. However, in general, CMS products often provide features such as skill-based routing, interactive voice response (IVR) menu creation, multi-media recording and quality monitoring, outbound dialing, agent presence information for customer transfers, monitoring and reporting tools, and so on.

When an agent logs into the SAP CRM Interaction Center at the start of a shift, the agent additionally logs into their CMS system — which is responsible for routing the telephone calls, emails, and chats to the agent in the SAP CRM Interaction Center. Based on rules defined in the CMS system, incoming customer communications are distributed to different SAP CRM Interaction Center agents using real-time screen pop. The actual user interface (agent desktop) is completely provided by the SAP CRM Interaction Center, which contains a toolbar that enables access to the underlying functionality of the CMS system. Not only does SAP provide the user interface, but SAP is also the system of record for logging customer information, appointments, interaction history, business transactions, and so on. SAP CRM provides all of the business functionality. The CMS runs in the background and is responsible for routing customer communications to the agent, as well as for managing the agent's work mode and providing the agent with adequate time to wrap up each customer interaction before accepting the next customer communication.

Some of the most commonly used CMS products across the SAP installed customer base include:

Commonly Used Communication Management Software

▶ SAP Business Communications Management (BCM)

▶ Genesys Customer Interaction Management (CIM) Platform, which includes Genesys T-Server

▶ Avaya Interaction Center (AIC), which includes Avaya Application Enablement Services (AES)

▶ Cisco Unified Intelligent Contact Management Enterprise/Cisco Unified Contact Center Enterprise

▶ Siemens HiPath ProCenter

▶ Ericsson Solidus eCare

▶ Cycos Multi Media Contact Center (MMCC)/mrs (Unified Communications Suite)

Please see the appendix for a detailed description of the features and functionality provided by some of the SAP partners listed previously including Genesys, Avaya, and others.

2.6   SAP Business Communications Management (BCM)

Although SAP historically has not provided a CMS product itself and instead relied exclusively on certified partners, SAP now offers it own CMS product called SAP Business Communications Management (BCM). SAP acquired a Finnish company, Wicom Communications (*http://www.wicom.com*), a leading provider of all-IP and software-based business communications solutions, which SAP has re-branded. SAP BCM provides an integrated, out of the box SAP alternative to third-party products. However, SAP BCM is not intended to replace or displace existing SAP partners like Genesys or Avaya. SAP's commitment to the partner ecosystems remains unchanged. SAP still maintains close partnerships with certified CMS vendors. Rather, SAP BCM is an *additional* option available for SAP CRM Interaction Center customers looking for multi-channel integration. For example, SAP BCM is an option particularly well suited for SAP customers seeking an out of the box, integrated solution or an "all SAP" footprint with minimal third-party software or proprietary hardware.

SAP BCM integrates to the SAP CRM Interaction Center via SAP's ICI — the same interface used to integrate third-party CMS products. SAP BCM provides routing services to route incoming telephone calls, emails, and chat requests to the most appropriate interaction center agent utilizing CRM business data as well as agent skills and availability information. SAP BCM also provides a full set of online monitoring and reporting capabilities that integrate out of the box with SAP BW/BI for blended analytics. Other SAP BCM capabilities, for example, include Directory and Presence services, Interactive Voice Response (IVR), Voice-mail, and Call Recording. SAP Business Communications Management software is currently positioned both as an integrated solution with SAP CRM Interaction Center and as a stand-alone application. The integration with SAP CRM Interaction Center is supported with CRM release 4.0 (Add-on for Services Industries) and higher.

> **Note**
>
> SAP BCM is a separate product from SAP CRM and is licensed and installed separately. SAP BCM is available for download from the SAP Service Marketplace (http://service. sap.com) under SAP Support, Portal Downloads, SAP Installations and Upgrades, Entry by Application Group, SAP Application Components, SAP BCM Software, SAP BCM Software 5.5 or SAP BCM Software 6.0 (or higher).
>
> SAP BCM is a .NET application that runs on Microsoft servers, databases, and browsers. It is currently available in English, German, Russian, Polish, Finnish, and Swedish. Support for additional hardware and languages is planned.

2.7 Adding CTI or Multi-Channel Integration to an Existing Project

CTI and multi-channel integration are powerful tools that can be somewhat pricy to implement initially, but which will usually pay for themselves in just a matter of years. If you are an existing SAP CRM Interaction Center customer who does not yet leverage CTI, or if you are a customer who is currently planning an SAP CRM Interaction Center project and are still unsure whether to include CTI in the current scope — the following information will help evaluate whether CTI and multi-channel integration might make sense for you at this time.

Currently, only a portion of SAP CRM Interaction Center customers use CTI or multi-channel integration — varying by industry, business model, and CRM release. However, due to the recent availability of advanced, cost-effective IP-based CTI products — which eliminate the need for expensive hardware while enabling multi-site networking — adoption of CTI is on the rise. CTI can provide a number of cost and efficiency benefits in the interaction center including real-time screen pop of customer data and history, caller identification via automated number identification (ANI), dialed number identification service (DNIS), skill-based routing, and transfer of customer data via call-attached data (CAD).

Another benefit of CTI is that it can help you optimize call volume across peaks and valleys by allowing callers, during busy periods, to schedule call backs for a less busy time instead of waiting on hold. Additionally, CTI can help utilize excess agent capacity via blended inbound/outbound calling by switching unoccupied inbound agents to outbound calling (or to offline email processing) during lulls in inbound call activity.

2.7.1 Building a Business Case for CTI/Multi-Channel Integration

The costs of CTI hardware and software can be quite significant, varying from a few hundred dollars per user, to a few thousand dollars per user, depending on the vendor and the scope and complexity of the project. Adding support for additional channels beyond simple telephony — such as email, chat, and universal routing — will increase costs as well. Additionally, if using a vendor other than SAP, you may incur additional integration expenses; with SAP BCM there are no additional integration costs because no third-party adapter or connector is required (although there is, of course, a license fee for SAP BCM separate from the standard SAP CRM license).

SAP recommends that CTI purchase decisions should be made based on a business case that compares the potential cost savings of the CTI or multi-channel project against the total costs of the hardware, software, implementation, and maintenance. For example, if you know the average amount of time your agents spend searching for customer records, the average length of each customer interaction, the average agent cost per minute, the average number of calls received per year, and the percentage of successful ANI hits you anticipate based on your industry and the health of your customer master data — you can easily calculate how much money you will save per year by implementing CTI. If the estimated cost savings associated with time reductions outweigh the total costs of the CTI project, then you should implement CTI. If on the other hand, the costs significantly outweigh the anticipated savings, then you should hold off on CTI and evaluate again at a later date.

Of course, some companies also like to include "soft" factors into their cost calculations as well, such as the increase in customer satisfaction and improvement in customer experience that will result by integrating CTI — including eliminating the need for each agent to repeatedly ask the customer for their customer information each time the customer is transferred from one agent or department to another. Some companies use CTI and multi-channel integration as part of the business strategy to differentiate themselves from competitors by providing superior customer experience.

2.7.2 Implementing CTI or Multi-Channel Integration

The amount of time required to implement a CTI or multi-channel solution will depend on the scope of the project and the size of the interaction center. A relatively small and simple CTI project designed simply to provide screen pop for a small 20- or 30-agent call center can probably be done in as short as three to four weeks. A larger, more complex project involving multiple sites, multiple communication channels, IVR integration with multiple "data dips" into the CRM database, and reporting for several large distributed contact centers with thousands of agents could take up to 9 or 12 months. However, for a typical CTI project without email or chat integration for an average 50-users call center, you should expect to spend at least ten weeks to install, test, and go live with the new system.

As with any CRM project, it is often best to start small with your most immediate pain points, and then gradually increase the scope and roll out additional functionality based on a prioritized list of requirements. Due to the modular nature of CTI and multi-channel integration, it is very easy to start with one area — such as IVR integration and routing of telephone calls — and then later incorporate additional communication channels such as email and chat. As long as you plan in advance and take care to design your system with future considerations in mind, it is generally quite easy to roll out additional capabilities after you first address your most immediate requirements. This is generally a much more successful strategy than trying to roll out everything at once.

Most CMS vendors either offer professional services or bundle professional services as part of their product. If your CMS vendor does not offer professional services, we strongly suggest that you seek out a consultant who has experience integrating CTI systems with the SAP CRM Interaction Center. Be sure that your consultant has experience with the SAP interface (i.e., SAPphone or ICI) that you select.

2.8   Summary

This chapter introduced the basics of telephony, computer telephony integration (CTI), and multi-channel integration. We learned about the different pieces of hardware and software involved in CTI or multi-channel integration including the telephone switch (PBX, ACD, hybrid PBX/ACD), the communication management software, and the SAP CRM Interaction Center. We discussed SAP's strategy around multi-channel integration and learned about SAP's certified interfaces, including ICI and SAPphone. We took a brief look at some of the most commonly used telephone switches and CMS products in the industry, including SAP's own CMS product — SAP Business Communications Management (BCM). Finally, we discussed how to create a business case for adding CTI or multi-channel integration to a new or existing SAP CRM Interaction Center implementation.

Some of the most important points to remember from this chapter are:

- Telephone switches and software provide features like queuing, call treatment, and routing.

- Communication management software (CMS) enables true integration between the telephone system and the interaction center, providing computer telephony integration (CTI) features such as screen pop and ANI lookup.

- The SAP CRM Interaction Center contains a softphone toolbar that can be used to access telephone system functionality such as answering a call, placing the caller on hold, conferencing in a third party, and so on.

- Using communication management software from SAP BCM, or from certified SAP partners such as Genesys, Avaya, and others, you can integrate numerous communication channels into the Interaction Center including telephone, email, Web chat, and more.

- Email can be pushed real-time to an agent through the ICI interface using communication management software, or email can be handled in a back-office or offline scenario without real-time integration using the Agent Inbox feature of the Interaction Center.

- The Agent Inbox can also be used to handle other communication channels including fax, postal letter, SMS, and so on. In addition, the SAP E-Mail Response Management System (ERMS) functionality leverages the Agent Inbox.

- As of CRM 2007 (SP02) the SAP CRM Interaction Center provides multi-chat capabilities, allowing an agent to chat with up to six different customers in parallel from the same screen.

In the next chapter, we will introduce you to the basic features of the Interaction Center, including the user interface and the underlying technology of the SAP CRM WebClient. We'll also look briefly at some relevant configuration and administration tools.

In this chapter, we will explore the basic features of the Interaction Center user interface. We will also look at the underlying CRM WebClient framework technology on which the Interaction Center is built.

3   IC User Interface and Technology

This chapter will introduce you to the features of the Interaction Center (IC) user interface. We will also examine the CRM WebClient framework on which the Interaction Center is built. As of CRM 2006s/CRM 2007 and above, all CRM online applications including the Interaction Center run on the CRM WebClient user interface. Readers who are already familiar with the Interaction Center WebClient in CRM 2005 (CRM 5.0) and earlier releases will likely recognize much of the material — because the CRM WebClient UI framework was based on the IC WebClient framework. However, there are of course some significant differences between the new CRM WebClient version of the Interaction Center (in CRM 2006s/CRM 2007 and above) and the Interaction Center WebClient in CRM 2005. We will point out the major differences as appropriate throughout the chapter. Note that readers who are familiar with older products such as the *IC WinClient* or the *R/3 Customer Interaction Center* will likely be pleasantly overwhelmed by the vast differences between these older products and the new CRM WebClient version of the Interaction Center.

We will start off by looking at the various elements of the Interaction Center user interface including the context area, scratch pad, communication toolbar, breadcrumbs, navigation bar, index, broadcast messaging, and agent dashboard. Then we will introduce you to the Interaction Record, which is centrally (and inextricably) involved in all Interaction Center scenarios and processes. We will then move on and discuss the underlying framework technology and architecture of the Interaction Center and the CRM WebClient. We won't go into too much detail since another, more comprehensive document called the Consultant's Cookbook is available from the Ramp-Up Knowledge Transfer (RKT) section of the SAP Service Marketplace. This document goes into great depth on the Interaction Center and

CRM WebClient framework and architecture. However, we will at least introduce you to the basic concepts.

3.1 Browser Versions and Settings

The IC WebClient is a *thin-client* application that runs in a standard web browser. Thin-client refers to the fact that it is not necessary to install any special software — such as SAP GUI — on the machines of end users, as was previously the case with older products like the IC WinClient. All data displayed in the browser is sent from the CRM Web Application Server (Web AS) via Hypertext Transfer Protocol (HTTP) to the browser client. With only a couple of noted exceptions, no additional browser plug-ins or custom browser settings are required. See the related note for further explanation.

> **Note**
>
> In most cases the IC WebClient can run with out of the box browser settings, without the need for any special browser plug-ins or settings. There are a couple of exceptions:
>
> ▶ It is necessary to enable browser *Active X* controls in order to use certain functionality in the Interaction Center E-Mail Editor including Fax and Letter integration or integration with Microsoft® Outlook email contacts. It is also necessary to enable Active X controls in order to use the Microsoft Excel™ Download feature in SAP CRM 2007. See SAP notes *1018674* and *929457* that describe how to enable the browser settings.
>
> ▶ Depending on your CRM version, you may require *Sun Java Runtime Engine* (JRE) to enable certain functionality like the Interactive Scripting Editor or the Broadcast Messaging. See notes *717921* and *1105843* for details.

The IC WebClient can only be run on Microsoft Internet Explorer™ in CRM releases 4.0 Add-on for Service Industries, CRM 2005, and CRM 2006s. In CRM 2007 it is also possible to use Mozilla® Firefox™. Support is currently not yet available for Apple® Safari™ or other web browsers. You can find information about which browser versions are supported for each CRM release in the SAP Product Availability Matrix on the SAP Service Marketplace (*http://service.sap.com/PAM*). You can also find information about supported browser versions in SAP notes, such as SAP note *1114557* for CRM 2007.

SAP recommends running the IC WebClient in the browser F11 full-screen mode, which allows the application to display in its entirety without any vertical scrollbars. The IC WebClient was designed to be run on at least a 17-inch monitor with a screen resolution of 1024 × 768 or greater as indicated in SAP note *764974*. However, as technology continues to improve and prices continue to drop — your company should purchase the best equipment you can afford. Recycle those old, blurry, flickering, antiquated cathode-ray tube (CRT) monitors and buy high-resolution, wide-screen, liquid crystal display (LCD) monitors.

> **Note**
>
> SAP recommends running the IC WebClient in the browser F11 full-screen mode to allow the application to display fully with no vertical scrollbars.

3.2   Interaction Center User Interface

Now that you are familiar with the required browser versions, plug-ins, and settings necessary to run the Interaction Center, let's look at the user interface (UI) of the Interaction Center. Some people have described the Interaction Center as an *inverse L-shape* user interface. However, as a general rule, let's avoid using mathematical terms and letters of the alphabet when trying to describe the user interface. Rather, let's say that the Interaction Center screen consists of several different areas, including a section on the top that provides various toolbars and other controls, a menu bar on the left-hand side, and a large workspace that takes up the rest of the screen (Figure 3.1).

As shown in Figure 3.1, the very top portion of the screen contains a *title bar* with corporate branding. Beneath the title bar is the *context area,* which consists of the *account info* area, *alerts* area, and *communication info* area. To the left of the context area is the *scratch pad*, which allows the agents to take quick notes for later use. Beneath the context area is a communication *softphone toolbar*. The left-hand area of the screen contains a menu structure known as the *navigation bar*, while the largest area of the screen consists of as the *workspace* where the agent accesses customer information, business transactions, and other information. The workspace also includes a navigation tool called *breadcrumbs* as well as an area for displaying *system messages* and a context-specific link to the SAP Application Help. At the very bottom of the screen there is a scrolling ticker known as *broadcast messaging* where the agent can receive text messages sent by a supervisor. In the lower right-hand corner of the screen, the current date and time are displayed; if the agent clicks on the date and time, a dialog box called the *agent dashboard* will open, which displays technical information about the *queue status* and communication channels.

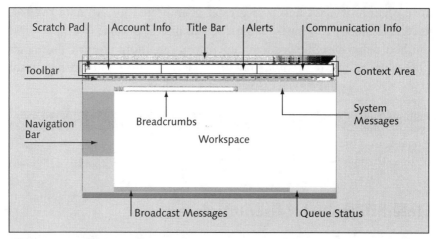

Figure 3.1 Overview of Interaction Center UI Components

3.2.1 Title Bar

The Title Bar appears at the top of the Interaction Center screen and displays the default text, "Interaction Center" as well as the SAP corporate logo. You can replace both the text and the logo with your own corporate branding. However, the process involves a modification of the code and therefore needs to be re-done after each upgrade. Instructions on how to replace the text and logo in the title bar can be found in the IC WebClient Consultant's Cookbook available on the SAP Service Marketplace. SAP is considering providing standard IMG configuration for re-branding the title bar in a future release after CRM 2007.

3.2.2 Context Area

The *context area* is located at the top of the Interaction Center screen beneath the title bar. The purpose of the context area is to ensure that important background information about the current customer and the current interaction is always displayed at the top part of the screen, regardless of which data or transactions are being worked on by the agent below in the main area of the Interaction Center. The context area is always present on the screen, and displays a combination of information including: (1) account info, (2) alerts, and (3) communication info.

The *account info* area displays information about the current account including the contact person and related company, if applicable (Figure 3.2). In a business-to-consumer (B2C) scenario the account info area only shows the name of the consumer. In a business-to-business (B2B) scenario, however, the account info area displays both the name of the contact person, as well as the name of the company that the contact person represents.

Figure 3.2 Context Area: Account Info

The *alerts* area displays text-based alert messages containing information pertaining to the current customer or interaction (Figure 3.3). Alerts are created by Interaction Center analysts using a tool called the Alert Editor, and then triggered based on business rules and events defined in the Rule Modeler. When an alert is no longer valid, it can be terminated via a business rule as well. If more than two alerts are present at one time, a small back arrow will appear allowing the agent to page down through the list of current alerts. If an alert contains a navigational hyperlink, the alert will be underlined when the agent places the cursor over the alert. Note that *alerts* are different than *system messages,* which display purely technical information generated by the software application itself.

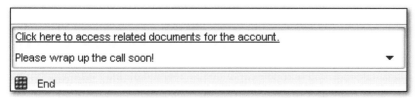

Figure 3.3 Context Area: Alerts

The *communication info* area displays information about the current *contact* (Figure 3.4). Note that whereas the term *interaction* describes the set of events and business transactions involved in the current business dealing with the customer, the term *contact* refers to data about the communication channel being used to interact with the customer in the current interaction. Some of the information displayed about the current contact includes the communication channel type (e.g., telephone or email) and direction (e.g., inbound or outbound). The contact address is also shown, such as the 1-800 number that the customer dialed, or the corporate email address to which the customer sent an email or chat request. In addition, the current contact state is displayed (e.g., ringing, connected, on hold), as well the duration of the current state and the total duration of the interaction. Finally, if more than one contact is involved (e.g., if the agent is in the process of composing a follow-up email to the customer who is on the phone), the number of open contacts is displayed for each channel.

Figure 3.4 Context Area: Communication Info

3.2.3 Communication Toolbar

The communication toolbar allows agents to accept incoming contacts (e.g., telephone calls, emails, and chat requests) and to perform other functions such as putting a caller on hold, transferring a chat session, or making a consultation call to a colleague while working on an email. Essentially, the communication toolbar provides a so-called *softphone* interface, allowing agents to control telephone functionality (e.g., answer, hold, retrieve, transfer) directly from the Interaction Center application without the need for an actual physical *hardphone* that sits on the agent's desk. The communication toolbar is not just limited to telephony functionality — it also offers a separate set of buttons (and corresponding functionality) for both chat and email. The Interaction Center automatically presents the appropriate toolbar based on the selected communication channel; an agent can also manually select the desired toolbar using the channel selector icon located on the left side of the toolbar (Figure 3.5). The communication toolbar also contains radio buttons that display the agent's current work mode — as maintained automatically by the communication management system or manually by the agent.

Figure 3.5 Communication Toolbar with Channel Selector

As of CRM 2007, there are more possibilities than in previous releases to configure the appearance and behavior of the buttons in the communication toolbar. You can still choose which buttons should be visible on the toolbar (and which should not) and in which order the buttons should appear, as you could do in CRM 2005. However, as of CRM 2007 you can also decide whether each button should be represented by an icon, text, or both an icon and text. This is configured in the IMG: CUSTOMER RELATIONSHIP MANAGEMENT • INTERACTION CENTER WEBCLIENT • BASIC FUNCTIONS • COMMUNICATION CHANNELS • DEFINE TOOLBAR PROFILES. If you want, you can even upload your own icons instead of using the default SAP icons. This can be configured in the IMG: CUSTOMER RELATIONSHIP MANAGEMENT • INTERACTION CENTER WEBCLIENT • CUSTOMER-SPECIFIC SYSTEM MODIFICATIONS • DEFINE TOOLBAR BUTTONS.

3.2.4 Scratch Pad

The *scratch pad* provides an area for the agent to type notes and other information that can later be imported into the notes field of the interaction record, service ticket, case, and other business transaction with a single button click. The idea behind the scratchpad is that often when a customer calls the Interaction Center, the first thing the customer wants to do is describe the issue they are experiencing and explain their reason for calling. However, typically the Interaction Center agent first needs to search for and locate the customer's account information before the agent can create an Interaction Record or other business transaction and log the customer's issue.

Rather than interrupt the customer and explain that the agent is not yet ready to hear about the customer's issue, many interaction center agents have historically used a paper notepad and pen or pencil to write down the problem. Later, the agent retypes the information into the computer system. The Interaction Center scratchpad on the other hand, provides an electronic notepad, allowing the agent to only type the information once rather than first writing it down and then later retyping it.

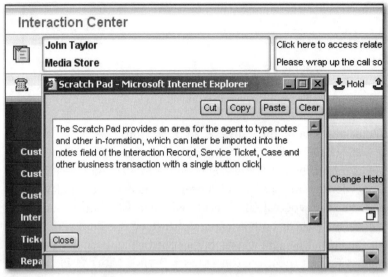

Figure 3.6 Scratch Pad

3.2.5   System Messages

The *system messages* area is actually located in the main workspace, beneath the workspace title. System messages contain technical information raised by the different application components of the Interaction Center. There are three types of system messages, each with its own icon: informational messages (green checkmark icon), warning messages (yellow triangle with exclamation point), and error messages (red circle with exclamation point). For example, after you confirm a main account, the system presents you with an informational message reminding you to optionally also confirm a contact person. On the other hand, a warning message is presented if multiple (alternative) organizational units are available for a particular business partner, while an error message will be raised if no organization unit is selected (Figure 3.7).

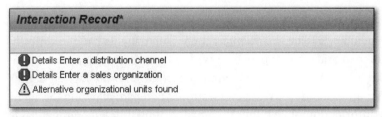

Figure 3.7 System Messages

3.2.6   Navigation Bar & Index Page

The *navigation bar* is the primary means by which Interaction Center agents access commonly used business transactions and other functionality from the Interaction Center. The *index* page is an alternative method for accessing less frequently used transactions and functionality. The navigation bar and the index page work in the same fashion. When an agent clicks on a link in the navigation bar or the index, the corresponding application component is launched in the main workspace. Typically, the most commonly used functions are included directly in the agent's navigation bar profile, while all of the rest of the less commonly used functions are accessed as needed from the index. Configuration of the navigation bar and index are discussed as part of the CRM framework in Section 3.4.2.

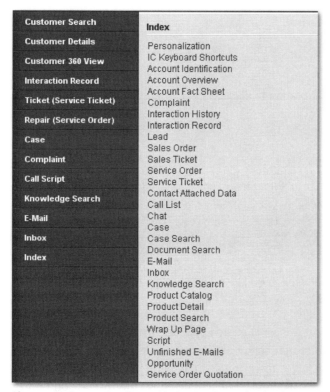

Figure 3.8   Interaction Center Navigation Bar and Index Page

In addition to providing a list of all navigation links available to an agent, the index page also offers links to the *IC Keyboard Shortcuts* page and the *Personalization* page.

The IC Keyboard Shortcuts page provides expert users with mouse-free access to Interaction Center-specific functionality, including communication toolbar, alerts, scratch pad, system messages, and agent dashboard. The list of IC keyboard shortcuts provided by SAP is shown in Figure 3.9.

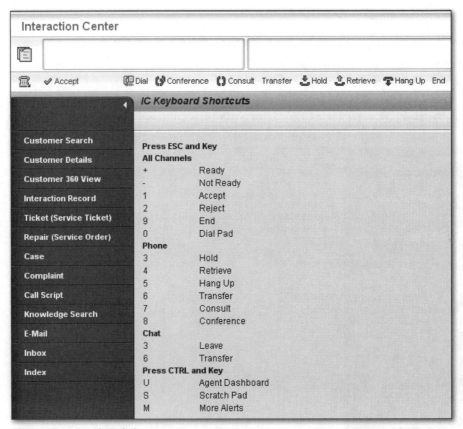

Figure 3.9 IC Keyboard Shortcuts

In addition to the Interaction Center-specific keyboard shortcuts, the index page also provides a link to the Personalization page, which offers general, non IC-specific keyboard shortcuts that focus on automatic navigation and automatic setting of the cursor position. These links can be personalized by the Interaction Center agent as desired (Figure 3.10). To access the keyboard personalization dialog box, the user clicks on the *Personalization* link in the index page and then clicks on the *Personalize Shortcuts* hyperlink in the personalization page. As seen in Figure 3.10, several other personalization options besides keyboard shortcuts are also available from the personalization page including groupware integration options, screen layout, and date and time formatting preferences.

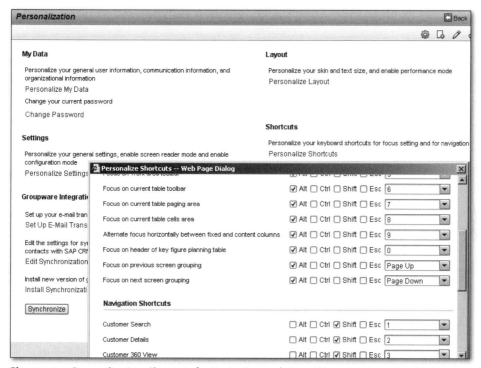

Figure 3.10 Personalization: Shortcuts for Navigation and Cursor Focus

Navigation Bar Differences Between CRM 2005 and CRM 2006s/CRM 2007

Readers familiar with the navigation bar and index page in CRM 2005 and earlier releases will notice a few differences in CRM 2006s/CRM 2007 and above. In CRM 2005, the navigation bar was divided into two sections: a standard section and a personalized section. Agents could add or remove items from the personalized section of the navigation bar from the index. However, in CRM 2006s/CRM 2007 the navigation bar does not include a user personalization section. Additionally, in CRM 2005 when an agent navigated to a transaction or other screen by clicking on link in the navigation bar, the selected link in the navigation bar stayed highlighted — giving the agent a visual reminder of which link had been clicked.

In CRM 2006s/CRM 2007, the navigation bar does not highlight selected links. Finally, users of CRM 2006s will notice that keyboard navigation shortcuts are not available; however, keyboard shortcuts are re-introduced again in CRM 2007 (as shown in Figure 3.10).

3.2.7 Breadcrumbs

Interaction Center agents can navigate back and forth between screens in the Interaction Center using *breadcrumbs* — a virtual navigational tool that tracks the agents *steps* during each customer interaction. As the agent moves through screens, the title of each screen is recorded. These recorded titles are called *breadcrumbs*. An agent can display history of all screens visited within the current customer interaction by clicking on the drop-down list box that appears in the breadcrumbs. Using the breadcrumbs, an agent can verify their current location or retrace their steps in the current interaction, as necessary. Breadcrumbs are cleared when the agent completes each interaction by pressing the *End* button.

In CRM 2005, the Interaction Center WebClient does not support the use of the back and forward buttons in the Web browser. Rather, as per SAP note *884976*, it is recommended to always run the Interaction Center in the browser full-screen (F11) mode and to use the breadcrumbs tool for all navigation between screens in the Interaction Center. As of CRM 2006s/CRM 2007, however, it is possible to enable navigation via the browser back and forward buttons by applying SAP note *1002385*.

3.2.8 Agent Dashboard

Agents can access the agent dashboard by clicking on the date/time display located in the lower right-hand corner of the Interaction Center. However, the agent dashboard is arguably not really a *dashboard* at all. For example, it does not display real-time data dynamically adjusted on the fly, nor does it offer any neat graphical gauges and meters as we might expect from an application referring to itself as a *dashboard*. Rather, the agent dashboard simply provides some rather static, very technical data about the agent, including the agent's CRM user ID, CRM business role (formerly IC profile), assigned channels and queues, and some other system information — such as the domain of the CRM application server (Figure 3.11).

Most of this information is probably of little use to an Interaction Center agent; rather, the information is probably more useful for analysts or IT professionals who need to help the agent debug and resolve any technical issues or problems.

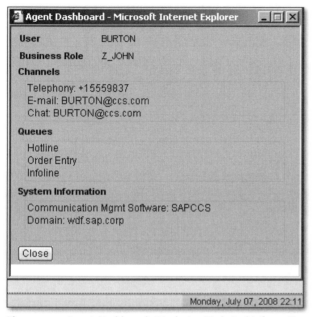

Figure 3.11 Agent Dashboard: Displaying Technical Information

3.2.9 Broadcast Messaging

At the bottom of the Interaction Center screen there is a small area called the messaging bar that displays scrolling text messages sent (i.e., broadcasted) by a supervisors to one or more agents. This functionality is referred to as *broadcast messaging* because it allows a supervisor to *broadcast* information out to all the agents the supervisor is responsible for (or some subset of the group) with a single message. Based on the time duration that the supervisor defines a message to be valid for (e.g., 30 minutes), the message will continue to scroll across the bottom of the agent's screen unless the agent explicitly clicks on the message and manually marks it as read (Figure 3.12). If more than one message has not yet been marked as read, the messages will all continue to scroll one at time; depending on the length (i.e., number of characters) of the messages, more than one message might be visible (or partially visible) at once. Messages that are marked as high priority will appear in bold font, while normal priority messages appear in regular font.

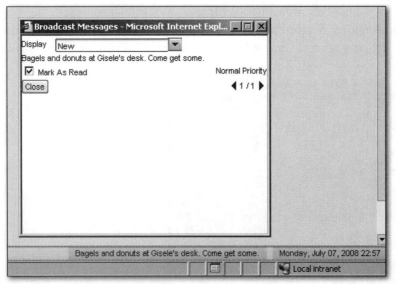

Figure 3.12 Broadcast Messaging

3.3 Interaction Record

Now that you have a good understanding of the Interaction Center user interface, let's discuss one of the most important concepts involved in actually using the Interaction Center — the interaction record. Every time an agent in the Interaction Center works with customer data — regardless of whether the agent is processing a telephone call, email, Web chat, fax, letter, or even an offline order in the back office — an *interaction* has occurred. For a variety of reasons, every interaction that occurs in the Interaction Center should always be categorized, recorded, and saved. Doing so will allow you to provide proper service to customers. It will also enable accurate measurement and reporting of your Interaction Center performance and metrics. It will even help you to evaluate and appropriately compensate your agents. On the other hand, if you aren't logging your interactions, you have no idea what your customers are contacting you about. You have no idea what your agents are working on. And essentially, you have no idea what is going on in your Interaction Center. The answer to all your record-keeping needs is a simple document (well, technically a rather elaborate business transaction) called the interaction record.

When an agent accepts an incoming contact (e.g., telephone call, email, chat request) or initiates an outbound contact via a call list or planned activity, an interaction record is automatically created by the system. In non-CTI scenarios where no communication management software (CMS) system is used, an interaction record is created when an agent confirms a customer account or contact person. When working in a back-office mode (i.e., processing business transaction from the agent inbox) an interaction record is created when the agent selects a transaction from the agent inbox and presses the *Interact* button. Similarly, an interaction record is created if the agent opens a transaction from the inbox in display mode, and then sends a new email to the customer (or replies to an existing email from the customer), or if the agent creates a dependent follow-on transaction to the original item. Not surprisingly, an interaction record is also created anytime the agent manually clicks the interaction record link in the navigation bar or index page. Basically, *any time an agent works with customer data* an interaction record is created.

So now that you know *when* an interaction record gets created, let's look at *what* the interaction record does. The interaction record acts as a file folder (or an old shoebox used for the same purpose), serving to keep together all relevant documents, business objects, and transactions involved in each individual customer interaction. The interaction record contains a storage area known as the *activity clipboard,* which links together all of the relevant business object repository (BOR) objects involved in the current customer interaction (Figure 3.13). These include account and contact person, solutions, emails, chat transcripts, all dependent business transactions — and of course — the interaction record itself. When the agent ends the interaction by pressing the *End* button (formerly the *End Contact* button), all the contents of the activity clipboard are linked to the interaction record.

Activity Clipboard

Description	Object Id	Process Type
Media Store	3271	
John Taylor	400012	
New interaction record	2243	Interaction Record
New service ticket	8000001605	Teleservice
sent Email	E-Mail	

Figure 3.13 Interaction Record: Activity Clipboard

> **Note**
>
> When reading about the interaction record in other resources (e.g., Web forums, online help, and other books) you may come across two additional terms: Business Data Context (BDC) and Business Data Display (BDD). The *BDC* is a virtual (non-visible) central data storage device used in the IC WebClient. The Interaction Record relies on the BDC to store data belonging to the activity clipboard. The contents of the BDC are refreshed at the end of each interaction when the End button is pressed.
>
> The *BDD* was the original name used for the activity clipboard, and is still in use in the older SAP GUI-based IC WinClient.

Suppression of Interaction Record Creation

One of the advantages of using the interaction record is that it acts as an anchor, keeping all of the other related objects tied firmly in place. Nothing is able to float away and get lost at sea. Yet, some SAP customers choose to not use the interaction record. Instead, these companies directly create other business transaction types as required — such as the service ticket — with no interaction record to provide object linking. Technically, it is possible to suppress the creation of interaction records via an enhancement to the standard code. The ABAP class *CL_ICCMP_CUCOIREC_IMPL* provides a method called named *GET_INTERACTION_RECORD*. This method includes a Business Add-In (BADI) named *CRM_IC_IARECORD* that can be used to suppress the creation of interaction records. See SAP note *828402* for full details.

However, while it is technically possible to do so, *SAP does not recommend suppressing the creation of interaction records*. Without the interaction record, the contents of the activity clipboard are not linked together at the end of an interaction. Without the interaction record, it becomes very difficult to keep track of all of the relevant business transactions and objects involved in each particular customer interaction. Additionally, the interaction record is utilized by several out of the box SAP reports such as the blended analytics reports.

Unlinking Items from the Activity Clipboard

In CRM 2006s/CRM 2007 and above, a new feature is available to allow Interaction Center agents to manually unlink selected items from the activity clipboard when the interaction record is saved at the end of an interaction. Based on configuration settings, a dialogue box appears on the screen after the *End* button is pressed, containing a list of all items from the activity clipboard of the interaction record (Figure 3.14). In the event that a business transaction or other document was inadvertently or incorrectly added to the activity clipboard during the interaction, the agent can select the item and prevent it from being linked when the interaction record is saved. Note that the item is not deleted (i.e., the actual transaction or other object still exists in the database), but rather the *link* between the item and the interaction record is deleted.

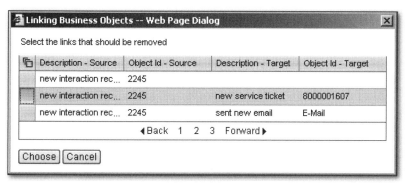

Figure 3.14 Unlinking Items from the Activity Clipboard of the Interaction Record

The following configuration is necessary to enable the activity clipboard unlinking feature. Run transaction *CRMC_UI_PARAMETERS*. In the folder *Parameter Definition* create a parameter with ID *SHOW_LINK_DIALOG*. In the folder *Profile Definition* create a profile with ID *PARAMPROFILE*. Select the newly created profile and double-click on the folder *Parameter Assignment*. Add a new entry with the parameter *SHOW_LINK_DIALOG* in the *Name* field and "X" in the *Value* field.

Now that you have created your parameter profile, you need to assign it to your business role. In the IMG, select the configuration activity *Define Business Role*. Select your business role and double-click on the folder *Assign Function Profiles*. Add a *function profile* with *PARAMETERS* as the *Function Profile ID*, and *PARAMPRO-FILE* as the *Profile Value*.

3.4   Getting the Interaction Center Up and Running

Now that you've learned about configuration (of the activity clipboard unlink functionality), let's examine the minimum requirements to get the Interaction Center up and running. Specifically, we will look briefly at the following topics: IC profile/CRM business role, navigation bar configuration, function profiles, and HR org data. We won't go too deeply into areas such as the CRM business roles and or navigation bar configuration – as these topics are covered in full detail in other sources such as the Consultant's Cookbook. However, we will at least make sure you are familiar with any IC specific functionality inside these areas.

As you probably realize by now, the SAP CRM Interaction Center is extremely flexible and supports a variety of different business scenarios, customer markets, and levels of sophistication. For example, some companies mainly conduct telemarketing and telesales, while other companies focus on customer service. Some companies work exclusively with consumers, while others companies operate primarily in the B2B market or do business with both consumers and business customers. Other companies might not even work with external customers at all but instead provide internal IT help desks and/or HR employee interaction centers. Some companies run high-volume professional interaction centers with thousands of users, while other companies staff small 20- or 30-person service centers. Some companies have telephony integration (or sophisticated multi-channel integration including telephony, email, and chat) while other companies don't have CTI at all, and work in a back-office mode.

Obviously, with so many different possibilities for leveraging the Interaction Center, companies need an easy way to configure which Interaction Center features and functionality should be available to agents. It doesn't make sense, for example, to give an Interaction Center agent access to internal HR data if the agent's job is to process sales orders from external business customers. Let's take a look at how you can use the roles, profiles, navigation bar configuration, and HR org data set up to control who has access to what functionality and features. We'll start with the CRM business role (formerly known as the IC WebClient profile).

3.4.1 CRM Business Role/IC WebClient Profile

The CRM business role is the central object that controls all aspects of what the agent sees on the Interaction Center screen, including the screen layout, the available navigation bar entries, and even the appearance and behavior of the functions selected from the navigation bar. The CRM business role is not IC specific, but rather is used across CRM for all business applications as of CRM 2006s/CRM 2007. Readers who are familiar with CRM 2005 and earlier releases will recognize that the CRM business role is basically an enhanced version of the IC WebClient profile — except that the CRM business role is now valid for all CRM online applications, not just the Interaction Center.

SAP delivers a number of out of the box CRM business roles including: IC Agent, IC Manager, Marketing Professional, Sales Professional, Service Professional, and so on. Essentially, a CRM business role is used to package the business content that a user needs to perform their specific job. Each role can have its own navigation bar profile, layout profile, PFCG authorization profile, and so on, that collectively control what functionality is available to the user (Figure 3.15). Roles are not directly assigned to users but rather to positions in the HR organizational model; users are then assigned to the positions. The process of assigning users to CRM business roles is covered in detail in Section 3.4.4.

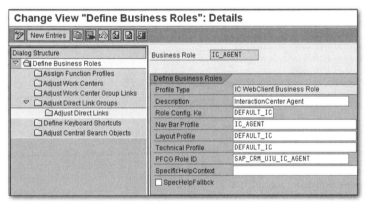

Figure 3.15   CRM Business Role Definition

Let's look at what's involved in defining a business role. The *Profile Type* is used to indicate whether the role belongs to a CRM application with special requirements — such as Interaction Center or CRM on Demand (CoD) — which differ from other standard CRM online business roles. The *Role Config. Key* allows you to incorporate screens (views) that have been specially configured for a particular business role. The *Nav Bar Profile* provides a master list of work centers, logical links, and direct link groups that are be used by a particular business role. The *Layout Profile* allows you to choose whether to include certain UI features — like the communication toolbar and context area — that are only relevant in IC specific roles but not used across the rest of CRM. The *Technical Profile* defines technical attributes such as memory consumption, cookies, start page, logoff page, and so on. Finally, the *PFCG Role ID* defines the authorization profile (maintained in transaction PFCG) that is associated with the business role. Note that there is a one-to-one mapping between PFCG profiles and business roles, in that each business role must have its own unique PFCG profile.

In addition to all of the technical attributes, each CRM business role also contains a collection of *function profiles* that control how each of the different functions of the relevant application behaves. For example, in the Interaction Center, the BPIDENT function profile controls which various settings and options are used in the business partner identification screen. Each function profile is configured separately in its own respective IMG transaction. In the Assign Function Profile step of the business role definition process you are merely choosing which of the already configured function profiles to assign to your business role. For example, for the selected entry, BPIDENT, you can see for example that many different business partner identification profiles have already been created and are available for selection (Figure 3.16).

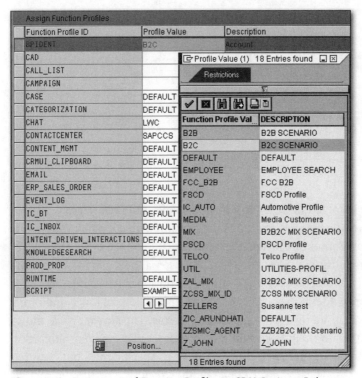

Figure 3.16 Assignment of Function Profiles to CRM Business Role

3.4.2 Navigation Bar

The navigation bar — together with the CRM business role — determine which functionality an Interaction Center agent is able to access. The *navigation bar pro-*

file provides a lot of different functionality, some of which is not particularly relevant for the agent-facing Interaction Center roles. Work center group links are only used in overview (home) pages, which are the landing pages for roles used by sales professionals, service professionals, or IC managers. Similarly, the default configuration for the Interaction Center does not make use of direct group links, which allow you to directly create a new account. Rather, in the Interaction Center you would typically first search for an existing account — and then create a new account if necessary — directly from the identify account search screen.

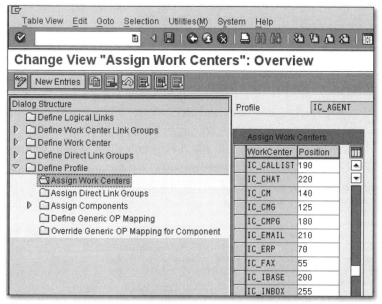

Figure 3.17 Navigation Bar Configuration

The two most important aspects of the navigation bar configuration relevant in the Interaction Center are the *Assign Work Centers* activity and the *Define Generic OP Mapping* activity — both located as sub-folders inside the folder *Define Profile*. The work center assignment activity is where you specify which work centers should potentially be available in the agent's navigation bar (although it is possible to later filter out undesired work centers at a higher level using the CRM business role profile). A work center is simply a link in the navigation bar that opens a particular application component in the main workspace area of the Interaction Center. In Figure 3.17, you can see that various work centers have been assigned to the navigation bar profile IC_AGENT. For each work center, you can also indicate the relative position in which it should appear in the list of navigation bar links. For example, a work center with position 55 will appear much higher in the list of links than a work center with position 200.

The *Define Generic OP Mapping* activity is one of the most important — yet also one of the most overlooked — configuration steps involved in the Interaction Center (Figure 3.18). You need to maintain an entry for every Interaction Center component that you want agents to be able to navigate to. Inbound and outbound plugs are technical terms used internally by SAP software developers. Yet, as is sometimes the case with SAP products, these technical terms find their way onto the user interface. Essentially, inbound and outbound plugs are what enable navigation between different components in the Interaction Center (or other CRM applications). In order for an agent to be able to navigate from one component to any other, a corresponding outbound plug mapping must be maintained in the agent's navigation bar profile. The outbound plug mapping basically consists of an *object type* (e.g., service ticket, fax, agent inbox) and *object action* (e.g., search, execute, create, edit, display), as well as the corresponding *target ID* to which the navigation should occur. A target ID is basically the technical ID of the inbound plug of the screen you want to access. Optionally, you can instead specify a *logical link* — which is a target ID that also includes a parameter (such as *transaction type* if calling the target ID for a service ticket).

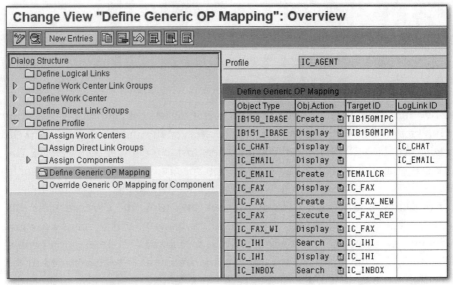

Figure 3.18 Define Generic Outbound Plug (OP) Mapping

Note

In order for your agents to navigate to anywhere in the Interaction Center, you must first maintain so-called *outbound plug* mappings for each component that they want access. In the outbound plug mapping, you specify the *object type/object action* and *target ID* or *logical link* (i.e., target ID with parameter) that the system should navigate to. This is required for all manual navigation — when the agent clicks on a link in the navigation bar, index, alert, or other application — as well as for automated navigation provided by Intent-Driven Interaction.

3.4.3   Transaction Launcher

The *transaction launcher* — and its IC WinClient predecessor, the *action box* — are tools that integrate non-IC transactions and applications into the Interaction Center. The transaction launcher can be used to launch a variety of applications including SAP GUI transactions, CRM business object repository (BOR) objects, URL-based Internet application (which run inside an HTML iFrame), and utilities industry solution (IS-U) front-office processes.

Sometimes an agent in the CRM Interaction Center needs to access a back-office transaction such as ERP sales order creation (transaction VA01) or ERP customer creation (transaction XD01). The transaction launcher can access these back-end R/3 of ERP SAP GUI transactions, and render them as HTML via Internet Transaction Server (ITS) technology. The transaction launcher can also integrate *CRM-based* SAP GUI transactions into the CRM WebClient (Figure 3.19). For example, certain administrative SAP GUI transactions — like creation of call lists or creation of solution database (SDB) problems and solutions — do not have a CRM WebClient equivalent and can only be accessed from the SAP GUI interface. Using the transaction launcher, however, you can access these transactions from the Interaction Center (or other CRM business roles of the CRM WebClient). Please note that the transaction launcher only works with transactions that are marked as supporting *SAPGUI for HTML*, which can be verified with transaction code SE93.

Note

Not all SAP GUI transactions work with the Transaction Launcher and the Internet Transaction Server (ITS). Only transactions that are marked as supporting the SAPGUI for HTML can be accessed in the CRM WebClient via the transaction launcher – which renders the SAP GUI transaction as an HTML page. For example, the Call List Generation transaction CRMD_CALL_LIST supports SAPGUI for HTML, but the Call List Maintenance Transaction CRMD_TM_CDLIST does not.

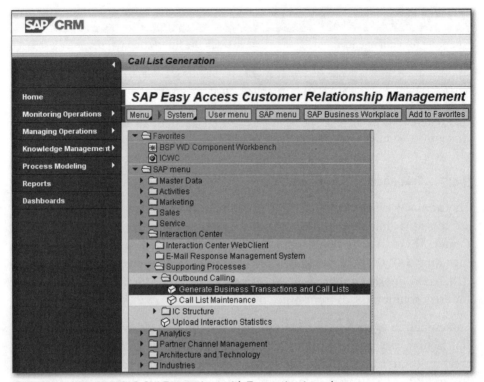

Figure 3.19 Accessing SAP GUI Transactions with Transaction Launcher

A wizard is provided in the IMG to help with the actual creation of *launch transactions*. You can access the wizard via IMG path: CUSTOMER RELATIONSHIP MANAGEMENT • INTERACTION CENTER WEBCLIENT • BASIC FUNCTIONS • TRANSACTION LAUNCHER • CONFIGURE TRANSACTION LAUNCHER (WIZARD). The wizard will guide you through all the necessary steps of creating the launch transaction. Once created, the launch transaction can be reused as many times as required by assigning it to the desired navigation bar profile. It is also possible to transport launch transactions across clients and systems, although technically only the meta-data is transported and the actual ABAP classes are regenerated in the target system using the instructions contained in the meta-data.

To assign a launch transaction to your navigation bar profile, you first need to define a new *logical link* using the launch transaction you have already created (Figure 3.20). Then you need to create a new *work center* that uses the logical link you just defined (Figure 3.21). And then you need to assign the new work center to your *navigation bar profile*.

Create Logical Link

▸ Access the *Define Navigation Bar Profile* activity from the IMG. Double-click on the folder *Define Logical Links*. Click the *New Entries* button.

▸ Provide a name for the new logical link you will be creating.

▸ Select "Launch Transaction" as the *Type*.

▸ Enter "EXECLTX" as the *Target ID*.

▸ In the *Parameter* field enter the ID of the launch transaction you previously created (Figure 3.20). Note that the F4 value help will not provide you with this value. You must either remember it or use the copy and paste technique.

▸ Enter, "CL_CRM_UI_LTX_NAVBAR_PARAM" in the Parameter Class field.

▸ Enter a title and description. Save.

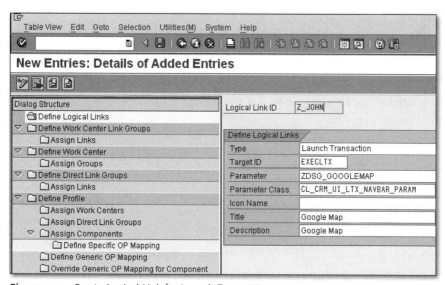

Figure 3.20 Create Logical Link for Launch Transaction

Create Work Center

Now that you have created a new logical link for your launch transaction, you need to assign the logical link to a work center. To do so, follow these steps:

▸ While still in the *Define Navigation Bar Profile* IMG activity, double-click the folder *Define Work Center*.

▸ Enter whatever you would like as your *Work Center ID*, *Title*, and *Description*.

▶ In the *Logical Link ID* field select the logical link that you previously created (Figure 3.21). Save.

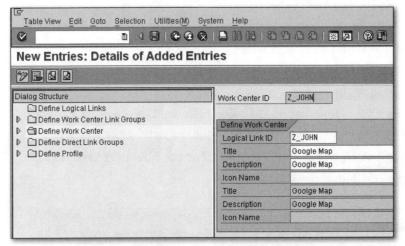

Figure 3.21 Define Work Center with Logical Link for Launch Transaction

Assign Work Center to Navigation Bar Profile

▶ While still in the *Define Navigation Bar Profile* IMG activity, double-click the folder *Define Profile*.

▶ Select the existing navigation bar profile where you would like to make your new launch transaction available.

▶ Double-click on the folder *Assign Work Centers*.

▶ Click the *New Entries* button.

▶ In the *Work Center* field, select the work center you previously created. Enter a position number where you would like the new work center link to appear in the navigation bar (e.g., 1 will be close to the top of the list while 255 will be near the bottom). Save.

Your work center will now appear in the navigation bar of the Interaction Center, allowing you to execute your new launch transaction.

> **Note**
>
> In CRM 2006s/CRM 2007 all navigation between components in the CRM WebClient and the Interaction Center make use of the transaction launcher technology. The previous *navigational link* concept is replaced by the new *target ID/logical link* concept.

3.4.4 HR Organizational Model

In order for Interaction Center agents to use the Interaction Center, the agents first have to be assigned to one or more positions in the HR organization model. The process of assigning users to CRM business roles is done in the HR organizational model, which can be accessed from the SAP Menu in SAP GUI via the following menu path: INTERACTION CENTER • SUPPORTING PROCESSES • IC STRUCTURE • CREATE ORGANIZATION AND STAFFING. Two other options are also provided for accessing the HR organizational model in display or edit mode as well. This process works exactly the same in CRM 2006s/CRM 2007 as in previous releases, with the only difference being that the CRM WebClient business role uses a different infotype than the ones formerly used by IC WebClient and IC WinClient.

After you have created your organizational model, including your positions and assignment of users, you select the menu path: GOTO • DETAIL OBJECT • ENHANCED OBJECT DESCRIPTION (Figure 3.22). In the subsequent screen, you select the new infotype *Business Role* and click the *Create Infotype (F5)* button to access another screen where you can select and assign the desired CRM business role (such as IC_ AGENT). Note that the older IC WinClient and IC WebClient infotype assignments might still be present in the system if you are upgrading from an older release. However, these older infotypes are no longer used by the system.

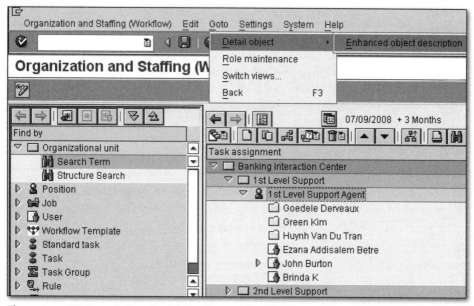

Figure 3.22 HR Organization Model Creation and User Assignment

3.5 Architecture and Technology

Now that you've learned about the basic configuration activities needed to get the Interaction Center up and running, let's jump right in and discuss the architecture and framework of the Interaction Center and the new CRM WebClient. If you are on the business side of the house and generally try to avoid purely technical IT stuff, please feel free to jump ahead to the summary at the end of the chapter or to skim through the following material as desired.

As of CRM 2006s/CRM 2007, the Interaction Center and the rest of the CRM online (i.e., everything except Mobile CRM and Web Channel, formerly E-Commerce) now share the same user interface. The CRM WebClient UI — which was actually built based on the existing framework of the Interaction Center WebClient — relies on CRM Web Application Server (WebAS) technology. Technically, the CRM WebClient UI uses Business Server Pages (BSP) technology on the frontend for rendering the user interface, and on ABAP coding on the backend for providing the application logic. Business server pages (BSPs) are a blend of ABAP code and Hypertext Markup Language Business (HTMLB) tags — with HTMLB being an SAP proprietary extension of HTML that provides additional features and extensibility over regular HTML. All data displayed in the web browser client is sent via Hypertext Transfer Protocol (HTTP) from the CRM application server.

> **Note**
>
> In SAP CRM 2006s/CRM 2007, the CRM WebClient is the only supported user interface for business users. SAP GUI (including the IC WinClient) and the People-Centric User Interface (PC-UI) are no longer available or supported for business users. SAP GUI is only supported for administrative tasks; PC-UI is no longer supported at all. For more information, see SAP note *1118231*.

3.5.1 BOL/GenIL

The CRM WebClient was designed using the widely accepted model-view-controller (MVC) software design paradigm, which clearly separates business logic from the user interface. In SAP CRM, this was achieved by separating the presentation layer, business layer, and business engine layer. As seen in Figure 3.23, the presentation layer is implemented via business server pages (BSP) technology; the business layer consists of a data model known as the Business Object Layer (BOL). The business engine layer involves the CRM database as well as a set of ABAP classes known collectively as the Generic Interaction Layer (GenIL), which are responsible for mapping the methods of the BOL to the underlying application programming interfaces (APIs) and function modules.

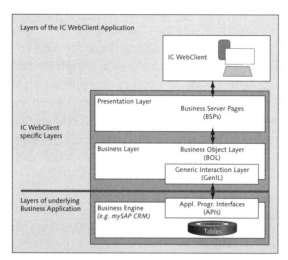

Figure 3.23 Model-View-Controller Concept: Three-Layered Architecture

---

Note: CRM 2006s/CRM 2007

The BOL/GenIL of CRM 2005 is still compatible with CRM 2006s/CRM 2007. However, there have been significant enhancements to the BOL/GenIL in CRM 2006s/CRM 2007.

The biggest change is that previously in CRM 2005 only the Interaction Center relevant business objects were included in the BOL. However, as of CRM 2006s/CRM 2007 all CRM business objects, relations, and attributes have been BOL enabled. For example, any fields that you manually added using the Easy Enhancement Workbench (EEW) will automatically be available in the respective BOL objects without manual coding effort in CRM 2006s/CRM 2007. This means that many project-based enhancements made to CRM 2005 may no longer be required in CRM 2006s/CRM 2007.

3.5.2 BSP Applications

In CRM 2005, the IC WebClient is launched by the BSP application *CRM_IC*, which also serves as the main BSP, providing most of the functionality of the Interaction Center. A second BSP application named *IC_BASE* provides the generic UI framework features such as the navigation bar, context area, breadcrumbs, and so on. In addition, there are some other BSP applications that provide the tools used by

Interaction Center managers (such as CRM_IC_ISE for the Interactive Script Editor). Additionally, there is also a *runtime repository* BSP application named *CRM_IC_RT_REP* that dynamically retrieves the correct views that should be displayed based on your configuration.

Each BSP application in CRM 2005 consists of views and controllers. The views handle the visual output. A view is responsible for rendering the output and relevant UI controls, such as data fields and push buttons. Views are implemented using HTMLB tags, which ensure a consistent look and feel of all views throughout the application. In addition to views, BSP applications also have controllers, which control the behavior of the views. For example, a controller is responsible for handling all the interaction logic and for providing a link between the view and the underlying data model.

What's Different in CRM 2006s/CRM 2007

In CRM 2005, the Interaction Center was the only CRM business application that was using the WebClient framework and architecture. However, as of CRM 2006s/CRM 2007 all CRM online applications share the same CRM WebClient framework and architecture. So, obviously, some changes and adjustments had to be made to make the WebClient suitable for all CRM business applications, and not just the Interaction Center. Let's have a look at some of the most important differences.

In CRM 2006s/CRM 2007, there have been some major changes to how BSP applications work. For example, there is a new main BSP application called *CRM_UI_FRAME* that is used to start the CRM WebClient. The Interaction Center–specific BSP application CRM_IC is no longer used; it has been separated into about 30 different IC-specific BSP components. Additionally, when starting the CRM WebClient, instead of only being able to choose from various Interaction Center profiles, you can now choose other profiles as well, such as the Sales Professional role, Service Professional role, or the IC Manager role. This is a nice improvement for Interaction Center users, because previously the IC Manager functionality was only accessible via SAP Enterprise Portal.

One of the nicest improvements between CRM 2005 and CRM 2006s/CRM 2007 is the availability of the new UI Configuration Tool as of CRM 2006s. The *UI Configuration Tool* provides an easy-to-use tool for adjusting the standard CRM views to fit your needs. Using the UI Configuration Tool, you can easily delete, add, or move fields around on the screen. You can also easily change captions and field labels. You even decide which fields should be mandatory and which fields should be editable or display only. Another great thing about the UI Configuration Tool is that it allows you to use parameters to save your configuration, so that two different business roles (such as the Interaction Center and the Sales Professional role) will use different configuration profiles, and therefore see different field, field positions, field labels, and so on — for the same underlying object.

Another big difference between the IC WebClient in CRM 2005 and the CRM WebClient in CRM 2006s/CRM 2007 and above is that original HTMLB tags from the IC WebClient have been replaced with a new *THTMLB* and *CHTMLB tag library*. These two new sets of tags enable greater flexibility in terms of easily configuring views and re-labeling fields via standard tools of the Component Workbench such as the UI Configuration Tool. The THTMLB tags (the T stands for thin) handle low-level *UI controls* such as input fields, tables, and trees, while the CHTMLB tags (C stands for configurable) enable easier arrangement and relabeling of fields on forms or in table controls.

One more new feature introduced in CRM 2006s/CRM 2007 is the addition of the *component* concept. A component is a meaningful bundle of view sets, views, and custom controllers, which can be reused by other BSP applications. Previously in CRM 2005, views were stored directly in a specific BSP application, preventing the view from being reused by other BSP applications. In CRM 2006s/CRM 2007, views are now stored in components, which can be reused across multiple BSP applications. Components contain an interface, referred to as a *window*, which is what actually enables the component to be reused. This offers a nice improvement over CRM 2005 where the views could not be directly reused.

At a technical level, a component is actually a type of BSP application. As such, each component now has its own *runtime repository*. This is quite different than in CRM 2005 where all BSP applications share the same runtime repository. Obviously, the CRM_IC_RT_REP runtime repository from CRM 2005 cannot be used with the new CRM WebClient UI framework.

Upgrading from IC WebClient to CRM WebClient

The major changes and incompatible features between the old IC WebClient application and the CRM WebClient naturally lead to questions about how upgrades should be performed and whether a standard upgrade can even be performed. What about custom BSP screens and other enhancements?

The short answer is yes, an upgrade is possible. Any custom BSP applications and views will survive the upgrade (i.e., they won't be lost or destroyed). However, due to the various changes in the CRM WebClient UI framework, existing BSP applications will not run out of the box in the new environment. You will unfortunately have to re-do all UI work. However, the good news is that in CRM 2006s/CRM 2007 and above it is much easier to make UI changes and adjustments due to powerful new tools included in the revamped BSP Component Workbench including the UI Configuration Tool.

3.6   Summary

In this chapter, we introduced the basic features of the Interaction Center user interface, including the navigation bar, context area, communication toolbar, and workspace. We talked about the importance of the Interaction Record business transaction, and the central role that it plays in the Interaction Center. We looked at the basic configuration tasks necessary to get the Interaction Center up and running. Finally, we talked about the technology and architecture of the Interaction Center with emphasis on differences between CRM 2005 and CRM 2006s/CRM 2007.

Some key points to remember are:

▸ The Interaction Center user interface provides several methods for bringing important information to an agent's attention, including system messages, alerts, and broadcast messaging.

▸ The Interaction Record is a central part of the Interaction Center as it links together all objects involved in a particular customer interaction. It is possible to suppress the creation of interaction records as described in SAP note *828402*, but SAP does not recommend doing so.

▸ As of CRM 2006s, you can enable a feature that allows agents to review and unlink items from the activity clipboard of the Interaction Record at the end of an interaction.

▸ The IC WebClient profile is replaced by the CRM WebClient business role as of CRM 2006s/CRM 2007.

▸ In order for an agent to navigate to any business transaction or other screen, an entry must exist in the agent's navigation bar profile, linking the relevant object type/object action with the desired target ID (or logical link) of the intended navigation destination.

▶ Many changes have been introduced in CRM 2006s/CRM 2007 that affect the Interaction Center, including reusable BSP views, more powerful tag libraries, and enhanced configuration tools.

In the next few chapters, you will begin your exploration of the core CRM business scenarios and processes supported by the Interaction Center — Marketing, Sales, and Service. We will start in Chapter 4 with Marketing, which involves activities such as setting up campaigns and call lists (including automated, outbound dialing), conducting surveys, processing leads, and making product recommendations.

If you're not marketing, you're probably not selling either. Read this chapter to learn how to use the SAP CRM Interaction Center to acquire new customers, retain your existing customers, and grow unprofitable customers into valuable assets.

4   IC Marketing

CRM begins with marketing. You can't sell products — or provide world-class customer service — if you don't have any customers. Marketing is about acquiring customers, protecting the valuable customers you already have, and growing your unprofitable customers into valuable assets. The role of marketing professionals — sometimes also known as "marketing managers" or simply as "marketers" — is to acquire, retain, and grow customers in order to increase sales revenue and profitability. Marketing professionals are typically responsible for a variety of marketing-related activities, including marketing planning and calendaring, campaign and promotion planning, customer segmentation, call list creation, and lead distribution.

A marketing plan represents a long-term, high-level, strategic framework for all of a company's marketing activities. Marketing plans typically consist of campaigns and promotions — which can be designed to generate awareness for a new product line, stimulate demand for an existing product, increase customer loyalty, prevent customer churn, and so on. Once a marketing campaign has been created, one or more target groups will be assigned to the campaign. A target group, also known as a customer segment, consists of customers with the same marketing attributes — such as similar demographic profiles (age, income, gender, location, and so on). Marketing campaigns can be executed via a variety of communication channels, including print media, radio and television, Internet, email, or telephone.

The SAP CRM Interaction Center can be used to support marketing activities by allowing interaction center agents to contact customers through communication channels, including telephone, email, and so on. For example, assume that a company is launching a new product line and creates a marketing campaign to generate interest among their existing customer base. The company might decide to target a particular customer segment with a special offer or promotion, such as a price reduction or perhaps even a free sample trial period. The company could proactively contact customers — perhaps via a targeted email or telephone call list. Or, the company could wait until existing customers contact the interaction center for service or support, and then offer the promotion to the customers after resolving the customer's service issues.

This chapter will outline the different options for using the SAP CRM Interaction Center to support CRM marketing activities. We will look at how marketing campaigns can be executed using call lists and outbound dialing integration. We will analyze the different options for outbound dialing, including manual outbound dialing as well as automated outbound dialing modes such as preview dialing, progressive/power dialing, and predictive dialing. We will also discuss how agent productivity tools such as Interactive Scripts can be used to guide the agent through complex or difficult interactions and to allow the agent to directly update marketing attributes of a customer. If a customer expresses interest in an offer, built-in surveys or questionnaires can be used to automatically create and qualify a lead in the background. We will also look at functionality for enabling cross-sell, up-sell, and retention offers including CRM Marketing Product Proposals as well as integration of SAP Real-Time Offer Management. Finally, we will discuss how marketing analytics like customer lifetime value (CLV) and customer churn rate can be embedded in the Interaction Center to optimize real-time decision making.

4.1 Campaigns

Once a marketing professional has created and released a campaign that is relevant for the Interaction Center, the campaign details can be made available to agents. In the SAP Implementation Guide (IMG) configuration, you can define search criteria to determine which campaign details are displayed in the Interaction Center. It is possible to create several different sets of search criteria relevant for different groups of agents using different campaign profiles, and to specify the maximum number of campaigns that should be displayed for each profile (see Figure 4.1). For example, you might have one group of agents who are responsible for campaigns in North America, and another group responsible for campaigns in Latin America. Or, you might have certain highly skilled agents who handle high priority campaigns. For each group of agents, you can control the maximum number of campaigns for which campaign details are displayed in the Interaction Center.

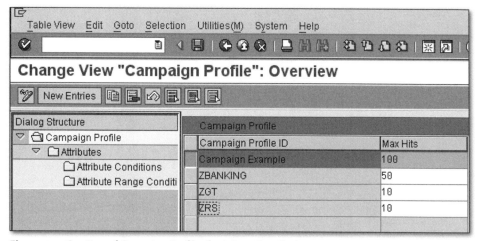

Figure 4.1 Creation of Campaign Profiles for Interaction Center

The campaign search is conducted using campaign attributes, which are defined by the marketing professional using the Marketing Planner tool. Campaign attributes could include campaign priority, tactics, communication channel, planned start date, planned finish data, and so on (see Figure 4.2). After completing the campaign profile, the profile should be assigned to the IC WebClient profile (CRM 2005 and below) or to the CRM WebClient business role (CRM 2006s/CRM 2007 and above).

Agents who are responsible for working with campaigns will typically take a few minutes each day before starting their work shift to review any newly assigned campaigns in order to familiarize themselves with the details of the new campaign or promotion (Figure 4.3). In addition, if the campaign has an attached script, the agent can click on the script hyperlink to open the actual script and view the details of the script.

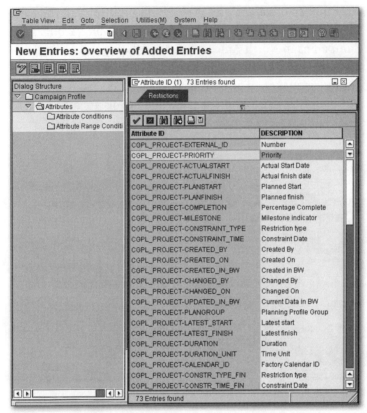

Figure 4.2 Assignment of Campaign Attributes to Interaction Center Campaign Profile

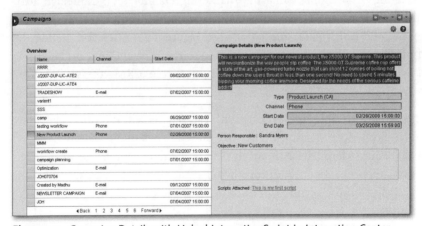

Figure 4.3 Campaign Details with Linked Interactive Script in Interaction Center

> **Note**
>
> Interactive scripts provide agents with step-by-step guidance for handling specific customer issues — such as providing information about a new product, promotion, or marketing campaign. The scripts can include questions with predefined answers. Based on the customer's response to each question, the script can move to another question, navigate to a particular screen, launch a Web URL, or even open a survey questionnaire. Scripts can be assigned to a campaign, allowing the agent to directly access the script from the campaign details screen.

When an agent receives a telephone call, email, or chat message from a customer referring to a particular campaign or promotion, the agent can manually record this information as part of the customer interaction. In the Interaction Record document, the "Campaign" field allows the agent to search for and enter the appropriate campaign (Figure 4.4).

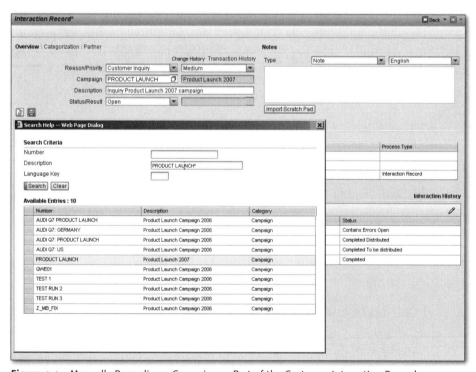

Figure 4.4 Manually Recording a Campaign as Part of the Customer Interaction Record

In addition, the system can automatically determine the campaign for emails that contain a campaign tracking ID. For example, assume that a company's marketing department sends out an email blast to a group of customers informing them about a new promotion. The email will contain a special tracking code that represents the campaign. When the customer replies to the email, the tracking code is detected by the system and the relevant campaign ID is automatically entered into the "Campaign" field of the Interaction Record once the email is processed by an agent. In order to enable this functionality, you must set the "Campaign Determination" flag in the "Define E-Mail/Fax Settings" IMG activity for the email address for which you want to enable automatic campaign determination (Figure 4.5). The IMG menu path is: SAP IMPLEMENTATION GUIDE • CUSTOMER RELATIONSHIP MANAGEMENT • INTERACTION CENTER WEBCLIENT • AGENT INBOX • SETTINGS FOR ASYNCHRONOUS INBOUND PROCESSING • DEFINE RECEIVING E-MAIL/FAX SETTINGS.

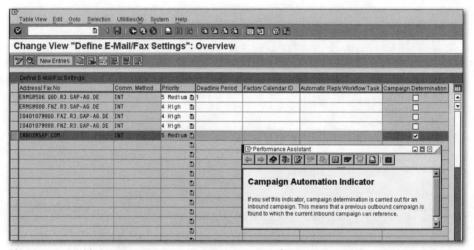

Figure 4.5 Enabling Automatic Campaign Determination for Customer Replies to Corporate Marketing E-Mails

4.2   Call Lists and Planned Activities

The Interaction Center can handle inbound telephone calls, outbound telephone calls, or both. The inbound scenario is pretty simple: A customer calls and an agent answers the phone. However, outbound calling can be more complicated. Which customers should you call? What's the best time to reach each customer? How many times should you try to reach a customer before giving up? Which customers are you not allowed to call?

Call lists and planned activities take the guess work out of outbound calling. A call list is a collection of customers along with their telephone number and preferred calling times. Call lists are useful for any marketing campaign that needs to be executed via telephone from the Interaction Center. Call lists can be used to support a variety of scenarios, including outbound telesales, telemarketing, fund-raising, and marketing surveys.

Some companies have interaction centers dedicated solely to telemarketing and call list activities. Other companies may support a blend of customer service, telesales, and telemarketing activities. Typically, these companies will often employ a strategy of having interaction center agents who work exclusively on inbound customer service issues during hours of peak customer activity, and then switch some agents over to outbound calling when customer activity slows down — often in the late morning, after lunch, and toward the end of the day or working week. It is important to note that call lists and outbound calling — while typically associated with marketing — can also be used outside for sales- and service-related activities such as collections, fundraising, telesales, service follow-ups, or appointment confirmations.

Call lists are assigned to a group of agents who share the call list and take turns calling the next customer from the top of the sorted list. Call lists can be dialed manually or integrated with automated outbound dialers. Call lists are ideal for large campaigns or promotions where hundreds or even thousands of customers need to be called by a large pool of agents fully dedicated to call list processing. However, for smaller, more targeted campaigns that can be executed by a single agent, it is sometimes more convenient to use planned activities. When working with planned activities, each agent is responsible for their own calls rather than working from a shared list.

4.2.1 Call List Creation

There are actually several different possible methods of generating call lists for the Interaction Center, depending on the use case. Marketing professionals can automatically generate call lists to accompany a campaign using segmented customer target groups. Call lists can also be created by sales professionals for regular reoccurring calls with their accounts. Finally, interaction center managers can also create their own call lists if necessary. After call lists have been created, assigned to the responsible agents, and released — the agents will be able to see the call lists in the Interaction Center when an agent logs into the Interaction Center and clicks on the "Call List" link in the Navigation bar. If using planned activities instead of call lists, the agent will be able to see the scheduled outbound calls in the Agent Inbox.

Marketing Planner

This option is typically used by marketing professionals in order to automatically generate call lists for campaigns based on segmented customer target groups. For example, a marketing professional might target leads collected from a recent trade show or event, in order to generate sales opportunities. This task would typically be done by a marketing professional. The actual assignment of the interaction center agents to the call list (and activation of the call list) would be done later in another step by the interaction center manager using the Call List Maintenance functionality.

The Marketing Planner functionality is available from SAP GUI transaction CRM_ MKTPL, accessible via SAP Menu path: SAP MENU • MARKETING • MARKETING PLAN- NING AND CAMPAIGN MANAGEMENT • MARKETING PLANNER in CRM release 2005 and below. In CRM 2006s/CRM 2007 and above, the Marketing Planner functionality can be accessed in the CRM WebClient with the business role MARKETINGPRO via Navigation bar menu path: MARKETING • MARKETING PLANS.

Generate Business Transactions and Call Lists

This option, which generates planned call lists based on calling hours that have been maintained for each business partner, is especially useful for sales profession- als who need to call their accounts on a regular, reoccurring basis. For example, this option works well for direct store delivery (DSD) scenarios often employed by beverage bottlers who make regular deliveries to their retail customers on a regular basis. It is possible to maintain the Reason field as part of the call list (Figure 4.6), which will automatically populate the Interaction Record reason field at runtime in the Interaction Center. The Generate Business Transactions and Call Lists func- tionality allows you to generate either call lists or planned activities (visible in the Agent Inbox) depending on whether you enable the "Generate Call List" flag or not. In either case, whether generating a call list or planned activities, this option works best if calling hours have been maintained as part of the business partner's master data. However, it is also possible to generate calls without calling times.

The Generate Business Transactions and Call Lists functionality is available from SAP GUI transaction code CRMD_CALL_LIST, accessible via the SAP Menu path SAP MENU • INTERACTION CENTER • SUPPORTING PROCESSES • OUTBOUND CALLING • GENERATE BUSINESS TRANSACTIONS AND CALL LISTS.

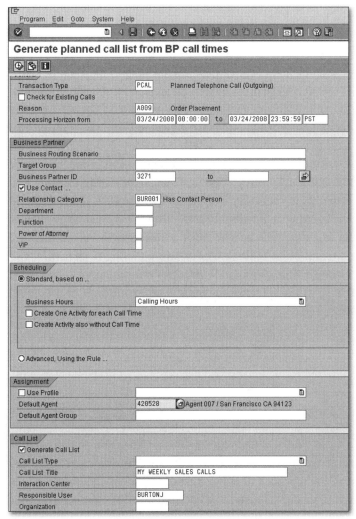

Figure 4.6 Generate Business Transactions or Call List Depending on Whether the "Generate Call List" Is Enabled

Call List Maintenance

This option allows interaction center managers to create their own call lists if necessary, perhaps for special situations. This tool requires that every call be added to the call list manually — one call at a time — and does not support automatic call list creation from target groups or business partner ranges. Hence, this tool is primarily useful when an interaction center manager needs to manually create a small call list to make sure agents follow up on a few open items.

The primary strength of the Call List Maintenance transaction is monitoring and managing call lists that have already been created — via the Marketing Planner, Create Business Transactions and Call Lists, or from the Call List Maintenance transaction. Interaction Center managers can use the Call List Maintenance transaction to assign agents to call lists that have been created automatically by a marketing professional, as well as to activate the call lists so that the lists can be executed by agents in the Interaction Center. It is possible to assign individual agents directly; however, the manager usually will assign a position or organizational unit rather than an individual user. The advantage of assigning the higher level organizational unit is that it is only necessary to make one assignment — the organization unit — rather than manually assigning each agent to the call list. In addition to assigning the agents responsible for executing the call list, the manager can also maintain other settings, such as whether the call list will be executed via manual dialing or via integration to automated outbound dialing (Figure 4.7). The Call List Maintenance transaction can also be used for monitoring the status of in-process call lists, as well as for splitting, merging, and exporting call lists to an external predictive dialer.

The Call List Maintenance functionality is available from the SAP GUI transaction code CRMD_TM_CLDIST, accessible via the path: SAP Menu path • SAP menu • Interaction Center • Supporting Processes • Outbound Calling • Call List Maintenance.

4.2.2 Planned Activities Creation

Planned activities provide an alternative to using call lists. This is a more personalized — and more flexible — approach that relies on the planned activity (business transaction) rather than the call list. Instead of sharing a call list with a group of other agents, each agent can view the calls that they are responsible for making from the Agent Inbox, with the calls represented as planned activities. Instead of clicking on Call Lists in the Navigation Bar, the agent navigates to the Agent Inbox and searches for activities that are assigned personally to that agent or agent group. The agent sees all activities that they are responsible for, including (but not limited to) planned calls. Using the Agent Inbox instead of the Call List view makes sense in most business to business situations where the agent is responsible for calling the same accounts on a regular basis, such as in the Direct Store Delivery model.

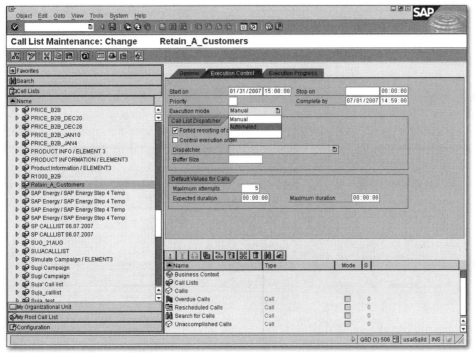

Figure 4.7 Creation of Call List via Call List Maintenance with Selection of Manual or Automated Dialing

To create planned activities (which will appear in the Agent Inbox) instead of a call list, it is necessary to deselect the "Generate Call List" flag in SAP GUI transaction CRMD_CALL_LIST when generating planned outbound calls. See Figure 4.6.

4.2.3 Processing Call Lists from the Interaction Center

After creating a call list, assigning agents, and activating the call list, agents will be able to see the call list when they click the "Call List" link in the Navigation Bar. If an agent is assigned to more than one call list, he will see all the currently active call lists to which he is assigned, as well as the execution mode (manual or auto-mated) and progress level for each call list. The agent can also view the details of the campaigns attached to the call lists. Click the "Next" button to automatically dial the next call from the top of the list of call, or view the complete list of calls attached to a call list (Figure 4.8).

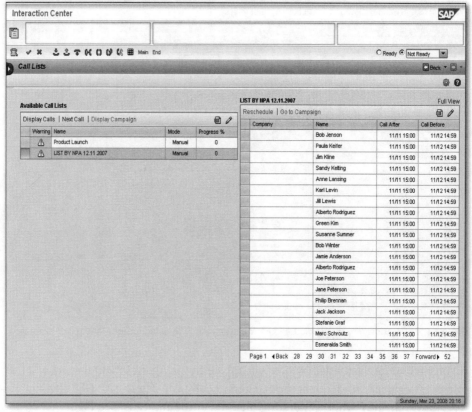

Figure 4.8 Displayed Calls for Selected Call List in the Interaction Center

Interaction Center agents can also click on the "Full View" hyperlink for any selected call list in order to switch to a larger full-screen view of the calls in order to see additional data such as the telephone number, the number of attempted calls, and the result of each call (Figure 4.9).

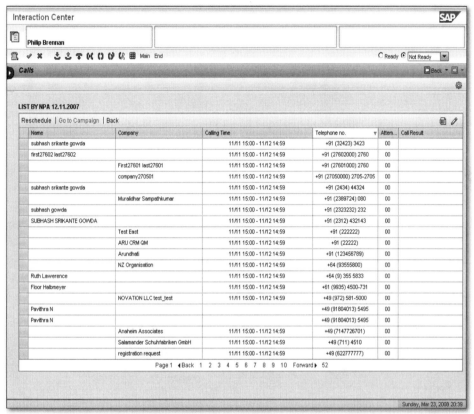

Figure 4.9 Full View Displaying Additional Data for Each Call

Depending on whether the call list is set to manual or automated dialing mode (via integration to an external automated dialer), the call will either be dialed automatically when the agent clicks the Next Call button or the agent will need to manually click the Dial button; however, the customer's telephone number will be automatically pre-populated from the call list details (Figure 4.10).

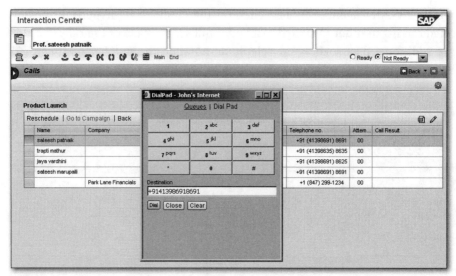

Figure 4.10 Dial Pad is Pre-populated with Customer's Telephone Number from Call List

After the call has been dialed — either manually or automatically — the telephone number, status, and length of time are displayed in upper-right hand corner of the Context Area in the communication information section (Figure 4.11).

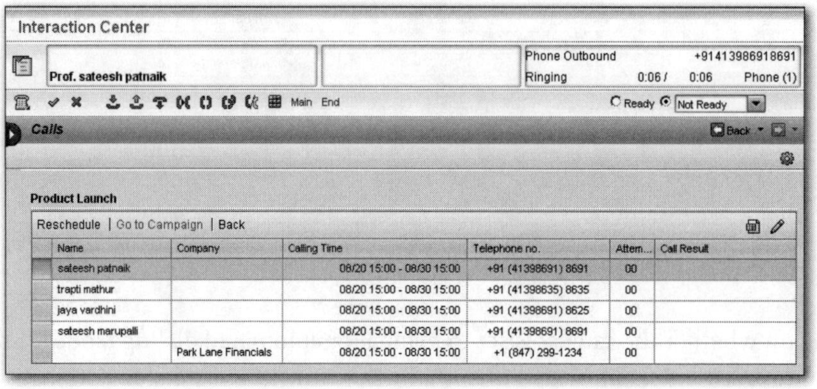

Figure 4.11 Outbound Call Information Displayed in Context Area

If the call is connected to a live person, the system will automatically flag the call as completed at the conclusion of the call unless the agent explicitly indicates that the call needs to be rescheduled. For example, if someone other than the intended contact person answered the phone, the agent could select the reschedule reason "Wrong Party." See Figure 4.12.

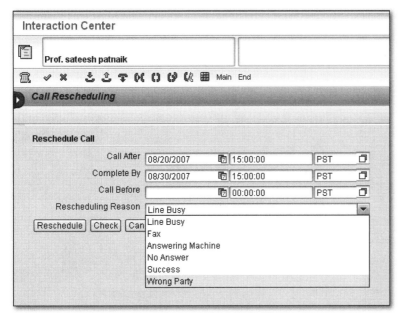

Figure 4.12   Reschedule Call

4.2.4   Do Not Call List Integration

Many countries and regions are adopting legislation that allows consumers to register their telephone numbers on a do not call list in order to avoid being contacted with unsolicited marketing offers. The United States government, under the Federal Trade Commission, enacted legislation in 2003 that established a National Do Not Call Registry. Customers can add their telephone number to the registry if they don't want to be contacted by marketers. Companies are required to subscribe to the list every month and update their records. Companies who attempt to call a customer who is registered with the do not call list face a substantial monetary fine ($11,000 per incident).

Other forms of communication, such as email and fax, are not yet covered under such legislation. However, clearly it makes sense for companies to respect the wishes of their customers. Even customers who have not registered with the do not call list may still prefer that you not contact them via telephone. If your customers would rather be contacted via email than telephone, or vice versa, you need a way to reflect this in your customer master data. SAP CRM provides a "do not use" flag as part of the customer master data for each maintained communication channel, including telephone, mobile phone, email, fax, and pager (Figure 4.13).

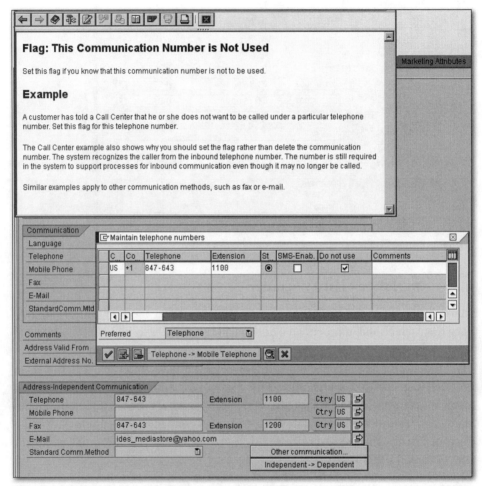

Figure 4.13 Maintenance of "Do not use" Flag in Master Data

The SAP CRM Interaction Center supports do not call efforts by allowing agents to flag the "Do not contact" field next to a customer's telephone number if the customer requests to be removed from the company's call list (Figure 4.14). It is more desirable to flag that the telephone number should not be used than to delete it, because the telephone number may still be beneficial for other purposes, such as automatically identifying the customer.

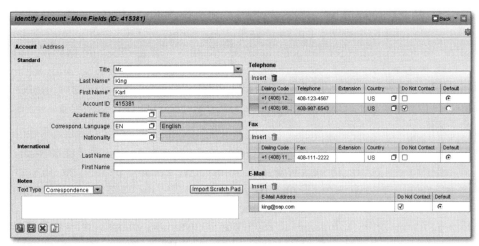

Figure 4.14 Maintenance of "Do not use" Flag in Interaction Center

4.3 Outbound Dialing

People tend to have negative associations with outbound dialing — especially *automated* outbound dialing. It is true that outbound dialing has historically been abused by marketers looking to maximize the number of consumers they reach while minimizing the cost and effort of doing so. However, due to increased complaints from consumers, many governments recently have enacted consumer protection and privacy legislations that limit the reach of telemarketing. Companies are still allowed to use technology like automated outbound dialing, but companies have to use this technology more responsibly. As we will discuss, automated outbound dialing can be used in a responsible manner to maximize your ability to reach out to your customers — without driving them away.

So what is automated outbound dialing, and how can it best be leveraged? Automated outbound dialing allows a computer telephone system to automatically execute an outbound marketing call list rather than having interaction center agents manually dial each call. In most *modes* of automated dialing, the dialer software automatically dials numerous telephone numbers and connects an agent whenever a call is answered by an actual person. In cases where the dialer encounters a busy signal, unanswered call, answering machines, or fax machine the dialer software does not bother connecting an agent, thus saving time and money. The person who answers the phone often experiences a delay of a few seconds while the dialer software connects an agent. In cases where no agent is actually available, the predictive dialer will drop the call — hanging up on the person who answered the call.

Automated outbound dialing is commonly used in scenarios such as collections, in order to contact customers whose accounts have become delinquent. In such situations, the auto dialer will often play a pre-recorded message for the customer asking them to call in and make a payment. Automated dialing is also often used to support marketing campaigns to reach out to customers whose service contracts are about to expire, in order to offer extensions to the contracts. The most common modes of automated outbound dialing include preview dialing, progressive/power dialing, and predictive dialing. In rare situations, *manual* outbound dialing is sometimes used; however, due to the inefficiencies involved with manually dialing each telephone call, this solution is not ideal for most interaction centers.

SAP CRM provides integration with external dialers, available from both the ICI and SAPphone interface. The integration allows you to perform an initial export of call lists from SAP CRM to the external dialer, as well as to perform delta updates from SAP CRM to the external dialer (e.g., to inform the dialer of unsuccessful calls that needed to be rescheduled). Although the solution can be used with either interface, the actual computer code behind the scenes is part of the SAPphone interface. Hence, the documentation for outbound dialing is described in the SAPphone interface specification.

> **Note**
>
> It is important to note that outbound dialing (both manual and automated) requires integration with third-party communication management software for computer telephony integration (CTI). The SAP CRM Interaction Center does not include out of the box outbound dialing software. You should also be aware that not all communication software vendors necessarily support all three outbound dialing modes (preview, power/progressive, and predictive). Check with your vendor to find out which modes they support.
>
> This book provides a separate chapter devoted entirely to CTI and multi-channel integration.

4.3.1　Manual Outbound Dialing

Manual outbound dialing is the least used — and the least efficient — mode of outbound dialing. Assuming that some form of CTI is used, manual dialing doesn't have to involve the agent actually keying in telephone numbers with their fingers all day. When using manual dialing in the SAP CRM Interaction Center, the agent only needs to manually press the "Dial" button to trigger each call; the agent does not need to manually key in the actual telephone number. The customer's telephone number is automatically populated into the dial pad from the customer master data. However, this form of dialing is very inefficient because the agent needs to wait while the phone rings, hoping that someone eventually answers. Unfortunately, much of the time no one answers, or an answering machine or voicemail system is reached. In such cases, valuable time is lost.

As a rule of thumb, for each 60 minutes that an agent spends doing manual outbound dialing, the agent will only actually spend about 20 minutes speaking with customers. The other 40 minutes are wasted on unanswered calls, voice mail, and answering machines. Manual dialing is perfectly acceptable for making an occasional outbound telephone call, but manual dialing is not well suited to heavy usage or for processing outbound call lists.

4.3.2　Preview Dialing/Auto Dialing

Definitions of preview dialing — sometimes also referred to as auto dialing — differ among vendors and products. However, in general, products that provide preview dialing show the details of the next planned call of a call list to the agent before the system automatically dials the call. This gives the agent time to review the customer information beforehand. When the agent is ready, the agent usually presses a button to have the dialer software initiate the call. Some products also provide a feature to let the agent press a button to skip the call and move on to the details of the next call instead. The main advantages of preview dialing over manual dialing is that the agent is able to review the customer details before making the call, and the agent saves the time that it would actually take to dial the telephone number.

The SAP CRM Interaction Center does not support preview dialing mode directly. However, it is possible to achieve similar functionality by manually pulling up the customer's information before making a call, and then using the Dial button to automatically dial the call. If the customer is not reached, the agent can reschedule the call using the reschedule button provided in the Interaction Center. In addition, several Interaction Center customers have enabled preview dialing on a project basis in order to allow for integrated call rescheduling.

4.3.3 Power Dialing/Progressive Dialing

Progressive dialers, also known as power dialers, work in a similar fashion to preview dialers – except that the agent is shown the customer information as the call is being dialed rather than beforehand. Additionally, no manual action or confirmation is required from the agent. The agent is able to listen along as the dialer "progresses" through the call list, dialing numbers and encountering busy signals, answering machines, fax machines, and unanswered calls until finally an actual person answers a call.

Power/progressive dialing can be integrated with the SAP CRM Interaction Center through SAP's ICI or SAPphone interface using certified communication management software products from third-party SAP partners such as Genesys, Avaya, or others.

4.3.4 Predictive Dialing

Predictive dialers automatically dial more telephone calls than there are actual agents available to receive calls, in order to make sure that no agent is ever sitting around idle waiting for a call. The predictive dialer uses a complex mathematical algorithm involving the number of agents, the average length of each call, and the average number of calls that need to be dialed to reach a live person. Ideally, as an agent is wrapping up their current call, the predictive dialer is already dialing several customers hoping that at least one customer will answer just as the agent is wrapping up the previous call. Thus, agents never spend any valuable time waiting idle while the system encounters busy signals, answering machines, fax machines, or unanswered calls.

Obviously, however, this can result in an unpleasant experience for callers who answer the telephone only to find that there is no one on the other end – or that the call has been dropped. Predictive dialers try to minimize this amount of "over dialing" by using sophisticated predictive algorithms that take into consideration statistics such as the average talk time of each call as well as the percentage of calls that are answered by an actual person (as opposed to busy signals, unanswered calls, or fax or answering machines) in order to estimate how many calls to over-dial. It is possible with most dialers to configure a maximum acceptable drop rate (in order to limit the number of calls that are dropped by the dialer) that temporarily slows down or suspends over-dialing until a large enough sample size of statistics exists to fully optimize over-dialing.

Predictive dialing can be integrated with the SAP CRM Interaction Center through SAP's ICI or SAPphone interface – depending on the particular communication management software vendor. Please note that some vendors require project-based effort in order to integrate with SAP.

4.4   Interactive Scripting

In today's busy world, it is getting increasingly more difficult to reach your customers and to hold their attention, especially in business to consumer (B2C) scenarios. Whether you are reaching out to customers as part of a marketing survey, promotion, or retention effort, you need to deliver your message clearly and efficiently, while also being able to flexibly respond to the reactions and cues of your customers. Interactive scripting provides you with the tools to model your customer interactions in structured yet flexible process flows. You can create predefined decision trees that provide agents with step-by-step instructions and pre-written dialogues to skillfully guide the agent through customer interactions.

Interactive scripts can support marketing efforts in a number of ways. Scripts can be created and attached to a marketing campaign as well as to individual call lists that are assigned to the campaign. Agents can access the script by manually clicking on the script from the campaign details screen. Or, if the script is attached to a call list, the script will be automatically launched each time an outbound call is dialed from the call list. Agents can also manually access scripts assigned to them via their profile or business role. Finally, you can even launch scripts automatically based on certain events that happen during the course of a customer conversation.

In addition to providing agents with situation-appropriate pre-written dialogues and other instruction, scripts can also be used to navigate to other screens, launch other business transactions, and even open Web pages. For example, you might want to update a customer's address, contact information, or marketing attributes in certain situations — such as when a customer calls to inquire about a new product or to place an order. This can be done directly from within a script by embedding the desired customer data fields inside the script. You can also embed marketing surveys into a script, allowing the agent to collect and record answers from the customer. It is even possible to automatically create and qualify leads based on the customers' responses to survey questions from inside a script (Figure 4.15). Interactive Scripting is discussed in full detail in Chapter 8.

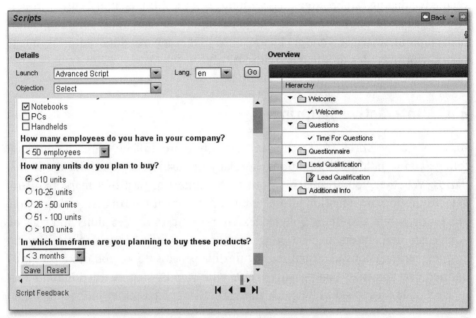

Figure 4.15   Lead Qualification via Marketing Questionnaire Script

4.5   Questionnaire/Survey and Lead Integration

Marketing questionnaires (also known as surveys) are commonly used by marketing departments to gauge the effectiveness of marketing efforts. However, questionnaires can also be marketing tools. As companies shift from the product-centric model of the past to today's customer-centric model, companies increasingly need to understand the needs and wants of their customers. Questionnaires provide an excellent way of learning what your customers really think and how they actually feel about your products and your company. Questionnaires allow you to collect demographic information in order to create more accurate marketing attributes and customer segments. Questionnaires can also help you find out whether customers are satisfied with your products and the post-sales service that you provide. Questionnaires can even be used as a sales tool to gauge the customer's level of interest in a product — and to automatically create and qualify a sales lead when appropriate.

A lead is a sales opportunity that has not yet been prioritized and qualified. Typically, leads are generated at trade shows and conferences, collected from a company's corporate website or interaction center, or rented or purchased from external companies. Leads contain information about the products or services a customer is interested in, the level of the customer's interest, and the customer's time frame for making a purchase decision. Leads can either be qualified manually by the Interaction Center agent, or, more commonly, qualified by the agent with the assistance of an embedded questionnaire. After a lead has been qualified and prioritized, the lead is typically routed to the sales organization and converted into an opportunity.

4.5.1 Survey Integration

There are two options for integrating marketing questionnaires into the Interaction Center. Questionnaires can be included inside the process flow of interactive scripts, or questionnaires can be accessed from inside the IC Lead screen. When including the questionnaire inside a script, it is possible to either simply collect the results of the questionnaire, or to use the results to automatically create and qualify a sales lead. Including questionnaires inside an interactive script is a convenient way to provide Interaction Center agents with access to questionnaires in situations where no lead should be created.

However, even in situations where you may want to create a lead based on the results of the questionnaire, you might still choose to use an interactive script rather than using the IC Lead screen if you want to create the lead in the background. This is a good option if the agents aren't familiar with the IC Lead screen and won't need to maintain any fields. However, if agents will be expected to work with the lead — such as entering notes or manually qualifying the lead priority — then it is better to access the questionnaire directly from the IC Lead screen rather than from an interactive script.

Regardless of whether you plan to access questionnaires from interactive scripts or from the IC Lead screen, you must first create the questionnaires the CRM Survey Tool, which is accessible from the SAP GUI transaction "CRM_SURVEY_SUITE." See Figure 4.16. See Chapter 8 for full details on how to integrate questionnaires with interactive scripts. Integrating questionnaires with leads is discussed in the next section on Lead Integration.

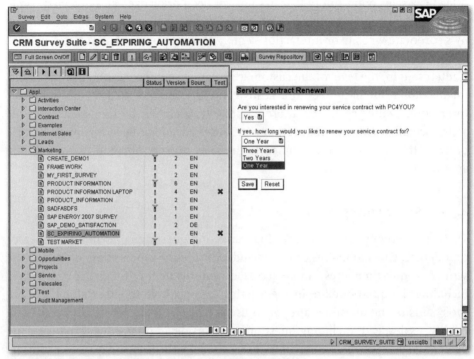

Figure 4.16 Creation of Questionnaires in CRM Survey Tool

4.5.2 Lead Integration

As with questionnaires, there are also two options for integrating leads into the Interaction Center — depending on your particular CRM release. Leads can be generated automatically in the background without any agent involvement based on the customers' responses to a questionnaire embedded inside an interactive script. Alternatively, leads can be created manually by agents, in CRM 2005 and above, by manually navigating to the lead transaction from the Interaction Center navigation bar. As mentioned previously, the interactive script option is ideal if the agents will only be using fully automated lead qualification based on survey integration; on the other hand, if the agents will need to manually qualify the lead and/or maintain other information (such as notes) then it is recommended to work with the lead transaction directly instead of creating leads in the background using interactive scripts.

> **Note**
>
> In CRM 4.0 it is only possible to create leads in the background via scripts; there is no option to create leads directly, because the Interaction Center does not provide an IC Lead screen in CRM 4.0. As of CRM 2005, an IC specific lead screen is available, allowing agents to create leads directly.

When creating a lead in the background from an interactive script, the lead will automatically be pre-filled with the description, "Lead Qualification." In addition, the start date will be populated with the current date and the status will be set to "Open." Based on the customers' responses to the survey questions, the lead will be automatically qualified by the system. The "Questionnaire Level" field will display the qualification (e.g., hot, warm, or cold) as well as the name of the survey that was used to qualify the lead.

The "Qualification Level" is a second field that can be used by an agent to additionally qualify the lead manually. This field will be left empty by default. The partner determination will be done automatically based on the confirmed account and contact person as well as the current Interaction Center agent. Figure 4.17 shows a lead that has been created automatically in the background by the system based on an interactive script containing the questionnaire, "Lead Questionnaire." Note that the questionnaire and the customer's responses are shown on the left side of the Lead screen.

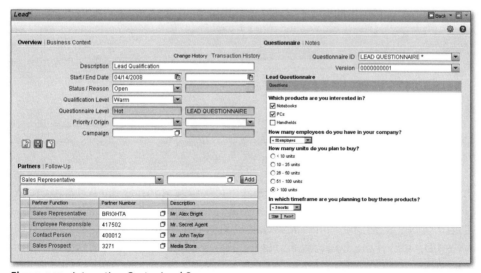

Figure 4.17 Interaction Center Lead Screen

In addition to creating leads automatically via interactive scripts with questionnaire integration, it is also possible for Interaction Center agents to create leads manually, and to manually edit leads that were created automatically in the background via interactive scripts. To edit an automatically created lead, the agent simply clicks on the lead from the Activity Clipboard of the Interaction Record. To create a new lead, the agent can click on the Leads entry in the Interaction Center navigation bar. The start date will be automatically populated with the current date and the status will be set to "Open" by default. The partner determination will be done automatically based on the confirmed account and contact person as well as the current Interaction Center agent. Depending on which questionnaires have been assigned to the lead, the agent will be able to select and open the appropriate questionnaire in order to automatically qualify the lead (Figure 4.18). Alternatively, the agent may either qualify the lead manually without using a questionnaire, or add a manual qualification in addition to the automatic qualification performed by the system based on the customer's responses to the selected questionnaire.

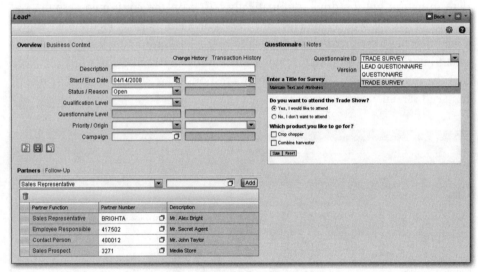

Figure 4.18 Selection of Assigned Questionnaires from IC Lead

In order to make a questionnaire available to an agent inside the IC Lead screen, you must assign the questionnaire to the lead in the IMG transaction "Define Determination for Questionnaires" via SAP GUI transaction code "SAPLCRM_SURVEY_CD," which can be accessed via the IMG path: SAP IMPLEMENTATION GUIDE • CUSTOMER RELATIONSHIP MANAGEMENT • TRANSACTIONS • SETTINGS FOR LEADS •

QUESTIONNAIRES FOR LEADS • DEFINE DETERMINATION FOR QUESTIONNAIRES. For each questionnaire that you want to make available, you enter the questionnaire ID along with the desired transaction type (e.g., LEAD, ZLEAD, etc.), an arbitrary determination procedure and description, optional validity dates, and so on (Figure 4.19).

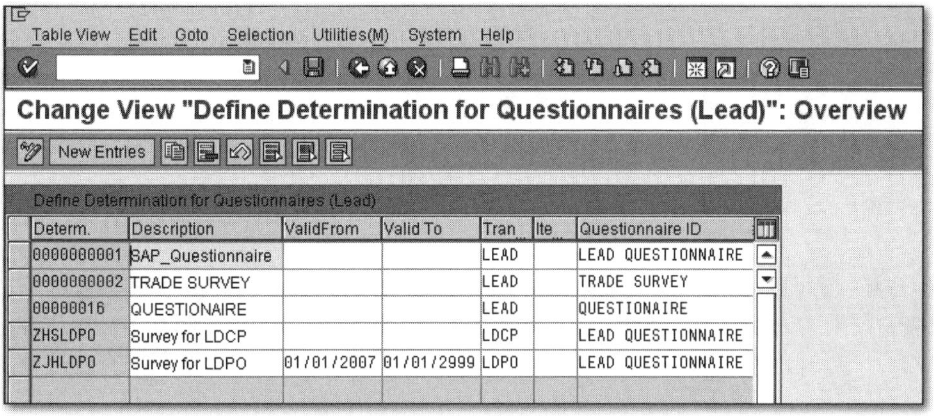

Determ.	Description	ValidFrom	Valid To	Tran	Ite	Questionnaire ID
0000000001	SAP_Questionnaire			LEAD		LEAD QUESTIONNAIRE
0000000002	TRADE SURVEY			LEAD		TRADE SURVEY
00000016	QUESTIONAIRE			LEAD		QUESTIONAIRE
ZHSLDPO	Survey for LDCP			LDCP		LEAD QUESTIONNAIRE
ZJHLDPO	Survey for LDPO	01/01/2007	01/01/2999	LDPO		LEAD QUESTIONNAIRE

Figure 4.19 Assignment of Questionnaires to Lead Transaction Type

In CRM 2006s/CRM 2007 and above, it is additionally possible to integrate the standard CRM WebClient Lead screen into the Interaction Center. Some customers may to prefer to work with the standard CRM Lead rather than the IC-specific Lead screen, because the CRM Lead contains more fields and information, including notes, attachments, transaction history, change log, and other information that is not available by default on the user interface of the IC Lead (Figure 4.20). However, the CRM Lead is not optimized for the Interaction Center as it has a vertical scrollbar that requires additional scrolling and more mouse clicks than an interaction center agent might be accustomed to. Additionally, the CRM Lead screen is not fully integrated with the Interaction Center in CRM 2007 (although SAP is considering doing so in a future release). This means that, for example, the business partner determination does not automatically occur based on the confirmed business partner. Similarly, the transaction must be saved manually (whereas the IC Lead is automatically saved when the End button is pressed on the communication toolbar).

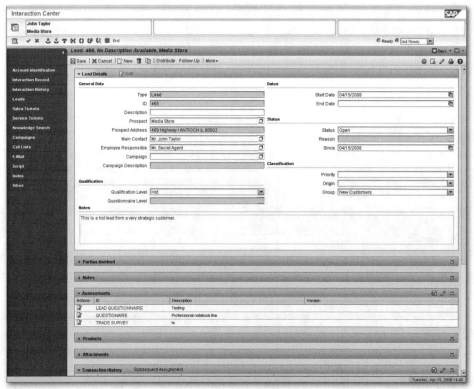

Figure 4.20 CRM UIU Lead Integration in Interaction Center

4.6 Marketing-Based Product Proposals

So far in this chapter you have learned about the role that marketing plays in the Interaction Center *prior* to the actual sales process, in terms of creating campaigns and call lists, contacting customers via outbound dialing, surveying customers, and qualifying prospective sales leads. However, marketing can also play a role in the Interaction Center during the actual sales process. In particular, marketing-based product proposals can be used to increase sales revenue, improve profitability, and deepen customer relationships by enabling the agent to recommend products that best suit the customer's needs. For example, the agent can propose accessories related to a reference product (e.g., the item that the customer is purchasing). The agent can also propose other cross-selling items that complement the item the customer is purchasing, such as extended service contracts, professional installation services, spare parts, components, or other peripheral products and services. Agents can also suggest up-selling items if the product that the customer is currently looking at does not seem well suited to the customer's needs. Finally, in situations where a product is beyond the customer's price range or a product is currently not available (e.g., out of stock) the agent can even recommend *down-selling* options to less expensive items.

Product proposals for accessories and spare parts work slightly differently than product proposals for cross-selling, up-selling, and down-selling. Accessories and spare parts for a particular reference product are maintained as part of the product details of the reference product; this is typically handled by a product expert. The cross-selling, up-selling, and down-selling rules on the other hand are maintained in separate product proposal rules, which are typically handled by one of the company's marketing managers. However, at runtime in the Interaction Center, agents are able to select all types of product proposals, including accessories and spare parts as well as cross-sellers, up-sellers, and down-sellers, regardless of how they are maintained. It is also important to note that the maintenance of product proposals for the IC WebClient works slightly differently than the maintenance of product proposals for other CRM applications such as E-Commerce or CRM Online Sales. Let's take a look at how product proposals are maintained in the IC WebClient.

4.6.1 Maintaining Accessories and Spare Parts (Service Parts)

Accessories and spare parts of a given reference product are mapped directly against the product details of the reference product in the product master record. In CRM release 2005 and below, you maintain accessories in the Product Workbench via SAP GUI transaction "COMMPR01" (Figure 4.21). In CRM 2006s/CRM 2007 and above, you maintain accessories via the MARKETINPRO business role (Figure 4.22). In order to maintain accessories or spare parts in CRM 2005 and below, you need to first click the "Relationships" button at the top of the screen; accessories can be added under the tab labeled "Accessories," while spare parts can be added under the tab labeled "Service Parts." To maintain accessories and spare parts in CRM 2006s/CRM 2007 and above, you simply expand the relevant assignment blocks.

At runtime in the IC WebClient, a function module called COM_PRODUCT_GETLIST_API is called to check the relationships assigned to the product master to determine the list of relevant accessories and spare parts to display to the agent.

143

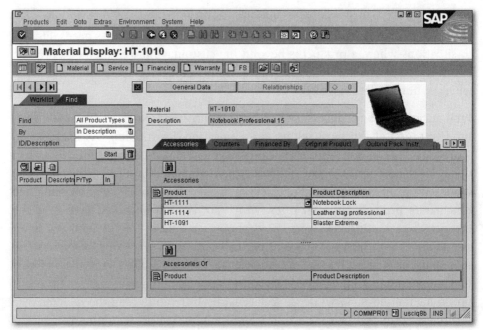

Figure 4.21 Maintenance of Accessories in Product Master in SAP GUI in CRM 2005

Figure 4.22 Maintenance of Accessories in Product Master in CRM WebClient in CRM 2007

> **Note**
>
> In addition to containing tabs for accessories and spare parts, the product master record also contains tabs or assignment blocks for cross-selling and up-selling. However, the IC WebClient does not make use of the values maintained in the product master for cross-selling and up-selling. Rather, the IC WebClient relies on product determination rules maintained in the SAP GUI transaction "CRMD_AR_MAINTAIN" along with the IMG configuration method schemas to determine the relevant cross-sell, up-sell, and down-sell products for a given reference product.

4.6.2 Maintaining Cross-Sellers, Up-Sellers, and Down-Sellers

Although the product master record also contains tabs or assignment blocks for cross-selling and up-selling, the IC WebClient does not make use of the values maintained in the product master for cross-selling and up-selling. Rather, the IC WebClient relies on product determination rules maintained in the SAP GUI transaction "CRMD_AR_MAINTAIN" (Figure 4.23) along with the IMG configuration method schemas to determine the relevant cross-sell, up-sell, and down-sell products for a given reference product. For cross-selling rules, you map one (but only one) leading product against one or more dependent products. Although transaction CRMD_AR_MAINTAIN actually allows you to maintain multiple leading products, the Interaction Center does not make use of this feature. In the Interaction Center, only one leading product is supported; however, one or more dependent products can be maintained for each leading product. In Figure 4.23, you can see an overview of two cross-selling rules in which different leading products, HT-1001 and HT-1010, each have one or more dependent products.

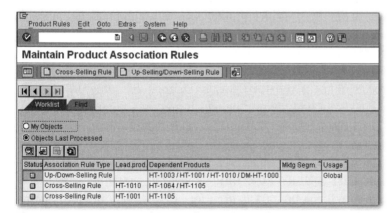

Figure 4.23 Maintenance of Cross-Selling and Up-Selling/Down-Selling Product Association Rules

In addition to cross-selling rules, you can also create up-selling/down-selling rules. Figure 4.24 shows an up-selling/down-selling rule involving the four different models of notebook computer. The "Rank" field indicates which products have the highest priority, with 4 being the highest and 1 being the lowest in this example. This means that at runtime in the Interaction Center, if the agent selects product HT-1010, which has a rank value of 2, product DM-HT-1000 with rank value 1 will be shown as a down-seller, and products HT-1001 and HT-1003 with values 3 and 4 will be shown as up-sellers.

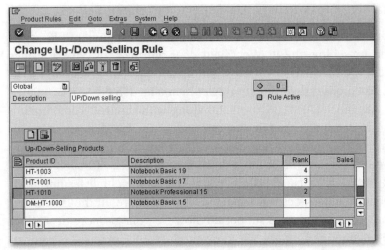

Figure 4.24 Maintenance of Up-Selling/Down-Selling Rules

It is possible to maintain product association rules globally, per target group or per profile. In order to determine which product association rules should be used, the Interaction Center relies on method schemas that have been configured in the IMG in transaction "SAPLCRM_MKTIMG_MS_CD," accessible via IMG menu path: SAP IMPLEMENTATION GUIDE • CUSTOMER RELATIONSHIP MANAGEMENT • MARKETING – PRODUCT PROPOSALS • CREATE METHOD SCHEMA (Figure 4.25). Other CRM applications outside the IC WebClient determine which method schema to use based on an additional IMG configuration that maps a sales organization and business transaction type to a particular schema. However, in the IC WebClient, the method schemas are actually hard coded in ABAP class CL_CRM_IC_PROD_EVENT_HAN-DLER, method PROCESS_QUERY_FURTHER_PRODUCTS, starting at line 137 (Figure 4.26). Method schema 000001 is used for cross-sellers, method schema 000002 is used for up-sellers, and method schema 000003 is used for down-sellers. Although the schema ID is hard coded, you are still free to configure the structure of each schema to determine which type of product association rules to use (global, target group, profile, or some combination of the three).

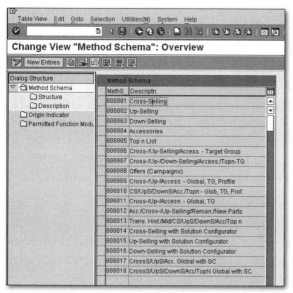

Figure 4.25 Method Schemas for Determining Product Association Rules

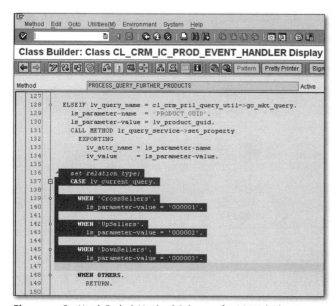

Figure 4.26 Hard Coded Method Schemas for IC WebClient

4.6.3 Using Product Proposals in the Interaction Center

Inside the Interaction Center, product proposals are presented both as part of the product details screen (Figure 4.27) as well as in the sales order transactions. This chapter focuses only on the integration of product proposals in the product details screen; integration of product proposals into the sales order transaction will be discussed later in more detail in Chapter 5, IC Sales.

An agent would typically access the product details by clicking on a product that has been added as a line item to a sales order. However, it is also possible to navigate to the product details directly from the product search screen. Once inside the product details screen, the agent can see a description and image of the product, as well as any notes and pricing information that have been maintained. It is even possible to add the product directly to a sales order from the product details screen.

On the right-hand side of the product details screen shown in Figure 4.27, the agent has access to any additional products (accessories, spare parts, cross-sellers, etc.), or alternative products (up-sellers and down-sellers) that have been maintained for the main product. If the agent selects an additional product such as an accessory, spare part, or cross-seller, the selected product will be added to the cart along with the main product. On the other hand, if the agent selects an alternative product, the previously selected main product will be exchanged with the selected alternative product — adding the alternative product to the sales order cart and removing the previously selected main product.

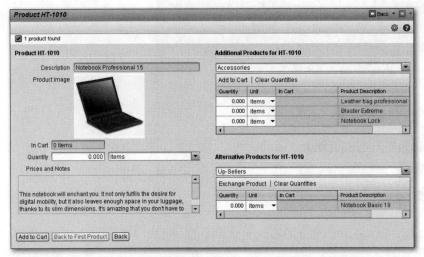

Figure 4.27 Product Accessories and Up-Sellers in the Interaction Center

4.7 SAP Real-Time Offer Management (RTOM)

Although marketing-based product proposals provide quite a bit of flexibility in how accessories and other product proposals are modeled, ultimately the product proposals themselves are relatively static. For example, if a customer already owns product A and B, then the customer will also be offered product C — regardless of why the customer is calling the interaction center, or how many times the customer has already called recently. While static product proposals are a great way to drive incremental sales and revenue, they do have some restrictions. For example, a product proposal is always mapped against a reference product; hence, if no reference product is selected or added to the cart, no product proposals are available. Also, there aren't learning algorithms associated with product proposals; hence, if the customer calls several times during the same business day to follow up on an open sales order or delivery, the customer will receive the same product proposal each time — even if the customer declines the order each time. Finally, product proposals are limited in their scope to actual, physical products and services; product proposals can't be used for triggering other types of marketing efforts such as retention offers or other marketing messages (e.g., "Use our website for faster service").

SAP offers SAP Real-Time Offer Management (RTOM) to integrate with SAP CRM to overcome the restrictions of the product proposals by allowing you to model offers — including product proposals, retention offers, and marketing messages — that are triggered dynamically based on information about what is happening in the current customer interaction. RTOM is built on the SAP CRM Real-Time Decisioning Engine (RTD), an advanced analytical decision-making framework. The engine connects to the SAP Interaction Center via a Web service and determines the most suitable offer(s) based on input from the current customer interaction, enriched with historical customer information, transaction data, and analytics. The offer recommendation is transferred back to the Interaction Center and indicated to the agent via an alert.

Agents can display the ranked list of recommended offers and navigate to the details of any recommended product. Alternatively, the recommended product can be automatically transferred to a sales order, depending on the configuration. Additionally, the list of relevant offers is continually refined in real time throughout the agent's interaction with the customer according to the customer's responses. At the end of the customer interaction, feedback about whether the customer accepted or rejected the offers is transferred back to the RTD and used by its learning engine to improve future recommendations. Default feedback is suggested by the system. For example, if the suggested offer was added to a sales order, the system marks the offer as having been accepted. If the agent clicked on the offer but the product was not added to the cart, the offer is marked as rejected. If the agent did not click on the offer, it is marked as having not been offered. Of course, the agent can modify or correct the feedback proposals set by the system before the agent submits the feedback.

Real-Time Offer Management is especially well suited to industries such as Telecommunications, Financial Services (Insurance and Banking), Utilities, High-Tech, or any other industry or business that typically offers multiple concurrent marketing efforts or promotions. However, even companies that don't make heavy use of marketing promotions can benefit from the retention management capabilities of RTOM. It is at least five to ten times more expensive (depending on the industry) to acquire new customers than to retain existing customers. Loyal customers are much more likely to spend more money, to buy more often, and to refer new customers. Hence, it is absolutely critical to detect customers who are likely to churn, and to trigger the most appropriate retention offer in hopes of saving the account and preventing a customer defection. RTOM can assist by detecting when customers are likely to defect and by promoting the best-suited retention offer for that particular customer.

> **Note**
>
> SAP Real-Time Offer Management (RTOM) is a separate product from SAP CRM and is licensed and installed separately from SAP CRM. RTOM is currently only available as part of an SAP Custom Development Project. However, as of November 2008, RTOM will be available as a regular product on the price list.

4.8 Summary

This chapter outlined the various options for using the SAP CRM Interaction Center to support marketing activities. We looked at how campaigns can be supported via call list and outbound dialing integration. We discussed how agent productivity tools like Interactive Scripting can support marketing efforts by enabling agents to execute surveys, process leads, and update customer marketing attributes. Finally, we explored the different options for creating marketing based product proposals and retention offers.

Some of the most important points to remember are:

▶ Marketing professionals normally generate the call lists for a campaign automatically based on target groups using the Marketing Planner tool. After a call list has been generated, the interaction center manager typically assigns the appropriate agents to the call list.

▶ In special situations, interaction center managers can manually create their own call lists using the Call List Maintenance tool. However, this is not an ideal tool for large call lists because the manager needs to manually assign each customer who should be called.

▶ It is also possible to create planned activities, in lieu of call lists, for situations in which a certain agent is responsible for calling specific customers, often on a reoccurring (e.g., weekly) basis.

▶ Automated outbound dialing modes, such as predictive dialing, can be integrated into the Interaction Center on a project basis using outbound dialer software from companies like Genesys or Avaya.

▶ Interactive Scripting can help guide your agents through the process of capturing survey data and automatically creating and qualifying sales leads.

▶ As of CRM 2005, agents can create leads directly in the Interaction Center. In earlier releases, including CRM 4.0, it was only possible to create leads in the background via interactive scripts; agents could not directly view or edit actual leads.

▶ Marketing-based product proposals are available in the sales order and product detail screens to help agents increase revenue and profitability by selling additional and/or more profitable products.

▶ SAP Real-Time Offer Management (RTOM) can provide intelligent, real-time offer recommendations, including marketing messages, product recommendations, next-best actions, and retention offers.

In the next chapter, we will look at the different options for using the SAP CRM to support your end-to-end sales processes from the Interaction Center.

"I'm just trying to make a dollar out of fifteen cents."
— *Tupac Shakur*

5 IC Sales

There is an expression in business that, "Sales is king." Marketing is key to finding new prospects and growing your existing customers; and of course customer service is absolutely critical to keeping your customers and generating repeat business. However, while marketing and customer service are both vital disciplines, both play supporting roles to the star of the show — *sales*. Even companies who pride themselves on providing world-class customer service will acknowledge that if they're not generating sales revenue, they probably won't stay in business very long. You need to be able to capture and fulfill customer orders quickly and accurately. Regardless of your industry, target market, or business model, if your order entry and fulfillment processes don't run smoothly and reliably, you'll experience fewer orders, more returns, and higher costs of sales.

One of the challenges in processing and fulfilling orders is that many companies find themselves with a fragmented IT landscape, consisting of multiple order entry systems. On average, companies tend to have at least six different systems for capturing customer orders. This can sometimes be the result of mergers and acquisitions where each company tends to keep using their own order capture system even after the companies have been consolidated. Other times, different departments within the same company might undertake their own projects — with or without the blessing of the company's IT department — and implement a system different from what is being used across the rest of the company. When disparate order entry systems are used across an organization, it makes it very difficult — if not impossible — to operate using a single set of standardized order management processes.

Another challenge in processing and fulfilling orders accurately is that many orders are created and saved with incomplete data and/or errors. In certain industries, such as consumer products, as many as 30% of orders contain errors that result in a similarly high percentage of product returns and credit memos. In addition to incomplete and inaccurate orders, there is also the challenge that customers frequently call and make changes to their order, even after the order has been processed — and sometimes even after the order has been shipped. Up to 40% of consumer-products orders get changed at some point. In certain B2B situations, a company may actually reuse a single order for the entire year: Each time the customer calls to order something, new line items are simply added to the existing order.

It is critical for companies to have an integrated end-to-end order management system, allowing front-end users in the interaction center to access sales orders that have already been released for fulfillment to the backend ERP system. As shown in Figure 5.1, there are numerous touch points between your frontend CRM order entry system and your backend ERP order fulfillment system. Obviously, if you are using a consolidated enterprise software application — such as the SAP Business Suite, which includes both SAP CRM and SAP ERP — then you don't need to worry about integrating disparate systems. On the other hand, if you are using SAP CRM with a non-SAP standalone or legacy order processing or order fulfillment system, then you will need to develop custom tools and procedures for ensuring seamless transfer and integration of orders from each system to the other.

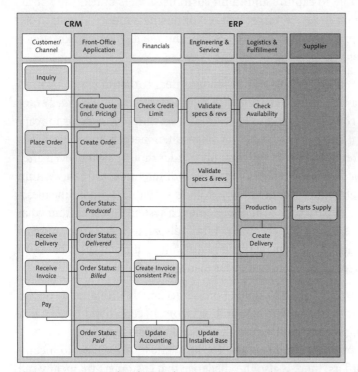

Figure 5.1 Integrated End-to-End Opportunity-to-Order Process

In this chapter, we will explore the various ways in which the SAP CRM Interaction Center can support your end-to-end opportunity-to-order process for B2C, B2B, or mixed (consumer and business buyer) scenarios. We will briefly look at how to create leads and opportunities. We will discuss the different approaches for conducting product searches, leveraging product proposals, and supporting configurable products. Then we will explore all of the various order entry possibilities supported by the Interaction Center across the different CRM releases, including: IC Sales Order, IC Sales Ticket, R/3 Sales Order (IC), ERP Sales Order (IC), ERP Sales Order (CRM WebClient), CRM WebClient Sales Order, and PC-UI Sales Order. Finally, we will briefly touch on the options for conducting available-to-promise (ATP) checks and pricing determination.

5.1 Leads and Opportunities

The first step in selling often involves generating customer demand (via marketing) and then capturing information about interested prospects via leads, which are then qualified and hopefully converted into sales opportunities. Leads and opportunities are used heavily in most industries — with perhaps the exception of regulated utilities and telecommunications, or consumer retail where there is typically no actual "sales cycle" and usually just involves a consumer logging into a website or placing a telephone call to make a purchase.

The creation of leads was described in detail in Chapter 4, IC Marketing. However, to briefly summarize, leads can be created in the Interaction Center either directly via the Lead screen, or leads can be created automatically in the background from a survey embedded into an interactive script. Once a lead has been qualified, either manually or automatically via marketing survey integration, the lead is dispatched to an appropriate sales person based on business rules defined in the SAP CRM Rule Modeler. Hot leads can then be converted into actual opportunities, either automatically via workflow or manually via a follow-up transaction, which are then entered into the sales pipeline and monitored by management.

Note
An IC-specific Lead screen is available as of CRM 2005. It is also possible to embed the PC-UI lead screen in the Interaction Center via the transaction launcher in CRM 2005. Prior to CRM 2005, no IC-specific Lead screen is available and it is only possible to use the PC-UI lead in the IC.

As of CRM 2006s/CRM 2007, it is possible to use either the IC Lead or the CRM Web-Client Lead. The PC-UI Lead is not available in CRM 2006s or CRM 2007 as PC-UI is no longer supported after CRM 2005.

Opportunities are often created from leads. Typically, the creation of an opportunity from a lead is performed by a sales professional (or performed automatically by the system using workflow). The SAP CRM Interaction Center does not provide an IC-specific Opportunity screen because the assumption is that interaction center agents should generally not be creating opportunities; this is the job of the sales professional. However, some companies do require their interaction center agents to create opportunities. In such cases, it is possible to use either the PC-UI Opportunity screen (in CRM 2005 and below) or the CRM WebClient Opportunity (in CRM 2006s/CRM 2007 and above). Figure 5.2 shows the CRM WebClient opportunity screen integrated into the Interaction Center.

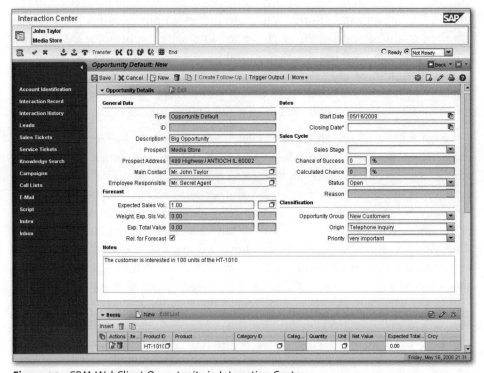

Figure 5.2 CRM WebClient Opportunity in Interaction Center

5.2   Searching for Products

Products are the things consumers and businesses buy and sell each day. Some products are geared toward end consumers, while other products are sold to businesses. Some products, like vehicles and computers, are configurable — allowing the customer to specify the exact options and features that they would like. Other products are not really physical products at all but rather services, such as auditing, accounting, or consulting. Regardless of the type of product, however, one thing is consistent: In order to sell a product, you have to be able to describe it, find it, and provide it to the customer at the requested cost, place, and time.

When a customer (or prospect) contacts a company's interaction center, they are often looking for information about a particular product or service, such as features and options, price, availability, or shipping conditions. An interaction center agent needs to be able to access this information quickly, even if the customer is not able to provide a perfect description of the product. For example, customers rarely know the SKU number or the exact product ID of the product they are calling about. It is crucial that the interaction center agent be able to search for products not only by ID and description but also by the marketing campaign or simply by browsing a product catalog.

There are several ways for an interaction center agent to search for and locate products using the SAP CRM Interaction Center. One way, which has traditionally been available since early releases of the SAP CRM Interaction Center, is by using the standard IC Product Search screen (Figure 5.3). As of CRM 2006s/CRM 2007, another screen called the Product Catalog was introduced to the Interaction Center, which provides additional search options including searching by product catalog, browsing by product catalog hierarchy, and searching for products via campaign.

> **Note**
>
> Please note that when talking about products and product searches in this chapter, we are referring to products as the items that are added to sales orders. We are not referring to *registered products* — such as the IBase or IObject — which are another concept altogether. Registered products are discussed in the chapter on IC Service.

5.2.1 Standard Product Search

The standard Product Search screen, which has been traditionally been available in the Interaction Center, allows an agent to search for products using a variety of criteria, including: product category, product ID or Global Trade Identification Number (GTIN), description, or combination of account ID and account product ID. The Show Category field can be used to display all the products that belong to a certain category (i.e., hierarchy node) in the product catalog. Optionally, you can also narrow down the list of products returned from the category search by using the Product ID/GTIN and/or Product Description fields. For example, if you searched for products belonging to the category with ID 001700010000000110 (i.e., Notebooks), you could filter the results to show products that start with ID "HT" and contain the word "professional" in the description (Figure 5.3).

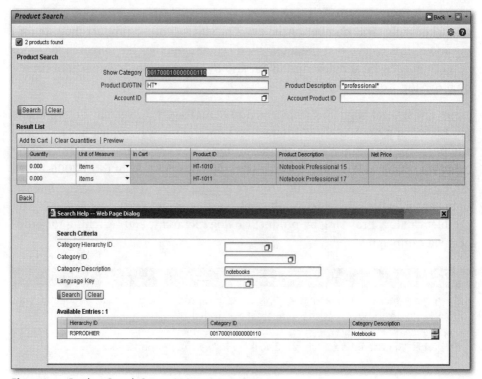

Figure 5.3 Product Search Screen in Interaction Center

Note

When searching for products using the Product Description field in the standard Product Search screen, you can use wildcards to better control your results. For example, a search for the next "Notebook" would only return a product with the exact description "Notebook." However, by using wildcards before and/or after the search term, you could also find products whose description contains the word "Notebook" such as "Notebook Basic 15."

Note that the three fields for category, product ID, and description can be used together, but that these fields cannot be used in conjunction with the fields Account ID and Account Product ID. The Account ID field and the Account Product ID field must be used together and cannot be used with any other fields. These two fields allow you to locate a product by searching with the ID that the customer uses to describe a product, rather than the material number that you assign to the product. For example, the company Media Store with Account ID 3271, refers to material number 371 with their own internal ID "1320." See Figure 5.4.

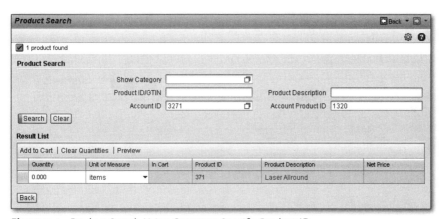

Figure 5.4 Product Search Using Customer-Specific Product ID

In order to use the Account Product ID search, you must have first maintained the customer-specific product name as part of the product master record. In CRM 2005 and below, this is done in transaction "COMMPR01" by selecting a product, clicking the "Relationships" button, choosing the "Customers" tab, and entering the account ID of the customer in the "BPartner" field and the name the customer uses for the product in the "Product ID of Business Partner" field. See Figure 5.5. In CRM 2006s/CRM 2007 and above, you maintain the Account Product ID via the product maintenance screen of the CRM Marketing Professional role in the "Customer Product ID" assignment block (Figure 5.6).

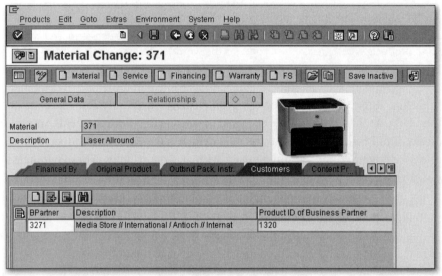

Figure 5.5 Maintenance of Customer Product ID in CRM 2005

Figure 5.6 Maintenance of Customer Product ID in CRM 2006s/2007

5.2.2 Product Catalog

In addition to the standard Product Search screen, as of CRM 2006s/CRM 2007 the Product Catalog search screen provides another set of options for searching for products in the Interaction Center. The Product Catalog search screen contains three tablinks: Product Search, Product Search by Catalog Hierarchy, and Product Search by Campaign. Each tablink provides different product search capabilities to locate products based on the product catalog or marketing campaigns to which they belong.

Product Catalog — Product Search

The Product Search tablink of the Product Catalog allows agents to search for products using catalogs, including catalog variants and catalog areas. For example, an interaction center agent of a high-tech company called PC4U would first choose the appropriate product catalog or variant (such as Fall 2008) and then optionally choose a particular product area such as computers, monitors, printers, scanners, software, or accessories. Based on the selected catalog and catalog area, the relevant products will be shown in the results list (Figure 5.7). The agent can further restrict the result list by entering a product description or product ID (or partial description or ID). For example, by entering the text "laser" in the description field, the result list would only show those printers that contain "laser" in the description.

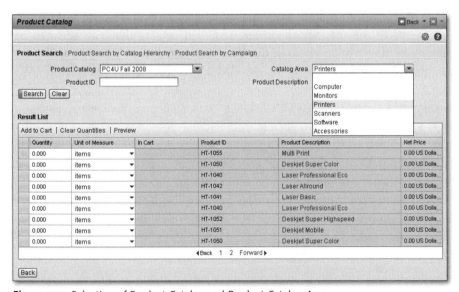

Figure 5.7 Selection of Product Catalog and Product Catalog Area

> **Note**
>
> The search in the description field of the Product Catalog — Product Search tab works slightly differently than the search in the description field of the standard Product Search screen. In the standard Product Search screen, the results list will only return results that match the exact search query you entered; optionally, you can use wildcards to expand your results list. In the Product Catalog search screen, however, the description field includes an implicit wildcard search, returning all results that contain your search query — even without explicitly entering any wildcard operators.

Product Catalog — Product Search by Catalog Hierarchy

In some situations it is more convenient for an interaction center agent to be able to actually browse through a catalog of products, organized into hierarchical groups rather than searching for a specific product by ID or description. For example, if a customer knows the general type of product they are interested in but does not already know the exact model, the agent can browse to the appropriate product category in the catalog and see which products are available in that category (Figure 5.8). The ability to browse product catalogs can also be useful if a customer calls and refers to a product contained in either a print catalog or a catalog located on the company's website. In this case, the agent can pull up the appropriate catalog and then locate the product in question.

In order for your agents to take advantage of the product search by catalog hierarchy feature, you must first decide which catalogs you would like to make available to agents in the interaction center. For each catalog that you want to be available, you maintain an entry in the IMG activity "Define Catalog Profiles for Product Search" (transaction code "SAPLCRM_IC_PS_CD") accessible via the IMG menu path: SAP IMPLEMENTATION GUIDE • CUSTOMER RELATIONSHIP MANAGEMENT • INTERACTION CENTER WEBCLIENT • MASTER DATA • PRODUCTS • DEFINE CATALOG PROFILES FOR PRODUCT SEARCH. See Figure 5.9. Once you have created a new catalog search profile, the assigned catalog will automatically be available for selection in the Interaction Center. Unlike the way the Interaction Center works for most other areas, it is not necessary (or possible) to assign the catalog search profile to the IC WebClient profile or CRM business role as a function profile; rather, every product search profile is automatically available from every IC WebClient profile or CRM business role.

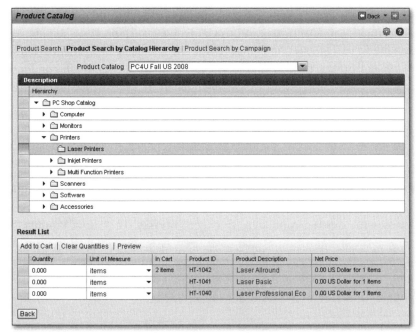

Figure 5.8 Browsing the Product Catalog Hierarchy

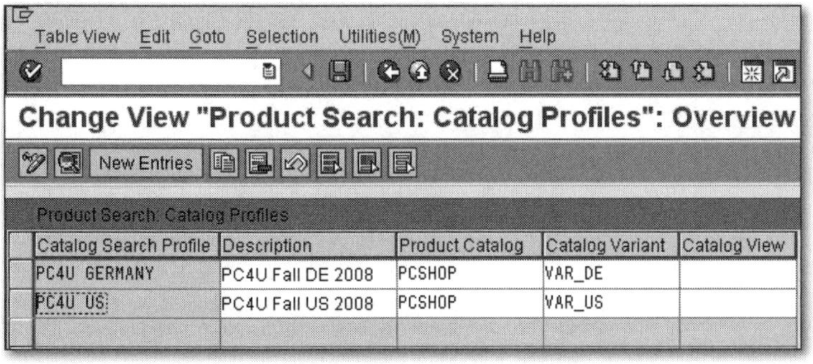

Figure 5.9 Assignment of Product Catalogs to Interaction Center

Product Catalog — Product Search by Campaign

Sometimes a customer might be interested in a product attached to a particular marketing campaign. Ideally, the marketing department would have already informed the interaction center management team in advance that a promotion was scheduled to be run, allowing the interaction center supervisors to schedule additional resources to handle the increased demand and to brief the agents about the new campaign. The agents would already be familiar with the details of the new campaign, including any related products. However, interaction managers can attest that life in the interaction center is not always ideal. Even if agents are already up to speed on the newest marketing campaigns, they can still conduct a quick search to locate the relevant products attached to a particular marketing campaign.

To locate the products attached to a particular campaign, the agent navigates to the Product Search by Campaign tab link of the Product Catalog screen and chooses the desired campaign from the list of campaigns presented in the drop-down list box. All campaigns in the system that have status "Released" and whose "Planned End Date" has not yet been reached will be presented in the drop-down list box. After the agent chooses the desired campaign, the agent presses the "Show Products" button to retrieve the list of products that have been assigned to the chosen campaign (Figure 5.10). The user can select one or more products, enter the desired quantity, and add the products to the cart. Later, these products can be imported into a sales transaction such as a sales order or sales ticket.

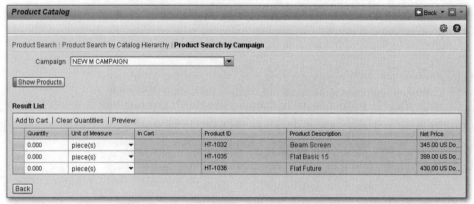

Figure 5.10 Searching for Products by Campaign

> **Note**
>
> The Product Search by Campaign drop-down list box does not utilize the Interaction Center campaign profile defined in the IMG. The Interaction Center campaign profile defined in the IMG is only used to determine which campaigns (and campaign details) are shown when the user selects the Campaign link in the Navigation Bar. The Interaction Center campaign profile — and its corresponding campaign attributes and attribute conditions — do not influence the entries that are shown in the Product Search by Campaign drop-down list box.

5.2.3 Add-to-Cart Button and Product List Preview

As of CRM release 2007, all of the product search screens include a product list "Preview" button that provides the ability to preview the details of multiple products from a single screen, without navigating back and forth between the product search result list and the product details screen. After conducting a search where multiple products are returned in the result list, the agent can click the Preview button to navigate to the Product Details screen where a split screen is available that shows the list of selected products on the left side, and the details of the selected product on the right side of the screen (Figure 5.11). As the user clicks on each product in the list, the details for the chosen product are displayed at the right. This is ideal in situations where a customer has questions about several different products and wants to compare options and costs between two or more products.

As of CRM release 2007, all of the product search screens also include an "Add to Cart" button that allows a product and quantity to be added to a temporary cart that can later be imported into a sales transaction such as the IC Sales Order or IC Sales Ticket. If the customer is interested in purchasing one or more products, the agent can enter the desired quantity for the appropriate product and click the "Add to Cart" button in order to add the products to a temporary shopping cart. Later, the products can be imported into a sales order from the cart.

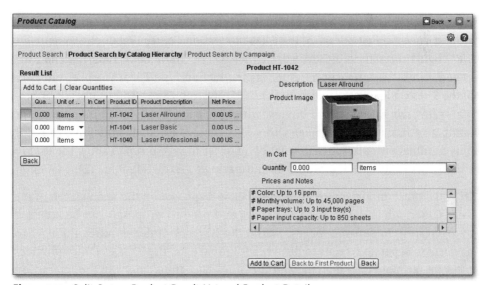

Figure 5.11 Split-Screen Product Result List and Product Details

5.3   IC Sales Transactions

After a customer has expressed interest in a product and the interaction center agent has satisfactorily answered the customer's questions, it is time to create a sales transaction. The SAP CRM Interaction Center offers access to various different options for sales order entry. One option is geared toward business buyers, while another option is optimized for consumers. Some options create the sales transactions in CRM (with the option to replicate the orders to ERP), while other options create the order directly in the backend ERP system. Each option has its own strengths — as well as its own limits and restrictions. In the following sections, we will take a look at each of the different options in detail.

However, despite the subtle differences in functionality provided by the different sales transactions, they all share some basic similarities. For example, every sales transaction, regardless of its transaction type, contains required information about partners, products and quantities, prices and other conditions, terms or delivery, and terms of payment. In addition, all sales transactions support critical functions such as credit check, product determination (material determination) and substitution, available-to-promise (ATP) check, and pricing check.

5.3.1   Sales Order for Interaction Center

The IC Sales Order screen has traditionally been the de facto standard for creating sales transactions from the Interaction Center in CRM. The IC Sales Order has been around since the first release of the CRM Interaction Center WebClient. Essentially, SAP copied the standard CRM Sales Order screen (transaction type TA) and integrated it into the Interaction Center (as transaction type TSA). The user interface of the Sales Order is particularly well suited toward business-to-business (B2B) scenarios involving professional buyers, where orders typically often involve a large number of line items. The Sales Order is optimized for such situations, showing only minimal order header information in order to save room to allow the user to add many products to the order without having to scroll (Figure 5.12).

Only the most important order header data is displayed on the main screen of the Sales Order, while details such as pricing and product proposals can be accessed by navigating to separate pages. While the IC Sales Order requires the user to navigate to separate screens to display additional data, the IC Sales Order provides access to far more data than most of the other sales transactions in the Interaction Center. For example, pricing information is available both on the IC Sales Order header level (Figure 5.13), as well as for the individual line items of the IC Sales Order (Figure 5.14).

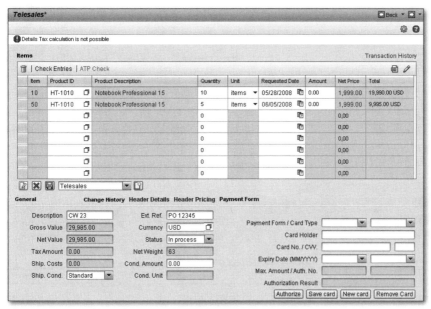

Figure 5.12 IC Sales Order

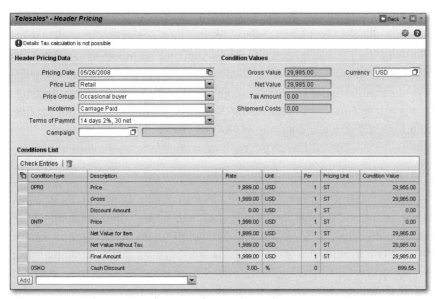

Figure 5.13 Header Pricing Information for IC Sales Order

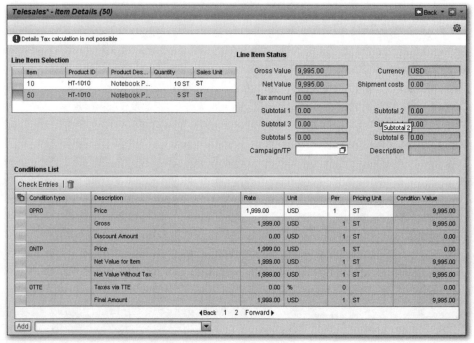

Figure 5.14 Line Item Pricing Information for IC Sales Order

When using the IC Sales Order option, the sales transaction is created directly in the frontend CRM system. Optionally, the sales transactions can also be replicated via CRM Middleware from the CRM system to the backend R/3 of ERP system for fulfillment — picking, packing, delivery, invoicing, and billing. Pricing (including variant configuration and pricing) is handled by the Internet Pricing and Configurator (IPC) — the standard tool for conducting pricing in CRM. Available-to-promise (ATP) checks are usually carried out using Advanced Planning and Optimization (APO), although ATP can also be done via R/3 or ERP if desired.

5.3.2 Sales Ticket for Interaction Center

The IC Sales *Ticket* screen was first introduced in the IC WebClient with CRM 2005. Whereas the standard IC Sales Order was designed with professional buyers in mind, who might be buying dozens or hundreds of products in the same order, the IC Sales Ticket is optimized for B2C scenarios. The IC Sales Ticket contains fewer line items (because consumers typically buy two or three items at a time rather than hundreds) and provides all necessary information on the main screen (Figure

5.15), reducing the need for the agent to navigate to other screens and facilitating faster order entry. This not only saves time, but also helps prevent order entry errors because the agent never loses sight of the item list of the order. Being able to create orders quickly and accurately is of paramount importance in consumer scenarios where customers want to get off the phone quickly.

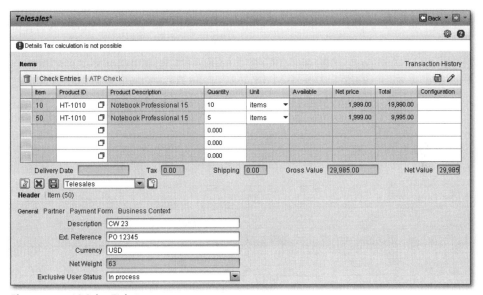

Figure 5.15   IC Sales Ticket

In addition to the fewer number of line items and the inclusion of all relevant data on the main screen, another technical difference between the IC Sales Ticket and the IC Sales Order is that the IC Sales Ticket displays less information (e.g., fewer fields) by default. The enhancement concept of IC WebClient enables you to easily add, remove, or replace fields on a project basis via custom coding without modification. In SAP CRM 2006s and 2007, this process is even easier because such layout adjustments are supported by a graphical editor called the UI Config Tool. From a technical perspective, the IC Sales Ticket uses the same underlying business object repository (BOR) object as the IC Sales Order and all other One Order business transactions – BOR object 2000116. However, the IC Sales Ticket uses a different transaction type than the IC Sales Order. While the IC Sales Order uses transaction type TSA, the IC Sales Ticket uses transaction type TSAC.

5.3.3 PC-UI Sales Order

The SAP People-Centric User Interface concept was introduced with SAP CRM 3.1 to provide a set of standard, pattern-based screens that business users could access via a Web browser from the SAP Enterprise Portal. PC-UI provided a Web-based, thin-client alternative to SAP GUI for most CRM scenarios, with the exception of the Interaction Center. PC-UI was not used for the Interaction Center, which already had a Web-based thin-client solution called the IC WebClient. However, in some cases, it made sense to leverage certain PC-UI screens for which no native IC WebClient screen was available, such as the CRM Opportunity, inside the Interaction Center without the Enterprise Portal using the Transaction Launcher. A couple of SAP CRM customers decided, for whatever reasons, to employ this technique to use the PC-UI Sales Order in the Interaction Center instead of using either the native IC Sales Order or IC Sales Ticket. Figure 5.16 shows the layout of the PC-UI Sales Order.

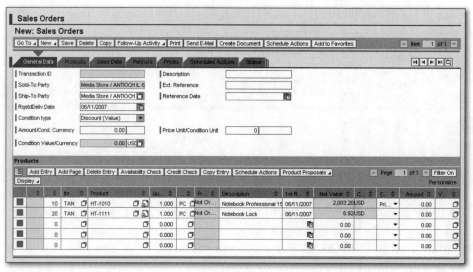

Figure 5.16 PC-UI Sales Order

However, there are some inherent difficulties with using the PC-UI Sales Order inside the Interaction Center. For one, integration between PC-UI and IC is not standard. Therefore, additional work is necessary to pass parameters back and forth between PC-UI and the IC (e.g., to add the newly created PC-UI sales order to the activity clipboard of the Interaction Record in the IC). Additionally, support for PC-UI in CRM is discontinued by SAP after CRM 2005. Therefore, unless you have a compelling need to use the PC-UI option, you should avoid this approach.

5.3.4   R/3 Sales Order for Interaction Center

Since the first release of the Interaction Center in SAP CRM, it has always been possible to incorporate the SAP R/3 Sales Order into the CRM Interaction Center by calling the appropriate R/3 transactions (e.g., VA01, VA02, etc.) via the Action Box/Transaction Launcher. This was deemed necessary because SAP CRM was a new product and existing customers had already implemented their sales processes in SAP R/3 via the Sales and Distribution (SD) functionality. Rather than reimplement all of their sales processes in CRM, customers wanted the ability to simply integrate their existing R/3 order entry screens into CRM. Even today, ten years after the first release of SAP CRM, it is still possible to integrate the R/3 or ERP transactions (such as the Sales Order) into the CRM Interaction Center as long as you are using R/3 4.6 or higher, or any version of SAP ERP. Despite its name, the R/3 Sales Order is not only limited to older SAP R/3 systems; it also works with newer SAP ERP systems such as ECC 5.0 and 6.0.

Note
Early versions of SAP CRM, including the IC WinClient, leveraged a tool called the Action Box to launch external applications, URLs, and backend R/3 transactions. The Action Box relied on underlying remote function call (RFC) technology. Newer versions of SAP CRM, including the IC WebClient, use a tool called the Transaction Launcher, which has replaced the Action Box as the means of launching external applications, URLs, and backend transactions inside CRM. The Transaction Launcher relies on underlying Internet Transaction Server (ITS) technology.

There are a number of reasons why companies may want to continue creating orders in their backend R/3 or ERP system instead of CRM. For example, if your company is already a heavy user of SAP R/3 or ERP but is just starting out with CRM, you may want to leave your sales order processing in R/3 or ERP for the time being at least, and consider a phased CRM rollout, perhaps starting with some marketing or customer service functionality. Another reason to potentially keep your sales order processing in R/3 or ERP is if you have already invested heavily in custom code and configuration, including custom fields, user exits, user statuses, or pricing conditions. In this case, there may not be any compelling reason to undertake the substantial rework required to migrate the existing ERP functionality to CRM and IPC. Finally, if your users are already comfortable and proficient with the R/3 or ERP Sales Order screens and don't have time now for retraining, it could make sense to leave the sales processing in ERP for the short term.

There are, however, some tradeoffs to consider if you are thinking about using the R/3 Sales Order from the CRM Interaction Center. The main downside of this approach is that it doesn't provide any integration with CRM marketing product-proposals. For example, when a product is added to the R/3 Sales Order, the CRM system is not aware of which product was added. Hence, the CRM system has no chance to propose a related cross-sell, up-sell, or accessory. Another consideration is that the R/3 Sales Order is not fully integrated with CRM. Basic integration with the Interaction Center is available out of the box, allowing the R/3 Sales Order to appear in the Agent Inbox and in the Activity Clipboard of the Interaction Record. However, custom project-based work would be required, for example, to display the R/3 sales orders in the IC Fact Sheet. Additionally, it would be necessary to replicate the R/3 orders to CRM in order to allow the orders to appear in other CRM applications outside of the Interaction Center such as Mobile Sales or Internet Sales.

5.3.5 ERP Sales Order for Interaction Center

An alternative to using the R/3 Sales Order is a new option available in the IC WebClient as of CRM 2005 called the ERP Sales Order. Like the R/3 Sales Order, the ERP Sales Order also creates the sales transaction directly in the backend ERP system. However, the main advantage of the ERP Sales Order over the R/3 Sales Order is that the ERP Sales Order is fully integrated with CRM Marketing product-proposal functionality. When using the ERP Sales Order, you have access to back-end ERP order processing capabilities, while also being able to leverage CRM product proposals for up-sells, cross-sells, and accessories.

Unlike the R/3 Sales Order option, which uses the Transaction Launcher to embed actual the R/3 or ERP transaction (e.g., VA01) inside the CRM Interaction Center, the ERP Sales Order uses a native CRM Interaction Center screen with standard CRM look and feel (Figure 5.17). The ERP Sales Order relies on an application programming interface (API) to actually create the order directly in the backend ERP system. This option is compatible with a backend ERP system of ECC 6.0 or higher, but cannot be used with older R/3 based systems. Several SAP customers have worked with the SAP Custom Development Project (CDP) organization to retrofit the ERP Sales Order to work with older backend systems including R/3 4.6C and higher.

Figure 5.17 ERP Sales Order for Interaction Center

There are some tradeoffs to consider when using the ERP Sales Order. Unlike the R/3 Sales Order that provides full access to all of the functionality of the backend transaction (by calling the transaction directly), the ERP Sales Order relies on an API that currently only supports some basic features of the order creation transaction. It is worth noting that SAP plans to continue developing the API, providing support for more features with each release. As of CRM 2006s/CRM 2007, the API of the ERP Sales Order for the Interaction Center currently does not support a number of advanced features, such as variant configuration and variant pricing or user statuses.

5.3.6 CRM WebClient ERP Sales Order

As of CRM 2006s/CRM 2007, the CRM Sales Professional role also provides its own version of the ERP Sales Order, similar to the ERP Sales Order available in the Interaction Center. Like the Interaction Center version of the ERP Sales Order, the version available in the Sales Professional role also involves a native CRM screen that creates the order in the backend ERP system via an API. One of the biggest differences between the two in terms of functionality is that the newer CRM Web-Client version of the ERP Sales Order (which was introduced in CRM 2006s/CRM 2007) supports a few more features than the older IC version (which was introduced in CRM 2005). Hence, some SAP CRM 2007 Interaction Center customers prefer to use the CRM WebClient ERP Sales Order from the Interaction Center, instead of using the IC version.

There are some other notable differences between the two transactions as well. One of the most visible differences is the actual screen layout. The CRM WebClient version of the order (Figure 5.18) uses the standard CRM vertical layout paradigm — with a main object on top of the screen (i.e., order details) followed by a long scroll list of related assignment blocks (i.e., line items, parties involved, organizational data, pricing, shipping, etc.). The Interaction Center version of the ERP Sales Order is optimized specifically for interaction center users — with the goal of having everything fit on the screen with very little or no scrolling, in order to maximize agent productivity (Figure 5.17). Hence, Interaction Center users who are concerned about usability and speed of order entry generally prefer the IC version of the ERP Order.

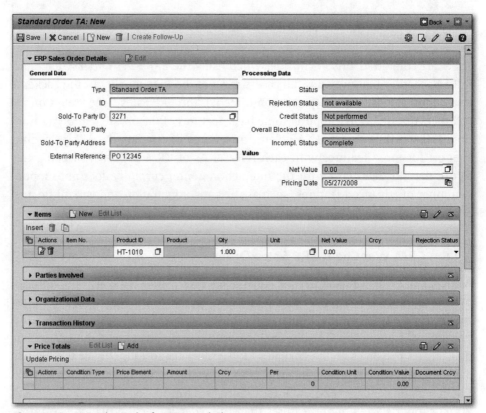

Figure 5.18 ERP Sales Order for CRM WebClient

If you already know that you want to create orders directly in the ERP backend (with ECC 6.0 or higher) and also want to leverage CRM marketing based product proposals, then you should consider one of the two versions of the ERP Sales Order. If you are more concerned with having a user interface optimized for the Interaction Center and you only require basic features, then the IC version of the ERP Order is probably right for you. On the other hand, if you need more advanced features and are open to the idea of using a slightly different user interface that is not specifically optimized for the Interaction Center, then the CRM Sales Professional version of the ERP Sales Order will likely be your choice.

5.3.7 CRM WebClient Sales Order

In CRM 2006s/CRM 2007 and above, the Sales Professional role in the CRM WebClient provides its own version of CRM Sales Order that has some significant differences from the IC Sales Order or IC Sales Ticket transactions available in the Interaction Center. Naturally, the physical appearance of the CRM WebClient Sales Order is quite different than the IC Sales Order or IC Sales Ticket. For example, whereas the IC transactions use a tiled layout that fits everything on the agent's screen without the need for scrolling, the CRM WebClient Sales Order follows the standard CRM WebClient design paradigm; the header details are presented on top of the screen followed by a long list of assignment blocks providing other data such as items, shipping information, billing, payment methods, transaction history, and so on.

It is technically possible to embed the CRM WebClient Sales Order inside the Interaction Center in CRM 2006 and CRM 2007 as shown in Figure 5.19. However, it is important to note that integration is limited. You can at least enable basic integration, such as passing of the confirmed account and contact person from the Interaction Center into the order, as well as linking the order into the Activity Clipboard of the Interaction Record after it is saved.

The CRM WebClient Sales Order will still behave differently than other native IC transactions. For example, a data-loss confirmation box will appear when navigating away from the order. When you return to the order, the order is presented in display mode rather than edit mode. Also, the order will not be saved automatically when pressing the End button on the toolbar, as happens with standard IC transactions. Additionally, the CRM WebClient Sales Order is not integrated with the standard IC product search, product details, and product catalog screens. It is planned to provide more out of the box integration between the CRM WebClient Sales Order and the IC in future releases.

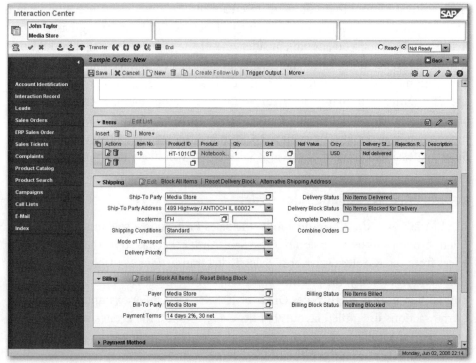

Figure 5.19 CRM WebClient Sales Order Inside the Interaction Center

5.4 Configurable Products

Customers today are sophisticated and demanding. They want high-quality products, of course. But they also want *personalized* products that are tailored to their specific usage needs and requirements. Today's consumers demand made-to-order *configurable products* that can be customized to match their specific tastes and preferences. Rather than settling for a standard off-the-shelf, off-the-lot, or off-the-menu products, many customers prefer to choose their own options and features. Increasingly, a greater number of products are being offered as configurable, including everything from cell phone plans to custom-printed T-shirts.

SAP CRM supports configurable products within the sales process, both in Web Channel E-Commerce (Internet Sales) as well as in the Interaction Center. The actual modeling of the configurable products is done by a product expert using SAP's Configuration Engine. In CRM 2005, a separate J2EE application called the Product Modeling Environment has to be installed to use the Configuration Engine; in CRM 2006s/CRM 2007, the Configuration Engine in accessible via the CRM WebClient user interface. Once a configurable product has been modeled, the product can be configured by end users in the Interaction Center whenever the product is added to a sales transaction.

When a configurable product is added to a sales transaction, a small wrench icon will show up in the "Configuration" column, indicating that the product can be configured. When the agent clicks on the configuration icon, the system navigates to the configuration page where the agent can configure the selected product (Figure 5.20). As the agent selects different options, the price of the product adjusts to reflect the current configuration. For example, adding more memory or a faster CPU to a computer will result in additional cost. The agent uses the "Take Snapshot" button of the current configuration, and then later selects different configuration options and compares the price and features of the two configurations via the "Compare to Snapshot" button.

Figure 5.20 Product Configuration in the Interaction Center

5.5   Product Proposals

In Chapter 4, IC Marketing, we discussed marketing-based product proposals in detail, including the maintenance of accessories and spare parts, as well as the setup of product-proposal rules for cross-selling, up-selling, and down-selling. However, we limited our discussion to the usage of product proposals within the Interaction Center Product Details screen. As shown in Table 5.1, all of the different types of product proposals that are supported in the IC product details screen are also supported in the various sales transactions at the line-item level of the transaction. This means that for each product that is added as a line item of a sales transaction, additional related products, such as accessories, up-sells, down-sells, and cross-sells, are available (if maintained). Furthermore, as shown, the ERP Sales Order (both the IC and CRM version) and the CRM Sales Order additionally supports several other types of product proposals at the header level of the sales order, which are obviously not available in the product details screen (because it is not a sales transaction and does not have an order "header").

	Sales Oder/ Ticket	ERP Sales Order	Product Details	CRM WebClient Sales Order
Header				
Top N List		X		X
Campaign Products				X
Order History CRM				X
Order History ERP		X		
Customer Listings		X		
Item				
Accessories	X	X	X	X
Up/Down Selling	X	X	X	X
Cross Selling	X	X	X	X
RTOM	X	X	X	

Table 5.1 Product Proposals Supported in the Interaction Center

The "Top N List" is essentially a list of top-selling products for a particular customer target group. The actual number of products is configurable and could be set to show the top 3, top 5, or top 10 selling products, for example. The creation of the Top N List is done by the marketing manager. Neither the IC Sales Order nor the IC Sales Ticket supports the Top N List; however, the Top N List is available in both the IC and CRM version of the ERP Sales Order, as well as in the standard CRM Sales Order (delivered with the Sales Professional role).

The "Marketing Products" functionality, which is exclusively available with the CRM WebClient Sales Order, allows you to select one or more marketing projects or campaigns for which you want to propose linked products. If products have been linked to the marketing project or campaign, the products can be transferred into product proposal screen of the order. The agent can select the desired products and quantities and transfer them to the actual order item list from the product proposal screen.

The "Order History" feature allows you to select past orders — either CRM or ERP orders depending on whether you are creating a CRM or ERP order — and use the item list from the historic order as the basis for product proposals in the current order. Product proposals based on the ERP order history are available from both the IC version of the ERP Sales Order as well as the CRM version of ERP Sales Order. Product proposals based on the CRM order history are only available in the CRM WebClient Sales Order. No order history-based product proposals are available from the IC Sales Order or the IC Sales Ticket.

The "Customer Listing" feature is only available in the ERP Sales Order. It is included with both the IC version of the ERP Sales Order, as well as the CRM version of the ERP Sales Order. The customer listing functionality provides a list of products that the current customer is authorized to purchase, based on the customer's sales contract or business agreement. This can be a very important feature, for example, in the retail beverage industry, where a particular retailer might only be allowed to purchase certain products from each distributor.

Product proposals based on accessories and alternative products (up-seller, down-sellers, and cross-sellers) are available in every sales transaction accessible from the Interaction Center including the various versions of the ERP Sales Order as well as the CRM WebClient Sales Order. An example of product proposals for alternative products inside the IC Sales Ticket can be seen in Figure 5.21. In addition to the various types of product proposals discussed so far, a new option is available in CRM 2006 and CRM 2007 and beyond to utilize SAP Real-Time Offer Management (RTOM) to provide product recommendations. RTOM tries to determine the one or two best offers for a customer, based on all available data and information about the customer, including the reason for the customer's current interaction with the company. As of CRM 2006s/CRM 2007, RTOM is integrated into all the IC specific sales transactions; however, RTOM is not yet available in the standard CRM WebClient sales order.

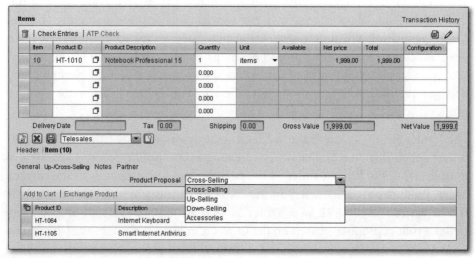

Figure 5.21 Product Proposals in IC Sales Ticket

5.6   Available-to-Promise (ATP) and Pricing

When using one of the approaches that create sales transactions in the frontend CRM system, such as the IC Sales Order or IC Sales Ticket, pricing (including variant pricing for variant configuration) is carried out using IPC, which is the standard pricing tool for CRM. Available-to-Promise (ATP) checks are performed using either APO, or a direct RFC call to the backend ERP system. After you create orders in the frontend SAP CRM system, you can automatically replicate the orders to the backend ERP system for processing and fulfillment via the CRM Middleware.

On the other hand, if you employ one of the approaches that creates the sales transactions directly in the backend R/3 or ERP system, then the pricing and ATP check are carried out in the backend R/3 or ERP system. Optionally, you can replicate the sales orders from the back-end system to CRM, although this is not required. Even if you don't replicate the orders from ERP to CRM, you can still access the ERP orders from the CRM Interaction Center via the Agent Inbox or Interaction History. However, it would be necessary to replicate the ERP orders to CRM if you want the orders to appear in other CRM applications outside of the Interaction Center, such as Mobile Sales or Internet Sales.

5.7 Summary

In this chapter, we looked at how you can use SAP CRM to support your end-to-end sales processes from the Interaction Center. We discussed the different approaches for handling sales order entry, including the best approaches for B2B and B2C scenarios. We also compared the options for creating orders directly in CRM, versus creating orders in the backend ERP system from CRM.

Some of the most important points to remember from this chapter are:

▶ Sales leads can be created in the Interaction Center automatically via Interactive Scripts using embedded marketing surveys. You can also create leads directly using the IC Lead screen (introduced in CRM 2005) or the PC-UI Lead screen (valid from CRM 3.1 to CRM 2005).

▶ The Product Catalog screen, introduced in CRM 2006s/CRM 2007, provides additional techniques for searching for products including seaching by product catalogs and catalog areas, browsing by product catalog hierachy, and searching for products by campaign.

▶ Other new features in CRM 2006s/CRM 2007 such as the "Add to Cart" button and the split-screen product results list and product preview screen simplify the process of finding products and creating sales orders.

▶ The IC Sales Order is very well suited for business-to-business sales scenarios, while the IC Sales Ticket is optimized for consumer sales scenarios.

▶ Several options are available for creating orders directly in the back-end ERP system from the IC including accessing the R/3 Sales Order (e.g., transaction VA01) via the Transaction Launcher, or using one of the new ERP Sales Order screens to create the order via API.

▶ Configurable products are fully supported in the Interaction Center, providing consistency with other CRM sales channels such as Internet Sales.

▶ Various product proposal options can be leveraged (depending on the particular order entry screen you use), potentially including accessories, alternative products (cross-sell, up-sell, and down-sell), Top N Lists, customer-specific product lists, and real-time offers.

In the next chapter, we will look at how the SAP CRM Interaction Center can support your CRM service initiatives, helping you to keep your customers happy and coming back for more.

"Maybe 'Customer Service' should be more than just one department."
— *SAP advertisement*

6   IC Service

Customer service, defined very simplistically (perhaps naively) means doing whatever is necessary to keep customers completely satisfied — and loyal. In practice however, customer service often involves doing just enough to keep the customer reasonably satisfied — at a *reasonable cost*. Customer expectations are continually rising, but so are investor expectations. Providing increasingly better service while keeping service costs low is good, but it is not enough. Now service departments must not only provide high-quality service, but they must also make money doing so. Traditionally, service departments of companies were run as cost centers; the service department directly contributed to the costs of the company without directly generating revenue. In today's business environment where both public and private companies are squeezed to grow revenues, even service organizations are asked to add more to the bottom line. Hence, service organizations must drive sales revenues (via cross-selling and up-selling) while improving quality, while at the same time reducing costs.

In this chapter, we will look at how companies drive down service costs while increasing service revenue, while still maintaining high-quality service. The trick involves doing things better and more efficiently: executing service processes with greater efficiency, automating non-core service-related activities, leveraging intelligent agent guidance for complex manual tasks, and making greater use of customer self-service tools. For example, alerts, scripts, and automatic navigation can be used to guide agents through complex customer issues in the most efficient manner. Reoccurring and easy-to-solve tasks such as password resets or routing tickets to the current processor can be handled via automated rules. Automatically suggested solutions and email/chat templates can help agents respond to customers faster and more accurately. By allowing customers to go online and resolve their own issues, companies can reduce the burden on their interaction center.

6.1   About Help Desks

As discussed in Chapter 1, there are many different types of interaction centers — outbound telemarketing and telesales, inbound B2B sales support centers, consumer help desks, IT help desks, employee interaction centers, and everything in between. However, the most common use of interaction centers is for customer service, also known as the help desk or service desk. In this chapter, we will look at the various forms of help desks, including information help desk, customer service desk, and customer IT service desk. So, why are there so many help desks? The answer to this question probably depends to some extent on who you ask. Industry veterans will likely point out that help desks are a product of history, originally established when consumers were much less informed and less product savvy than they are today. Other experts, who possess a couple ounces of insight and a few grams of cynicism, might comment that the reason there are so many help desks is because most products are overly complex, difficult to use, and prone to error. Finally, Web 2.0 technocrats (like the author of this book) suggest that perhaps someday soon we will no longer need help desks at all, due to the free flow of information on the Internet and the preponderance of Web self-service–based applications.

However, regardless of why they originated and whether they are still necessary, help desks (or service desks as they are sometimes also called) are still widely used. Almost every company you can think of runs a help desk. Even companies whose business models are built exclusively on the Internet, such as Amazon.com or eBay offer telephone help desks for their customers, or at least for certain segments of their customers (i.e., power sellers, VIP customers, etc.). A help desk can play many different roles within a company's customer service department, such as providing answers to basic questions, handling product and warranty registration, diagnosing and resolving complex technical issues, scheduling appointments for maintenance or installations, or handling customer complaints and returns. The SAP CRM Interaction Center supports all of these processes. Let's start off by taking a look at one of the most common help desk processes: information help desk.

6.2   Information Help Desk

The goal of the information help desk process is to provide customers with required information and answers as quickly, accurately, and efficiently as possible. Many issues that are handled by information help desks involve providing basic information or services such as account balances and payment information, reservation confirmations, password resets, order statuses, return policies, shipping charges, methods of payment, catalog requests, store hours, retail locations, and driving directions. Granted, any of these routine issues could probably be automated via a good self-service website, but this book is about interaction centers, not Web self-service (though we will say a few words about Web self-service at the end of this chapter). Of course, not all issues are routine or easy to solve. Customers also contact the information help desk with complex or difficult to solve issues including billing questions, payment disputes, complaints, or technical issues.

Let's assume that, using the 80/20 rule, 80% of customer contacts involve some basic, easy to resolve issues such as product registration, account balances, or password resets; the other 20% of issues may involve more complex issues such as technical trouble shooting, billing or payment disputes, or complaints from unhappy customers. Ideally, you want to be able to handle the 80% of easy to resolve issues as quickly, efficiently, and cheaply as possible, allowing you to focus your time, resources, and money on the more critical 20% of more difficult issues.

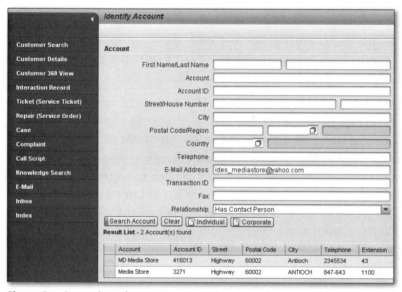

Figure 6.1 Screenshot of Navigation Bar Tailored to Information Help Desk

The SAP CRM Interaction Center supports the information help desk process, by providing tools to enable Interaction Center agents to easily register new customers and products, quickly locate information and other documents, and efficiently create responses to customers. Figure 6.1 shows a screenshot of the Interaction

Center tailored to support the information help desk process. The navigation bar contains links for viewing customer details, conducting knowledge searches, emailing documents to customers, creating various types of service requests including service tickets and service orders, opening cases, logging complaints, and so on.

6.2.1 Customer Identification and Registration

The first step in the information help desk process is generally to retrieve the customer details of the person you are speaking with, or, in cases where no customer record yet exists, to register the customer. CRM is about managing customer relationships; however, before you can effectively manage customer *relationships*, you have to be able to manage customer *data*. For many companies, customer data often proves to be the biggest challenge in their CRM project. Some companies have too much data, literally, with duplicate records for the same customers. This tends to happen when agents cannot easily locate existing customer records, and instead create new (duplicate) records. On the other hand, some companies have the opposite problem of too little data — and have no idea who their customers are. This often happens when customers buy products through a retailer or reseller, and the brand owner is not informed about the sale. Thus, the brand owner might never hear from the customer until the customer contacts the help desk for service or support.

The challenge for a help desk agent is to be able to locate existing records quickly (while the customer is on the phone), and to be able to easily register new customers, without creating duplicate records. Using the SAP CRM Interaction Center, agents can search for existing customer accounts via a variety of common fields including account ID, account name, first name, last name, address, or even using the transaction ID of a previous order, service request, or complaint. For high-performance professional call centers where every second counts — and call volume is high and talk time is short — it is possible to super-charge the standard customer search using the High-Speed Business Partner Search or the Index-Based Business Partner Search options.

If the customer has already been registered, the agent will be able to locate the customer record by searching against one or more of the appropriate fields. Depending on the settings in the system, the agent can either manually confirm the customer after, for example, verifying the customer's address and telephone number, or the account can be confirmed automatically by the system. In B2B scenarios where an employee or other representative of a company is contacting the interaction center on behalf of the company, the agent will first confirm the main account and then confirm the contact person (or other related partner).

Note

There are a couple of options for enhancing the standard performance of the business partner search in the Interaction Center. One option is to use the High-Speed Business Partner Search feature introduced in CRM 4.0 Add-On for Service Industries. The *High-Speed Business Partner Search* stores and indexes business partner master data in main memory via the SAP Software Agent Framework and TREX search engine. This option is more efficient than the standard search when searching large numbers of business partner records and when using complex search queries involving wildcards. However, this option involves a bit of overhead and may therefore actually be slower than the standard search if using simple search queries and searching a small number of records.

A second option for accelerating the standard business partner search is provided by the *Index-Based Business Partner Search* introduced in CRM 2006s/CRM 2007. The index based search provides faster search results by allowing you to create your own index tables for frequently used search fields. Instead of using the standard search (which relies on something called the reporting framework), the index based search uses a BADI to by-pass the reporting framework-based search. This option is ideal if your IC agents often search using the same couple of fields each time.

In situations where no customer record yet exists, agents can create a new account (Figure 6.2). When creating the account, the agent can specify the role of the new account, such as a "Consumer" in a B2C scenario, or "Prospect" or "Sold-to-Party" in a B2B scenario. Obviously however, many companies, particularly B2B companies, have strict policies in place regarding the creation and maintenance of customer master data. These companies may want to use R/3 or ERP as the system of record for all creation and maintenance of customer data. For example, these companies might configure the system so that Interaction Center agents can only create new "prospects" in CRM. The prospects would then be replicated to the backend R/3 or ERP system where someone else would create the actual customer record after doing a credit check and contacting the customer for more details. Afterward, the newly created customer record could then be replicated back up to the CRM system.

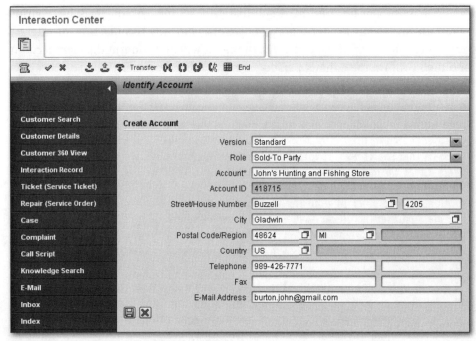

Figure 6.2 Creation of New Customer Account

Agents are also able to create contact persons for new (or existing) accounts in the event that the person calling (or chatting or emailing) is not already maintained in the system as a contact person for the account. As of CRM 2006s/CRM 2007, the SAP CRM Interaction Center supports additional relationship categories in addition to the contact person. When creating a new related partner for a main account, the agent can select from any of the relationship categories that have been maintained in the system and explicitly added to the account identification profile. See Figure 6.3.

Additionally, in CRM 2006s/CRM 2007 several other useful features are provided for creating new accounts and contact persons, which were not available in previous releases such as CRM 2005. For example, when creating a new account, agents can use the address validation feature to provide validity checking of postal code, city, and street name. Agents can also take advantage of duplicate checking (if enabled) to avoid creating a duplicate record in case a similar record already exists but was not found by the agent during a manual search.

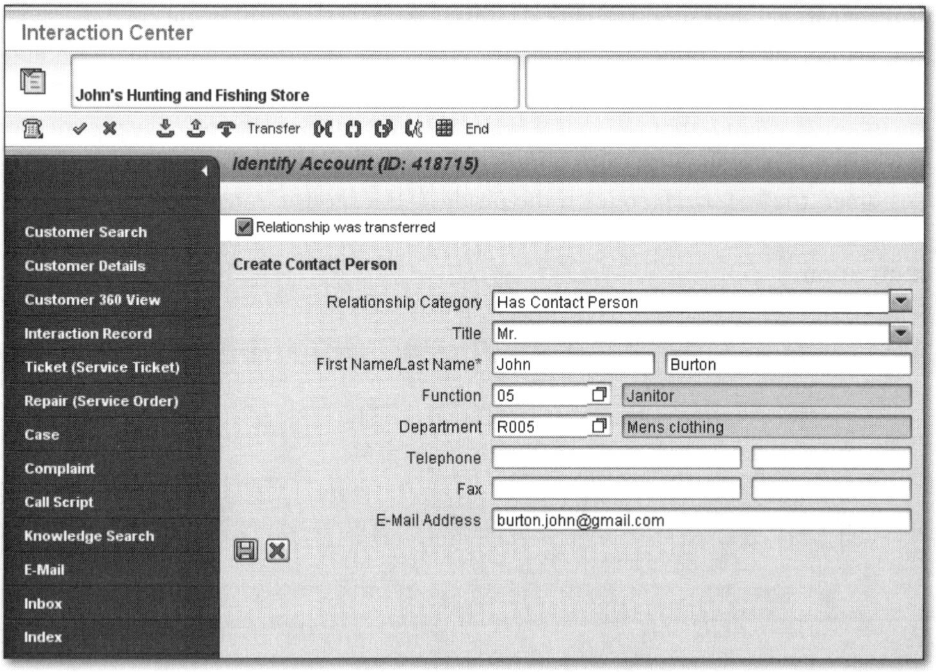

Figure 6.3 Creation of New Contact Person for New or Existing Account

6.2.2 Product Identification and Registration

When contacting the help desk, a customer typically has an issue or question regarding a particular product or service that the customer has purchased. In order for the agent to retrieve the relevant product information and trouble-shooting documentation and to check whether the customer is entitled to service, the Interaction Center agent needs to find out whether the customer has registered the product or not. In B2B scenarios, there is a good chance that the product will already have been registered, because most companies want to ensure that they are entitled to service for the (often expensive) products they purchase; in fact, many companies additionally purchase extended service contracts on top of the standard warranties provided by the manufacturer. However, in B2C scenarios, unless the customer has previously contacted the help desk for service on the same product, the product will often not already be registered; many consumers do not send in their warranty registration cards or register products online.

If the customer and product have already been registered, after the customer and contact person (if applicable) are confirmed, a list of registered products belonging to the customer will be displayed in the search results list (Figure 6.4). If the customer is calling about a specific product, the agent clicks on that product in the results list to view the product details. After verifying the product with the customer, the agent can confirm the product. If a service transaction is created at some later point, the confirmed product will automatically be transferred to the transaction.

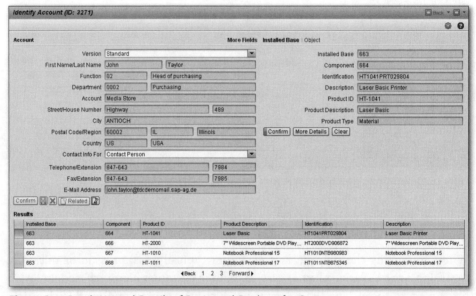

Figure 6.4 Result List and Details of Registered Products for Customer

If the product has not yet been registered, the agent can register the product on behalf of the customer. SAP CRM provides two options for representing registered products in the Interaction Center: the IBase (Installed Base) and the IObject (Individual Object). The IBase is the way that registered products have traditionally been modeled in the Interaction Center, and is the only out of the box option supported with CRM 2005 and below. The IBase provides a hierarchical representation of the products installed on a customer's site. For example, if dealing with HVAC (heating, ventilation, and air conditioning) equipment on a multi-site campus, the campus might be modeled as the top node of the hierarchy with subnodes for each building on the campus. Each building in turn might have subnodes for each floor, and each floor might have sub-nodes representing each piece of equipment installed on that floor.

Support for the IObject (sometimes also referred to simply as Object rather than IObject) was added to the Interaction Center with CRM 2006s/CRM 2007. Unlike the IBase, which represents a hierarchy of all the equipment that a customer has installed at particular site, the IObject represents a single piece of (usually serialized) equipment. For example, each notebook computer or BlackBerry® device that a company owns might be represented as a unique IObject. In CRM 2006s/CRM 2007, the registered product search area, located to the right of the customer search area on the main Identify Account screen, is now configurable and can displays separate tablinks for Base or IObject, or both (Figure 6.5).

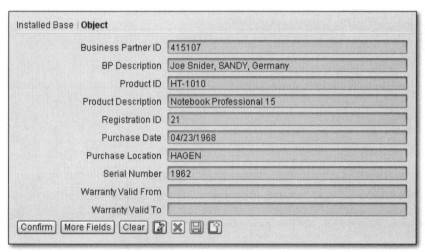

Figure 6.5 IObject Integration in Interaction Center

Currently, only the equipment family is available out of the box for the standard IC scenarios and processes like the information help desk. However, other objects such as the Vehicle IObject are supported in certain industry options of the Interaction Center, such as the Automotive solution. (Note: Industry solutions are discussed separately in Chapter 10, Back-Office Interaction Centers for Industries and Shared Services. Additionally, on a project basis you could create your own user interface screen to support other IObject families if desired. Before IObjects can be used in the Interaction Center, you must first assign set types for your IObject family (e.g., Equipment) in transaction COMM_HIERARCHY as described in IMG documentation (Figure 6.6). You must also assign a partner function (such as Sold-to-Party) to your IObject family in the IMG activity "Define Object Profiles" accessible via Customer Relationship Management • Interaction Center WebClient • Define Object Profiles (Figure 6.7).

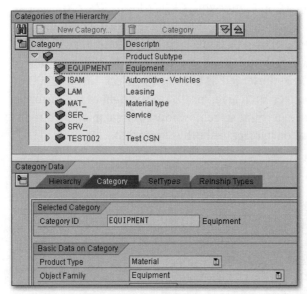

Figure 6.6 Assign SetTypes for IObject Equipment Family

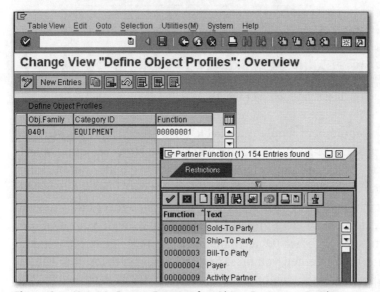

Figure 6.7 Maintain Partner Function for IObject Equipment Family

In the IMG configuration of the "Define Account Identification Profiles," a new folder "Object Components" is available in CRM 2006s/CRM 2007 that allows you to specify which objects should be available for customer searches. You can choose either the IBase or IObject, or even both — assuming that both have been properly set up and configured. (You can also choose other search objects such as Contracts, Business Agreements, or Vehicles.) For each object that you want to make available in the identify account search you provide a sequence number, an optional auto search flag, and an object search approach. The sequence number controls the order in which the tablinks appear on the screen. The Auto Search flag controls whether the search for the IBase or IObject is conducted automatically based on the confirmed business partner. The Object Approach selection controls whether a search for IObject or IBase (either an automatic or manual search) is based on the main account, the related contact person, or both as seen in Figure 6.8.

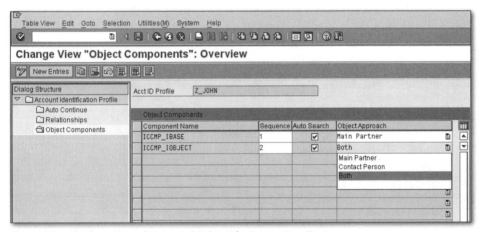

Figure 6.8 Configuration of IBase and IObject for Interaction Center

6.2.3 Customer Overview and Details

So far, we have talked about the steps involved in locating existing customer and products, and registering new customers and products when necessary. Now, let's turn our attention to some of the ways that Interaction Center agents can retrieve more detailed information about a customer's account and activities in order to resolve common customer questions and concerns. After the Interaction Center agent has confirmed the customer and the appropriate registered product (if applicable), quite often the agent will want to pull up an overview of the customer's account activity or display specific customer details. For example, if the customer is calling about an unresolved trouble-ticket, service request, sales order, or complaint, the agent may want to view the customer's order history and pull up the relevant transaction. On the other hand, if the customer wants to make changes to their account data such as address, contact information, or marketing attributes, the agent will want to access the customer details directly.

After confirming an account and contact person (if applicable) the Interaction Center agent can press the "More Fields" link on the top of the Identify Account screen to navigate to another screen with three tablinks that display additional information about the confirmed contact person and account. For example, the "Contact Person" tablink displays more fields for contact person than are shown on the default Identify Account screen, such as Function and Department. Additionally, this screen shows all different communication channels that have been maintained for the contact person, including multiple telephone numbers, email addresses, and fax numbers (if applicable). This screen also displays any notes that have been maintained about the contact person (Figure 6.9). Similarly, the "Account" tablink displays the same type of information for the main account.

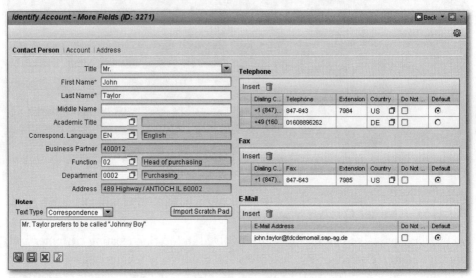

Figure 6.9 Additional Account Details Shown From "More Fields" Link

In CRM 2006s/CRM 2007, there is an additional option available for displaying even more details about a customer. You can call the standard CRM customer account screen (included in the CRM WebClient roles such as Marketing Professional) from inside the Interaction Center (Figure 6.10). This screen provides access to additional information that is not normally included in the standard Interaction Center view of the customer, such as marketing attributes. While many companies do not require their Interaction Center agents to have access to such information, this can be useful for companies with unique requirements in this area.

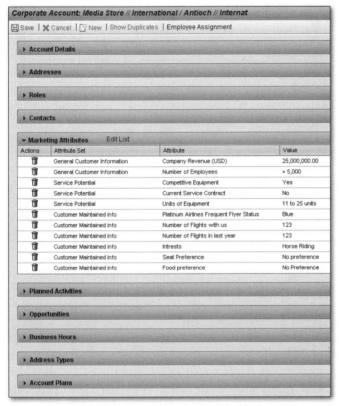

Figure 6.10   CRM WebClient Account Screen Inside Interaction Center

In addition to viewing specific details about an account, sometimes an Interaction Center agent needs an overview of the customer's account activity including unresolved service requests, recent orders, open complaints, and so on. An all-inclusive, comprehensive view of the customer can be achieved using the configurable customer fact sheet. When configuring the fact sheet, you decide which information should be presented about the customer. For example, you might want to provide a list of products that the customer owns. You might also want to include a history of the customer's most recent interactions, as well as lists of open service orders, service tickets, complaints, and sales orders (Figure 6.11).

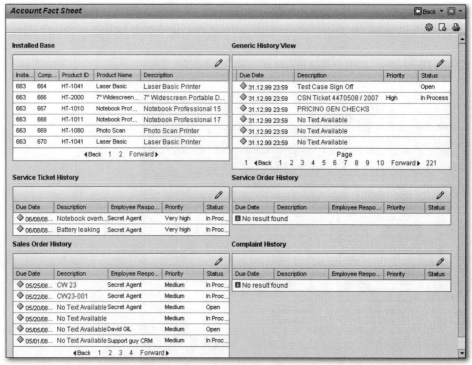

Figure 6.11 Configurable All-Inclusive View Customer Fact Sheet

The fact sheet is configured in the SAP Implementation Guide (IMG) under the path: CUSTOMER RELATIONSHIP MANAGEMENT • UI FRAMEWORK • UI FRAMEWORK DEFINITION • MAINTAIN FACT SHEET. You list all of the different views that you might potentially want to include in your fact sheet (or fact sheets). Then you define the different screen layout options that you would potentially like to use, such as two columns by three rows (as shown in Figure 6.11), one column by eight rows, and so on. At this point, you are only defining the views and layouts that you might want to use when you actually create your fact sheet later. The actual selection of views and screen layout is done in the BSP Component Workbench tool (transaction code BSP_WD_WORKBENCH) using BSP component BSP_DLC_FS. See Figure 6.12.

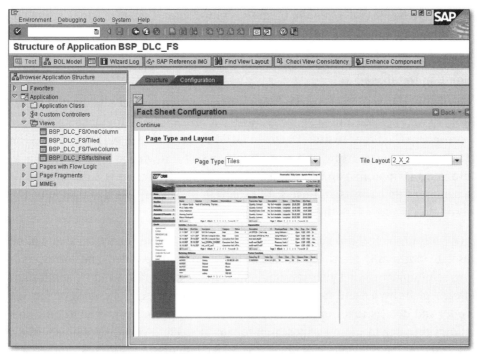

Figure 6.12 Configuration of Fact Sheet in BSP WD Workbench

6.2.4 Knowledge Search

So far in this chapter, we have talked mainly about the maintenance and usage of *customer* information. However, let's now look at the role that other types of information can play in the help desk as part of the IC Service process. The information help desk processes essentially involve providing customers with answers, solution documents, FAQs, and other relevant information. Let's look at the different knowledge management tools that the Interaction Center provides for organizing, indexing, and retrieving information, including information stored in external third-party knowledge repositories.

The knowledge search process in the Interaction Center is enabled by several different components that work together to facilitate the retrieval and presentation of information to the Interaction Center agent. These components include: a knowledge repository such as the SAP Solution Database (SDB), the SAP Software Agent Framework (SAF) architecture, and SAP's TREX (Search and Classification) search engine, formerly known as Text Retrieval and Information Extraction. Together, these components enable agents to search for solutions and other documents from the Knowledge Search screen in the Interaction Center. Let's take a look at each of the three components in detail.

Solution Database

The first step in setting up any knowledge management project is to create a repository of well-defined and organized knowledge articles. SAP provides a knowledge repository called the Solution Database (SDB) that is included with SAP CRM. The SDB allows you to create and store two types of knowledge articles known as problems (symptoms) and solutions. The problem document is a description of a symptom that affects end users; the solution document is a description of the resolution that resolves the problem.

For both problems and solutions, you can define various attributes that can be used to more easily search for and locate the appropriate problem and corresponding solution. Attributes that can be defined include priority, validity, application area, type, subtype, and so on. You can also create a hierarchical catalog of damage codes and defects that can be linked to the various problems and solutions. This allows the user to more easily search for problems and corresponding solutions by entering the relevant error code. The SDB configuration is located in the IMG under CUSTOMER RELATIONSHIP MANAGEMENT • ENTERPRISE INTELLIGENCE • SOLUTION DATABASE. It is also possible to use external or third-party knowledge repositories instead of (or in addition to) the SDB, but this requires integration with SAP NetWeaver PI (formerly XI) on a consulting project basis.

After you have done the necessary IMG configuration for the SDB, you can create, edit, and display problems and solutions using SAP GUI transaction code IS01 (Figure 6.13). This transaction is designed to be used by a knowledge administrator who is responsible for creating and maintaining knowledge articles in the Solution Database. In addition to creating problems and solutions manually, the knowledge administrator can also create them via reference from existing problems or solutions. A wizard is also available to guide the knowledge administrator through the process of creating new problems and solutions, or for searching for, displaying, or editing already existing ones. An advanced search screen can also be accessed by the knowledge administrator in order to search for existing problems and solutions using free text as well as any of the defined attributes such as priority, validity, application area, type, and so on.

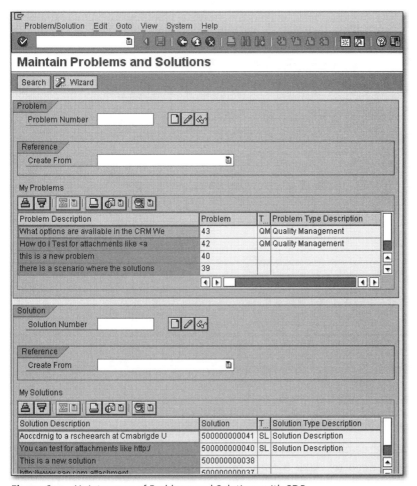

Figure 6.13 Maintenance of Problems and Solutions with SDB

Knowledge administrators need to constantly keep knowledge articles up to date and accurate. If agents give feedback that a problem or solution is no longer accurate — or if the problem or solution is flagged in an automated report indicating that the knowledge article is receiving little use anymore — the knowledge administrator may want to modify (or archive) the problem or solution. Figure 6.14 shows the maintenance of an existing problem and solution pair. In this example, a problem (problem ID 43) and a solution (solution ID 41) have been linked together; the knowledge administrator is extending the valid-to date of the solution to indicate that it should be applicable until June 8, 2010.

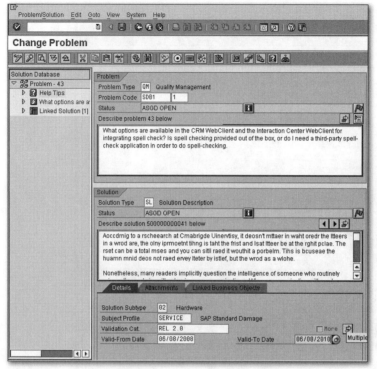

Figure 6.14 Creation of Problem and Solution with SDB

Software Agent Framework (SAF)

Once you have created knowledge articles in the SDB (or another knowledge repository), you need to make the documents available for searching in the IC WebClient. This process, known as compilation, is executed by the SAP Software Agent Framework, a component of SAP CRM previously known in older releases as the "Interactive Intelligent Agent (IIA)." The Software Agent Framework (SAF) provides an open architecture that integrates tools such as compilation, classification, and searching with a variety of data sources and knowledge repositories including the SDB. However, the SAF can also be used to index and search other types of knowledge articles, including CRM business transactions such as Service Tickets or Cases.

The SAF is included with SAP CRM. Prior to CRM 2005, the SAF required installation of a separate J2EE component; however, with CRM 2005 and above no separate installation of SAF itself is required. However, in all releases, in order to use the SAF you need to separately install SAP TREX, which requires its own

J2EE server. The configuration for the SAF can be accessed in the IMG under the path: Customer Relationship Management • Enterprise Intelligence • Software Agent Framework.

> **Note**
>
> SAP NetWeaver Search and Classification (TREX) is a search engine and text mining engine that is responsible for executing search queries entered from the IC WebClient Knowledge Search screen. To use the Knowledge Search feature in the Interaction Center with CRM 2007, you need to install SAP NetWeaver 7.0 Search and Classification (TREX 6.1) or higher. See the SAP Solution Manager: Basic Configuration • Configuration Structures • SAP NetWeaver 7.0 • Standalone Engines • TREX Post-Installation Configuration.

After you have installed and configured TREX and the Software Agent Framework, you need to set up your knowledge bases and compile the knowledge articles into searchable indexes. The knowledgebase setup and compilation process is done from the SAF Compilation Administration screen of the IC Manager role, located under the menu item Knowledge Management. From the SAF Compilation Administration screen you can select one or more knowledge repositories and perform an initial knowledge base set up by clicking the button "Set Up Knowledge Bases." Once a knowledge base has been set up, you can perform a full compilation to create the necessary index files used by the TREX search engine. After an initial set up and full compilation has been executed for the knowledge base, you need only run periodic delta compilations in order to keep the knowledge base current by indexing any newly added, changed, or deleted knowledge articles (such as problems and solutions). See Figure 6.15.

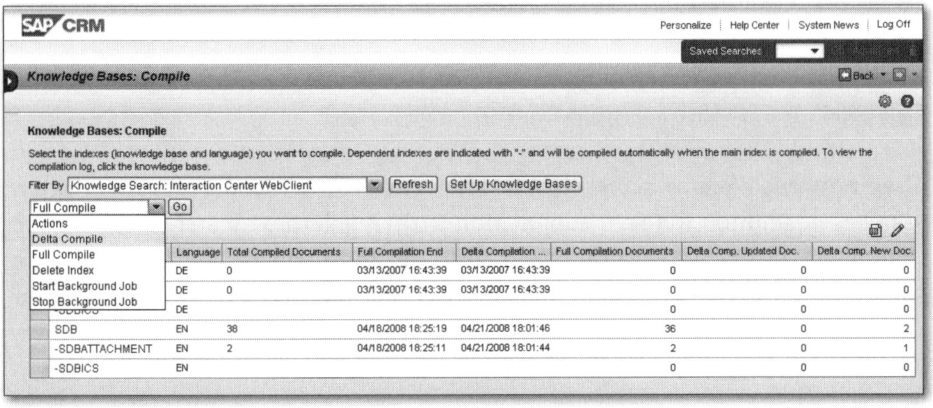

Figure 6.15 Maintenance of Knowledge Repositories by IC Manager

Knowledge Search

Once you have set up and compiled a knowledge repository such as the SDB, the knowledge articles (e.g., solutions) will be available for searching from the Interaction Center via the Knowledge Search screen (Figure 6.16). To conduct a search, the Interaction Center agent optionally selects the desired knowledgebase and language (or uses the default options) and enters a text search query and/or attribute search query. Several types of text searches are possible. The most commonly used text search option is the "Search Terms" field, which works similarly to Google and other Internet search engines by returning any results that contain some or all of the words in the query. Agents can also search with more precision by using the "Exact Phrase" search, which only returns results that contain the exact term or phrase entered. Finally, the "Exclude Terms" search option, which must be used in conjunction with one of the other two text search options or the attribute search option, returns results that satisfy the other search queries and do not contain any of the terms entered in the excluded terms field.

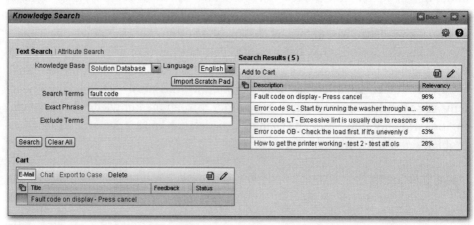

Figure 6.16 Text Search in Interaction Center Knowledge Search

The Knowledge Search screen in the Interaction Center also supports attribute searches in addition to (or in conjunction with) regular text searches. An Interaction Center agent can select one or multiple desired attributes and corresponding values. For example, as shown in Figure 6.17 an agent has selected two different attributes supported by the Solution Database: Problem Type (with value Service/ Plant Management) and Problem Subtype (with value Hardware). Based on this search query, various solutions are returned in the results list.

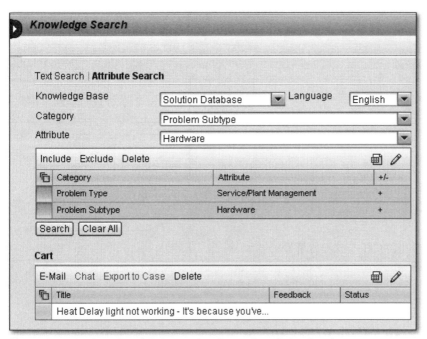

Figure 6.17 Attribute Search in Interaction Center Knowledge Search

Regardless of which type of search was used (attribute, text, or both), the Interaction Center agent can select one or more solutions from the result list and add them to the cart as shown in Figure 6.17. After being added to the cart, solutions will also be linked to the Interaction Record Activity Clipboard and thus saved as part of the customer's interaction. Additionally, once a solution has been added to the cart, the agent can click a button to insert the solution into an outgoing email (Figure 6.18) or to a chat message (not pictured). If the agent is working with cases (a specific type of SAP CRM business transaction) the agent could directly open the case from the cart and navigate to the case itself via the "Export to Case" button (Figure 6.17).

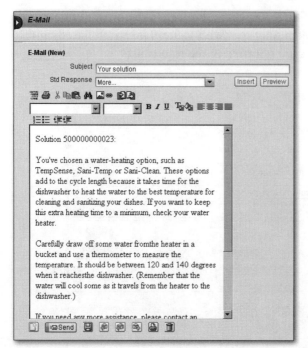

Figure 6.18 Solution Inserted into Interaction Center E-Mail Editor

6.3   Service Order Management

So far in this chapter, we have talked about the information help desk, which allows companies to handle customer and product registration, and to provide basic answers and information to customers. Now, let's discuss a slightly more sophisticated type of help desk, the customer service desk. Then, we will look at an even more advanced type of help desk, the customer IT service desk.

When customers have a product that needs to be installed or repaired, or which requires routine maintenance, they typically contact a company's service center. The customer service desk, which in former times was an actual desk or counter inside a brick-and-mortar office, is now usually run via telephone or Internet as an Interaction Center. The primary function of the customer service desk is to schedule appointments for installation, maintenance, or repairs of products, either in-house at the company's service depot or via field service at the customer site. In the SAP CRM Interaction Center, such service tasks are represented using a business transaction known as the IC Service Order.

6.3.1 IC Service Order

The service order is used within the Interaction Center for situations in which some follow-up action is necessary, such as installation, maintenance, or repair. The service order is created as a follow-on document to the Interaction Record (Activity), which is used to document the reason and result of the customer interaction. In a typically configured SAP CRM system, an interaction record is automatically created as the leading document for every customer contact. Then, if a follow-on service task is required, the Interaction Center agent manually creates a service order. The service order ID will be automatically added to the activity clipboard of the interaction record, and conversely the interaction record ID will be added to the business context of the service order. The business context area of the service order is used to store and display links to all business documents that are assigned to the order.

The service order enables agents to perform detailed technical analysis of problems, and to assign the correct spare parts and service products. When creating a service order, after having already confirmed an account and registered product (IBase or IObject), the Product ID field and either the Component (IBase) or the Object (IObject) field are filled automatically based on the confirmed product. Additionally, the service order can be used to trigger field service processes and repairs. As shown in the example in Figure 6.19, both a spare part (a new LCD display screen) and a service product (repair service) have been added to the service order as separate line items.

Agents can display the details of any line item, including entitlement and SLA information by selecting the individual line item and clicking the Item Detail button. As shown in the example, in Figure 6.20, line item 10 (Repair Service) has been selected and the item details are visible. In the item details, several additional tablinks appear, including the SLA Info tablink. Clicking the tablink reveals whether the customer has any contract for the given product. In the example in Figure 6.20, no contract exists for this product, and hence no service profile or response profile is determined. Because the customer is not entitled to free of charge service, the agent can enter the appropriate Valuation Type (i.e., 10% markup because an expert is required) and Account Indicator (e.g., 50% discount for VIP customer). Pricing and payment information can be entered back on the header level of the order after exiting the line item details. Also visible in the line item details is another tablink called Appointments. Clicking on the Appointments tablink would navigate the agent to a screen where they could select an available appointment time block (e.g., Friday 8 a.m. to noon) based on the customer's service level agreement and preferences.

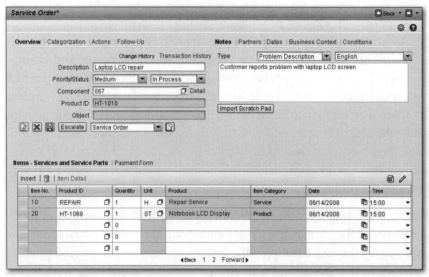

Figure 6.19 IC Service Order with Spare Part and Service Product

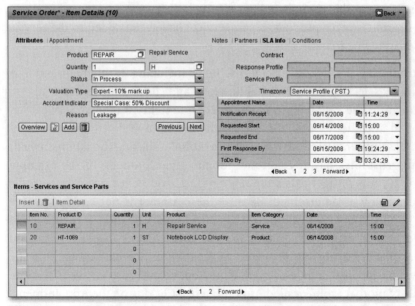

Figure 6.20 Line Item Details Including SLA and Appointment Tablink

Readers who are already familiar with the SAP CRM may notice the IC Service Order is slightly different than the standard CRM Service Order. This is because while both service orders are built on the same underlying Business Object Repository (BOR) object, BUS2000116 (also known as the CRM Business Activity or "One Order"), the two orders use different transaction types. The CRM Service Order uses transaction type SRVO, while the IC Service Order uses transaction type TSVO. For readers who are not familiar with the concept of BOR objects and transaction types, BOR objects control which fields and methods (i.e., functions) are available, while the transaction type defines properties and characteristics such as partner determination procedure, text determination procedure, organizational data profile, and status profile. As the CRM Service Order and the IC Service Order are used in different channels (CRM Enterprise versus the Interaction Center) and have different end users (service professionals versus Interaction Center agents) it makes sense that the two orders behave differently and therefore use different transaction types.

The IC Service Order, like all other "One Order" business transactions that share the underlying BOR object BUS2000116, is able to take advantage of SAP NetWeaver Post Processing Framework (PPF) actions in order to schedule and execute predefined processes from the service order. For example, an action could be set up to automatically send out an email confirmation to a customer whenever a service order has been set to status complete. Actions can be triggered automatically by the system based on predefined conditions, or manually by agents using the Actions tablink in the IC Service Order. Figure 6.21 shows an example of an action that has been triggered in order to generate a product service letter (PSL), which informs a dealer or other business partner about a potential issue with a product, including the recommended resolution.

In CRM 2005, several enhancements were introduced to the IC Service Order. A feature called the Reference Object Hierarchy was incorporated, giving the Interaction Center agent an overview of the hierarchical structure of the objects involved in the Service Order. Additionally, support for appointment scheduling was also added in CRM 2005, allowing agents to schedule appointments for installation or repairs based on customer preference and service level agreements.

> **Note**
>
> When scheduling an appointment in the Service Order, only the reservation of a time block is performed in the Interaction Center; the actual dispatching of a service technician to the appointment is handled outside the Interaction Center via a separate SAP CRM resource planning tool.

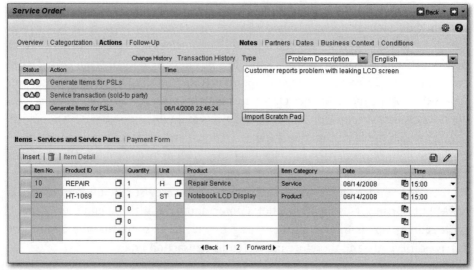

Figure 6.21 Service Order with CRM PPF Actions

6.4 Service Desk (for External Customers)

We just examined the IC Service Order, which is used within the Interaction Center for scheduling installations and repairs and for assigning spare parts and service products. Now, let's look at another transaction type called the IC Service Ticket, which is used in situations where external customers report technical issues with products manufactured or sold by your company, particularly high-tech products. (Later in Chapter 10, Back-Office Interaction Centers for Industries and Shared Services, we will discuss internal service desks where your employees contact you with issues about their IT infrastructure such as computers, software, and telecommunications equipment.) The unique thing about high-tech products, and especially software, is that unlike traditional products, if something is not working you don't necessarily need to bring the product in for repair (or schedule a field service visit). Rather, many high-tech products and software issues can be resolved on the fly by changing some configuration settings or coding, or by downloading and applying a relevant hot fix, patch, support package, or correction instruction.

The IC Service Ticket is ideal for situations in which a customer reports a bug or technical issue and you need to perform technical trouble-shooting and analysis and then respond with a solution within a predefined SLA time frame. The service ticket is great for situations in which it is not necessary to perform any actual repair and where there is no need for spare parts or service products. You can still use the service ticket as part of your service flow in such situations, but then you will also need to additionally create a follow-up service order to handle the repairs, spare parts, and service products. As will be explained, the service ticket is not designed for handling repairs or maintenance because the service ticket does not offer any visible line items for entering spare parts or service products.

The IC Service Ticket was developed as part of the CRM 4.0 Add-on for Services Industries. The IC Service Ticket uses the same underlying BOR object as the IC Service Order, but utilizes a different transaction type (TSRV). One of the main differences between the IC Service Ticket and the IC Service Order is that the service ticket does not contain any line items, just order header information (Figure 6.22). The reason for this is that many SAP customers gave feedback that they were confused by the need to enter a line item with a service product each time they wanted to log a service order for some technical issue. In most cases, because an actual repair or spare part was not needed, customers would enter a dummy line item with a fictitious service product. To get around this, SAP introduced the IC Service Ticket, which uses a hard-coded dummy line item behind the scenes that is not visible on the user interface.

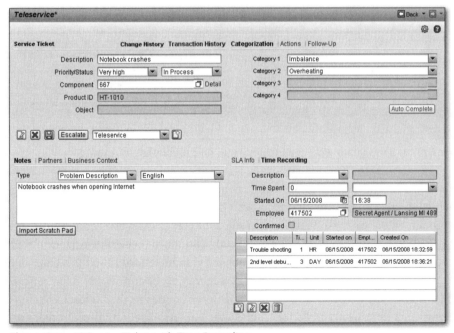

Figure 6.22 IC Service Ticket with Time Recording

However, the lack of line items is not the only difference between the IC Service Ticket and the IC Service Order. The service ticket also provides the ability for agents to record the time they spend working on an issue. If multiple people are involved in an issue, such as a first-level support person and two different second-level technicians or engineers, each can record their individual time spent (Figure 6.22). To enable service ticket time recording, you must first define activity descriptions in the IMG under the path: CUSTOMER RELATIONSHIP MANAGEMENT • INTERACTION CENTER WEBCLIENT • BUSINESS TRANSACTION • SERVICE TICKET • DEFINE ACTIVITY DESCRIPTIONS, as seen in Figure 6.23. When employees log their time spent working on each service ticket, the time records are stored in database table CRMD_TIMEREP. You can generate service confirmations by running report CRM_TIMEREP_CREATE_SERVCONF. Time recording is only available in the service ticket; it is not supported in other transaction types such as the service order.

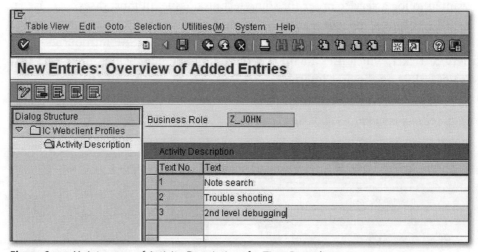

Figure 6.23 Maintenance of Activity Descriptions for Time Recording

There are also a few other new features introduced with the IC Service Ticket, which have later been extended to other One Order transactions like the IC Service Order. Some of these features include multi-level categorization, auto-completion, and routing (dispatching/escalation). The multi-level categorization and auto-complete functionality are both enabled by another tool called the Category Modeler, in which a business user creates a hierarchy of commonly experienced problems and maps various objects to the different nodes in the hierarchy including templates (for auto-completion), solutions (for auto-suggested solutions), and other objects. Set up of the Category Modeler is covered separately in Chapter 7, IC Management and Analytics. The routing (dispatching/escalation) functionality leverages a tool called the Rule Modeler, where a business user defines routing rules that dispatch the service ticket to the appropriate agent or engineer. Set up of the Rule Modeler is also covered in the chapter on IC Management.

Multi-level categorization, pictured in Figure 6.22, allows an agent to categorize an issue using a hierarchy of dependent categories. As the agent selects a value for the first level of the hierarchy (e.g., category 1) the values for the next level down will be dynamically determined based on what was selected at the top level. For example, imagine that a high-tech company used a three-level schema to categorize all problems based on area, product, and problem. The agent would select the problem area first, where possible values might include hardware, software, or accessories. Then, based on the area selected at the first level (e.g., hardware) the values available for product in the second level might include router, server, or PC. Then, based on the selected product (e.g., PC) the values for problems in the third level might include things like start-up failure or intermittent crash. Multi-level categorization is very useful for a number of things such as reporting, automatic suggestion of relevant solutions, and auto completion of tickets using templates.

The solution auto-suggest feature triggers an alert in the context area of the Interaction Center whenever the system detects that one or more solutions are linked to the categories selected in the Interaction Center multi-level categorization (Figure 6.24). The alert that is displayed can be configured to include a description of the number of relevant solutions (e.g., "2 Solutions Detected"). When the Interaction Center agent clicks on the alert, the system automatically navigates the agent to the Knowledge Search screen of the Interaction Center showing the relevant auto-suggested solutions (Figure 6.25). The agent selects one of more of the automatically suggested solutions, or clears the result list and performs a manual search using freely definable search criteria. Set up of automatically suggested solutions is described in Chapter 7, IC Management and Analytics.

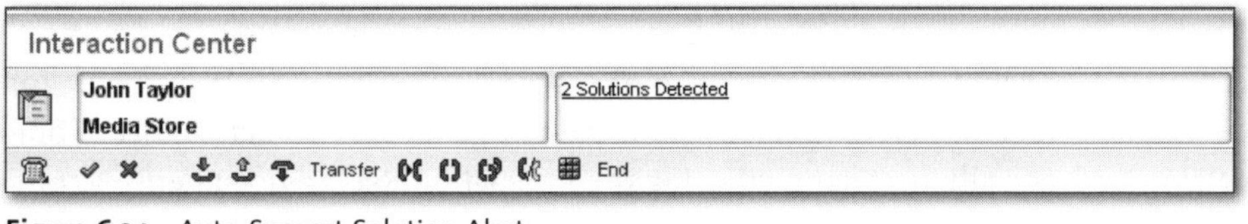

Figure 6.24 Auto-Suggest Solution Alert

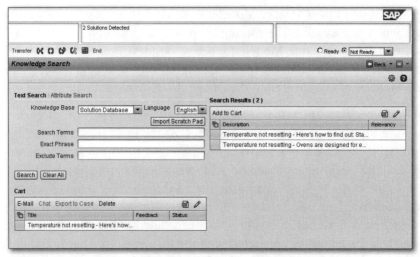

Figure 6.25 Auto-Suggested Solutions in Knowledge Search Result List

Auto-completion allows an agent to automatically fill in all relevant fields of a service ticket with the push of a button. When the Auto Complete button is pressed, the system checks in the Category Modeler and retrieves a service ticket template attached to the node in the hierarchy that corresponds to the current selection in the service ticket multi-level categorization. Based on the values maintained in the service ticket template, all of the fields in the current service ticket will be automatically populated and the service ticket will be set to complete. This is very useful for situations that involve reoccurring and easy to solve issues, such as a request to reset a password. By automating such routine processes, agents increase their efficiency and save time, which can be used to work on other more strategic tasks.

6.5   Complaint Management

In SAP terminology, the term "complaint" has a very specific meaning. The IC Complaint is a business transaction that has a specific financial or logistical impact, such as a return or refund. The IC Complaint document is *not* used in situations where an unhappy customer contacts the organization to complain about, for example, a rude customer service agent. Rather, general customer service "complaints" are actually best handled using the Interaction Record document. A complaint is always created in reference to existing business transactions, most commonly to a sales order (though potentially on a project basis, complaints can also be created in reference to other transactions such as invoices).

The complaint screen in the SAP CRM Interaction Center provides built-in integration with SAP R/3 or ERP for various processes including returns, replacement shipments, credit memos (when no goods are sent back), and QM notifications. For example, in situations where the wrong product has been delivered, the customer can request a return material authorization (RMA) in order to return the product. In returns processing, the returned goods undergo a quality evaluation after they are received from the customer and placed into blocked stock. Afterwards, the goods are then either returned to unrestricted stock from blocked stock, or else moved from blocked stock to scrap, depending on the result of the evaluation. In situations where a customer did not receive all of the ordered items, the customer may choose to request credit for the missing items; in such cases, a credit memo can be created from the complaint. If, on the other hand, the customer still needs the missing items, a free-of-charge replacement shipment can be triggered. Finally, if the order contains non-conforming or defective items, the Interaction Center agent can trigger a quality notification (QM notification), which then notifies the production department about the issue so that it can be corrected.

When the agent creates a new complaint as a follow-on transaction to the interaction record, the first thing the agent does is to search for the reference transaction against which the complaint should be created (Figure 6.26). By clicking on the value-help icon in the reference transaction field, the agent is navigated to the Agent Inbox where the agent can search for and select the existing sales transaction (Figure 6.27).

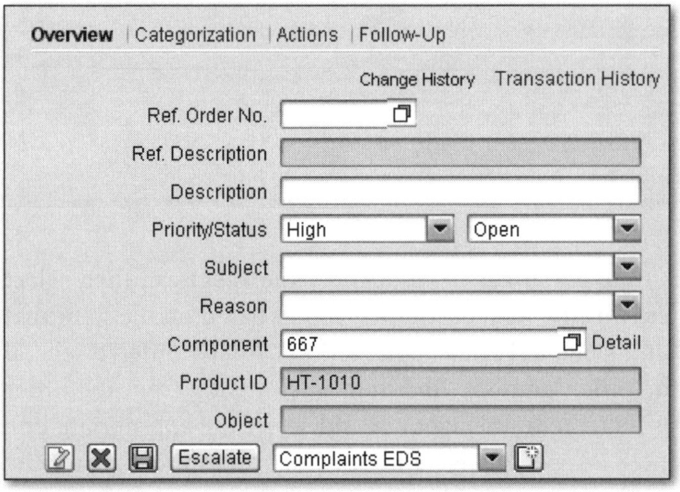

Figure 6.26 IC Complaint Screen with Value Help for Reference Order No.

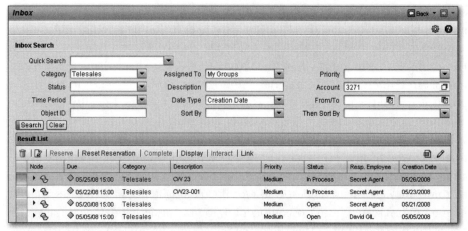

Figure 6.27 Search for Reference Order from Agent Inbox

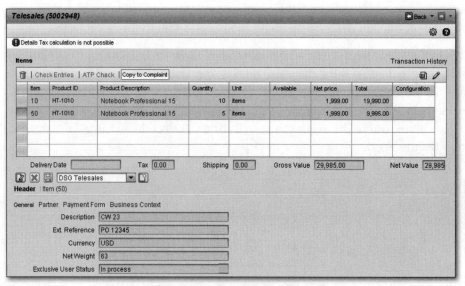

Figure 6.28 Copying Line Item from Sales Order to Complaint

Once the historic sales transaction has been opened, the agent can then select the appropriate line item (or line items) from the order, based on the item that the customer is complaining about. For example, if the customer ordered several line items as part of the order, and one line item was missing from the order (or the wrong item was delivered), the agent would select the appropriate line item from the order and click the "Copy to Complaint" button to transfer the line item into the complaint (Figure 6.28). The Interaction Center agent then navigates the agent back to the complaint, and the selected line item (or items) from the sales transactions are added to the line item area of the complaint (Figure 6.29).

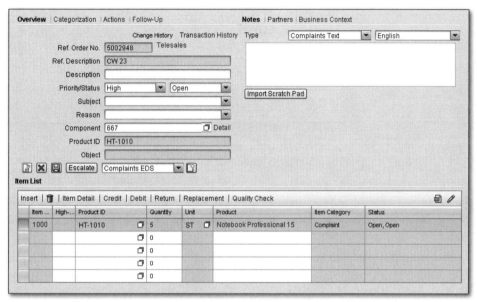

Figure 6.29 Line Item Transferred from Sales Order to the Complaint

Once one or more line items have been transferred from a sales transaction into a complaint, the agent can select the line items and decide which type of follow-on task to perform. For example, if the customer had ordered 100 units of a particular product (e.g., ceramic tile) and two arrived broken, the agent could choose to issue a credit memo to refund the cost of the two units to the customer. However, if the customer was not interested in a refund but instead needs the two additional tiles, the agent could decide to issue a free of charge shipment and send two more tiles to the customer. On the other hand, let's assume the customer ordered blue tiles but received all red tiles. In this case, the customer might want to return the red tiles and instead receive a new shipment of blue tiles. In this case, the agent would issue a return and generate a return materials authorization (RMA) for the customer, allowing the customer to return the red tiles. Figure 6.30 shows an example of a product return being entered as a line item in the complaint.

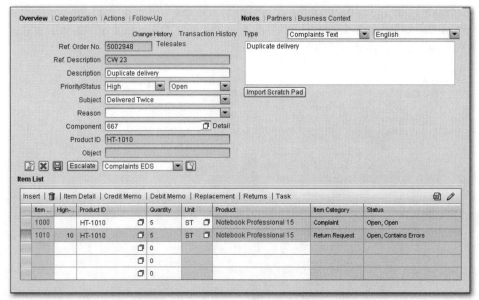

Figure 6.30 Request for Product Return Created as Line Item in Complaint

6.6   Case Management

In SAP terminology, the term "case" has a very specific meaning. The IC Case business transaction is used to group together related issues. For example, a case might be used to track multiple service tickets that are part of the same related issue such as a service outage, product recall, storm or disaster, and so on. You can think of the Case as a "master service ticket" or "super service ticket." Other software vendors use the term "case" synonymously with "ticket" and create a case to log each incident or service request. However, please keep in mind that in SAP the Case is not used for logging individual issues but rather as a means of relating individual issues that have the same root cause or problem.

Most Interaction Centers have some preferred method of communicating to agents that a new case has been created. For example, when there is a major service outage that affects a group of customers, an Interaction Center supervisor will often create a new case and then notify agents that the case has been created. For example, the supervisor might send a message to the agents via broadcast messaging (the scrolling text that appears at the bottom of the agent's Interaction Center screen). Once the agent knows that a case exists, the agent can search for and locate the appropriate case whenever the agent receives a call (or email, chat, etc.) from a customer related to this case. Figure 6.31 shows the Case search screen, which provides numerous search fields such as description, case ID, product ID, and so on. Agents can even search for cases that have been assigned to the agent or the agent's group using "My Cases" search criteria.

Figure 6.31 Case Search Screen in the Interaction Center

Let's look at an example of a service outage affecting the city of Palo Alto, California. The Interaction Center takes a new call from a customer who complains that service is out. The Interaction Center agent confirms the customer and registered product and then logs a new service ticket. After creating the service ticket, the agent does a search for the existing case. After opening the case, the agent checks the notes area of the case and informs the customer of the current status, for example, service will be restored in five minutes (Figure 6.32). The agent can then automatically add the current customer, registered product, and service ticket to the existing case by simply pressing the "Activity Clipboard" button at the bottom of the case, which inserts all of the entries from the activity clipboard of the Interaction Record into the Case (Figure 6.33). Once the case has been resolved, all of the individual customers affected by the case can be informed of the resolution, either manually or perhaps via a scheduled post processing framework (PPF) action.

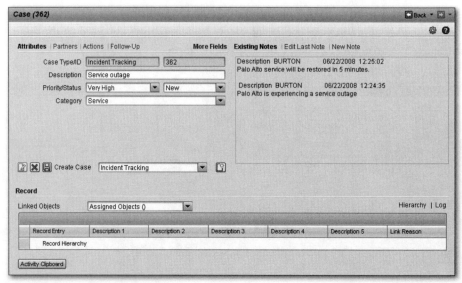

Figure 6.32 Case with Notes History

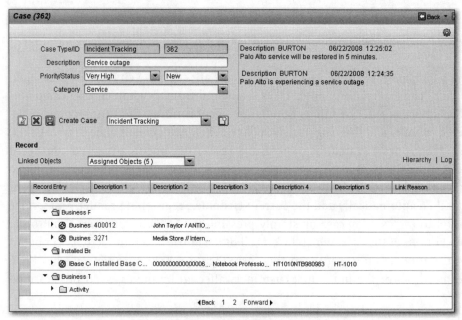

Figure 6.33 Insertion of Objects Into Case from Interaction Record

6.7   A Few Words About Self Service

The preceding sections gave you a thorough understanding of the various options available with the SAP CRM Interaction Center for conducting customer service. However, before we conclude our discussion on service, let's talk briefly about a related topic, Internet customer self-service, because it often goes hand in hand with the interaction center.

Web self-service can be a great way for an organization to provide customers (or at least certain types of customers) with low-cost, yet convenient, service. However, self-service should not be used to completely replace your interaction center. Self-service is not a panacea and is not relevant in all situations. Ideally, both the inter-action center and Web self-service should be part of your company's service strat-egy. While the interaction center is ideal for complicated or hard to solve issues (like technical trouble shooting) or for very high-value customers who require high-touch customer service, Web self-service is a fast and convenient way for customers to handle simple tasks like checking their account balances, updating their account information, or finding information. In addition, Web self-service is a very cost-effective channel for providing customer service for low-margin prod-ucts or unprofitable customers.

While you can certainly nudge certain customers to one channel or another, in the end it makes sense to let customers choose which channel they find most convenient for their needs. Companies should not force customers to a particular channel, such as the Web, against the customer's will. In fact, companies should be thrilled whenever a customer contacts the interaction center. This gives the com-pany an opportunity to interact with a captive customer who is ready to talk about the company's products and services. Perhaps the company's marketing depart-ment has even been frantically trying to reach this very same customer for months regarding a new promotion. Now the customer is on the phone ready to talk busi-ness. This is the perfect opportunity to increase customer loyalty by resolving the customer's issue quickly and accurately. It could also be a good opportunity to generate additional revenue from cross-sell or up-sell of related products, acces-sories, or maintenance contracts. This opportunity should not be squandered by trying to get the customer off the phone quickly, or by pressuring the customer to move to lower-cost Web self-service channel.

6.8 Summary

In this chapter, we examined the different options for providing world-class customer service using the SAP CRM Interaction Center. We discussed various different types of service including help desk, service desk, IT service desk, complaint management, and case management.

Some of the most important points to remember from this chapter are:

▶ Two options are available for enhancing the out of the box performance of the customer search screen including the High-Speed Business Partner Search and the Index-Based Business Partner Search options.

▶ A more recent version of SAP CRM provides additional possibilities for conducting customer searches including search by registered serialized product (IObject), contract, business agreement, vehicle, and so on.

▶ A configurable customer fact sheet is available, which can provide an all-inclusive view of customers including things like open orders, recent complaints, sales history, and so on.

▶ The Interaction Center includes knowledge management functionality that can automatically suggest solutions based on multi-level categorization of a service request. *SAP NetWeaver 7.0 Search and Classification (TREX 6.1) or higher is required for this functionality.*

▶ The IC Service Order transaction is ideal for installations, repairs, or maintenance activities, while the IC Service Ticket is more appropriate for technical analysis and trouble-shooting activities.

▶ Complaint Management is integrated with backend R/3 and ERP processes for returns management, replacement deliveries, credit memos, and QM notifications.

▶ Case Management provides tracking of multiple service requests related to the same underlying cause and is ideal for service outages, product recalls, storms and disasters, and so on.

So far in the book, we have talked about the agent facing tools provided by the SAP CRM Interaction Center. In the next chapter, we will discuss IC Management and Analytics, taking an in-depth look at the various tools and reports available to the people who are in charge of keeping the interaction center running smoothly — managers, analysts, and supervisors.

"What I need is a list of specific unknown problems we will encounter."
— *Anonymous manager*

7   IC Management and Analytics

Up until this point in the book, we primarily have been focused on the people who work on the front lines of the interaction center — the *agents*. Whether we refer to them as agents, customer service reps, technical support reps, or sales reps, — these are the people resolving customer issues, handling complaints, generating leads, and booking sales orders. Without agents, you couldn't even run your interaction center. Yet, that being said, someone needs to hire, train, schedule, supervise, and monitor the agents. Someone has to be in charge of making sure the interaction center runs smoothly. To ensure that things run smoothly, the person (or people) in charge needs as much information as possible, including current real-time operational data as well as aggregated historical data and analytics. Of course, it would also be nice to have a list of all unknown problems that will be encountered.

SAP delivers a default business role called IC Manager that provides the tools and reports needed to keep the interaction center running. The term "IC Manager" might tend to give the (false) impression that there is one single person who can single-handedly run an entire interaction center, including: planning, budgeting, hiring, training, scheduling, supervising, monitoring, and analyzing. In reality however, most interaction centers (even small ones) have multiple people and multiple roles involved in keeping the interaction center up and running. For the sake of simplicity, let's assume that there are three main types of roles that contribute to the "management" of the interaction center: (1) supervisors, (2) analysts, and (3) directors.

Supervisors, also sometimes known as team leaders (or team leads), typically supervise a team of anywhere from 5 to 25 agents, depending on the type of interaction center. Supervisors are usually responsible for hiring, training, performance appraisals, and so on. Yet, supervisors also work very closely with their team of agents — answering any questions the agents might have and even helping out with (or taking over) difficult customer calls. Typically, supervisors were previously top-performing agents who were promoted to team lead or supervisor. To do their job, supervisors need tools that allow them to monitor the *real-time* activity and performance of the agents they are responsible for, as well as tools to communicate with the agents when necessary. In the following sections, we will look at the tools that SAP provides in this area, including the IC Manager dashboard, broadcast messaging, and numerous real-time reports and performance metrics.

In addition to front-line supervisors, interaction centers also need people who set up the business rules and monitor the performance of the interaction center from behind the scenes. These people are referred to as analysts. Some analysts specialize in particular topics such as workforce management (forecasting, scheduling, optimization), training, quality monitoring, or statistical analysis. Other analysts are responsible for creating and maintaining call scripts, business rules, mail templates, alerts, and other tools that help optimize agent productivity. To accomplish their daily tasks, analysts require access to tools that help them model and enforce organizational business rules and processes across the interaction center. We'll look at relevant SAP CRM tools such as the Rule Modeler, Category Modeler, Interactive Script Editor, Alert Editor, and Mailform Template tool. We'll also look at applicable toolsets offered by SAP partners for areas like Workforce Management (WFM) and Workforce Optimization (WFO) and skills-based routing.

Finally, no interaction center is complete without senior leadership. Interaction center managers, who typically have the title director, are ultimately responsible for the overall quality, service level, and profitability of the interaction center. The director oversees the departmental budget and manages the interaction center staff to achieve desired performance standards. The director typically reports to senior management and aligns with the other line of business owners from the marketing, sales, and customer service departments. To effectively run the entire interaction center, the director needs access to *historical* reports and analytics (rather than *real-time* performance metrics required by supervisors). We'll look at some of the SAP NetWeaver BI reports and analytics available to interaction center directors.

Now that we have described the three main types of "managers" involved in setting up and running the interaction center — supervisors, analysts, and directors — let's take a look at the different tools and reports available to support them. For the sake of convenience and ease-of-use, SAP delivers a default IC Manager role that is organized into five areas, as seen in Figure 7.1:

- Monitoring operations
- Managing operations
- Knowledge management
- Process modeling
- Reports

Each of these areas contains specific functionality designed to support a particular objective such as monitoring real-time agent activity and performance, taking corrective action, organizing and publishing organizational knowledge, setting up business rules, and viewing historical reports. Let's start with where all the action is — monitoring real-time agent activity and performance with Monitoring Operations.

> **Note**
>
> In CRM 2005 and below, the IC Manager functionality is accessed via a web browser in the SAP Enterprise Portal. In most cases, it is also possible to access the individual applications that make up the IC Manager role by directly calling the appropriate BSP (Business Server Page) application component. See Chapter 3 for more information about Business Server Pages (and other technology topics).
>
> In CRM 2006s/CRM 2007 and above, the IC Manager functionality is delivered via the IC_MANAGER business role, which can be accessed in a web browser via the CRM WebClient. The Enterprise Portal is no longer required but may optionally be used. See Chapter 3 for more information about the CRM WebClient user interface (and other technology topics).

Figure 7.1 Home Page of IC Manager Business Role in CRM 2007

223

7.1 Monitoring Operations

The Monitoring Operations functionality of the IC Manager role is geared toward interaction center supervisors who need access to *real-time* data about the activities and performance metrics of the agents they supervise. The IC Manager role provides several tools that can be used to monitor and optimize the activities and performance of interaction center agents (Figure 7.2). Supervisors can search for and re-assign activities from one agent group (or queue) to another using the Business Transaction Assignment feature. If CTI or multi-channel integration is used within the interaction center, in conjunction with SAP BCM or another certified partner, supervisors can monitor the call volume and agent activity in each queue via the IC Manager Dashboard. Finally, if SAP E-Mail Response Management System (ERMS) is implemented, supervisors can access an overview of how many emails have been received and processed via ERMS during the current business day.

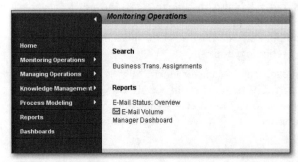

Figure 7.2 IC Manager Monitoring Operations Work Center Page

7.1.1 Business Transaction Assignment

The Business Transaction Assignment feature is a tool used primarily by supervisors. It allows a supervisor to search for and reassign business transactions (e.g., service tickets, sales orders, etc.) from one agent group to another. This can be useful, for example, in a 24 hour/7 day per week "follow the sun" interaction center where the supervisor needs to reassign all open issues to another location at the end of the working day. The Business Transaction Assignment functionality can also be useful if a supervisor simply wants to find certain items and reassign them from one agent to another. For example, the supervisor might search for a service ticket that has a certain status such as open (Figure 7.3), and then reassign the ticket from the current processor to another employee (Figure 7.4). This could be especially useful, for example, if one employee gets sick, goes on vacation, or leaves the company and the supervisor needs to quickly locate and reassign all unresolved business transactions to another agent.

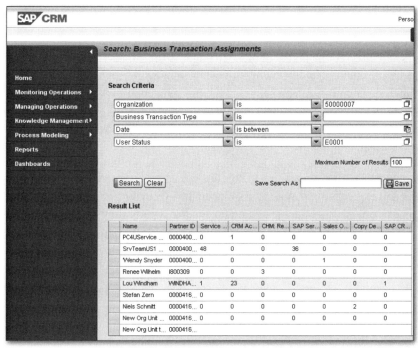

Figure 7.3 Supervisor Searches for Open Tickets

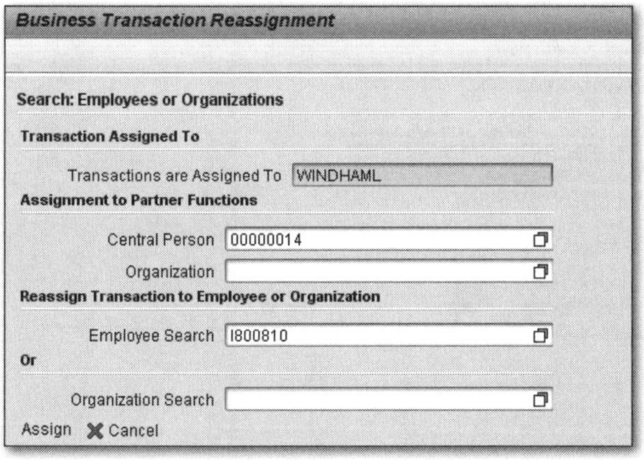

Figure 7.4 Supervisor Reassigns Open Tickets to Another Employee

7.1.2 IC Manager Dashboard

The IC Manager Dashboard is another tool used primarily by interaction center supervisors. It allows supervisors to monitor the status and performance of the interaction center throughout the day, and can help point out sudden trends or potential emergencies. Supervisors can view how many customers are waiting in each queue across all communication channels such as telephone, email, or chat. Supervisors can also see the status of all of the agents the supervisor is responsible for, including what each agent is working on (a telephone call, email, chat, etc.) and how long the agent has been working on the item. Please note however that this feature can be disabled via configuration in countries where government legislation or local customs prohibit or discourage monitoring of individual employees without their explicit consent.

The IC Manager Dashboard can be configured (i.e., personalized) directly by the responsible supervisors themselves. However, for security purposes — so that supervisors are only allowed to see the data for the agents they personally manage — a business analyst typically "personalizes" the dashboard for each of the supervisors. A wizard is available to guide the analyst through the configuration (Figure 7.5).

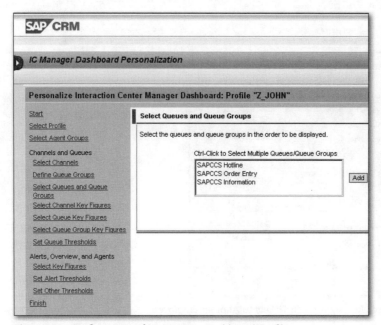

Figure 7.5 Configuration of IC Manager Dashboard Profile

As one of the first steps of the configuration process, the analyst creates a unique profile and selects which agent groups should included in the profile. The system provides a list of agent groups for selection based on data maintained in the HR-ORG (Human Resources Organizational Management). The analyst then chooses which communication channels and queues (both provided by the CMS software) to include in the profile (e.g., telephony, email, or chat). Finally, the analyst chooses the desired key figures and threshold values to include in the profile. Some key figures are provided by SAP as part of the IC Manager Dashboard, including total number of agents and number of customers waiting in the queue. Other key figures are provided by the CTI system such as average handling time and average speed of answer. The threshold values specify when a key figure should be considered in violation (e.g., too many customers waiting in queue, average speed of answer too slow, etc.).

> **Note**
>
> The IC Manager Dashboard displays real-time information provided by an external communication management software (CMS) system via the SAP Integrated Communication Interface (ICI). To use the IC Manager Dashboard you must install and configure a CMS system such as SAP BCM, Genesys, or other vendor.

After the IC Manager Dashboard has been configured by the analyst, it can be accessed by supervisors. As per the configuration (or personalization), each supervisor will see the agent groups that they are responsible for managing (Figure 7.6). If the supervisor manages more than one queue, the supervisor can select to view each queue individually or opt for a consolidated view across all queues. The supervisor can see the number of customers in queue for each communication channel, as well as the number of agents serving each queue. For each agent, the supervisor can see which communication channel the agent is working in and the length of time the agent has been working on the current item. If necessary, the supervisor could contact an individual agent by selecting the agent's name and clicking the *Message* or *Call* buttons, or listen in on the agent's current telephone conversation (if supported by the CMS system).

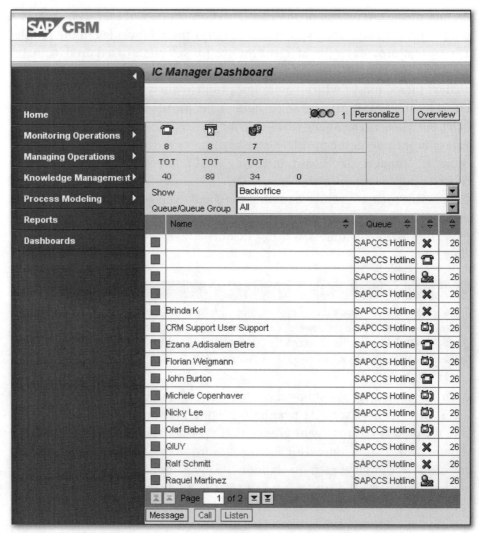

Figure 7.6 Display of Real-Time Queue and Agent Data

It is worth noting that most CMS systems come with their own dashboards that provide comparable functionality and features. Additionally, the dashboards provided by each CMS vendor tend to be optimized specifically for that vendor, whereas the IC Manager Dashboard from SAP was designed to be vendor neutral. For these reasons, most SAP customers have traditionally opted to use the dashboard provided by their CMS vendor than to use the IC Manager Dashboard of

SAP. However, one advantage of using SAP's IC Manager Dashboard is that as of CRM 2006s/CRM 2007 the dashboard can integrate data from multiple, disparate CMS vendors. Most companies today, especially large, international or global companies, have multiple software systems from multiple vendors. Rather than having to open several different CMS dashboards from several different vendors, a supervisor can simply use SAP's IC Manager Dashboard to view the consolidated data from each of the different CMS systems.

> **Note**
>
> In CRM 2005 and prior, there was a restriction that the IC Manager could only be integrated to a single CMS system. However, as of CRM 2006s/CRM 2007, the IC Manager Dashboard can integrate to as many CMS systems as desired, providing a supervisor with a consolidated view of the all the queues the supervisor is responsible for — without regard to the backend CTI software (CMS system).

7.1.3 E-Mail Status Overview & E-Mail Volume

As explained in Chapter 2, which covered CTI and multi-channel integration, there are two different techniques for integrating email into the SAP CRM Interaction Center. The first option is to use a supplemental communication management software (CMS) product, like SAP BCM, Genesys, Avaya, or others, to route each email to an agent in real-time using a screen pop; this option utilizes the SAP ICI interface and stores the actual email outside the SAP system on the server of the CMS system. The second option is to not use any CMS product but to instead route the emails to a virtual queue, where agents access the emails via the Agent Inbox inside the SAP CRM Interaction Center; this option uses the SAP SAPconnect interface and stores the emails in the tables of the SAP CRM system. The E-Mail Status Overview feature and the E-Mail Volume report only work with the second option. That is, you can only use the E-Mail Status Overview and E-Mail Volume report if you are using SAPconnect and the Agent Inbox for email processing.

The E-Mail Status Overview and E-Mail Volume report were designed specifically for the SAP E-Mail Response Management System (ERMS) solution, which allows companies to partially or fully automate email processing. Companies can leverage the E-Mail Volume report and the E-Mail Status Overview to gain a better understanding of how many emails are being received, and how well the ERMS system is automating email processing and handling. The two features work together. The

E-Mail Status Overview provides a daily snapshot of how many emails have been received and processed during the current business day; the E-Mail Volume report provides historical data and analysis of how many emails have been received and processed for a particular week, month, or year.

These two features would typically be used by the interaction center analyst to determine whether the ERMS configuration or business rules need to be adjusted. However, these two features could also be used by interaction center supervisors and directors. For example, a supervisor might rely on the daily E-Mail Status Overview to see how many emails are sitting in the queue, whereas an interaction center director would probably be more interested in viewing monthly or yearly email trends via the E-Mail Volume report.

E-Mail Status Overview

The E-Mail Status Overview displays real-time information about ERMS emails received during the current business day (Figure 7.7). This data is extracted directly from the CRM system and does not rely on any SAP NetWeaver BI functionality. The E-Mail Status Overview helps analysts better understand how well the ERMS rules are working. If, for example, most emails are being manually processed by agents, and very few emails are being automatically handled by ERMS, then the analyst may need to modify the current ERMS configuration and business rules. The Email Status Overview breaks down and displays daily email volume both by organization (i.e., HR-ORG. Management) and incoming email address. For example, a company may have several email addresses, perhaps one for regular customers and another for VIP customers. In addition to seeing how many emails are in the queue and how many are being processed automatically via ERMS versus manually by agents, the E-Mail Status Overview also reveals if emails are not being processed within the defined SLAs and get escalated to management.

E-Mail Status

Status by Organization

Group	Today's E-Mails	In Queue	In Process	Responded	Auto Responded
Unassigned	0	161	3	0	0
PC4U Global	0	4	0	0	0
Backoffice Agents	0	7	0	0	0
CRM Tester Organization	0	275	34	0	0
Test11	0	1	0	0	0
CRM Interaction Center	0	8	2	0	0
New organizational unit	0	1	0	0	0
test_29.3	0	1	0	0	0
New organizational unit	0	0	1	0	0
testo123	0	0	1	0	0

◀Back 1 2 Forward▶

Status by Incoming E-Mail Address

Group	Today's E-Mails	In Queue	In Process	Responded	Auto Responded
erms@506.q8d.r3.sap-ag.de	0	459	43	0	0
erms@800.faz.r3.sap-ag.de	0	1	0	0	0
erms@800.fnz.r3.sap-ag.de	0	32	0	0	0

Escalations by Organization

Group	Escalated E-Mails	Average Violation(Hours)	Avg.Rule Violation(Hours)
Unassigned	56	6,231.35	8,245.63
CRM Tester Organization	342	4,722.76	4,961.88
Test11	1	8,277.03	0.00
CRM Interaction Center	10	3,405.56	0.00

Figure 7.7 E-Mail Status Overview Showing Daily E-Mail Volume

The E-Mail Volume Report

Whereas the E-Mail Status Overview displays real-time information (directly from the CRM system) about ERMS emails received during the current business day, the E-Mail Volume Report provides historical data aggregated via SAP NetWeaver BI (Figure 7.8). This information could be useful to either an analyst or a director of an interaction center. For example, after making some recent changes to the ERMS configuration or business rules, an analyst might want to check whether things have improved in the last week since making the changes. A director of an interaction center might want to compare email volumes for the current quarter or year against volumes from the previous year as part of the planning, budgeting, or evaluation process.

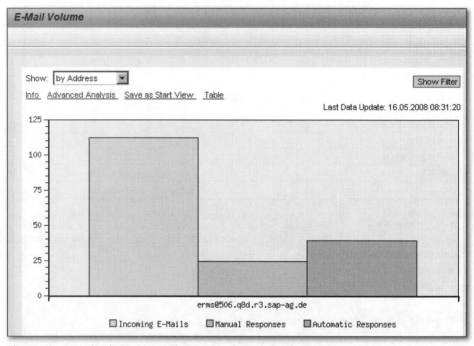

Figure 7.8 E-Mail Volume Report Showing Yearly E-Mail Volume

> **Note**
>
> The E-Mail Volume report is enabled via SAP NetWeaver BI. In order to use any of the standard reports provided by the IC Manager role, including the E-Mail Volume report, it is necessary to first install and configure SAP BI.
>
> As of CRM 2006s/CRM 2007 several CRM-based reports, known as CRM Interactive reports, are available that do not require installation of SAP NetWeaver BI. These reports are also sometimes referred to as OLTP (online transaction processing) reports due to the fact that the transactional data is retrieved directly from the CRM system rather than from a consolidated data warehouse like SAP NetWeaver BI. These reports are discussed in Section 7.5 on Reports.

7.2   Managing Operations

The Managing Operations functionality of the IC Manager role is geared toward both supervisors and analysts, each of whom need to access different administrative tools for planning, scheduling, and making on-the-fly adjustments to the Interaction Center. For example, analysts can do things like display or adjust the assignment of business roles to org structures, view the daily email volume and handling metrics, and perform simulations on recently changed email processing rules to make sure the new rules will work as expected. Interaction center supervisors can reassign emails and business transactions from one agent or agent group to another, create new outbound call lists, and send messages to specific agents (or agent groups) working in the Interaction Center, as seen in Figure 7.9.

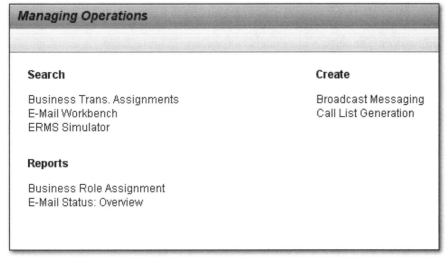

Figure 7.9   IC Manager Managing Operations Work Center Page

7.2.1   Business Transaction Assignment

The Business Transaction Assignment (BTA) functionality allows interaction center supervisors to search for and reassign business transactions from one interaction agent group to another. This functionality appears in both the Monitoring Operations and Managing Operations section of the IC Manager role because it allows supervisors to monitor currently assigned transactions, as well as to manage (reas-

sign) transactions. Please see Section 7.1.1 of this chapter for more details on the
BTA functionality.

7.2.2 E-Mail Workbench

The E-Mail Workbench works very similarly to the BTA functionality, in that the
E-Mail Workbench allows a supervisor to monitor and re-assign *emails* from one
agent (or agent group) to another, just as the BTA functionality allows you to reassign business transactions. The tool provides a variety of attributes that can be
used — in combination if desired — to locate emails. For example, in Figure 7.10
a supervisor is searching for emails assigned to a specific Interaction Center agent
named Gert Tackaert whose user ID is "Gert Tackaert." After conducting a search,
the supervisor can select one or more emails from the result list and execute a
desired action such as re-assigning the emails to another agent, routing the emails
to another org unit, forwarding the emails to an external email address outside the
SAP CRM system, or setting the emails to complete (Figure 7.11).

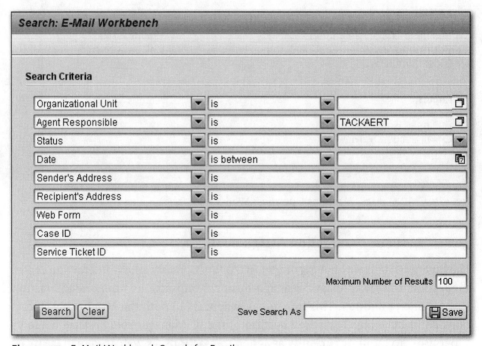

Figure 7.10 E-Mail Workbench Search for Emails

Search: E-Mail Workbench

Result List   Show Search Fields

🗑 | Assign To | Route To | Forward | Send Copy |Set to Complete| | Display All | Display Selection

Sender's Address	Status	Subject	Created On Date	Agent Responsible	Business Partner
john.burton@sap.com	In Process	B ZJOHN Z_JOHN Forward	05/29/2008	TACKAERT	50001175
octavian.iancu@sap.com	In Queue	ZJOHN 1	05/29/2008	TACKAERT	50001175
octavian.iancu@sap.com	In Queue	Test 1	05/28/2008	TACKAERT	50001175
kamalraj.j.kuppal@sap.com	In Queue	Test Mail	05/05/2008	TACKAERT	416794
venkata.krishna.motumarri@sap.com	In Queue	Smart responce	04/30/2008	TACKAERT	416794
sapconnect	In Queue	Returned mail: User unknown	04/30/2008	TACKAERT	416794
kamalraj.j.kuppal@sap.com	In Queue	Test Email	04/29/2008	TACKAERT	416794
sapconnect	In Queue	Returned mail: User unknown	04/29/2008	TACKAERT	416794
sapconnect	In Queue	Returned mail: User unknown	04/23/2008	TACKAERT	416794
jagadeesh.kantharaju@sap.com	In Queue	testing	04/18/2008	TACKAERT	416794
john.burton@sap.com	In Queue	Email, email, email	02/20/2008	TACKAERT	416794
parul@506.q8d.r3.sap-ag.de	In Queue	Cannot be sent: Test for email error	09/25/2007	TACKAERT	416794
erms@506.q8d.r3.sap-ag.de	In Queue	RE: RE: tht	09/22/2007	TACKAERT	416794
lokesh.manikantha.aldi@sap.com	In Queue		09/21/2007	TACKAERT	416794
rashmi.c@sap.com	In Queue	Route to	09/20/2007	TACKAERT	419260

Figure 7.11 Setting Multiple Selected Emails to Status Complete

In addition to doing things like reassigning, routing, or forwarding emails, a supervisor can also drill down into the details of an individual email. The supervisor can, of course, see standard information such as the contents and attachments of the email (Figure 7.12). Additionally, however, the supervisor can also see other useful information such as the responsible org unit and agent to which the email has been assigned. The supervisor can also view the results of the automated ERMS email processing, including the results of the ERMS rule evaluation as well as the content of the ERMS Factbase (i.e., runtime repository). Additionally, if the ERMS system had been able to automatically categorize or classify the incoming email based on content analysis, the resulting categories would also be displayed. If you don't have any idea what is meant by "Factbase" or "content analysis" don't worry, we'll explain it all in the section on ERMS. For now, you just need to know that all of the ERMS relevant data for an email can be viewed from the E-Mail Workbench.

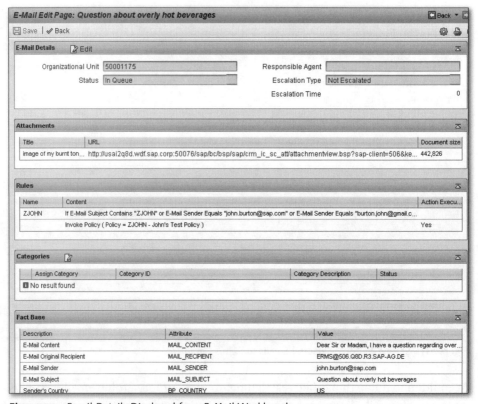

Figure 7.12 Email Details Displayed from E-Mail Workbench

7.2.3 ERMS Simulator

As discussed in Chapter 9, Rule Modeler and Category Modeler, the goal of ERMS is to allow analysts to create business rules to help automate the processing of inbound customer emails. For example, rules could be created to automatically reply to certain types of emails with an automated response, and to route other types of emails to a specific agent or agent group for processing (perhaps based on the content or keywords in the email subject or body). Obviously, extensive testing is necessary after creating new rules before you activate the rules in the production system. However, handling small changes to existing rules can be trickier. For example, if a couple of rules are not working quite as intended or producing undesirable results, you can easily change the rule by creating a new set of draft rules. But how do you know if the new draft rules will work as intended once they are activated? This is difficult to do unless you can somehow reuse the exact same data that was used for the original rules. But, clearly, you can't ask all of your customers to email you a second time describing their original problems.

The ERMS Simulator provides the solution to this dilemma, allowing use to simulate — using actual historic customer emails — how the new *draft* rules would have been performed if they had been *active* at the time the original emails were sent. To use the ERMS Simulator, an analyst would select the desired ERMS Service Manager profile to be tested (Figure 7.13). Note that the analyst does not select individual rules or even a rule collection (policy) but rather selects the underlying technical Service Manager profile that controls which rule policy or policies are invoked. The analyst then selects other parameters, including whether to use draft rules (if available) and the sample size of emails to be simulated (e.g., every email, every 10th email, every 100th, etc.). The analyst could optionally choose to execute the simulation in the background (for performance reasons, such as to not disrupt the performance of the customer-facing Interaction Center agents) or to have a copy of the simulation results sent via email.

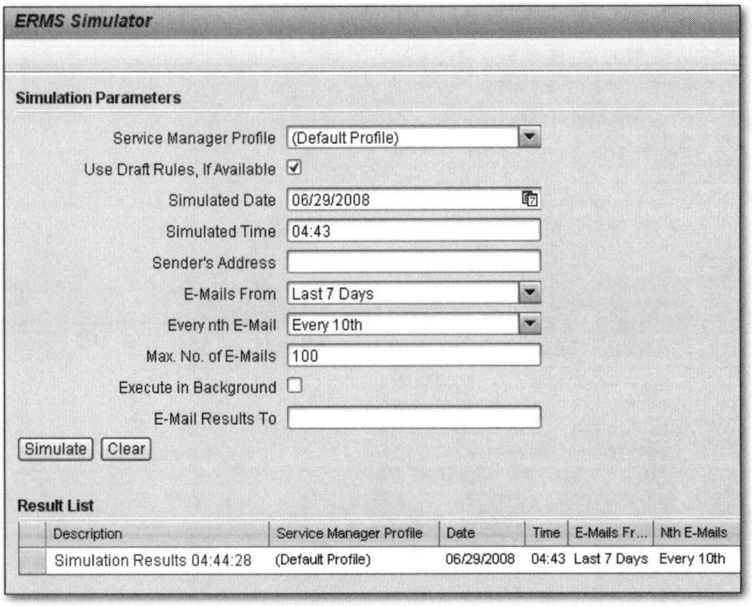

Figure 7.13 ERMS Simulator Parameter Selection Screen

The results of the simulation are added to the Result List at the bottom of the ERMS Simulator parameter simulation screen. The analyst can conduct multiple simulations. For example, it might be helpful to compare the simulated results of the new draft rules against the (simulated) results of the active rules. However, only the results of one simulation can be viewed at a time. To view the results of a simulation, the analyst simply clicks on the blue description field of the desired simulation results. The system then navigates to the ERMS Simulator detail screen where the analyst can see what would have happened if the selected rules had been used with real customer data (Figure 7.14). For example, in the simulation results shown in Figure 7.14, you can see which rule policies and actions were invoked for the 36 simulated emails. If the analyst is pleased with the results of the simulation, the analyst can activate the draft rules. Otherwise, the analyst goes back to work and tries additional modifications to the existing rules.

ERMS Simulator

Statistics	Count
Emails Processed	36

Action	Parameter	Count
Invoke Policy	Policy="RASH_AUTORESPOND"	1
Invoke Policy	Policy="RASH_SMARTRESPON"	1
Invoke Policy	Policy="RASH_WEBFORM"	5
Invoke Policy	Policy="ZJOHN - John's Test Policy"	4
Invoke Policy	Policy="ZRULEPOLICY - Test Rule Policy"	2
Send Auto Acknowledgement	Mail Form = "ERMS_RASH" Outgoing E-Mail Address = "erms@506.q8d.r3.sap-ag.de" Create Interaction Record = "No" Create Service Order = "No"	5
Send Auto Acknowledgement	Mail Form = "" Outgoing E-Mail Address = "erms@506.q8d.r3.sap-ag.de" Create Interaction Record = "Yes" Create Service Order = "Yes"	2
Auto Respond	Category Schema = "ERMS Categories" Mail Form = "ZRASH_SERVICE_TICKET" Outgoing E-Mail Address = "erms@506.q8d.r3.sap-ag.de" Create Interaction Record = "No" Route To (On Exception) = "O:50001175" Inline = "No"	1
Auto Respond	Category Schema = "ERMS Categories" Mail Form = "ZERMS_RASH" Outgoing E-Mail Address = "erms@506.q8d.r3.sap-ag.de" Create Interaction Record = "Yes" Route To (On Exception) = "O:50001175" Inline = "No"	1
Forward EMail	Forward To = "venkata.krishna.motumarri@sap.com" Forward From = "erms@506.q8d.r3.sap-ag.de"	5

Figure 7.14 Simulation of ERMS Rule Processing Using Draft Rules

7.2.4   Business Role Assignment

The Business Role Assignment report — though officially classified as a report — actually offers powerful functionality that goes far beyond mere reporting. This tool can be used by an analyst or supervisor to display all the CRM business profiles (or IC WebClient profiles, depending on your release) that are linked to any particular user. For example, an analyst might create a new CRM business role (or IC WebClient profile), which should be assigned to a particular user or user group. Using the Business Role Assignment report, the analyst can find out which organization a user is assigned to. The analyst can then also see — and change — the business role assigned to the selected organizational unit, as seen in Figure 7.15. This procedure often proves much quicker (and easier) than going into the standard HR-ORG Maintenance transaction, such as transaction code PPOMW.

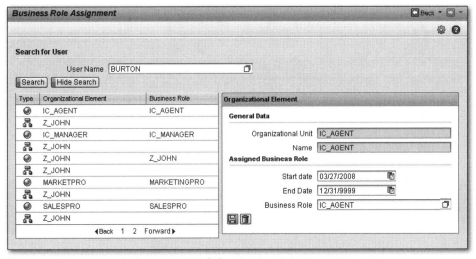

Figure 7.15   Business Role Assignment Tool Showing Agent Assignments

7.2.5   E-Mail Status Overview

As mentioned in Section 7.1.3, the E-Mail Status Overview displays real-time information about ERMS emails received during the current business day. The ERMS email data is stored and extracted directly from the CRM system and does not require any separate installation of SAP NetWeaver BI. Please see Section 7.1.3 for complete details about the E-Mail Status Overview feature.

7.2.6   Broadcast Messaging

Broadcast messaging is an extremely important feature in interaction centers and is used by supervisors and team leaders to push important, time-sensitive information to the agents in their teams. Using the Broadcast Messaging tool, an analyst would typically create a distribution list for each supervisor that includes all of the members assigned to the supervisor's team (Figure 7.16). Optionally, the analyst might also create additional distribution lists, each containing only one member of the supervisor's team; this would give the supervisor more flexibility when sending messages (i.e., the ability to send a message to one person rather than the whole team).

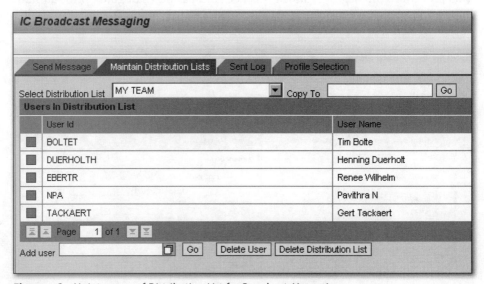

Figure 7.16   Maintenance of Distribution List for Broadcast Messaging

Once the distribution lists have been created by an analyst, a supervisor can each select their team (or optionally, individual team members) and send a broadcast message. For example, a supervisor might want to notify their team that a television commercial is airing as part of a new marketing campaign, and that the interaction center is expecting a temporary spike in incoming call volume (Figure 7.17). Once the message is sent, the text of the message will show up and scroll across the bottom of the screen of the selected recipients in the Interaction Center. The supervisor can select a duration for the message (e.g., 15 minutes) to control how long the message should continue to scroll (until the message is manually confirmed and removed by the agent). The supervisor can also indicate if the message should be high priority or normal priority; high priority messages will be presented to the agents as bold text.

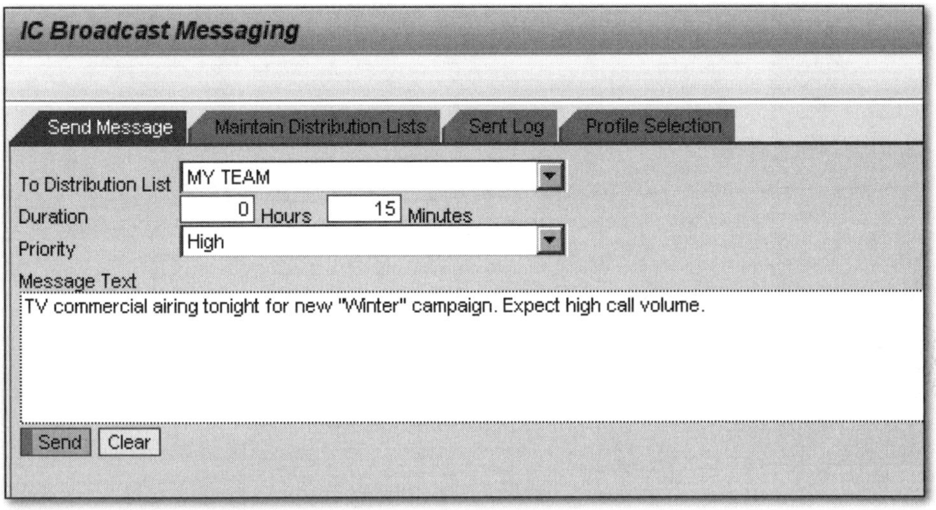

Figure 7.17 Sending of Broadcast Message by Supervisor

7.2.7 Call List Generation

In CRM 2006s/CRM 2007 and beyond, most business user transaction and functionality was moved from SAP GUI to the new CRM WebClient user interface. However, there are still a few transactions and tools, which a business user might need, still available in SAP GUI and do not need their own native CRM WebClient screen. Transaction CRMD_CALL_LIST, Generate Business Transactions and Call Lists, is one such example. However, business users don't need to install the SAP GUI Logon application on their computers in order to log in to SAP GUI to create call lists. Rather, business users can still access this functionality from the CRM WebClient via the IC Manager role (Figure 7.18). Technically, behind the scenes, the system uses the Transaction Launcher and ITS to make a HTML representation of the screen available.

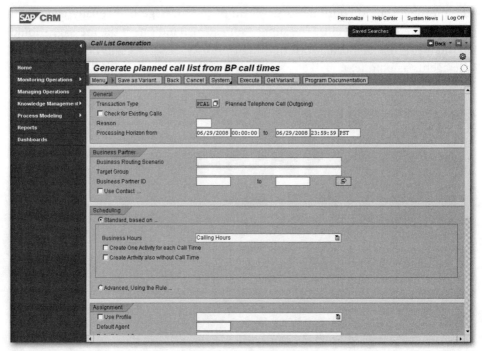

Figure 7.18 Generate Business Transactions and Call Lists

The Call List Generation tool allows interaction center managers to create their own call lists for special situations; typically, call lists are created automatically from a target list of a campaign by a marketing manager. The Call List Generation tool requires that every call be added to the call list manually — one call at a time — and does not support automatic call list creation from target groups or business partner ranges. Hence, this tool is primarily useful when an interaction center supervisor needs to manually create a small call list to make sure agents follow up on a few open items. The Generate Business Transactions and Call Lists were covered in great detail Chapter 4, IC Marketing.

7.3 Knowledge Management

Let's move on to a very different topic — Knowledge Management. You might recall that Monitoring Operations was essentially about checking the status of phone calls, emails, and business transactions, while Managing Operations was concerned with administrative tasks necessary to empower supervisors. Knowledge Management, on the other hand, focuses on making sure interaction center agents always have the information they need to resolve customer issues. The Knowledge Management functionality of the IC Manager role provides tools for structuring and organizing FAQs, solutions, procedures, templates, and other documents (see Figure 7.19). This type of work is most often handled by a special type of interaction center analyst, known as a knowledge administrator (or knowledge manager).

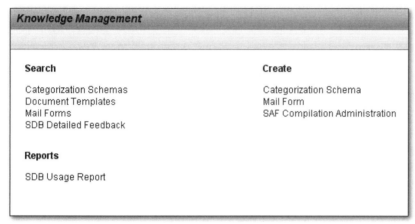

Figure 7.19   IC Manager Knowledge Management Work Center Page

7.3.1   Categorization Schemas

The Category Modeler is a tool that allows you to create and structure groups of multi-level related categories (known as *categorization schemas*) that you plan to use in classifying your service-related business transactions such as service tickets, complaints, and so on. Typically, companies will create hierarchies of related multi-level categories with various dependent levels, such as product line, product, problem type, or error code. Category schemas make it very fast and easy to classify customer issues using standard sets of criteria, which in turn ensure consistent reporting as well. Additionally, multi-level categorization can also be used to drive certain automated and semi-automated features inside the Interaction Center, such as automatic suggestion of solutions, auto-completion of service-related business transactions using stored templates, automatic classification of incoming emails, and so on. Categorization Schemas are discussed in full detail in Chapter 9, which covers the CRM Rule Modeler and Category Modeler.

7.3.2 Document Templates

Often, when creating a new object in CRM, whether that object is a business partner, product, sales lead, service contract, or warranty claim — it is often desirable to create the new object from a saved template document rather than creating the object completely from scratch. Not only does this save time and increase efficiency, but it also reduces the likelihood of errors and omissions. Using the Document Template functionality in the IC Manager role, an analyst can search for an existing document template to use when creating a new object.

7.3.3 Mail Forms

Mail forms are essentially email templates that can be used by an Interaction Center agent when sending an email, SMS, or fax. Mail forms are especially useful for agents who deal with customer emails on a regular basis, because it is much faster (and less error prone) to compose an email by inserting one or more email templates than to write each email completely by hand. Agents can access mail forms from both the E-Mail Editor and the Chat Editor inside the Interaction Center using the so-called "standard response" functionality. Mail Forms can also be inserted automatically into emails — both for manually and automatically responded emails — as part of the ERMS functionality.

The Mail Forms functionality in the IC Manager role is useful for analysts who need to create new email templates or modify existing templates. To locate an existing template, the analyst can search by a variety of fields including mail form ID, description, usage, language, and so on. For example, let's say an analyst wanted to locate and modify the generic signature template that is shared by all Interaction Center agents. The analyst might search for Mail Forms that contain the word "signature" in the description (Figure 7.20).

After locating the desired mail form, the analyst might want to, for example, add the corporate logo to the bottom of the signature (Figure 7.21). Note that in the email template pictured, the Attribute Context has been set to "ERMS." This is necessary to make all of the ERMS-related attributes (variables) available inside the mail form. ERMS provides certain ERMS-specific attributes, which depending on your specific version of CRM could include service ticket tracking ID, case tracking ID, account balance due, and so on. As of CRM 2006s/CRM 2007, SAP introduced several attributes such as agent title, first name, last name, agent email address, and agent phone number that can be used to create a generic email signature template that can be shared by all agents.

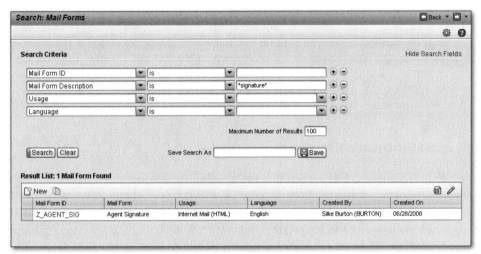

Figure 7.20 Search for Existing Mail Form (Email Template)

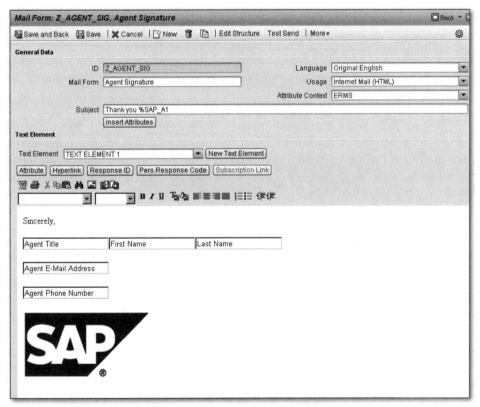

Figure 7.21 Generic Agent Signature Mail Form (Email Template)

> **Note**
>
> In CRM 2006s/CRM 2007, SAP introduced various Interaction Center agent-specific attributes that can be used in a mail form to enable a generic email signature template for all agents. These attributes appear under the Additional Fields attribute category of the Insert Attributes — Web Page Dialogue screen; however, to make these fields appear you must first select the Attribute Context "ERMS" in the General Data area above.

7.3.4 SDB Detailed Feedback

The primary task of a knowledge administrator is to create and maintain solutions and other documents that help agents resolve customer service issues. For example, the knowledge administrator is responsible for authoring and publishing a new solution in the knowledge database whenever a new reoccurring issue is detected. Similarly, the knowledge administrator is responsible for keeping the knowledge database current and accurate; seldom-used documents need to be updated or pruned (deleted) from the knowledge database if they are no longer relevant. The SDB Detailed Feedback functionality assists a knowledge administrator with these tasks by letting the administrator search for the most frequently and least frequently used solutions, solutions that have been sent out via a particular communication change, and solutions that agents have marked as "not useful."

Knowledge Administrators can select from one of the two rankings — Least Used or Most Used — to view solutions that have been frequently (or infrequently) added to the cart in the Interaction Center Knowledge Search screen. In the result list, the Individual Count field will display the number of times that agents have selected the solution and added it to the cart (Figure 7.22). This information can be useful if a knowledge administrator wants to update or delete the least used solutions.

Additionally, knowledge administrators often want to know which solutions are still being selected and added to the cart on a regular basis, but that are marked as "Not Useful" by agents. An agent might mark a solution as unhelpful if the solution is confusing or poorly written, or if the solution does not actually solve the problem it is supposed to address. The Individual Count field in the result list indicates the number of Interaction Center agents who have marked the solution as not useful (Figure 7.23).

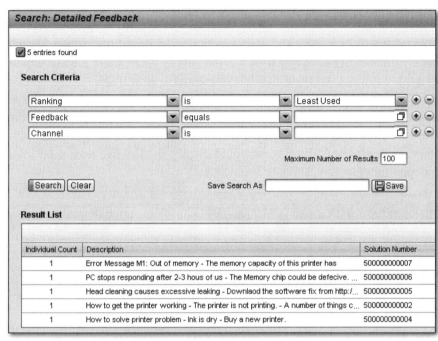

Figure 7.22 SDB Detailed Feedback: Least Used Solutions

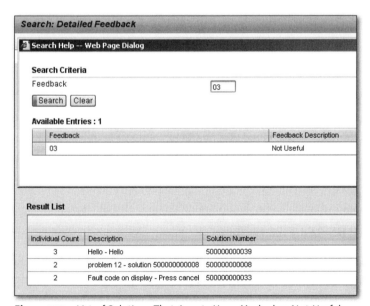

Figure 7.23 List of Solutions That Agents Have Marked as Not Useful

7.3.5   SDB Usage Report

The SDB Usage Report is basically just a preconfigured report that allows knowledge administrators an easier way to access the data of the SDB Detailed Feedback functionality without having to conduct a manual search (Figure 7.24). When a knowledge administrator clicks on one of the predefined queries, the system automatically navigates to the SDB Detailed Feedback screen and displays the results of the predefined search query. For example, if the knowledge administrator clicked on Least Used, the system would display the top five least-used solutions, as shown in Figure 7.22.

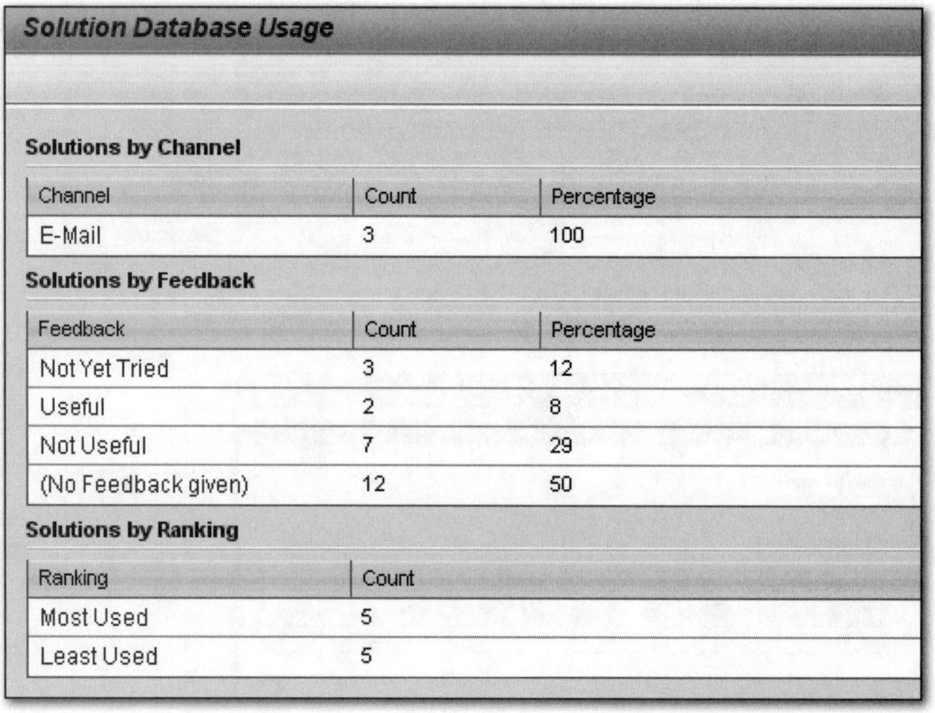

Solution Database Usage

Solutions by Channel

Channel	Count	Percentage
E-Mail	3	100

Solutions by Feedback

Feedback	Count	Percentage
Not Yet Tried	3	12
Useful	2	8
Not Useful	7	29
(No Feedback given)	12	50

Solutions by Ranking

Ranking	Count
Most Used	5
Least Used	5

Figure 7.24   SDB Usage Report

7.3.6   SAF Compilation Administration

As mentioned in Chapter 6, Section 6.2.4, the Software Agent Framework (SAF) provides an open architecture for enabling setting up, compiling, and searching of a variety of knowledge repositories including the SAP Solution Database (SDB). From the SAF Compilation Administration functionality, a knowledge administrator can select a knowledge repository, such as the SDB, and execute various actions. The administrator could perform a one-time initial database set-up. Or, if the database has already been set up, the administrator could compile the database to make the documents searchable. A full compilation should be used the first time a database is compiled after the initial set up procedure; after that, delta compilations can be performed to index any recently changed or created documents. If the database were corrupted for some reason, the administrator could delete the index and begin again with a new set-up. After any action has been executed, the results of the process can be seen in the compilation log that shows, for example, whether the process was successful or resulted in errors, as well as the number of compiled documents, user name, and time stamp (Figure 7.25).

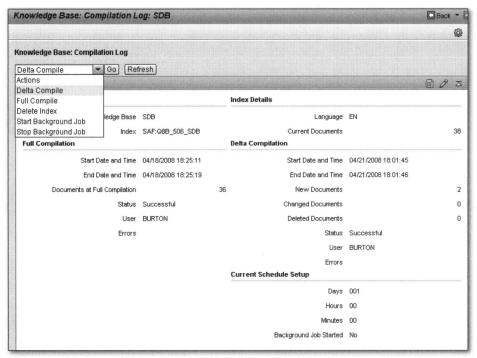

Figure 7.25 Compilation Log Showing Results of Successful Compilation

7.4 Process Modeling

The Process Modeling functionality of the IC Manager business role is intended for analysts who need to configure business rules, call scripts, and alert messages for the Interaction Center. For example, an analyst might need to create rules to enable automated processing of emails via ERMS, automated dispatching of service requests via Order Routing, or automated agent guidance via Intent-Driven Interaction. An analyst could also want to set up call scripts and/or text messages that guide agents through customer conversations or complex processes using Interactive Scripting and the Alert Editor (see Figure 7.26).

Figure 7.26   IC Manager Process Modeling Work Center Page

7.4.1 Alerts

Alerts are text messages that can be displayed to agents in the Context Area of the Interaction Center. Alerts can contain attributes (variables) that are dynamically inserted at runtime, such as the name of the customer. Alerts can also include navigable hyperlinks that take the agent to another screen when the alert is clicked, such as to an open service ticket, expiring service contract or warranty, or past due account balance. Alerts are triggered based on business rules and triggering events, like the clicking of a certain button by an agent in the Interaction Center. In CRM 2005 and prior releases, alerts were triggered via a tool called the Alert Modeler, which utilized ABAP condition tables (CRM 2005) or XML coding (CRM 4.0). In CRM 2006s/CRM 2007, a graphical modeling tool called the Alert Editor has replaced the former Alert Modeler. The Alert Editor, shown in Figure 7.27, provides a number of advantages over the former Alert Modeler tool.

In previous CRM releases, SAP was able to deliver certain default alerts. For example, a default alert was provided to notify agents if related documents were available for a confirmed customer. Similarly, a default alert was delivered to inform agents if the system was able to automatically determine one or more solutions that might be relevant for a customer's current issue. However, with the new Alert Editor it is not possible for SAP to deliver any default alerts. Therefore, you need to manually create all desired alerts yourself.

One of the main advantages of the Alert Editor is that you can create reusable alerts that can be triggered via the Rule Modeler using different sets of rules and events. Previously with the Alert Modeler, each alert was configured directly against a specific triggering event and could not be reused. The Alert Editor also provides all of the features that an analyst would expect, including mouse-over tool tips, support for attributes (variables) that are inserted at runtime, and the ability to navigate to any screen or application in SAP CRM. In the alert shown in Figure 7.27, the alert has been configured to show the number of automatically suggested solutions returned by the Software Agent Framework using a variable [Event$AutoSuggestStart:NumberOfSolutions]. The alert also contains a hyperlink that will navigate to the Knowledge Search screen, where the automatically suggested solutions will be displayed to the agent.

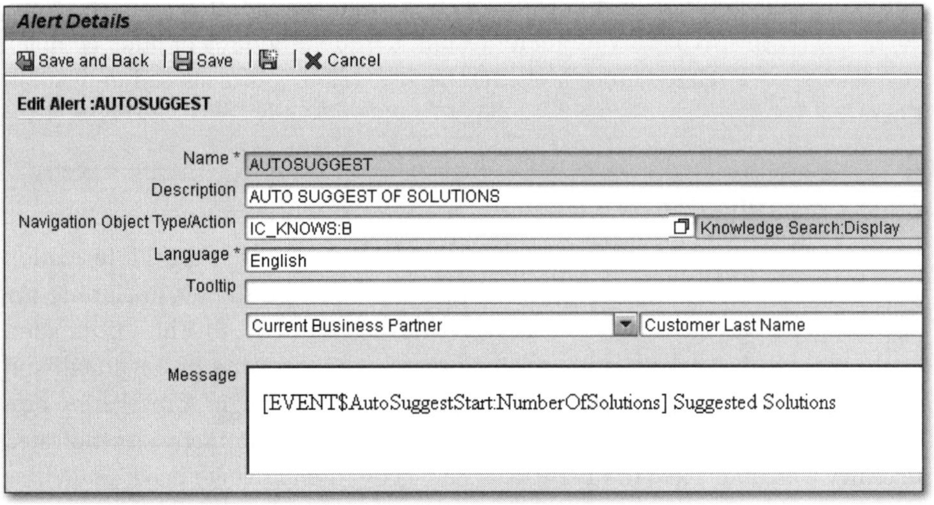

Figure 7.27 Alert Editor: Graphical Creation Tool for Alerts

7.4.2   Rule Policies

The Rule Modeler is one of the most powerful features included in SAP CRM. It allows analysts to define business rules that automate (or semi-automate) various Interaction Center processes from email handling to service ticket escalation and automated agent guidance. The Rule Modeler can be used to automatically acknowledge or reply to customer emails, or to prepare a response email for an agent automatically. The Rule Modeler can be used to dispatch or escalate service tickets to the responsible organization or employee based on things like product, priority, or status. You can even use the Rule Modeler to automatically guide your agents through a customer interaction with rule-based scripts, alerts, and automated document creation and navigation. The Rule Modeler is discussed in detail in Chapter 9.

7.4.3   Interactive Script Editor

Interactive scripts provide step-by-step procedures that can guide interaction center agents through customer conversations as well as complex or unfamiliar procedures. Using interactive scripts you improve the likelihood that your customers will receive a consistent customer experience regardless of the skill level or experience of the agent handling the interaction. Scripts are commonly used in outbound call scenarios to support marketing, sales, or collections efforts. However, scripts can also be very useful for technical troubleshooting or other complex customer-service related procedures. Interactive Scripting is discussed in detail in Chapter 8.

7.4.4   Scripting Evaluation

Interactive Scripting Evaluation is a feature that allows you to export information about scripts that have been executed in the Interaction Center (including the answers given by customers) to SAP NetWeaver BI (Figure 7.28). This information could potentially be interesting to, for example, a marketing professional who wants to create new target group of customers for a campaign. A marketing professional might want to create a new target group for all customers who indicated that they were interested in a particular product but didn't plan to make a purchase decision within the next three months.

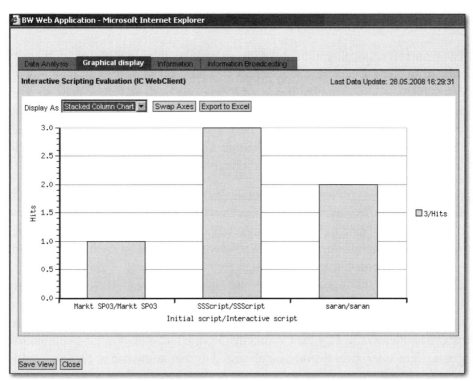

Figure 7.28 Interactive Scripting Evaluation

Interactive Scripting Evaluation was originally developed with SAP CRM 3.0 specifically for the IC WinClient product. So, the evaluation functionality was optimized for the IC WinClient version of Interactive Scripting, which works differently than Interactive Scripting in the IC WebClient (and the CRM WebClient). As a result, although Interactive Scripting Evaluation can be used with the IC WebClient, not all features of IC WebClient scripts are supported by Interactive Scripting Evaluation. For example, IC WebClient scripts can include various different types of answers, including push buttons, radio buttons, checkboxes, and text fields. However, only pushbuttons were available in IC WinClient scripts, and therefore Interactive Scripting Evaluation only records answers associated with pushbuttons. If you utilize other answer types (including radio buttons, check boxes, or text fields) in your IC WebClient scripts, these answers will not be exported or available in the Interactive Scripting Evaluation reports in SAP NetWeaver BI.

7.5 Reports

The reports functionality of the IC Manager business role are useful for all types of Interaction Center managers — supervisors, analysts, and directors. These reports help supervisors spot sudden trends with email and CTI, and allow them to react appropriately to avert a crisis. The reports also provide analysts with insight into the volume of incoming emails and service requests. Finally, the reports give directors and line of business managers the information they need about whether the Interaction Center is meeting the defined service levels.

All the standard reports available in the IC Manager role utilize SAP NetWeaver BI to retrieve data. These reports, like all SAP NetWeaver BI enabled reports to rely on standard SAP NetWeaver BI components such as queries, infocubes, and extractors. You can easily identify standard SAP NetWeaver BI reports by the distinctive icon, which shows a blue line graph as seen in Figure 7.29. However, as of CRM 2006s/ CRM 2007, SAP additionally provides the capability to create OLTP-based reports that use live, real-time data from the CRM system rather than extracted, historic data from SAP NetWeaver BI. These reports, known as CRM Interactive Reports, can be easily identified by their distinctive icon, which shows a multi-colored bar graph. CRM Interactive Reports are discussed further at the end of Section 7.5.1.

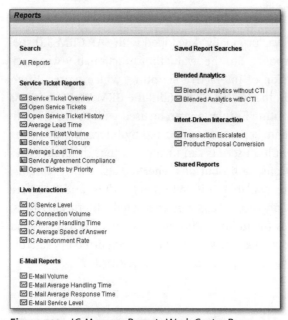

Figure 7.29 IC Manager Reports Work Center Page

7.5.1 Service Ticket Reports

The *Service Ticket Reports* functionality is useful to supervisors, analysts, and directors of the Interaction Center. These reports provide a wealth of information about the service tickets assigned to the various organizations associated with the Interaction Center. The *Service Ticket Overview* report offers information about currently open ticket balances, closed tickets, and ticket closure rate (Figure 7.30). The *Open Service Tickets* report lets you display the number of open tickets by lifetime (e.g., how many open tickets are 0 to 7 days, 8 to 30, over 30) or priority (e.g., how many open tickets are high, medium, low). The *Open Service Ticket History* report shows the number of open tickets over time (e.g., how many tickets were open during January 2009 compared to December 2008). Finally, the *Average Lead Time* report lets managers know how long, on average, it takes each organization to resolve and close their service tickets. Note the two versions of each report are available: a standard SAP NetWeaver BI-based report and an equivalent CRM OLTP-based version.

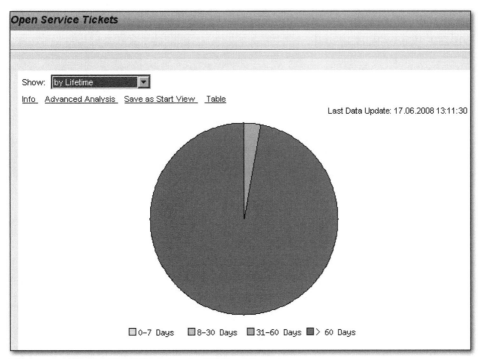

Figure 7.30 Service Ticket Overview (by Lifetime) Report

CRM Interactive Reports (OLTP Reports)

As of CRM 2006s/CRM 2007, SAP introduced CRM Interactive Reports, essentially OLTP-based reports that rely directly on live data stored in the CRM system without the need for a separate SAP NetWeaver BI installation. For the IC Manager role, the standard service ticket reports are now also offered via CRM Interactive Reports (Figure 7.31). These reports can be easily identified by their distinctive icon, which shows a multi-colored bar graph. You can use any of the default delivered CRM Interactive Reports, or you can create your own interactive reports using a provided wizard available via the ANALYTICSPRO business role (Figure 7.32). The wizard provides a six-step guided procedure for creating a new report by selecting the desired fields, choosing the layout, and deciding with which users the report should be shared.

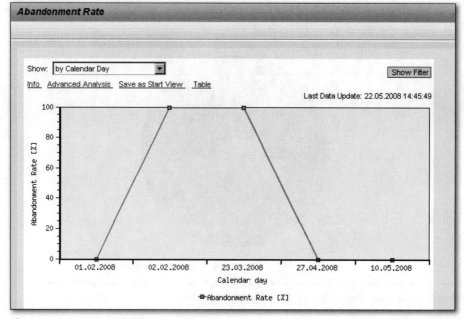

Figure 7.31 OLTP-Based CRM Interactive Reports

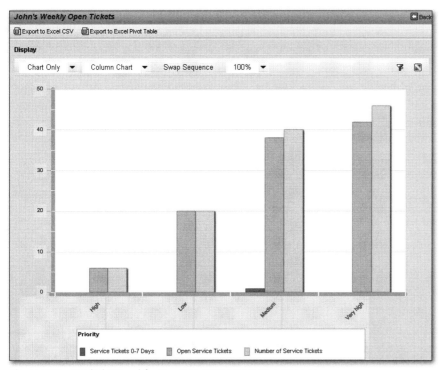

Figure 7.32 Guided Wizard for Creating CRM Interactive Reports

7.5.2 Live Interaction Reports

The Live Interactions functionality provides Interaction Center supervisors with a snapshot of how well the CTI aspects of the Interaction Center are running including traditional CTI metrics like Service Level, Connection Volume, Average Handling Time, Average Speed of Answer, and Abandonment Rate (Figure 7.31). SAP delivers these out-of-the-box reports using SAP NetWeaver BI. The reports are based on communication data that you import into SAP CRM from the Communication Management Software (CMS) system (such as SAP BCM, Genesys, etc.). The system then enriches the data with CRM business data from the SAP CRM system and exports the consolidated data to SAP NetWeaver BI. For more information, including detailed instructions on how to configure Live Interactions, please see the article, "Activate CTI Analytics to Better Monitor Your Interaction Center" by John Burton, which appears in the October 2007 issue of CRM Expert available at *http://www.crmexpertonline.com*.

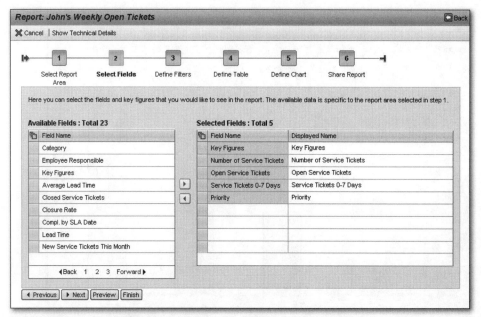

Figure 7.33 Live Interactions Abandonment Rate by Calendar Day Report

7.5.3 E-Mail Reports

E-Mail Reports, discussed in Section 7.1.3, were looked at in depth in the E-Mail Volume Report. Additionally, several other email reports are also available, including average response time (how long it takes from when the customer sends an email until they receive a response), average handling time (the actual amount of time where an agent was actively processing the email), and service level (whether customer SLAs are being met).

These reports can be utilized by all types of Interaction Center managers, including supervisors, analysts, and directors. As mentioned in Section 7.1.3, the E-Mail Reports functionality is designed specifically for the ERMS scenario, which relies on the SAPconnect interface and the Agent Inbox in the Interaction Center. For information about the reporting capabilities for real-time emails routed by additional communication management software (CMS) system, please refer to the Live Interactions reporting discussed in Section 7.5.2.

7.5.4 Blended Analytics

The IC Manager business role also provides something called Blended Analytics reports. The Blended Analytics reports extend the Live Interactions (CTI) reports, allowing supervisors to take standard CTI reports like Average Handling Time and drill down by service ticket categorization. For example, a supervisor might want to see which type of customer issues lead to the longest agent talk times. The Blended Analytics reports are available both with actual CTI integration (imported from the communication management software) as well as simulated CTI data (using Interaction Record time stamp logs to estimate when a call began and ended).

7.5.5 Intent-Driven Interaction

The last type of available reports is the Intent-Driven Interaction reports. Intent-Driven Interaction, which is covered in detail in Chapter 9, involves using the CRM Rule Modeler to automate certain types of agent guidance in the Interaction Center, such as automated alerts, scripts, and navigation. As part of Intent-Driven Interaction, analysts can optionally log all events that occur in the Interaction Center, and then export the event log to SAP NetWeaver BI for analysis. Additionally, business data such as the Interaction Record, confirmed customer and product, and business transactions can also be linked to the event logs and exported. This allows you to create your own reports in SAP NetWeaver BI, and to slice and dice the data as you see fit. Two sample reports, which you should probably not attempt to use in a productive environment, are provided to serve as a proof of concept for creating your own reports.

7.6 Dashboards

With the acquisition of Business Objects, SAP has acquired additional reporting and analytical capabilities. Many new features and products are currently being developed, even as this book was being written and sent to press. One example of the type of new functionality that Business Objects brings to SAP is something known as a dashboard (Figure 7.34). Dashboards provide business users with a very easy to understand and visually pleasing representation of real-time data. In principle, any OLTP-based CRM Interactive Report (as discussed in Section 7.5.1) could be converted into a real-time dashboard using Xcelsius technology from Business Objects.

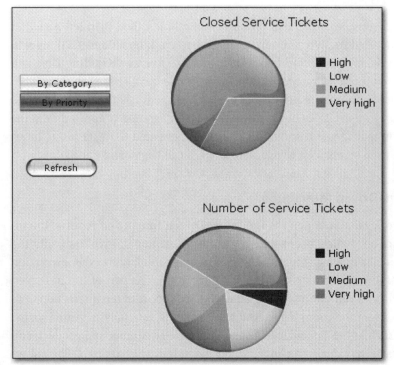

Figure 7.34 Example of Business Objects Xcelsius Dashboard

7.7 Summary

In this chapter, we discussed the topic of IC Management and Analytics. We looked at the different tools and reports available as part of the IC Manager business role, which comes standard with SAP CRM. We also discussed the different responsibilities of the various types of managers — including supervisors, analysts, and directors — responsible for running the Interaction Center.

Some of the most important points to remember from this chapter are:

▶ In CRM 2005 and CRM 4.0, the IC Manager functionality is accessed via the IC Manager role in the Enterprise Portal or SAP GUI. With CRM 2006s/CRM

2007, the IC Manager functionality is accessed via the CRM WebClient user interface.

▶ The basic areas of functionality for IC Managers include: Monitoring Operations, Managing Operations, Knowledge Management, Process Modeling, and Reports/Dashboards.

▶ The E-Mail Status Overview uses data from the CRM system to provide insight into the number of ERMS emails received and processed during the current business day. The E-Mail Volume report uses data from SAP NetWeaver BI to provide insight into the number of ERMS emails received and processed for longer, historical time periods.

▶ Broadcast messaging allows supervisors to send messages to specific agents or agent groups via scrolling text at the bottom of the agent's screen.

▶ The SAF Compilation Administration tool is required for setting up and compiling any knowledge repository for which you want agents to be able to search against from the Interaction Center, such as SAP's default knowledge repository, the Solution Database (SDB).

▶ The Alert Editor is a graphical tool for creating reusable alerts, which replaces the previous Alert Modeler configuration tool.

▶ In addition to the standard IC Manager reports, which utilize cached data from SAP NetWeaver BI, new options are available for reporting directly against live, up-to-date data in the CRM system including OLTP-based CRM Interactive Reports and Business Objects Xcelsius dashboards.

▶ Some IC Management topics such as the Interactive Script Editor, and the Rule Modeler and Category Modeler, will be discussed in separate chapters.

In the next two chapters, we will continue our analysis of IC Management functionality by diving deep into a couple of topics associated with one of the most important trends in contact center management — automated agent guidance and productivity tools. In Chapter 8, we will look at Interactive Scripting, including the Interactive Script Editor, which allows Interaction Center analysts to create detailed call scripts to guide agents through complex processes and customer interactions. Then, in Chapter 9, we will explore the Rule Modeler and Category Modeler tools, which enable various types of intelligent automation in the Interaction Center, including automated handling and processing of emails, automatic routing and escalation of service tickets, and intelligent guidance of agent navigation in the Interaction Center.

Interactive Scripts help enforce corporate standards and provide consistent customer experiences by providing agents with step-by-step scripts to guide them through customer interactions — whether via telephone, Web chat, or even emails and other offline, back-office processes.

8   Interactive Scripting

Interactive scripts provide step-by-step procedures to guide agents through customer conversations, marketing surveys, lead qualifications, sales opportunities, complex procedures, and unfamiliar processes. The goal of using scripts is to standardize the telemarketing, telesales, and customer service processes provided by your interaction center, based on best practices and centralized corporate procedures. Using scripts, you can improve the likelihood that your customers will receive uniform messaging and consistent customer experience, regardless of the skill level or experience of the agent handling the interaction. Scripts are commonly used to support marketing, sales, and collections efforts, especially in outbound call scenarios. Scripts can also be useful to walk agents through complex customer-service related procedures, like technical troubleshooting.

Your use of scripting will likely depend on the type of interaction center you are running and the skill level and experience of your agents. For example, telemarketing and telesales often rely on scripting much heavier than customer service operations. Additionally, newer, less-experienced agents typically benefit from heavy scripting more than highly-trained, experienced agents. In some situations, particularly when dealing with new agents, companies may prefer to use highly detailed scripts, instructing the agents to read verbatim from the script text. In other situations, companies may create loose scripts that only provide a rough outline for the agents to follow, allowing the agents to improvise and speak naturally using their own words.

Scripts can be as simple or as advanced as you like. For example, a script can contain basic pre-written dialogues and canned texts to guide an agent through a customer conversation. On the other hand, scripts can also be used to support more advanced tasks like helping agents overcome sales objections, qualifying sales leads, capturing post-service customer satisfaction surveys, or updating customer information and marketing attributes. Scripts typically include predefined questions and answers, as well as rebuttals to common objections. Based on the customer's response to each question, the script moves to another question, provides a rebuttal to a sales objection, navigates to a particular Interaction Center screen, opens a marketing survey/questionnaire, creates a sales lead, or launches a Web URL.

Scripts can be manually accessed by agents as required. In addition, scripts can be automatically pushed to agents based on business rules or events, such as a customer asking to open a new account, update their address or telephone number, return a product, or cancel an account. You can attach a script to a campaign, allowing the agent to directly access the script from the campaign details screen. You can also attach a script directly to a call list, causing the script to be automatically launched each time an outbound call from the call list is dialed.

> **Note**
>
> When upgrading to CRM 2006s/CRM 2007 and above from previous releases of CRM, you must manually recreate all of your scripts. Scripts created in CRM 2005 are not compatible with higher releases of CRM and will not function correctly.

8.1 Interactive Script Editor

Interactive scripts are created using a tool called the Interactive Scripting Editor. Scripts are typically created by interaction center managers. Less commonly, scripts could also be created by the marketing department. However, in such cases the marketing professional should work closely with the interaction center to make sure the scripts are appropriate. Few things annoy an interaction center agent more than being forced to use a script that clearly doesn't reflect the requirements and nuances of the interaction center.

8.1.1 Accessing the Interactive Script Editor

The Interactive Script Editor is included in the IC Manager role. In CRM 2005 and below, the IC Manager role is accessed via the Enterprise Portal under the path: PROCESS MODELING • INTERACTIVE SCRIPTING. In CRM 2006 and above, the IC Manager role is accessed via the CRM WebClient user interface; the Interactive Script is located under the menu option: PROCESS MODELING • INTERACTIVE SCRIPTING. There is a second entry under Process Modeling called Interactive Scripting (IC WinClient) that is used for SAP's older SAP GUI-based Interaction Center product.

Like several other SAP CRM graphical modeling tools, including the Workflow Editor, Campaign Automation, and Marketing Calendar, the Interactive Script Editor was built on Java-based technology from an SAP partner, Tensegrity Software (*http://www.tensigrity-software.com*). Because the Interactive Script Editor utilizes a Java Applet, it requires installation of the Sun Java Runtime Environment (JRE) on the computer of each person who will create or edit scripts. However, Sun JRE is not required to run the scripts and there is not needed to install Sun JRE on the computers of each agent.

> **Note**
>
> One of the most common issues encountered by users attempting to start the Interactive Script Editor for the first time is that Editor does not load, saying "Loading 0%".
>
> The Interactive Script Editor relies on a server-side Java Applet. In order to start the Editor, it is necessary to first install a specific version of Sun JRE. See SAP notes *717921* and *1105843* for more information on the required Sun JRE version and Java JAR (Java Archive) files for your particular CRM release.

8.1.2 Working with the Interactive Script Editor

The Interactive Script Editor consists of four separate screen areas: the script repository and toolbar, the search and navigator tool, the graphical modeling workspace and toolbar, and the properties area. See Figure 8.1.

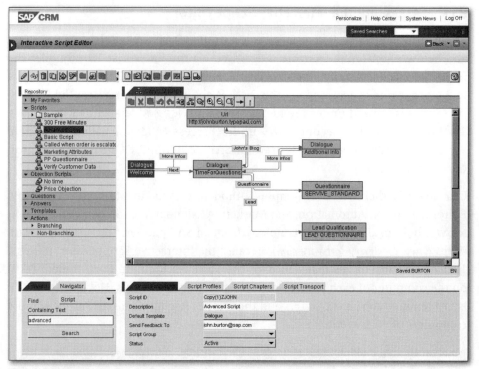

Figure 8.1 Interactive Script Editor Overview

Script Repository Area

The first screen area, located in the upper-left, contains the Repository and the Repository toolbar. The Repository is a tree structure used to store and organize your scripts (including a Favorites folder) as well as the various elements of your scripts including objection scripts, questions, answers, templates, and actions. The Repository toolbar contains buttons to provide standard functionality such as editing, displaying, copying, deleting, and renaming scripts. The toolbar also allows you to create new subfolders, add and remove scripts from the "My Favorites" folder, and access the interface for manually translating scripts. The script translation tool allows a translator to open a particular script and manually translate all of the script elements from one language to another (Figure 8.2).

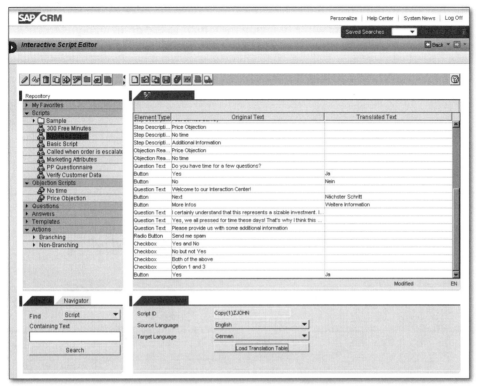

Figure 8.2 Tool for Manually Translating Script Elements of Selected Script

> **Note**
>
> Before you use the translation feature of the Interactive Script Editor, you must apply SAP note *1066900*.

Search and Navigator Area

The Search and Navigator tabs are located in the lower left. The search tool helps users quickly locate scripts or script elements via simple text search. For example, the user could type in "advanced" and the system would locate and highlight the script with the title "advanced script." The Navigator tool allows a user to focus in on a certain portion of a script by moving the purple rectangle in the Navigator area over the desired section of the script; to move the Navigator, a user simply places the cursor over the middle of the rectangle and then clicks and holds the mouse while dragging the cursor to the desired location. The user can also zoom in or out on a script or section of script by resizing the purple rectangle; to resize the Navigator, the user would place the cursor over the edge of the rectangle and click and hold the mouse while dragging the cursor to the desired zoom level (e.g., 80%, 100%, 200%, etc.), as seen in Figure 8.3.

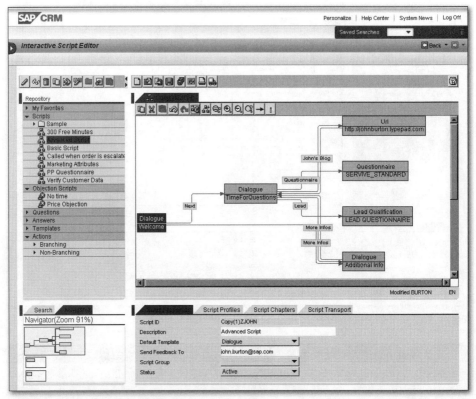

Figure 8.3 Navigator Zoom Feature

Graphical Modeling Workspace Area

The graphical modeling workspace takes up the largest section of the screen and appears on the upper right. The workspace provides visualization of the selected scripts and script elements. When working with a script, you can see the complete process flow of the script, including the decision-tree structure and the links between questions (see Figure 8.4). When working with other script elements such as questions you can see the text of the question as well as any answers, including text fields, pushbuttons, drop-down list boxes, radio buttons, or checkboxes that have been included with the question.

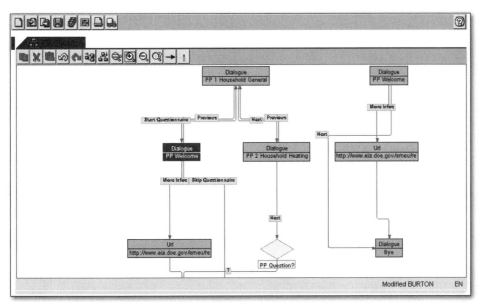

Figure 8.4 Graphical Visualization of Script Process Flow

The graphical modeling workspace contains two toolbars: a generic application toolbar with functions relevant across all script elements, and a specific toolbar with functions unique to the selected script element. The generic toolbar provides features such as New (to create a new Question, Button, Action, Script, Objection Script, or Field), Upload and Download (for saving a backup of the script locally on your computer as XML file), Save, Save All, Close, Print, and Transport (for transporting a script from, for example, a sandbox system to a test system). The second toolbar, with functions specific to the selected script element, provides different buttons depending on the selected object. For example, when working with a script, you will have buttons such as Copy, Cut, Paste, Undo, Redo, Horizontal Layout, Vertical Layout, Fit Graph to Window, Zoom In, Zoom Out, Interactive Zoom (which allows you to zoom in on a selected node), Insert Link (for linking questions together), and Status (which activates and deactivates a script). When selecting a question, several different buttons will be available in the toolbar such as Add Question, Add Answer Area, and Add Button Area.

Properties Area

The script properties area displays the details and properties of the selected script or script element. When working with a script, for example, the properties area will display various tabs such as the script properties (ID, description, default template, email address for feedback, script group, and status), list of profiles to which the script is assigned, chapters of the script, and script transport request details. If an individual node of a script is selected, the properties area will additionally display the node properties (description, template, chapter, and flag to indicate whether it is the starting node of the script) and, if a template is selected, the parameters of the template (such questionnaire ID for Questionnaires, transaction type for Leads, or URL and new window flag for Web URLs). See Figure 8.5.

Figure 8.5 Properties Area Showing Properties of Selected Script and Script Elements

8.1.3 Creating Scripts

An interactive script consists of a series of questions and related answers. The answers can be represented as push buttons, radio buttons, check boxes, text fields, or drop-down list boxes. In addition, scripts can include other elements such as actions (ABAP classes that perform some calculation or process some data) and templates (predefined sets of attributes that define the appearance and behavior or scripts). Before you begin creating a script, you first need to create the various elements that you plan to use in the script. The best place to start is with the questions.

Questions are the blocks of texts that the agent will read to the customer. Although we refer to these text blocks as questions, they could just as well be statements rather than actual questions. By default, each new question that you create will contain an area to enter the text that the agent will read to the customer. It is possible to include variables, such as the customer's name, in the text of the question by dragging and dropping the relevant text fields from the Repository into the text area. Oddly enough, the "Text Fields" folder containing the variables is located under the "Answers" folder rather than the "Questions" folder in the Repository.

In addition to the text of the question, you can also assign answers directly to the question via the "Add Answer Area" and "Add Button Area" buttons in the

Question toolbar (Figure 8.6). The answer area, which can contain text fields, drop-down list boxes, check boxes, or radio buttons, are useful for questions that require an actual response from the customer. Based on the values entered by the agent, the script can automatically branch to another question using a predefined action referred to as a "branching action." Additionally, the system could optionally update the customer's data based on the information entered.

However, not all answers require the agent to solicit detailed feedback from the customer. In some cases, a simple short answer such as "Yes or No" answer may suffice. In other cases where no actual response is required from the customer, a simple "Next" button is useful. In these situations, push buttons provide the ideal solution. The recommended best practice is to assign the desired push buttons directly to the question. This way, when later linking two questions, the system will automatically propose the push buttons you have assigned. If you don't assign push buttons directly to the question, you can always manually assign a push button to the link between the two questions; however, this process is cumbersome and not recommended.

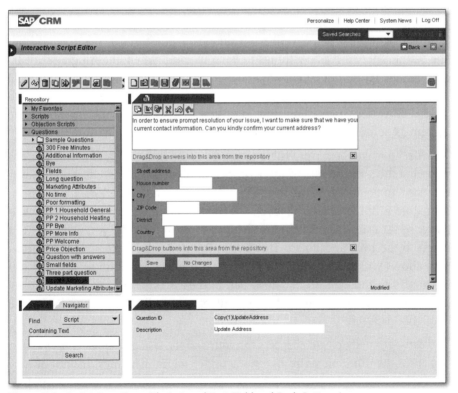

Figure 8.6 Script Question with Assigned Text Field and Push Button Answers

Once you have created all the questions (with assigned answers and buttons) that you plan to use in your script, you can begin creating the script. Drag and drop each question into the new, blank script. The first question you add to the script will be marked as the "Starting Node." However, you can always change this by clicking on a different question and marking that question as the starting node in the script properties area. To link the questions and create your process flow, click the "Insert Link" button. Now place the mouse over your starting node and click and hold the mouse down while dragging the cursor to the question that you want to link. As you release the mouse, the two questions will be connected. The system will prompt you to select a button to use to connect the questions. However, as mentioned, you can also manually drag and drop a button from the Repository onto the link — in which case the button will appear as part of the question when the agent accesses the script at runtime in the Interaction Center.

After you have created the process flow of your script, you need to maintain the script properties and the properties of the individual nodes.

▶ For each script, you need to maintain the script ID, description, and status. You can optionally also maintain a script authorization group and an email address to which agents can send feedback if they have questions or comments about the script. There are a few things to keep in mind when choosing a script ID because the ID cannot be changed once it is saved: The script ID should be 32 characters or less and should contain alpha numeric characters only with no special characters such as ampersand or brackets, which are interpreted by the system as being HTML or XML characters.

▶ In order to make the script visible to agents in the Interaction Center, you need to assign the script to one or more scripts profiles, with the script profile being assigned to an IC WebClient Profile (CRM 2005 and below) or a CRM Business Role (CRM 2006s and above). If you have not created a script profile and assigned it to an IC WebClient Profile or CRM Business Role, you will first need to go to the IMG and do so. The "Script Profiles" tab in the script properties area allows you to assign the script to one or more script profiles. You can also set a valid-to and valid-from date as part of the assignment. If you don't set any dates, the script will be immediately available and will continue to be available until 12/31/9999.

▶ You can optionally create chapters for your scripts. Using chapters allow you to structure the different script questions under logical headings, making it easy for Interaction Center agents to see where they currently are in the script process flow. Additionally, experienced agents can use the script overview control in the Interaction Center to jump ahead or back within a script to a particular question by chapter. To create new chapters, click on the "Script Chapters" tab in the script properties area. For each chapter you want to add, click the Add icon and enter the title of the chapter. Once you have created all of chapters, click on a question node and assign the desired chapter using the drop-down list box in the properties area.

▸ You can set authorization levels for scripts in the Interactive Script Editor in case you only want to give certain user groups access to only display scripts but not to edit or delete scripts. Script authorization groups are defined in the IMG with transaction "CRMC_ISE_GRP" accessible via the IMG menu path: SAP IMPLEMENTATION GUIDE • CUSTOMER RELATIONSHIP MANAGEMENT • INTERACTION CENTER WEBCLIENT • ADDITIONAL FUNCTIONS • DEFINE SCRIPT AUTHORIZATION GROUPS. Then the script authorization groups are assigned to the authorization profile for a chosen CRM business role in transaction PFCG with the authorization object CRM_IC_SCR.

8.1.4 Creating Objection Scripts

Objection Scripts are a special type of script. Objection scripts cannot be launched directly, but rather are selected from within another script. Typically, objection scripts are used to provide rebuttals to common objections or concerns that a customer might voice during the processing of a script. For example, if the script is designed to solicit orders for a new service, that customer might object, stating that they don't have time right now or that the price is too high. The objection scripts could contain guidance to the agent on how to potentially overcome these objections. To make an objection script available to agents as part of another script, simply drag and drop the desired objection scripts from the script repository into a script that is being edited. The objection scripts can be linked into the script like normal questions, but it is not necessary to do so. Once an objection script is added to a main script, the objection script will be available for selection by the agents when they are processing the main script. In the following example, you can see two objection scripts — price objection and time objection — on the right side of the script that is being edited. Note that the objection scripts are not connected into the normal process flow of the main script (Figure 8.7).

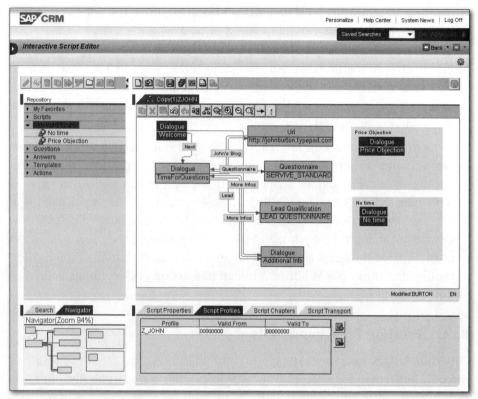

Figure 8.7 Objection Scripts

8.1.5 Transporting Scripts

It is possible to transport scripts from one SAP CRM system or client to another system or client. In order to transport a script, you first have to make the script inactive. Once you select an inactive script in the Repository and click the Transport button, a transport request will be created for your user in the background, assuming that your user has authorization to generate transport requests in the SAP GUI Transports Organizer (i.e., transaction SE09). The user is not able to manually select an existing transport request, but rather a new transport request will be created for each script that is to be transported. When the transported button is pressed, the entire script, including all questions, answers, buttons, fields, actions, and profiles, will be selected and added to the transport request.

In addition to transporting scripts, you can also download and upload scripts to your local drive. Downloading scripts allows you to create backup versions of your scripts locally, which are stored as XML files. This can be very useful for analyzing and troubleshooting scripts. It is also possible to use the download and upload functionality to actually upload scripts from your local drive to the same (or another) CRM system or client. Some companies use the script download and upload functionality in lieu of the script transport functionality. Please be aware however that you can only download and upload complete scripts not individual elements of a script such as a question or answer. Also, if the target system already has a script with the same ID, the script will not be uploaded. Finally, after downloading and uploading the script, you will need to redo the script profile assignment because only the script data itself is transported not the related IMG configuration such as the assigned script profiles.

For the mentioned reasons, SAP recommends using the transport functionality, rather than the download and upload functionality, for transporting scripts between systems. Additionally, depending on the policies and procedures of your company's IT organization, business users (like marketing professionals and interaction center managers) may be prohibited from transporting or uploading scripts into certain systems, such as a production system. To ensure full compliance and visibility with their IT departments, many companies prefer to use the script transport functionality rather than the upload and download functionality. Many companies only allow their business users to create scripts, and request that the transport of scripts be initiated by an SAP technical consultant, and that the release of the transport request be handled by a SAP basis consultant. Regardless of the approach you decide on, transport or upload, once you manage to get your scripts into the system you are ready to test them out. Let's look at how interactive scripts can be launched.

8.2 Launching Interactive Scripts in the Interaction Center

Once you have created your scripts in the Interactive Script Editor and assigned the scripts to the script profiles, interaction center agents will be able to select and access the scripts at runtime. By default, all agents will be able to manually select scripts that are included in the profiles to which they are assigned. Agents can also manually access scripts that are attached to campaigns. In addition, there are various options for automatically launching scripts based on call lists, Interaction Center events, or combinations of events and business data; these options will depend on your particular version of SAP CRM.

8.2.1 Manual Selection of Scripts

Allowing agents to manually select scripts is an ideal strategy for users who only need occasional access to scripts, and who need to be able to choose from several different scripts. For example, an agent might need to pull up a script if a customer wants to make a change to their account, such as updating their address, contact information, preferences, or marketing attributes. Scripts can also be a useful tool for helping agents respond to inquiries for the latest company information regarding topics like shipping rates or return policies. To access an interactive script, the agent clicks on the "Scripts" link in the navigation bar and then click on the "Launch: Script Name" drop-down list box and select the desired script (Figure 8.8).

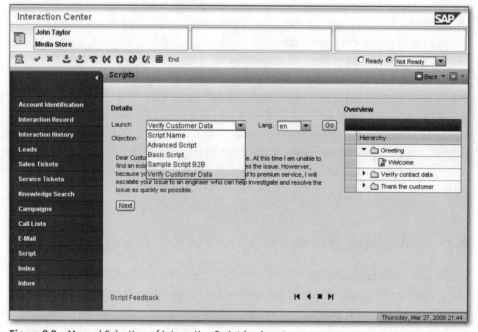

Figure 8.8 Manual Selection of Interactive Script by Agent

In addition, it is also possible to open scripts that have been assigned to a marketing campaign by clicking on the script name (which appears as a hyperlink) in the campaign details screen. This can be useful if a customer refers to a particular campaign or promotion, allowing the agent to quickly and easily pull up the linked script. It would be very inconvenient, especially if a large number of campaigns are executed in parallel with a company, to cluster the script selection drop-down list box with a separate script for each campaign and to force the user to search through the long list for the correct script.

8.2.2 Automatically Launching Scripts

Allowing agents to manually access scripts on an occasional basis as required is a great strategy for users who only need to access scripts infrequently and who need to be able to select from several different scripts. On the other hand, for heavy users of scripts, or for users who need to access the same script for each customer interaction, it is generally preferable to automatically launch the desired script with each interaction, rather than forcing the agent to spend time manually opening scripts many times each day. There are a couple of options for automatically launching scripts, depending on your business process and your CRM release. In all releases, you can automatically launch a script when dialing outbound calls from a call list. Depending on which CRM release you are using, you may have the ability to automatically launch scripts based either on Interaction Center events, or based on business rules (using a combination of Interaction Center events and business data).

Launching Scripts via Call Lists

If you are using call lists as part of an outbound marketing campaign, you can attach a particular script directly to the call list so that the script is automatically launched each time and outbound call from the call list is dialed and connected with the recipient. If using the "Generate Business Transactions and Call Lists" functionality (SAP GUI transaction code CRMD_CALL_LIST), you can assign the script in the area of the screen entitled "Call List" in the field "IC WebClient Script." See Figure 8.9.

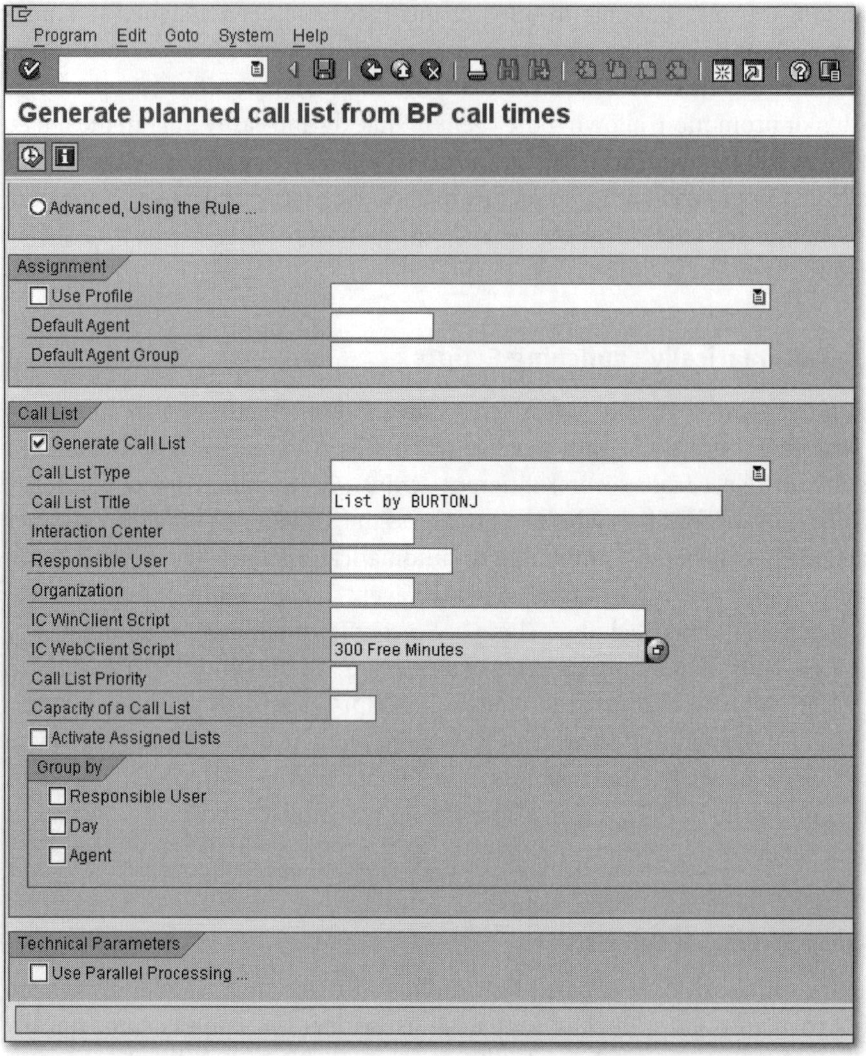

Figure 8.9 Attaching Interactive Script to Call List via Generate Business Transactions and Call Lists

If using the "Call List Maintenance" functionality (SAP GUI transaction code CRMD_CALL_LIST), you can assign the script by clicking on the "Business Context" section of a selected call list and clicking the icon with the tooltip "Add IC WebClient Script." See Figure 8.10.

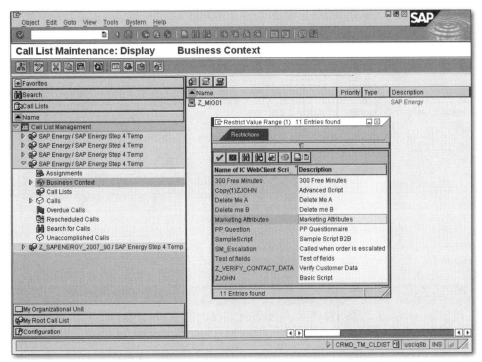

Figure 8.10 Attaching Script to Call List via Call List Maintenance

Launching Scripts via IC Events (CRM 2005 and CRM 4.0 Add-on for Service Industries)

In CRM 2005 and CRM 4.0 Add-on for Service Industries, it is possible to launch a specific script whenever a certain IC event is raised. For example, perhaps you want to trigger a script that displays the customer's marketing attributes after a customer is confirmed in the Account Identification area, and you want to trigger a different script whenever a Chat message arrives from a customer. To map an interactive script to an IC event, assign both the script and the event to an entry in the "Events" folder in transaction CRMC_IC_SCRIPT accessible via the IMG menu path: SAP IMPLEMENTATION GUIDE • CUSTOMER RELATIONSHIP MANAGEMENT • INTERACTION CENTER WEBCLIENT • BASIC FUNCTIONS – DEFINE SCRIPT PROFILES (Figure 8.11). In addition, it is possible to specify that the script should only be launched when certain conditions are true. This can be done by using optional parameters. For example, you could create your own custom ABAP event class that has a parameter called "Customer Type." Then, in the configuration shown in Figure 8.11, you could indicate that the script should only be launched if the desired IC event is triggered and if the customer type equals "Gold" for example.

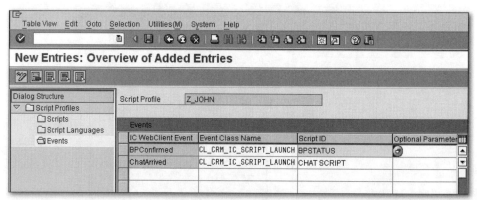

Figure 8.11 Launch Interactive Scripts via Mapped IC Events

Launching Scripts via Business Rules (CRM 2006s and above)

In CRM 2006s and above, the IMG configuration for launching interactive scripts based on IC events has been replaced with more powerful functionality that uses the SAP CRM Rule Modeler to launch scripts based on business rules. This ability to launch scripts based on business rules is part of a new CRM capability called Intent-Driven Interaction, which can perform a variety of rule-based Interaction Center related actions, such as launching scripts, triggering and terminating alerts, adding items to an agent to-do reminder list, and automatically creating new business transactions and navigating agents to other screens. Intent-Driven Interaction is discussed in detail in Chapter 7, IC Management and Analytics. Here, we will only focus on the script launching capabilities of Intent-Driven Interaction.

To launch scripts using Intent-Driven Interaction, you need to create business rules using a tool called the Rule Modeler. In CRM 2005, the Rule Modeler can be accessed in the Enterprise Portal with the IC Manager role under the menu path: PROCESS MODELING • RULE MODELER. You can also start the Rule Modeler application directly in CRM 2005 without using the Enterprise Portal by launching the

BSP application "CRMM_ERM_RULES" directly from transaction SE80. In CRM 2006s and above, the Rule Modeler can be accessed in the CRM WebClient via the IC_MANAGER business role under the menu path: PROCESS MODELING • CREATE: RULE POLICY.

The CRM Rule Modeler is used across SAP CRM by many different applications for many several purposes, including E-Mail Response Management System (ERMS), Marketing E-Mail Bounce Management, Order Routing, Lead Distribution, Opportunity Distribution, Account Assignment, and Intent-Driven Interaction in the Interaction Center. Each of the applications, or *contexts,* provides its own set of out of the box functionality. Therefore, when you start the Rule Modeler you must first specify which context you will be working with before you can create a new set of rules or search for an existing rule policy. In this case, we will be working with the context Intent-Driven Interaction (IC WebClient), which is the context used for launching scripts, as well as for other Interaction Center–specific actions such as triggering alerts, adding items to the agent wrap-up list, automatically navigating the agent to different screens, and so on. See Figure 8.12.

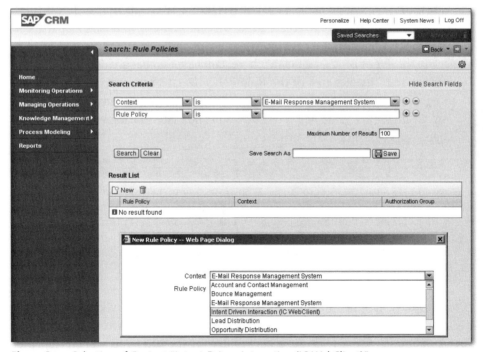

Figure 8.12 Selection of Context "Intent-Driven Interaction (IC WebClient)"

To create a new rule policy, select the context Intent-Driven Interaction (IC Web-Client), and enter a name for your new rule policy. A new policy will be created with an active variant and an empty set of draft rules (see Chapter 9, Rule Modeler and Category Modeler, for more details on variants and draft rules). You can provide a description for your policy variant such as "standard rules," "holiday rules," and so on. You can also choose a default language. The rest of the fields, such as "Created On," will be filled by the system.

The first, and most important, step to creating your rules is to click on the root node in the tree hierarchy on the left side of the screen (i.e., the name of your new policy) where you will maintain the Rule Policy Details, Business Roles, and IC Events. These settings are absolutely critical.

▶ The Business Roles area allows you to specify for which CRM business roles the policy should be used. This will ultimately dictate which agents or agents groups are affected by the rules. If you don't assign any business roles to the policy, the rules won't actually be used by anyone.

▶ The IC Events area is also very important in that this is where you declare the IC events that you plan to later use as the triggering events in your business rules. For example, if you plan to create a rule that automatically launches a particular script every time customer is confirmed by an agent, then you would need to declare the event BP_CONFIRMED here. Only events that are declared up front here in the IC Events area of the Rule Policy Details screen will later be available for use when creating rules. If you don't declare any events here, you will only see an empty value help drop-down list box later during you rule creation when you try to pick a triggering event for your rule.

Note

When creating business rules to launch scripts, you will trigger each rule with a particular IC event and then optionally evaluate additional business data. When selecting the triggering IC events, you can use any of the out of the box IC events or you can create your own events in transaction CRMC_IC_EVENT_REP. See the section on Intent-Driven Interaction in Chapter 9, Rule Modeler and Category Modeler, for more information on how to define your own IC events.

After you have assigned the desired business roles to the policy and declared the events that you plan to use, you can now select the draft rules node and click the Create Subnode button to create a new folder for the rules you will create. After giving the folder a name and description, click the Create Subnode button again to actually create a new blank rule. After you provide a name and description, it is time to create the condition for your rule. If you think of a rule as an if-then statement, the condition is the "if" statement that determines whether the rule evaluates to true and whether the corresponding action (or actions) in the rule get executed. Click the Add Entry button in the Conditions area to begin adding a new condition to the new rule. A blank condition will be added (Figure 8.13).

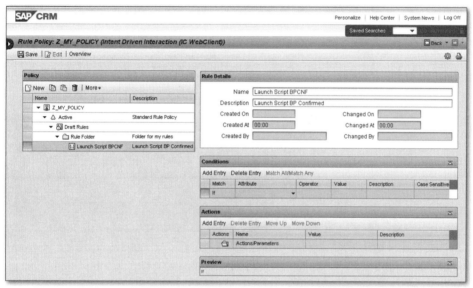

Figure 8.13 Adding New Condition to Rule

The next step is to choose the attribute "CurrentEvent." All rules in the Intent-Driven Interaction context must start with this attribute. Leave the value of the operator as "Equals" and then select the IC event that you want to use in your rule. The drop-down list box will provide a list of IC events based on the events you declared earlier in the rule policy node. If you don't see any events listed, or you don't see the event you want to use, go back to the policy node and declare the desired events. In this example, we want to launch a particular script each time a new customer calls in and is confirmed by the agent, so we will choose the event "BPConfirmed." See Figure 8.14. Optionally, we could add additional rule conditions, for example, to check whether the customer has a certain status (e.g., Gold).

> **Note**
>
> This is very important. All rules in the Intent-Driven Context must begin with the attribute "CurrentEvent" in order to work properly. You may optionally add additional attributes to check other business data (such as the priority of a service ticket of the marketing attributes of a customer) but the first attribute must always be "CurrentEvent."

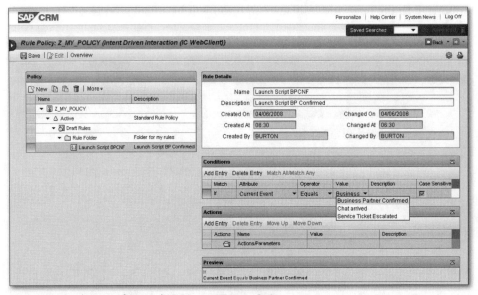

Figure 8.14 Selection of Desired IC Event to Trigger Script

The next, and most important, step is to add an action to launch the desired script. You can do this by clicking the "Add Entry" button on the Actions area and choosing the action "Launch Script" and then choosing the name of the script you want to be launched (Figure 8.15). Finally, you would save your policy, check and release your draft rules (using the "More" button), and then re-save your policy again. Your policy will now be released and your rules will be active. Whenever an agent, who is assigned to the business role you linked to the policy, confirms a customer, the selected interactive script will be automatically launched.

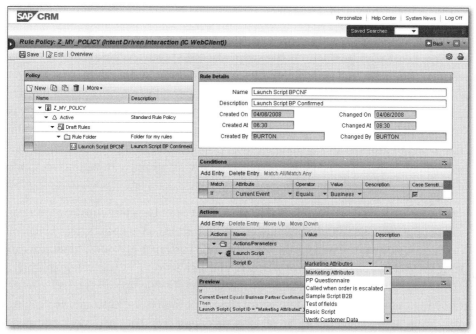

Figure 8.15 Selection of Desired Interactive Script to be Launched

8.3 Using Interactive Scripts in the Interaction Center

When an agent accesses a script, regardless of which method the script was launched, the script will provide the agent with questions or other information to read to the customer. Based on the customer's response, the script automatically navigates the agent to the appropriate next question, objection rebuttal screen, URL, or business transaction, such as a survey or lead. For agents who engage in Web chats with customers, the script can automatically insert text into the Web chat editor. In the event the agent needs to transfer the customer to another agent or department during the middle of a script, the script and any recorded customer information will be transferred along with the telephone, Web chat, or email. Finally, once an agent reaches the end of a script, the script can automatically navigate the agent back to any other Interaction Center screen or transaction.

8.3.1 Questions and Answers

Interactive scripts provide agents with step-by-step guidance for navigating through a customer interaction. The script can either provide the agent with exact text that should be read verbatim to the customer, or the script can merely provide a framework with general guidance to assist the agent if needed. The texts that are presented to the agent — presumably to read to the customer — are referred to as script *questions,* although they need not be in actual questions; they could also be statements or affirmations ("Thank you for doing business with us," or "Yes, I can help you with that," for example). Scripts can provide agents with various methods of capturing the responses of the customer.

The customer responses are referred to *answers* and can be represented by a variety of input options, including push buttons, radio buttons, checkboxes, text fields, or drop down listboxes. Based on the answer of the customer provides, the script can navigate to another question, or perform another action like launching an object script, navigating to another screen or transaction, or opening a Web URL. In the following example, in the first question the agent thanks the customer for calling and asking how the agent can be of assistance; based on the customer's response the agent can navigate to product information, make changes or updates to the customer's account information, create a sales order, or transfer the customer to the account retention team (Figure 8.16).

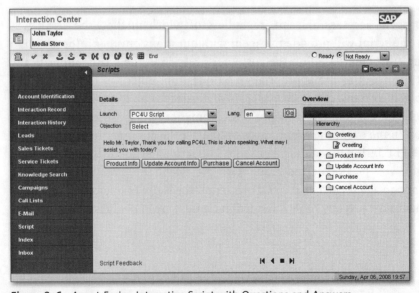

Figure 8.16 Agent-Facing Interactive Script with Questions and Answers

8.3.2 Objection Scripts

Even the best designed scripts don't work 100% of the time. Whether you are executing a marketing campaign, telesales drive, or performing technical trouble-shooting, sometimes customers aren't interested, change their minds, or don't want to participate. For example, a customer might say that he doesn't have time, your prices are too high, he's already doing business with someone else, doesn't need your product or service, and so on. You can model rebuttals to these types of common objections and make the rebuttals available to agents within the main script via objection scripts. If one or more objection scripts have been attached to the main script that the agent is executing, the agent can view and launch the objection scripts from the Objection drop-down listbox (Figure 8.17). The objection script can contain one or multiple questions and can optionally be connected back to the main script by the person designing the script in the Interactive Script Editor. However, even if the objection script does not link back to the main script, the agent can navigate back to the appropriate question in the main script by clicking on the appropriate chapter in the script overview on the right-hand side of the script area. The overview continues to show the chapters of the main script, not the objection script.

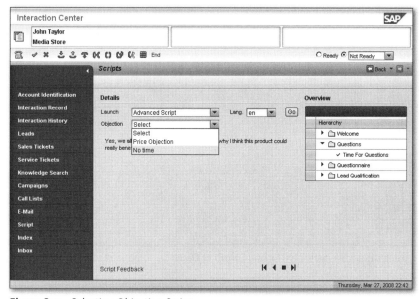

Figure 8.17   Selecting Objection Script

8.3.3 Updating Master Data and Marketing Attributes

Interactive Scripting can speed up and simplify the process of updating customer data. Quite commonly, customers may want to make changes to the contact information or account preferences. In addition, companies always want to make sure they have current addresses and contact information for customers, especially in situations where a field service technician or customer support person might need to make a site visit or contact the customer. Using scripts, agents can update customer data directly from within the script without navigating to the customer details screen in order to update address data or marketing attributes. In the following example, the customer address information has been brought into the script, allowing the agent to update any of the address fields as necessary (Figure 8.18). Similarly, it is possible to pull in other data as well, such as customer marketing attributes.

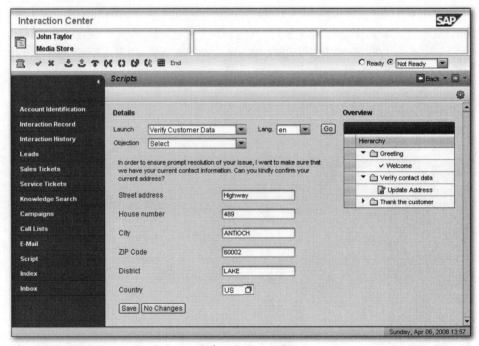

Figure 8.18 Using Interactive Script to Update Customer Data

8.3.4 Survey Integration

It is possible to integrate surveys, polls, and questionnaires into an Interactive Script using the Survey template provided in the Interactive Script Editor. The interaction center manager or marketing professional creating the script can specify the application ID, questionnaire ID, and version for the desired survey. It is important to note that in order to include surveys in a script, the surveys must first be created in a separate tool called the Survey Suite, accessible in SAP GUI via transaction "CRM_SURVEY_SUITE" or IMG menu path: SAP IMPLEMENTATION GUIDE • CUSTOMER RELATIONSHIP MANAGEMENT • TRANSACTIONS • SETTINGS FOR LEADS • QUESTIONNAIRES FOR LEADS • DEFINE QUESTIONNAIRES. For example, in Figure 8.19, you can see a survey called Service Contract Renewal created in the folder Service. In Figure 8.20, you can see that this same survey has been integrated into an Interactive Script, allowing the agent to utilize this survey to check whether a customer is potentially interested in renewing their service contract for another one, two, or three years.

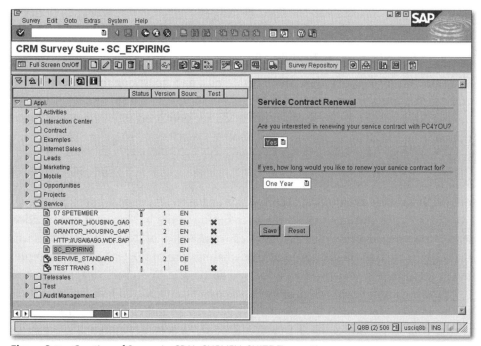

Figure 8.19 Creation of Survey in CRM_SURVEY_SUITE Transaction

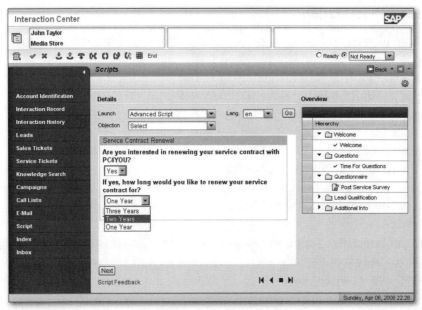

Figure 8.20 Integration of Survey into Interactive Script

8.3.5 Creating and Qualifying Leads

In addition to integrating regular surveys, polls, and questionnaires into a script, you can also integrate special lead qualification surveys to automatically create and qualify a lead via an interactive script. To do so, you need to create a lead questionnaire in SAP GUI transaction CRM_SURVEY_SUITE and assign the lead to your script using the Lead template in the Interactive Script Editor.

When an Interaction Center agent accesses a script that contains a built-in lead questionnaire, the agent can fill out the survey based on the customers input (Figure 8.21). When the agent clicks the Save button at the bottom of the embedded lead questionnaire in the script, a business transaction of type Lead will be automatically created in the background. The qualification of the lead as, for example, hot, warm, or cold will also be performed automatically in the background. The Interaction Center agent can display the automatically created lead by navigating to the Interaction Record link in the Navigation Bar and clicking on the Lead in the Activity Clipboard of the Interaction Record. As seen in Figure 8.22, the automatically created lead contains the survey data filled in by the agent as well as the qualification level of the lead determined by the system. Based on the qualification level, the lead would later be distributed by a lead dispatcher to a sales professional, such as an inside sales rep.

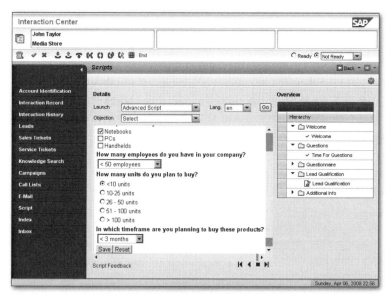

Figure 8.21 Integration of Lead Qualification Questionnaire in Script

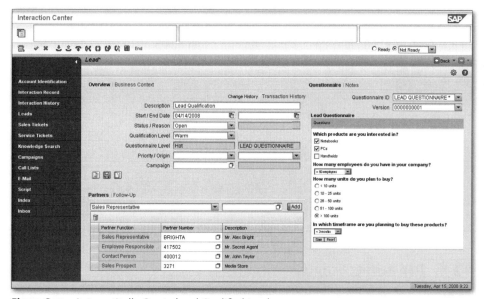

Figure 8.22 Automatically Created and Qualified Lead

8.3.6 Chat Integration

Interactive Scripting is not just for telephone calls. Scripts can also be useful in other situations as well, such as when interacting with customers via Web chat. When defining your scripts in the Interactive Script Editor, you can change the template used for any question from the standard "Dialogue" template to the "Chat node" template. Setting the chat node for a script question will cause the text of the question to be automatically inserted into the chat editor screen if the agent is in an active chat session. Automatically inserting text saves time for the agent, increases accuracy and consistency of responses, and reduces spelling and grammar mistakes by eliminating, or at least significantly reducing, the need for the agents to manually type chat responses. Of course, even though the text is automatically inserted into the chat editor from the script question, the agent still has the opportunity to modify or change the text before pressing the Send button. See Figure 8.23.

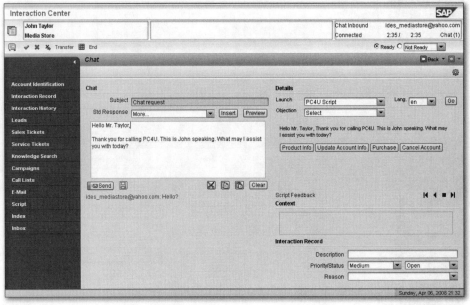

Figure 8.23 Interactive Script with Chat Integration

8.3.7 Transferring Scripts

Sometimes an agent is not able to resolve a customer's issue and needs to transfer the customer to another agent, or to another department. When transferring customers from one agent to another using the SAP CRM Interaction Center, by default, all of the business objects involved in the current interaction (i.e., everything listed in the Activity Clipboard of the Interaction Record) are transferred along with the telephone call, chat, or email. However, typically any other screens or information is not transferred. For example, if the agent is doing a knowledge search, the search query and the results list of the search will not be transferred; only solutions that have been added to cart and placed into the Activity Clipboard will be transferred. However, Interactive Scripting is an exception to this rule. When transferring a partially completed (in process) script, the script information is transferred along with the other information. When the new agent receives the transferred call, chat, or email, the script is opened to the step where the first agent left off.

8.4 Summary

In this chapter, we looked at the capabilities and benefits of Interactive Scripting. We learned about the requirements for accessing and using the Interactive Script Editor in order to create and edit scripts. We also covered the basic layout and functions of the Interactive Script Editor including how to create, translate, transport, and upload and download scripts. Finally, we discussed the different options for accessing and using scripts in the Interaction Center.

Some of the most important points to remember from this chapter are:

▶ Interactive scripts provide your Interaction Center agents with step-by-step procedures to assist agents in executing telemarketing promotions, telesales campaigns, and customer service efforts.

▶ Scripts help ensure that your agents provide uniform and consistent messaging to customers, regardless of agent skill level.

▶ The Interactive Script Editor tool allows managers to create and reuse elements of scripts including questions, answers, actions, custom fields, and templates.

▶ You can use interactive scripts in the Interaction Center to capture customer surveys, and to automatically create and qualify sales leads using lead questionnaires.

▶ Scripts can be accessed manually by agents, either by clicking on the link attached to a marketing campaign, or by selecting the desired script from a list of scripts to which the agent has been assigned. Scripts can also be launched automatically based on IC events or business rules.

In the next chapter, we will look at two additional modeling tools available to Interaction Center managers that help provide intelligent, rule-based guidance to Interaction Center agents, the Rule Modeler and the Category Modeler.

"Rules and models destroy genius and art."
— *William Hazlitt*

9   Rule Modeler and Category Modeler

Business Rules Management (BRM) and Business Rules Engines (BRE) have been industry hot topics for the past few years. Fundamentally, these concepts are about standardizing and automating your company's work processes in order to make correct (and consistent) decisions with limited human intervention. This is especially relevant to the Interaction Center, where you always want customers to receive the same high-quality service, answers and solutions, regardless of the skill and experience of the agent they are dealing with. By creating business rules based on corporate best practices, you remove the need for each agent to make their own decisions about how to handle specific situations, thus increasing quality and consistency (though perhaps at the cost of "genius and art"). Granted, this does not mean that your agents can now shut off their brains completely, or that you can replace all your agents with robots. Rather, this simply means that your company can model certain processes and decisions, providing your agents with rule-based recommendations and other tools to help achieve your desired business outcomes.

The Rule Modeler and Category Modeler are two tools, which work together, to provide intelligent agent guidance and automation in the Interaction Center. Both tools are configured by Interaction Center analysts from the IC Manager business role. The Rule Modeler is used for creating, maintaining, and administering rules and rule policies (collections of related rules) that ultimately control the behavior of the Interaction Center application. Areas of the Interaction Center that rely upon the Rule Modeler include E-Mail Response Management System (ERMS), Order Routing (dispatching and escalation of service tickets), and Intent-Driven Interaction (rule-based agent guidance). The Category Modeler is used for creating multi-level hierarchies of categories that can be used within business transactions (e.g., service tickets) in the Interaction Center to accurately classify issues — and ultimately to trigger automatic suggestion of solutions and one-click auto completion of business transactions via linked templates.

9.1   Rule Modeler

The CRM Rule Modeler was first introduced in CRM 4.0 Add-on for Service Industries Extension as part of SAP CRM E-Mail Response Management System (ERMS). Originally, the Rule Modeler was developed exclusively for use with ERMS, but was later extended for use in various other applications including Marketing Bounce Management, Lead Distribution, Opportunity Distribution, Order Routing (dispatching and escalation of service tickets), and so on. The Rule Modeler is targeted at business users such as analysts who need a graphical, natural language-based tool that doesn't require complicated coding, algorithms, calculations, or functional derivations. The idea behind the CRM Rule Modeler, compared to other business rules management tools, is that you shouldn't need a Ph.D. in Computer Science or Computational Mathematics to create a few simple business rules.

The Rule Modeler provides a flexible, powerful, and easy-to-use environment that allows you to author, maintain, and administrate your business rules. When using the Rule Modeler, you create policies, which contain rules that combine conditions with actions. A *policy* can be thought of as a collection of related rules. A *rule* is essentially a type of if-then statement where, based on whether one or more conditions are true, you execute one or more actions. Figure 9.1 shows an example of a rule policy and a selected rule in the CRM Rule Modeler.

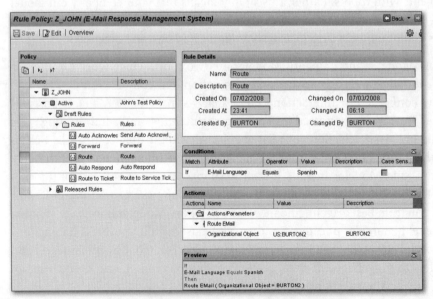

Figure 9.1   Rule Details for a Selected Rule in the CRM Rule Modeler

A rule *condition* is a combination of an attribute, an operator, and a value. A typical condition can be an expression like, "If the service ticket is high priority," or "If the email subject or body contains keywords A and B, and not C." The *attribute* is the thing you are checking against (e.g., service ticket priority, email subject, etc.). The *operator* compares the attribute with the value; typical operators are: is, is not, contains, does not contain, is greater, is less than, is greater than or equal to, is less than or equal to, etc. The *value* is the result you want to check against (e.g., high priority; keyword A, B, C; etc.). An *action* is a predefined service that you want to execute such as automatically replying to an email, routing a service ticket to a new processor, or automatically navigating an IC agent to a particular screen or transaction. Actions can have *parameters,* which influence the execution of the action. For example, for the Send Auto Acknowledgement action one of the parameter would be the ID of the email template that you want to use for the automated acknowledgement (Figure 9.4).

The Rule Modeler is delivered with a default *Repository* containing out of the box attributes (conditions), logical operators, and actions that you can use in the creation of your rules. You can extend the repository with your own attributes and actions if desired, by creating your own services (i.e., ABAP classes). You can view the Repository from the IMG via path: SAP IMPLEMENTATION GUIDE • CUSTOMER RELATIONSHIP MANAGEMENT • E-MAIL RESPONSE MANAGEMENT SYSTEM • DEFINE REPOSITORY. An Interaction Center analysts or other business user will not typically need to access the repository; rather, configuration of available attributes, operators, and actions in the repository is something that would be done by a technical consultant or other IT user.

The Rule Modeler is also delivered out of the box with *Service manager profiles* for each Rule Modeler context. For example, the default service manager profile for ERMS is literally named "DEFAULT," the default service manager profile for Order Routing is "SAP_ORDERROUTING," and the default service manager profile for Intent-Driven Interaction is "IDI_DEFAULT." The service manager profile essentially controls the Rule Modeler by specifying, for example, which rule policy should be used. The service manager profile also controls other aspects of the Rule Modeler as well, such as indicating in ERMS which transaction type (e.g., TSVO or TSRV) should be used when automatically creating new service orders/tickets via an action. You can access the service manager profile via the IMG path: SAP IMPLEMENTATION GUIDE • CUSTOMER RELATIONSHIP MANAGEMENT • E-MAIL RESPONSE MANAGEMENT SYSTEM • DEFINE SERVICE MANAGER PROFILES (**Figure 9.2**).

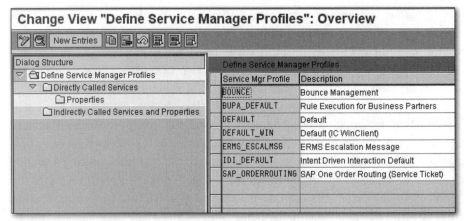

Figure 9.2 Define Service Manager Profiles for Rule Modeler

The Rule Modeler tool can be accessed from the IC Manager business role under the menu option Process Modeling. This tool is generally used by Interaction Center analysts or other CRM business users who are responsible for a particular line of business such as email handling, leads and opportunity routing, service request escalation, and so on. After accessing the Rule Modeler, you need to first specify for which application (referred to as the *Context*) you want to use the Rule Modeler (Figure 9.3). In the following sections, we will look at three contexts.

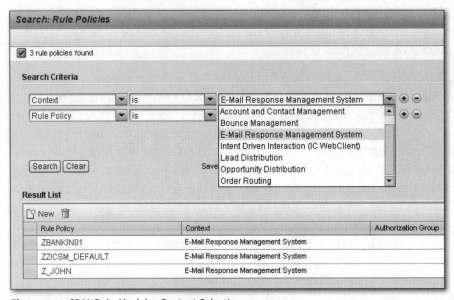

Figure 9.3 CRM Rule Modeler Context Selection

9.2   E-Mail Response Management System (ERMS)

SAP's CRM E-Mail Response Management System (ERMS) was designed to help companies deal with the increasingly large number of emails (and Web forms) received on a daily basis. Without an automated system to lighten some of the burden, Interaction Centers quickly become overwhelmed trying to manually route, process, and respond to the thousands of emails that they receive each day.

ERMS provides companies with a toolset for automatically organizing and processing incoming emails, as well as for monitoring and reporting of email volumes and results across the organization. Using ERMS, you can automatically send personalized acknowledgements to customers when each email is received. You can also automatically classify incoming emails into defined categories, and then respond with the appropriate documents or solutions using predefined templates. ERMS also includes out of the box reporting capabilities that provide Interaction Center supervisors with detailed, daily information about incoming email volumes and distribution, as well as average handling and response times.

ERMS can add value to your Interaction Center operations in several ways. First, using ERMS will reduce the number of emails that agents need to automatically respond to by automatically replying to easy to solve, frequently occurring issues and requests, such as questions about store hours, retail locations, driving directions, shipping and return policies, delivery information, shipping notifications, service request status updates, and so on. Additionally, ERMS increases the quality and the consistency of service received by your customers. By using automatically suggested e-mail templates, solutions, and other documents, you ensure that all customers receive the same high-quality response independent of the skill level and experience of your Interaction Center agents.

By automating as much of the initial email handling and processing as possible, ERMS helps free up your Interaction Center agents to perform more value-added work than just typing the same email over and over again. Your agents shouldn't be sitting around cutting-and-pasting emails all day; rather, your agents should be interacting with customers, building relationships, selling incremental products and services, and promoting your company's brand. Let's discuss some of the ways ERMS can help you achieve this. In particular, let's look at auto-acknowledgement, auto-response, auto-prepare, and email routing features of ERMS; and let's also discuss the benefits of incorporating Web-based mail forms into your ERMS system in addition to (or in lieu of) standard free-form emails.

9.2.1 Send Auto Acknowledgement

The *Send Auto Acknowledgement* feature of ERMS allows you to send an automated reply email to a customer letting the customer know that you have received their email. This action contains a number of parameters including: the ID of the mail form template that you would like to use as the basis of the reply, the outgoing email address that you want the email to be sent from, and optionally whether or not you want to automatically generate an Interaction Record and/or Service Ticket as well (Figure 9.4). As this action relies on the use of a mail form as the basis of the reply, it is therefore necessary to first create the mail form you plan to use. For more information about creating mail forms, see Section 7.3.3, in Chapter 7, IC Management and Analytics.

Figure 9.4 ERMS Send Auto Acknowledgement Action with Parameters

Certain ERMS actions, including Send Auto Acknowledgement, offer the possibility to automatically create a service order (or service ticket) as a parameter of the action. You can even configure which transaction type is used, such as TSRV for service tickets or TSVO for service orders, in the IMG activity *Define Service Manager Profiles*. Once inside the transaction, when you click on the folder Indirectly Called Services and Properties, you will see a list of service IDs (which correspond to certain ERMS actions). In the Property field, you enter the appropriate transaction type based on your requirements (Figure 9.5).

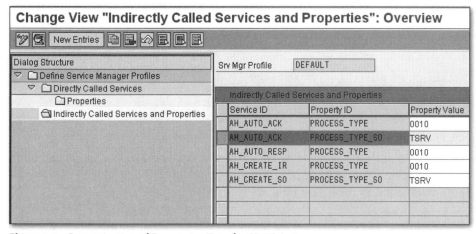

Change View "Indirectly Called Services and Properties": Overview

Service ID	Property ID	Property Value
AH_AUTO_ACK	PROCESS_TYPE	0010
AH_AUTO_ACK	PROCESS_TYPE_SO	TSRV
AH_AUTO_RESP	PROCESS_TYPE	0010
AH_CREATE_IR	PROCESS_TYPE	0010
AH_CREATE_SO	PROCESS_TYPE_SO	TSRV

Figure 9.5 Determination of Transaction Type for ERMS Actions

Note

If creating service tickets, ensure that SAP Note *1142948* is applied in your system. Without this note, any automatically created service tickets will be created without a line item, causing certain functionality such as SLA determination and date profile determination to not work correctly.

9.2.2 Auto Respond

The *Auto Respond* action is similar to, but slightly more powerful than, the Send Auto Acknowledgement action. The idea behind the Auto Respond action is that you use this action to automatically reply to a customer's email when the ERMS system has a high degree of confidence that it has correctly "understood" the customer's email and it has identified an appropriate solution. The main observable differences are that the Auto Respond action does not have an optional parameter to create a service ticket, and that it instead has an additional parameter called *Cat-*

egory Schema (Figure 9.6). Category schemas will be explained in Section 9.5 along with the related concepts of content analysis and multi-level categorization.

Philosophically, the difference between the Send Auto Acknowledgement action and the Auto Respond action is that you generally use an auto acknowledgement when you can't resolve the customer's issue directly and need to create a service ticket for follow-up; and in contrast, you use an auto response when you are confident that you can automatically answer the customer's question via ERMS and can therefore close the issue without creating a service ticket. Typically, auto responses are used for easy-to-solve, reoccurring issues such as password resets or requests for product information, store hours, retail locations, driving directions, shipping and return policies, and so on.

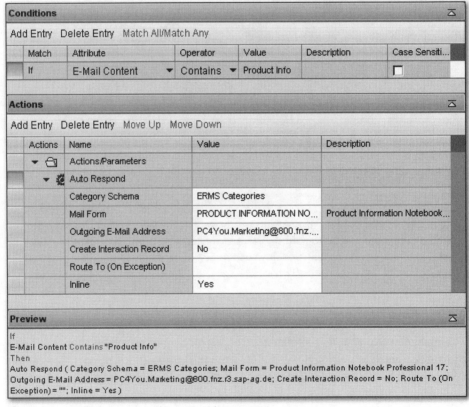

Figure 9.6 ERMS Auto Respond Action with Parameters

9.2.3 Auto Prepare

The Auto Prepare action works almost exactly like the Auto Respond action, with the difference that instead of automatically sending a reply email directly to the original email sender without any human intervention, the system creates a draft response that must first be approved by an agent in the Interaction Center. This can be useful in situations where you want an actual person to look over the email to make any necessary adjustments before clicking the send button. For example, a company might have a policy that auto responses should not be used in certain markets where customers are more likely to defect if they perceive they are not getting personal attention. Such a company might instead choose to use auto preparation instead of auto responses in these markets (Figure 9.7).

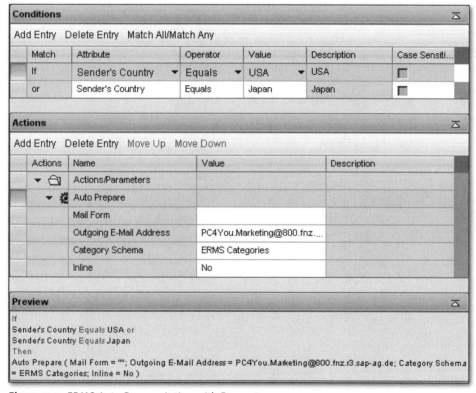

Figure 9.7 ERMS Auto Prepare Action with Parameters

When an agent opens the original customer email using the Interact button from the Agent Inbox and clicks the reply button in the E-Mail Editor, the system action populates the E-Mail Editor screen with a draft email created by the Auto Prepare action using one or more mail forms. If a mail form was included in the parameter of the action, this mail form will be used as the basis for the email reply. However, additional mail forms will also be appended to the email reply based on the Category Schema entered in the parameter of the action. Based on content analysis and categorization of the email (described in Section 9.5) the system will determine any additional applicable mail forms.

The typical strategy for using mail forms in conjunction with the Auto Prepare action is to assign a generic mail form directly to the parameter of the action. This mail form usually contains generic text that is not specific to any particular issues or topics but simply includes the standard company greeting for example. Then, based on the results of the content analysis and categorization, the system will insert additional mail forms that are linked to relevant categories in the Category Modeler. These additional mail forms contain information related to a specific issue or topic mentioned in the email (such as requested information about store locations, shipping rates, return policies, and so on).

9.2.4   Routing Actions

ERMS provides several out of the box actions for routing inbound emails to the appropriate Interaction Center agent or agent group (organization or position). Routing an email to the responsible user or organization on the first attempt is critical, because each required reroute results in lost time and reduced efficiency, which can result in missed SLAs and reduced customer satisfaction. You don't need to worry about routing emails for which you used the Auto Respond action, obviously (or for those emails for which you used the Delete E-Mail action). However, for all other actions, including Auto Prepare, you also need to use an ERMS routing action like Route E-Mail, Route to Service Ticket Responsible, or Route to Case Processor.

Route E-Mail

The Route E-Mail action is a fairly simple action. The one parameter offered is the organizational object (org unit, position, or user) to which you want to route the email. Typically, companies base their routing decisions on some attribute (or combination of attributes) such as product line, customer language, country, email address domain, and so forth. For example, a European consumer electronics company may route emails based on product line, sending emails about DVD players to one group, while sending emails about GPS devices to another group. Similarly, a U.S. high-tech company may route emails to different groups of agents based on the correspondence language of the customer — emails from English-speaking customers go to one agent group, while emails from Spanish-speaking customers go to another group staffed by Spanish-speaking bilingual agents.

Route to Service Ticket Responsible/Route to Case Processor

While the Route E-Mail action is good for handling initial customer inquiries, a more advanced action is necessary for handling a customer reply that references an existing service ticket or case tracking ID. The Route to Service Ticket Responsible action and the Route to Case Processor action are ideal for such situations. These actions are part of a broader concept called "email threading," which involves inserting a tracking ID when replying to a customer's email. Then, if the customer replies back again, the ERMS system can detect the tracking ID and route the new reply to whoever is assigned as the processor of the service ticket or case, while additionally linking the reply email to the existing email thread, which itself is attached to the service ticket or case.

In order to use the ERMS threading concept, it is first necessary to create a mail form that includes an attribute for the desired service ticket or case tracking ID (Figure 9.8). The mail form tool is accessed from the IC Manager role via the Knowledge Management functionality, as described in Section 7.3.3. To insert any of the ERMS-specific attributes such as Service Ticket/Order Tracking Text or Case Tracking Text, click the Attribute button and choose Additional Fields from the Attribute Category drop-down list box (Figure 9.9). However, you must first ensure that you have selected "ERMS" for the Attribute Context in the General Data area of your mail form.

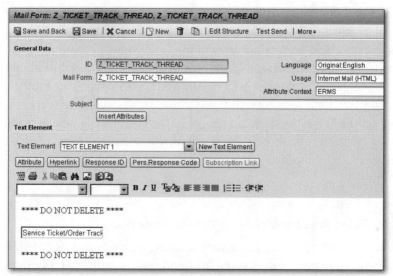

Figure 9.8 Inserting Tracking Text into Mail Form for E-Mail Threading

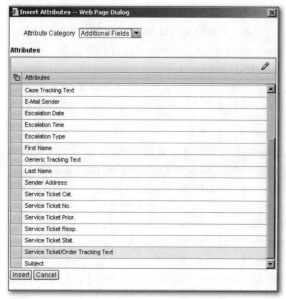

Figure 9.9 Selection of Service Ticket/Order Tracking Text Attribute

As shown in Figure 9.8, it is also wise to insert some additional text in your mail form, such as "Do Not Delete" to ensure that the customer does not delete the tracking ID when replying to the email; this tracking ID is required for the ERMS threading and Route to Ticket Responsible or Route to Case Processor actions to work. Although the tracking ID variable shows up in the mail form as "Service Ticket/Order Tracking Text," the actual ID of the service ticket or case will be substituted at runtime when the mail form is inserted into an email, either manually by an Interaction Center agent or automatically by the ERMS system via an action such as Auto Acknowledge (Figure 9.10).

Figure 9.10 Insertion of Service Ticket Tracking Text into Email

When a customer replies to an email that contains a tracking text, ERMS will automatically link the customer's reply email to the existing email thread. ERMS will also then route the customer's email to whichever organization or agent are currently assigned to the business transaction as the responsible organization or responsible employee. When the responsible employee or a member of the responsible organization conducts a search in the Interaction Center Agent Inbox for the items they are responsible for, they will see the new email in their list of emails, and they will also see the new email linked beneath the relevant business transaction that they are assigned to.

> **Note**
>
> Depending on your particular CRM release and support package version, you may need to apply one or more SAP notes to correctly enable the Service Ticket Tracking Text functionality for ERMS and the Interaction Center. You may want to confirm whether the following notes are applied in your system:
>
> ▶ *954060* (service ticket tracking text not available in mail forms)
>
> ▶ *989349* (service ticket tracking text missing in newly created emails)
>
> ▶ *990267* (service ticket tracking text cannot be inserted manually)

> **Additional Resource**
>
> For more information about using email threading to link service tickets and emails, see the article "Email Threading Gives IC Agents Quick Access to Customer's Email History," that appears in the March 2007 CRM Expert, available online at *http://www.CRMExpertOnline.com.*

ERMS Technical Information

The ERMS solution involves a number of different pieces of technology from across the SAP landscape. Let's look at how an email from one of your customers arrives in ERMS and is processed and routed to an agent. The customer most likely clicks on a link on your website, which opens a new email in the customer's default email client (such as Microsoft® Outlook™) with the email address of your ERMS already in the recipient field. When the customer clicks Send, the email arrives at your SMTP-compliant corporate email server (e.g., Microsoft Exchange™), which then passes the email along to the SAP Web Application Server 6.10 or higher. The email travels through your TCP/IP port and enters the SAP Internet Communication Manager (ICM) via the SMTP plug-in. From this point, the email arrives at the SAPconnect interface.

SAPconnect is the interface used by ERMS and the Agent Inbox in the Interaction Center; this is a different interface than the ICI, which is used for real-time pushing of email to agents via a screen pop. From SAPconnect, the email passes through the SAP Business Communication Services (BCS)/Business Communications Interface (BCI). At this point, ERMS finally gets involved. In transaction SO28, you map each ERMS inbound email address to a specific BOR object (ERMSSUPRT2). This BOR object converts the email text into a SAPoffice document and attaches it to a CRM workflow work item. ERMS executes the workflow tasks associated with the ERMS workflow (ERMS1). SAP recommends that you never modify this workflow.

Rather, all necessary adjustments to ERMS can be controlled by something called the *service manager profile*.

The service manager profile ultimately controls how the various ERMS workflow tasks behave. For example, the service manager profile is where you determine which Rule Modeler policy will be used by ERMS (Figure 9.11). The Rule Modeler policy is determined via the service manager profile. But, how is the service manager profile determined, that is, how does ERMS know which service manager profile to use for ERMS in the event more than one Service Manager Profile has been maintained in the IMG for the ERMS context? The answer actually depends on your version of CRM. In CRM 4.0, the service manager profile "Default" was hard-coded in the ERMS workflow template WS00200001. In CRM 2005 and above, you can map each incoming ERMS email address to a desired service manager profile in the IMG activity Assign Service Manager Profiles (Figure 9.12).

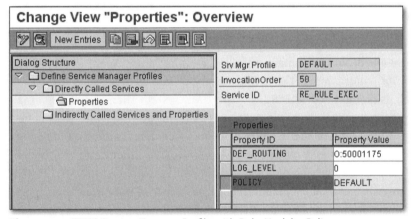

Figure 9.11 ERMS Service Manager Profile with Rule Modeler Policy

Change View "Assign Service Manager Profiles": Overview

Address/Number	ObjectID	Service Mgr Profile
ERMS@506.Q8D.R3.SAP-AG.DE	0	DEFAULT
ERMS@800.FAZ.R3.SAP-AG.DE	0	BOUNCE
ERMS@800.FNZ.R3.SAP-AG.DE	0	ERMS_ESCALMSG

Figure 9.12 Assignment of ERMS Addresses to Service Manager Profiles

Additional Resource

For detailed information about the technical architecture of ERMS and configuration tasks, see the article "ERMS Under the Hood: Configuration Tasks and the Service Manager Profile," that appeared in the January, 2007 CRM Expert available online at *http://www.CRMExpertOnline.com*.

ERMS Push

While ERMS always relies on the SAPconnect interface, as of CRM 2006s/CRM 2007, an enhancement is available called *ERMS Push* that allows you to route ERMS emails to an Interaction Center agent via a screen pop using the ICI interface. The ERMS Push solution involves a hybrid approach in that the original ERMS email still arrives via the SAPconnect interface and is still processed by ERMS in the normal fashion, allowing you to perform standard ERMS actions such as sending auto acknowledgments, sending auto responses, and creating automatic email replies for agents via auto preparation.

The key difference involves the actual routing of the email. Instead of using ERMS routing rules and routing the email to the Interaction Center Agent Inbox, ERMS Push hands the email over to the communication management software (CMS) system (such as Genesys or SAP BCM). The CMS system then routes the email to an online agent, in real time, via a screen pop using routing rules maintained in the CMS system. One of the benefits of this approach is that you can leverage skills-based routing options provided by CMS vendors. Another important benefit of this approach is that the ERMS Push emails will be stored in the SAP system (which is always the case with SAPconnect emails) instead of being stored in the external CMS server (which is usually the case with ICI emails). For many customers, it is desirable to store the emails in SAP CRM rather than an external email server because storing the emails in CRM guarantees that the email will always be available when, for example, looking at a previous email, interaction record, or service ticket from the Interaction Center.

9.2.5   Integrating ERMS with Web Forms

As discussed, ERMS can add value to an organization by automating (or at least partially automating) many issues that don't necessarily require human intervention, or which perhaps only need minimal human intervention, such as proofreading and sending an email reply that was automatically composed by the ERMS system. Much of the time, ERMS successfully "interprets" the meaning of an email based on analysis of the email subject line and email body contents by detecting certain predefined keywords that have been mapped to categories in the Category Modeler (as discussed in Section 9.5).

However, there are also many situations in which text classification tools are not able to successfully "interpret" an email. For example, today's tools struggle with emails that ask more than one question, particularly if the two issues are unrelated (e.g., What is the status of my order 8000001234, and what are your shipping rates for next day air?). Similarly, today's tools also struggle with emails that contain blocks of texts written in more than one language, which can be the case with long email threads in international companies. Perhaps even more commonly, a customer may simply omit to include a vital piece of information in the email such as account number, order number, product ID, etc. In these cases, ERMS is often not able to correctly classify the email and there is little or no chance to take advantage of ERMS capabilities such as auto-response, auto-prepare, and routing. Usually, in such situations all you can do is send an automated acknowledgement and route the email to a general queue where an employee has to read the email and decide to whom it should be routed.

However, one way to overcome the above issues encountered in email is to use Web forms instead of free-form emails. Not to be confused with "mail forms" (i.e., email templates), which were discussed in Section 7.3.3, a *Web form* is an Web page that you host on your corporate website or other Web-based application. The Web form includes fields (such as text fields, drop-down list boxes, check boxes, and radio buttons) for users to enter all relevant information required to properly submit a question or a request. For example, the Web form might have text fields for customer email address, full name, and problem description along with more structured fields (e.g., drop-down list boxes) for product ID and error code. All of this information would then be submitted to the ERMS system via an email (with an XML attachment) by the Web application hosting the Web form. ERMS would then have all the information it requires to make proper decisions regarding auto-response, auto-prepare, and routing.

9.3 Order Routing (Ticket Dispatching/Escalation)

So far, we have mainly focused on the use of the Rule Modeler for email handling as part of ERMS. Now, let's take a look at another way in which the Rule Modeler can be used within the Interaction Center, routing service tickets to the responsible agent or agent group. Often in the Interaction Center a first-level support agent will log a service ticket and then re-assign the ticket to a second-level support agent or agent group for processing; this is known as *escalation*. Similarly, a second level support person may need to reassign the message to another colleague in the same department; this is referred to as *dispatching*. In both cases, typically the person reassigning the ticket doesn't necessarily know to whom the ticket should be assigned, because in large companies there are often many different groups responsible for various different product lines, products, and issues. Hence, it is desirable to have an automated system that assigns the ticket to the appropriate processor based on business rules maintained by an analyst. This is where Order Routing comes in.

The *Order Routing* context of the Rule Modeler reassigns a service ticket to the most appropriate resource based on business rules defined in the Rule Modeler. Order Routing is manually invoked by an Interaction Center agent by pressing the "Dispatch/Escalate" button located on the Service Ticket screen (Figure 9.13). The agent can of course reassign a service ticket by hand without using the Rule Modeler simply by changing the name of the user or organization maintained in the Employee Responsible and Responsible Group partner functions. However, manual reassignment is rarely used except in very small companies where all of the agents and second-level support technicians know each other. Otherwise, most companies prefer to use rule-based, automated order routing.

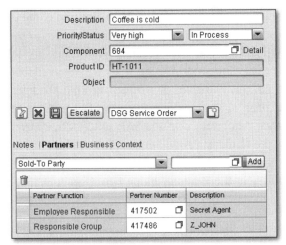

Figure 9.13 Rule-Based Partner Function Assignment via Escalate Button

The business rules for reassigning service tickets are defined in the Rule Modeler using the Order Routing context (Figure 9.14). Be careful when creating a new Order Routing policy or searching for an existing Order Routing policy because the default option in the Rule Policy drop-down list box is E-Mail Response Management System.

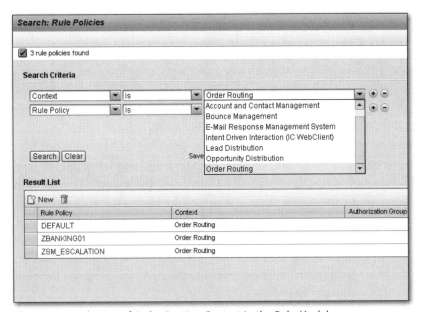

Figure 9.14 Selection of Order Routing Context in the Rule Modeler

Another very important thing to be aware of regarding the Order Routing context is that the SAP_ORDERROUTING service manager profile is hard coded. Therefore, you must use SAP_ORDERROUTING rather than creating your own service manager profile. In order to ensure that your order routing rules will be available for agents to use in the Interaction Center, you have to assign your Rule Modeler rule policy to the service manager profile. This is done from the Define Service Manager Profiles activity in the IMG. After selecting the SAP_ORDERROUTING service manager profile, you select the Directly Called Services folder and choose the service ID RE_RULE_EXEC. Then you select the Properties folder and enter the name of your Rule Modeler rule policy in the Property Value field (Figure 9.15).

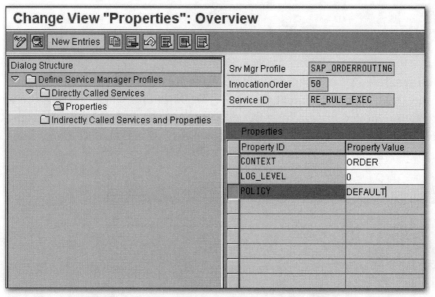

Figure 9.15 Assign Your Rule Policy to SAP_ORDERROUTING Profile

Unlike ERMS, which contains many actions, each with its own set of parameters, Order Routing is relatively straightforward. The mainly used action is *Routing*, and it basically does what its name implies — it routes the business transaction (e.g., service ticket) to the agent or agent group specified in the parameter of the action (Figure 9.16). Technically, the business transaction doesn't actually get "routed" anywhere of course; rather, the action simply manipulates the relevant partner function of the business transaction (e.g., replacing the currently assigned Responsible Group with a different one).

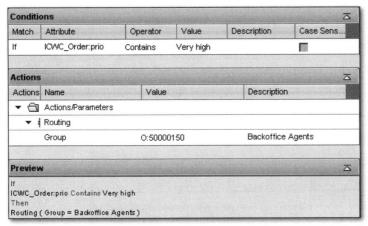

Figure 9.16 Rule Modeler Rule for Service Ticket Escalation

9.4 Intent-Driven Interaction (IDI)

So far, we have discussed ERMS and Order Routing, two powerful features of the Rule Modeler that can be used in the Interaction Center for automating email handling and reassigning service tickets. Now, let's discuss Intent-Driven Interaction — perhaps the most powerful of all features provided by the Rule Modeler that can be used in the Interaction Center. Intent-Driven Interaction, which was introduced in CRM 2006s/CRM 2007, allows you to provide business rule-based guidance to your Interaction Center agents in the form of automatically suggested solutions, automatic triggering and termination of alerts, automatic launching of scripts and other objects, and even automatic navigation to any screen or transaction anywhere in CRM from inside the Interaction Center.

Setting up Intent-Driven Interaction

Intent-Driven Interaction (IDI) is configured in the Rule Modeler like ERMS and Order Routing. However, IDI works slightly differently than the other Rule Modeler contexts. There are some very important differences to be aware of and to remember.

► To enable Intent-Driven Interaction (IDI) for agents in the Interaction Center, you need to create an IDI profile and assign the IDI profile to the CRM business role used by your agents (Figure 9.17). The IDI profile basically just includes

a mapping to your service manager profile (Figure 9.18). Contrary to expectations, the service manager profile actually does not control which rule policy
is used by IDI. Rather, the service manager profile just includes the necessary
services to make IDI work correctly. On most projects, you won't need to make
any changes to the IDI service manager profile, and you can simply use the SAP
default delivered profile IDI_DEFAULT.

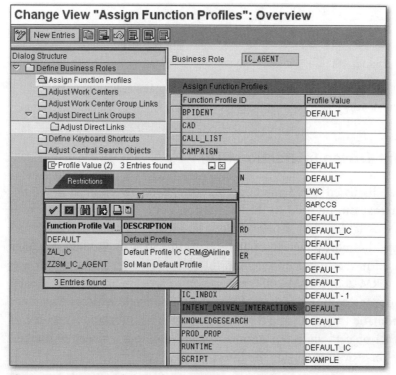

Figure 9.17 Mapping of IDI Profile to CRM Business Role

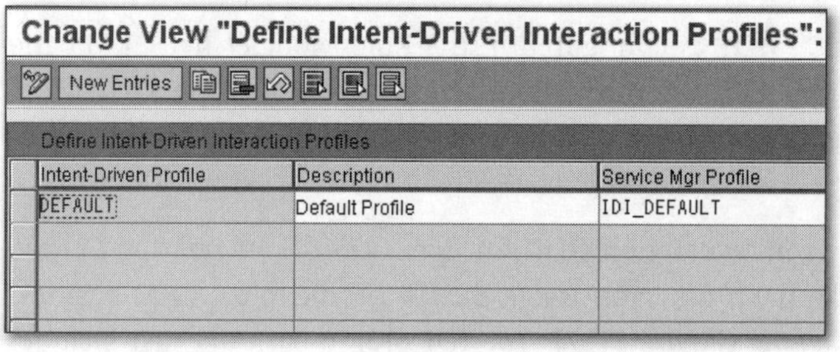

Figure 9.18 Mapping of Service Manager Profile to IDI Profile

▶ To determine which rules are used by IDI for your agents in the Interaction Center, you need to assign the appropriate CRM business roles directly to the desired rule policy in the Rule Modeler. The linking of a rule policy to a CRM business role is not done in the IMG. Rather, the assignment of the CRM business role to a rule policy is done in the Rule Modeler, in the Rule Policy Details screen (Figure 9.19). When you link one or more CRM business roles to an IDI rule policy, the rules in the policy will now affect all users who are assigned to any of the CRM business roles that you have linked to the policy.

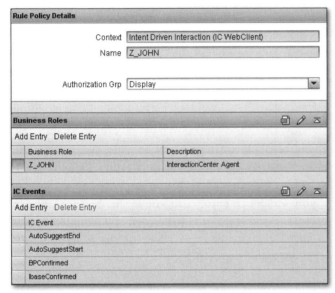

Figure 9.19 Linking of CRM Business Role to Rule Policy

▶ To create working IDI rules, you begin each IDI rule with a condition that uses the attribute Current Event. (Figure 9.20). If your rules do not start with this attribute condition, your rules will not work. This requirement is due to the fact that IDI uses an event-driven architecture. That is to say, IDI rules are triggered by events that happen in the Interaction Center, such as the confirmation of a business partner or IBase product by an agent, or by a programmatic event such as the detection of one or more potential solutions for a problem based on multi-level categorization of a service ticket. An initial condition might look something like, "If Current Event Equals IBase Confirmed," which would then be followed by the desired action (such as Navigate to Service Ticket create screen). After including the obligatory Current Event attribute in your first condition, you may then optionally include additional conditions that use attributes other than Current Event. For example, you might add a second condition that uses the attribute Current IBase to check whether a particular IBase product (or product range) has been confirmed.

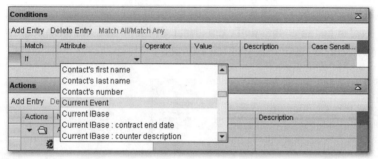

Figure 9.20 All IDI Rules Must Start with Condition "If Current Event"

▶ In order for any events to show up in the drop-down list box for the Value field (once you have selected the attribute Current Event in your condition), you must first have assigned the desired events in the Rule Policy Details screen under the area labeled IC Events (Figure 9.19). If you neglected to assign any events in the rule policy, you will get an empty drop-down list box as shown in the top portion of Figure 9.21. However, if you have correctly assigned one or more events to the rule policy, you will see those events in the drop-down list box as shown in the lower portion of Figure 9.21.

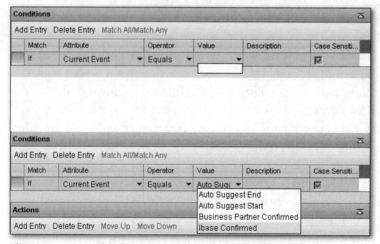

Figure 9.21 Example of Incorrect and Correct Configuration for Events

9.4.1 Triggering and Terminating Alerts

Now that you know how IDI works, let's look at some of the actions it can perform. One very useful action is the triggering and the termination of alerts. As described in Chapter 3, alerts are text messages that provide information and guidance to Interaction Center agents. The alerts show up in the Context Area of the Interaction Center and can have hyperlinks that navigate to other screens or transactions. IDI provides two separate actions — one for triggering the display of an alert, and other action for terminating (removing) the alert. To trigger an alert via an IDI rule, simply select the action Trigger Alert (Figure 9.22) and then select the alert that you want to trigger via the Alert Name drop-down list box (Figure 9.23). To cancel or remove an alert that you have already triggered, simply create another rule using the action Terminate Alert while again providing the name of the alert to be terminated.

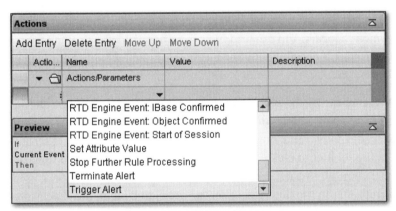

Figure 9.22 Selection of IDI Action to Trigger Alert

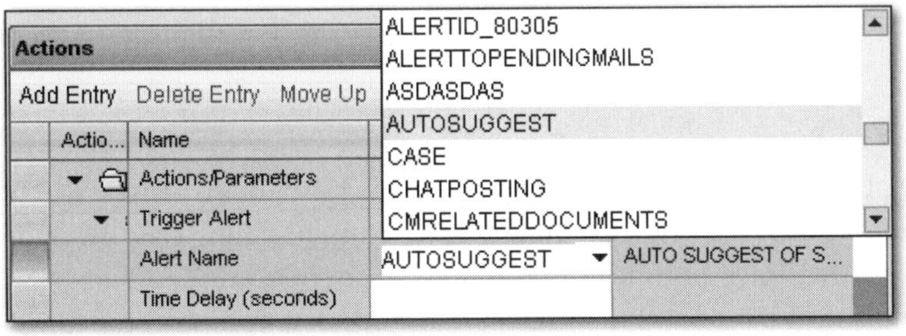

Figure 9.23 Selection of Desired Alert to be Triggered

> **Note**
>
> In SAP CRM 2005 and earlier, alerts were defined in a tool called the Alert Modeler, which relied on either XML configuration or ABAP table conditions depending on your release of CRM. With CRM 2006s/CRM 2007, the Alert Modeler has been replaced by a new graphical tool called the Alert Editor that allows you to create reusable alerts. See Section 7.4.1 for more details.

9.4.2 Launching Scripts

The first step to using Intent-Driven Interaction to launch scripts using business rules is to locate or define the IC events that you plan to use as the triggers for launching your scripts. You can use existing out of the box IC events or you can create your own IC events based on any UI element, such as a button on a screen; then, whenever the UI element is invoked (i.e., when the button is clicked) the new IC event will be raised. To define your own IC events (based on a UI element), you first have to know the name of the BSP application component and the view where the UI element appears. You can find the component and view name for any screen in the Interaction Center WebClient by pressing the F2 button to display the technical data.

Once you know the name of the BSP component, go to IMG transaction "Define Events in Repository" (transaction code CRMC_IC_EVENT_REP). Select the event application CRM_IC_EVENT and double-click the Events folder. Click the New Entries button in the toolbar to create a new event. Enter an event ID and description (choose an ID you will recognize later just in case the SAP developers used the technical ID rather than the description on the user interface in the Rule Modeler). Enter the name of the BSP component from the F2 technical data. Enter the name of the BSP view as well, or alternatively use the F4 value help to find the name of the view. Then use the F4 value help to find the name of the button or other UI element for which you want to create your event. Now you've created your own event.

Now that you know how to create the IC events, you are ready to create rules to launch your scripts. To launch an interactive script using the Intent-Driven Interaction context in the Rule Modeler, you first create your condition and then add an action via the New Entry button in the Actions area (Figure 9.24). Then you select the action Launch Script and then select the script that you want to launch from the Script ID drop-down list box (Figure 9.25). When the specified conditions occur in the Interaction Center, the system will automatically navigate the Interaction Center agent to the Interactive Scripting screen and automatically launch the specified script.

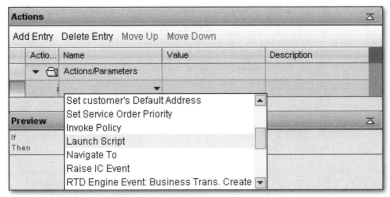

Figure 9.24 Select Launch Script Action

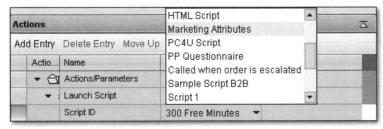

Figure 9.25 Select Desired Script to be Launched

9.4.3 Navigation

In addition to raising/terminating alerts and launching scripts, another useful feature of Intent-Driven Interaction is the ability to automatically navigate an Interaction Center agent to any CRM screen or business transaction. You can imagine how useful this feature could be for satisfying various business requirements. For example, in a customer service help desk whose primary function is to log service tickets, you might create a rule to automatically navigate a new service ticket after the agent confirms an IObject or IBase product. Or, perhaps you want to create a rule to navigate to the product service letter (PSL) search screen when a VIP customer orders a new product, in case there are any known issues and corresponding fixes available for this product. To navigate to a specific screen or transaction using the Intent-Driven Interaction context in the Rule Modeler, you select the action Navigate To (Figure 9.26) and then select the desired navigation object type and object action from the Navigation Object type:Action drop-down list box (Figure 9.27).

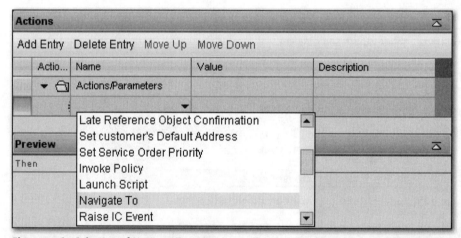

Figure 9.26   Selection of Navigate To Action

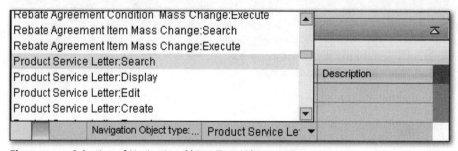

Figure 9.27   Selection of Navigation Object Type/Object Action

One very important thing to be aware of is that any navigation target used in your rules must also be included in the outbound plug mapping of your Navigation Bar profile. For example in Figure 9.28, you can see that an entry exists in the Navigation Bar profile for the product service letter search: Object Type BT120_PSL and Object Action Search. This entry corresponds to the selected object type and object action used in the Rule Modeler navigation action. If you try to use an object type and object action in your rule without also adding it to the outbound plug mapping of the appropriate Navigation Bar profile, the action will fail to navigate.

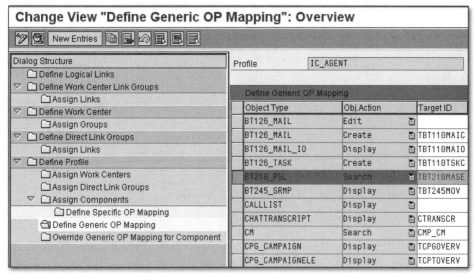

Figure 9.28 Object Type/Object Action Entry in Navigation Bar Profile

9.4.4 Additional Actions

In addition to the three main actions that we have looked at (Launch Script, Trigger Alert, and Navigate To), Intent-Driven Interaction actually offers many more out of the box actions as shown in Figure 9.29. We unfortunately don't have time to discuss all of the actions here. However, a few of the actions that you might want to check include the Set Service Order Priority action, which can be used to, for example, raise the priority of a service ticket if particular conditions are met. A few other interesting actions include the Add Object to Wrap-Up List and Add Product to Wrap-Up List. These two actions can be used inside the Interaction Center with the Wrap Up List screen that was newly introduced with CRM 2006s/CRM 2007. The Wrap-Up List essentially acts as a to-do reminder list for the agent, providing the agent with a list of activities that must be done before ending the conversation with the customer and before wrapping up the interaction. Please see related note for information about how to get more details on the Wrap-Up List and the two actions that add objects and products to the list.

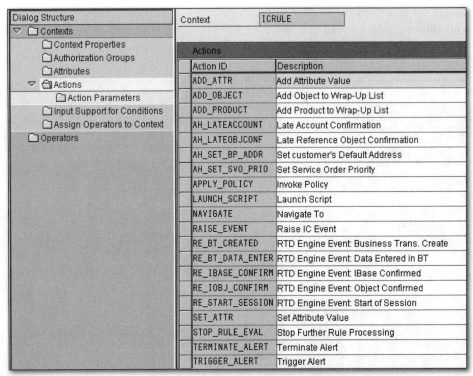

Dialog Structure	Context	ICRULE
▽ ☐ Contexts		
☐ Context Properties	**Actions**	
☐ Authorization Groups		
☐ Attributes	Action ID	Description
▽ ☐ Actions	ADD_ATTR	Add Attribute Value
☐ Action Parameters	ADD_OBJECT	Add Object to Wrap-Up List
☐ Input Support for Conditions	ADD_PRODUCT	Add Product to Wrap-Up List
☐ Assign Operators to Context	AH_LATEACCOUNT	Late Account Confirmation
☐ Operators	AH_LATEOBJCONF	Late Reference Object Confirmation
	AH_SET_BP_ADDR	Set customer's Default Address
	AH_SET_SVO_PRIO	Set Service Order Priority
	APPLY_POLICY	Invoke Policy
	LAUNCH_SCRIPT	Launch Script
	NAVIGATE	Navigate To
	RAISE_EVENT	Raise IC Event
	RE_BT_CREATED	RTD Engine Event: Business Trans. Create
	RE_BT_DATA_ENTER	RTD Engine Event: Data Entered in BT
	RE_IBASE_CONFIRM	RTD Engine Event: IBase Confirmed
	RE_IOBJ_CONFIRM	RTD Engine Event: Object Confirmed
	RE_START_SESSION	RTD Engine Event: Start of Session
	SET_ATTR	Set Attribute Value
	STOP_RULE_EVAL	Stop Further Rule Processing
	TERMINATE_ALERT	Terminate Alert
	TRIGGER_ALERT	Trigger Alert

Figure 9.29 Out of the Box Actions Available for Intent-Driven Interaction

> **Note**
>
> For more information on using Intent-Driven Interaction to add objects and products to the Wrap-Up List in the Interaction Center, please see the article, "Wrap-Up List Ensures Smooth Interactions," that appears in the December 2007 CRM Expert available online at *http://www.CRMExpertOnline.com*.

9.5 Category Modeler

The Category Modeler is a tool that allows Interaction Center analysts and other business users to create multi-level hierarchies of categories that can be used to classify issues when creating business transactions (like the service ticket or complaint) inside the Interaction Center. Other applications can also leverage your categories. For example, ERMS searches the categories in order to find the most appropriate email template to use for automatically creating replies to customer emails. The Interaction Center also relies on the Category Modeler. For example, when using multi-level categorization to categorize a business transaction, the system checks the appropriate Category Modeler schema order to trigger automated functionality such as automatic suggestion of mapped solutions, or automatic completion of business transactions using mapped templates.

A sample categorization schema is pictured in Figure 9.30, showing a hierarchy of categories on the left-hand side and the details of a selected hierarchy node on the right-hand side. Notice that for each selected node in the hierarchy you can map various documents including search queries (for ERMS content analysis), standard response (for ERMS automated reply emails), problems and solutions (for automatically suggested solutions), service order templates (for auto-completion), and many other objects (Figure 9.30).

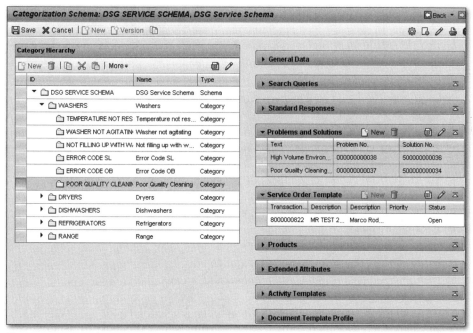

Figure 9.30 Sample Categorization Schema

The Category Modeler is delivered as part of the IC Manager business role and can be found on the Knowledge Management work center page via Categorization Schemas. A *categorization schema* is a collection of related categories in the Category Modeler, similar to how a rule policy is a collection of related rules in the Rule Modeler. Schemas can additionally have time-dependent versions. Each version of a schema is valid for a specific date and time interval, and no two versions are ever allowed to overlap. That is, if one version has the status Active, all other versions have a different status such as Draft (not yet released), Released (validity date/time in the future), or Deployed (validity date/time in the past). See Figure 9.31.

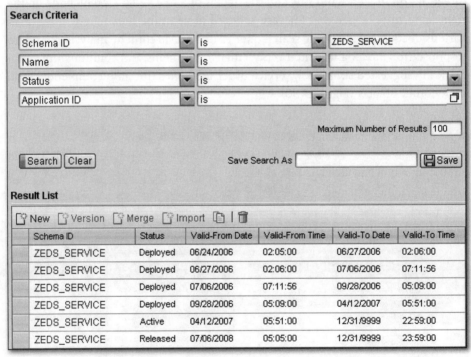

Figure 9.31 Time-Dependent Category Schema Versions

Creating Schema Versions

To create a new version of an existing schema that you want to automatically become active at a specified future date and time, select the existing schema version and click the Version button to copy the existing schema version. After making any desired changes to the categories in the new version, you change the Status field from Draft to Released in the area of the screen labeled General, after selecting a From Date and Valid From Time that are both in the future (Figure 9.32). After changing the status from Draft to Released, the Schema will now have status Deployed. Once the specified future date and time are reached, the status of the Schema will automatically change from Deployed to Active.

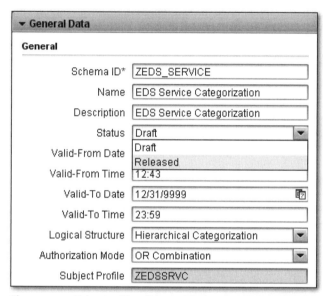

Figure 9.32 Releasing New Schema Version

Deciding How to Structure Your Schemas

In theory, the Category Modeler supports an unlimited number of hierarchies. However, in reality you should apply common sense when designing your category schemas because you need to consider potential bottlenecks in your design such as:

▸ Screen size: Can you really fit e.g., 20 category levels on the screen?

▸ Usability: Will your Interaction Center agents really take the time to select 20 values, especially if there is a system roundtrip (screen refresh) after each selection at every level?

▶ System and network performance: Do you have enough bandwidth in your network to handle the large data exchange required to support so many categories?

By default, business transactions display four categories, although you can extend this if desired. You can adjust this setting in the IMG configuration activity, Define Categorization Profiles by selecting the desired business transaction in the Categorization Contexts folder and clicking the Details button, and then enter the desired number of hierachies that you want to display in the Hierarchy Levels field under the heading Categorization Dropdown Listboxes. However, care should be taken when deciding how many category levels to support. For example, having too many categories slows down agent performance because a server roundtrip and screen refresh normally occur with each category selection. On the other hand, having too few categories (with too many values per category) decreases system perfomance because the system has to transfer more data between the browser and the CRM server with each category selection.

9.5.1 Multi-Level Categorization of Business Transactions

Multi-level categorization can be used in conjunction with most business transactions in the Interaction Center including the Interaction Record, Service Ticket, Service Order, Complaint, and Case as of CRM 2005. In earlier releases of CRM, business transactions such as the Service Ticket had only two fields for classifying an issue — subject and reason. These two fields were not dependent, meaning that if you selected one particular value for the Subject of a service ticket, the selected value did not have any effect on the list of available values available for the Reason field. However, with multi-level categorization, the hierarchy levels are dependent, meaning that as you select a value at each level, the values available in the lower category levels are adjusted accordingly as per your category schema.

Linking Categorization Schema to Transaction Types

When you create a categorization schema in the Category Modeler, you need to go through a two-step configuration process to make the schema available for multi-level categorization in your business transactions. The first step is to assign a subject profile directly to your categorization schema inside the Category Modeler as shown in Figure 9.32. The second step is to assign the chosen subject profile to all desired transaction types where you want to use multi-level categorization.

This is done in the IMG configuration activity Assign Subject Profiles to Transaction Types (Figure 9.33).

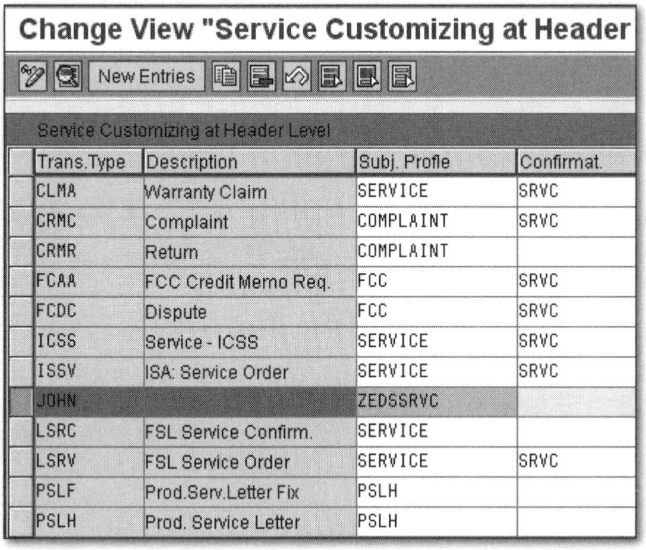

Change View "Service Customizing at Header

New Entries

Service Customizing at Header Level

Trans.Type	Description	Subj. Profile	Confirmat.
CLMA	Warranty Claim	SERVICE	SRVC
CRMC	Complaint	COMPLAINT	SRVC
CRMR	Return	COMPLAINT	
FCAA	FCC Credit Memo Req.	FCC	SRVC
FCDC	Dispute	FCC	SRVC
ICSS	Service - ICSS	SERVICE	SRVC
ISSV	ISA: Service Order	SERVICE	SRVC
JOHN		ZEDSSRVC	
LSRC	FSL Service Confirm.	SERVICE	
LSRV	FSL Service Order	SERVICE	SRVC
PSLF	Prod.Serv.Letter Fix	PSLH	
PSLH	Prod. Service Letter	PSLH	

Figure 9.33 Assignment of Subject Profile to Transaction Type

Configuring Category Labels in Interaction Center

As of CRM 2007, it is possible to change the text of category labels in the Interaction Center. Unlike most other fields in the CRM WebClient that can be changed using the UI Config Tool, category labels require a special two-step configuration approach because they are dynamically generated (based on the number of category levels that you configure). The first step is to define all the category labels that you will potentially use in your different multi-level categorization schemas. You do this in the IMG configuration activity Define Categorization Labels located via the IMG path: SAP Implementation Guide • Customer Relationship Management • CRM Cross-Application Components • Multilevel Categorization • Define Categorization Labels (Figure 9.34). The second step is to choose the labels you want and assign them in the Labels area of each categorization schema in the Category Modeler; you don't necessarily have to select all of the categories that you defined nor do you necessarily have to use them in same order as defined (Figure 9.35). Whatever labels you select and assign in the categorization schema will then show up in the Interaction Center as shown in Figure 9.36.

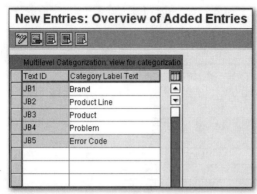

Figure 9.34 Define Categorization Labels in the IMG

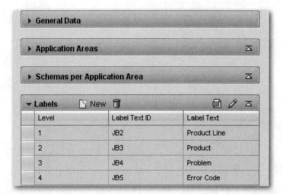

Figure 9.35 Assign Labels to Category Schema in Category Modeler

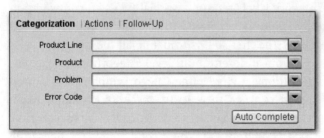

Figure 9.36 Category Labels Appear in IC Business Transaction

Transporting Categorization Schemas

You can transport category schemas between one SAP system or client and another by directly transporting the appropriate table entries as described in SAP note *864439*. However, to avoid database inconsistencies, the transport does not include linked objects like standard responses, solutions, service order templates, applications area assignments, and so on. These linked objects must all be reassigned by hand afterward in the target system to which the category schema was transported. For technical folks, this is why tables CRMC_ERMS_CAT_OK and CRMA_ERMS_CAT_LN (which are not mentioned in the note) are not transported. However, you can also include these two tables in your transport if you are careful — meaning, if you always transport from one unique source system and don't make any changes in the target system. In this case, you can transport everything and it is not necessary to make any adjustments after the transport in the target system.

9.5.2 Interaction Center Automation Using Categorization Schemas

Multi-level categorization, enabled by the Category Modeler, provides several benefits to a company. Being able to accurately classify issues and problems with a sufficient level of detail, and then later generate reports is wonderful. However, there are a couple of other benefits as well, which are specific to the Interaction Center. These include auto-suggested solutions, auto-completion of service tickets based on stored templates, and auto-preparation of emails.

Solution Auto Suggest

The Auto Suggest Solution functionality notifies an Interaction Center agent who is processing a service ticket (or service order) that relevant solutions are available for the issue they are working on. Based on the values that are selected in the multi-level categorization of the service ticket, the system triggers an alert notifying the agent that one or more solutions are available. When the agent clicks on the alert, the system automatically navigates the agent to the Knowledge Search screen where the solutions are displayed in the results list of the Knowledge Search area. The agent can select one or more of the automatically suggested solutions and add them to the cart — and then optionally insert the solutions from the cart into an outgoing email.

To enable automatic suggestions of solutions, you map one or more solutions to the appropriate nodes of your categorization schema in the Category Modeler (Figure 9.37). You can also control whether only the solutions assigned to the current category are proposed, or whether solutions belonging to higher or lower dependent categories are also shown. For example, assume the selected categories in the Service Ticket are as follows: The top level category in the service ticket is "printer," the second level is "installation," the third level is "software," and the fourth level is "utilities." Do you only want to propose the solutions assigned directly to the lowest node (utilities), or do you also want to propose any solutions assigned to the higher level nodes "software," "installation," and "printer." This will obviously depend on your business requirements and how you have modeled your categories. The configuration for these settings is maintained in the IMG configuration activity Define Categorization Profiles located under: INTERACTION CENTER WEBCLIENT • BUSINESS TRANSACTION (see Figure 9.38).

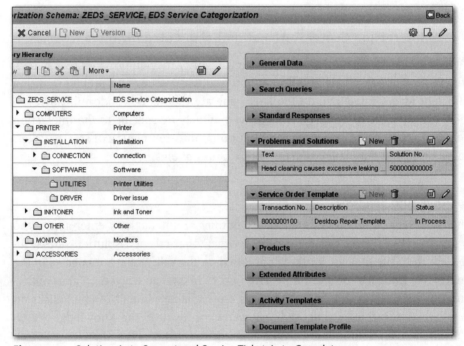

Figure 9.37   Solution Auto Suggest and Service Ticket Auto Complete

Auto-Complete for Service Orders/Tickets

The Auto Complete functionality allows an Interaction Center agent to automatically populate all the fields of a service ticket (or service order) with the click of a button. Based on the values that are selected in the multi-level categorization of the service ticket, when the agent clicks the Auto Complete button inside the Service Ticket, the system retrieves the corresponding service ticket template.

This process is especially ideal for commonly occurring issues like requests for password resets, where the agent doesn't want to waste time filling in the same information for every service ticket but instead wants to use a saved template to expedite the process.

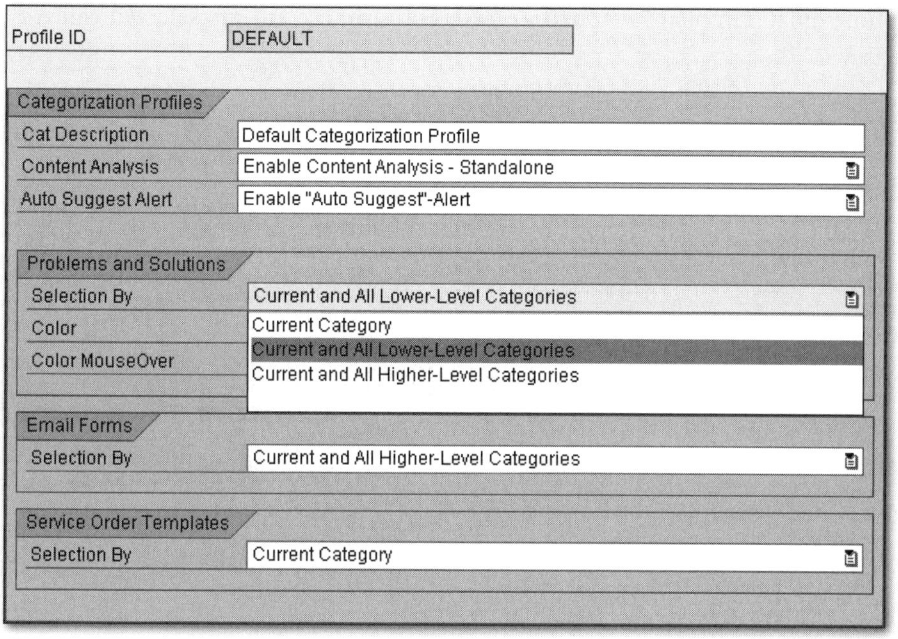

Figure 9.38 Define Categorization Profiles for Business Transactions

To enable automatic completion for service tickets, map the desired service ticket template to the appropriate node of your categorization schema in the Category Modeler (Figure 9.37). You can also control whether only the template assigned to the current category is proposed, or whether a template from the next higher nodes is selected (in the event no template is assigned to the lowest selected node). The configuration for these settings is maintained in the IMG configuration activity DEFINE CATEGORIZATION PROFILES located under: INTERACTION CENTER WEBCLIENT • BUSINESS TRANSACTION (see Figure 9.38).

Auto Pre-Prepare for Email Responses

The ERMS Auto Prepare functionality, as discussed in Section 9.2.3, uses search queries and email standard response templates attached to the Category Modeler to automatically compose reply emails on behalf of an agent based on an incoming customer email. ERMS relies on SAP NetWeaver TREX to scan an incoming email and perform so-called content analysis, which basically involves checking the email for certain keywords that are mapped as search queries in the category modeler (Figure 9.39). If TREX determines a good match between the contents of the email and a specific category, the system can generate a reply email using one or more email templates mapped as standard responses to the selected category (Figure 9.39).

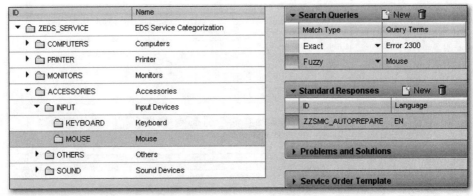

Figure 9.39 Search Queries and Standard Responses

9.6 Summary

In this chapter, we looked at how you can use the Rule Modeler and Category Modeler to standardize and automate work processes in the Interaction Center in order to improve agent efficiency and to provide customers with consistent high-quality service.

Some of the most important points to remember are:

- The Rule Modeler is used for creating business rules across a variety of Interaction Center processes including: E-Mail Response Management System (ERMS), Order Routing (dispatching and escalation of service tickets), and Intent-Driven Interaction (rule-based agent guidance).

- Using the Rule Modeler, you create rules that are essentially if-then statements that contain a condition and an action. A condition is comprised of an attribute, an operator, and a value. If the condition evaluates to true, then the corresponding action is executed.

▶ ERMS allows companies to send auto-acknowledgements and auto-responses to incoming customer emails without any human involvement from agents. ERMS can also assist agents by creating a draft email reply that the agent can send with a single mouse click (or modify as necessary).

▶ Order Routing allows an employee (such as a first level Interaction Center agent) to automatically dispatch or escalate a service request to the appropriate agent or group based on defined business routing rules.

▶ Intent-Driven Interaction provides intelligent guidance to Interaction Center agents including rule-based scripts, alert messages, and automatic navigation.

▶ The Category Modeler allows you to create multi-level hierarchies of categories that can be used within business transactions such as the Service Ticket in the Interaction Center to provide agents with guidance and support.

▶ Using the Category Modeler, you can automatically suggest solutions to agents, enable one-click auto-completion of service tickets, and facilitate auto-preparation of email replies for agents.

In the next chapter, we will explore how you can use the Interaction Center as the *front office* for your back-office operations. First, we will look at how you can integrate shared services for traditional back-office functions like IT, HR, and accounting into your Interaction Center as shared service centers. Then we will move on and examine how the Interaction Center can be used to support the requirements of certain industries that have strong back-office integration requirements such as utilities, telecommunications (Telco), and insurance.

This chapter looks at how you can use the Interaction Center as the front office for your back-office operations.

10 Back-Office Interaction Centers for Industries and Shared Services

In this chapter, we will explore specialized usages of the Interaction Center that diverge from the standard front-office, customer-facing help desk and telemarketing/telesales scenarios we have discussed so far. We will look at how the CRM Interaction Center can be used to integrate scenarios and processes that are typically associated with the back office, such as IT, HR, and accounting. We will also look at how the CRM Interaction Center can be used to support the requirements of certain vertical industries that have traditionally relied very heavily on back-office functionality such as utilities, telecommunications, and automotive.

In the first part of the chapter, we will introduce you to the concept of *shared services*, which involves consolidating internal back-office processes such as information technology (IT), human resources (HR), or finance and accounting across your company globally. We will explore how creating these so-called *shared service centers* can drive cost reductions by allowing you to leverage economies of scale and eliminate redundant infrastructure and work. We will also look at what SAP provides out of the box to enable shared service centers, including the standard IT help desk, employee interaction center, and accounting interaction center scenarios.

In the second part of the chapter, we will shift our attention to *vertical industries* that have unique industry-specific requirements often involving back-office ERP functionality. A *vertical industry* — or vertical market — describes companies who are involved in the same type of business, offering similar products and services to the same group of target customers. We will examine how the SAP CRM Interaction Center can be used to support some of these vertical industries, by integrating back-office functionality such as accounts receivables and contract accounting into the Interaction Center. Specifically, we will look at the Interaction Center capabilities provided for the utilities, telecommunications (Telco), and automotive industries.

10.1 Shared Service Centers

As mentioned in the introduction, shared service centers offer companies a way to reduce costs by eliminating redundant work and infrastructure. The concept behind shared services is that companies should consolidate their various regional back-office interaction centers (that serve their local user base) with a consolidated shared service center that serves all users globally. For example, rather than running six separate regional HR, IT, or accounting help desks for North America, Latin America, Europe, Asia Pacific, Japan, and Australia, a company would consolidate all of its regional help desks into a single help desk that serves all regions.

The main benefit of shared service centers is cost reduction. Not surprisingly, cost reduction is also usually the main driver behind shared service center projects, which tend to be championed by the offices of the chief financial officer (CFO) and treasurer. By consolidating regional interaction centers into a shared-service interaction centers, you can leverage economies of scale while also reducing inefficiencies and redundancy through business process re-engineering. Obviously, if each regional interaction center has its own separate support infrastructure in place but is basically doing the same type of work, then consolidating these disparate centers into a global shared service center will eliminate redundant infrastructure and work. Additionally, by consolidating into a single shared service center, companies can standardize technology, increase efficiency, and benefit from economies of scale.

Companies first moved toward shared service centers during the 1980s as part of re-engineering efforts that were sweeping across the enterprise software market. While there was some slow down during the financially prosperous 1990s, shared service centers are gaining momentum again as companies feel pressure to cut costs and improve profitability. Currently, many companies are transitioning their independent back-office interaction centers into consolidated shared service centers. From an operational perspective, the goal is to share resources (as well as the costs of those resources) across the company. For example, typically, the fixed costs of operation are shared throughout the organization, while the variable costs are assigned directly to the groups that consume the services, proportionately to their level of use.

People tend to automatically associate outsourcing with shared service. One of the advantages of consolidating and standardizing your operations is that you then have the option to outsource these activities if desired. There are indeed companies who offer outsourcing and are happy to take over your IT, HR, or accounting operations for you. Some of these companies — like BASF IT, ADP, and Bayer — actually use the SAP CRM Interaction Center as their platform for outsourcing their shared service centers. However, it is not necessary to outsource, or even to offshore your operations to lower-cost locations, in order to use the shared service center model. In fact, studies have shown that only 10% to 20% of all related cost savings associated with shared service centers are related to outsourcing or offshoring. Rather, a 2004 study by J.P. Morgan showed that the majority of costs savings are associated with business-process re-engineering (80%) and economies of scale (20%).

Assuming that you decide that shared services are right for you, SAP provides the tools to help you implement and adopt the shared service center (SSC) model. As of CRM 2006s/CRM 2007, two SSC scenarios are delivered out of the box with the SAP CRM Interaction Center: IT help desk and employee interaction center (EIC). Additionally, a third scenario — the accounting interaction center (AIC) — is available via a consulting solution. Although the benefits and cost savings associated with implementing an SSC are amplified as you roll in each additional scenario, it probably makes the most sense to start with one scenario, based on your most pressing pain points and requirements. Let's start off by looking at the IT Help Desk scenario, which is often one of the first places that companies begin their shared services efforts.

10.1.1   IT Help Desk

In Chapter 6, which talked about IC Service, we covered the concept of the service desk, which is a customer-facing help desk geared toward resolving technical issues reported by *customers* about *your company's products*. However, in this chapter we will introduce the concept of the IT help desk, which is usually geared toward resolving technical issues reported by your *employees* regarding the *IT infrastructure and equipment* they use to do their daily jobs (such as computers, accessories, software, network access, passwords, etc.). The IT help desk scenario conforms to the standards defined by the Information Technology Infrastructure Library (ITIL), a set of best practices for managing IT help desk issues defined by the United Kingdom's Office of Government Commerce (OGC) and accepted worldwide.

SAP delivers an out of the box business role (e.g., profile) for the IT help desk scenario as part of the standard Interaction Center product. The IT help desk is the central point of contact for all IT-related requests and incidents, ensuring that service is provided in compliance with internally defined service level agreements (SLAs). The IT help desk is also fully integrated with the back-end SAP ERP system, allowing you to integrate back-office change management and configuration management processes. For example, as depicted in the IT help desk process flow diagram shown in Figure 10.1, after an incident and problem are identified, you advance to the change management process — where you might, for example, create a request for change (RFC) document.

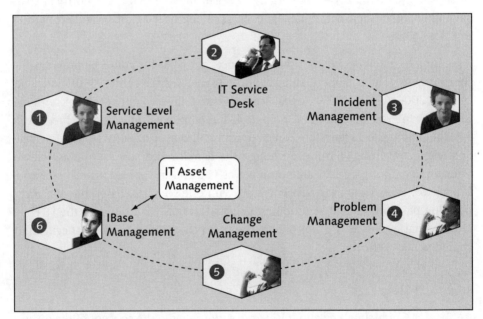

Figure 10.1 IT Help Desk Process Flow

Service Level Management

The IT help desk scenario allows shared services organizations to specify which services they want to provide to their clients (e.g., employees or external customers), as well as the desired availability or response times for those services. This information is available to agents in the Interaction Center at all times. Service contracts are first created to outline the service levels to which a client is entitled, including response profiles and price agreements. Then, when actual incidents are reported, a service ticket is created to record the incident. The service ticket performs an automatic contract validation to determine the SLA information, including the response profile and service profile (Figure 10.2). If an SLA is breached, escalation management can be automatically triggered via scheduled actions.

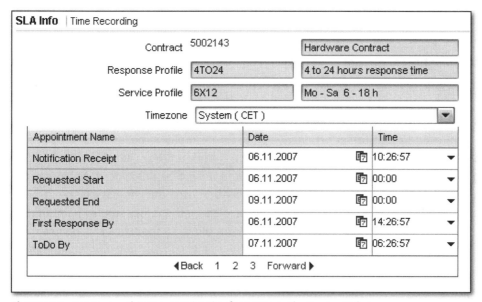

Figure 10.2 Service Level Agreement (SLA) Information in the Service Ticket

IT Service Desk

The IT help desk scenario, which is delivered using the standard SAP CRM Interaction Center product, provides agents with a multifunctional agent desktop, which includes all of the tools commonly associated with service-desk products. For example, the Interaction Center offers role-based profiles, allowing different groups of agents to access different screens and functions based on their profile. This means that your company can run several different interaction centers (e.g., a consumer help desk, a B2B sales order entry desk, and an internal IT help desk) using the same SAP CRM Interaction Center software but with different configurations.

The Interaction Center allows agents to identify customers or installed products by a number of search criteria, and to view the full interaction history of an identified customer. Agents can log service tickets, locate relevant solutions, and send the solutions (with attachments) via email. Agents can also process inbound customer emails manually via the Agent Inbox, or rely on the automated ERMS system to assist with automated or semi-automated emails. Interactive scripts are also available to coach and guide agents. If necessary, agents can access back-office ERP transactions via the transaction launcher. These individual tools were covered in detail in Chapter 6, IC Service.

Incident Management

The IT help desk scenario also supports the ability to manage incidents. The term *incident* is part of the official nomenclature of ITIL. As defined by ITIL, an incident is essentially any unexpected product behavior that disrupts service or reduces quality and/or customer productivity. So, for example, if the letter "i" keypad button on your new BlackBerry mobile doesn't work properly, that would constitute an incident. The non-working button would indeed be unexpected behavior, and it obviously would also reduce productivity because now you have to avoid using the letter "i" in all text messages and instead adopt the rather strange habit of constantly referring to yourself in the first person plural by typing "we" whenever you would normally just type "I".

In the IT help desk scenario using the Interaction Center, an incident is recorded using the service ticket business transaction. The service ticket provides standard fields to indicate the status and priority of the issue. These fields can be renamed to reflect urgency and impact in order to more closely align with the ITIL lexicon. In addition, the service ticket also provides a configurable hierarchy of dependent categories that allow you to further classify or categorize the incident (Figure 10.3). Based on predefined business rules set up in the Rule Modeler, the incident (i.e., service ticket) can be dispatched using the appropriate escalation procedures. Additionally, for commonly reoccurring issues, the Auto Complete button can be used to pre-fill the various fields of the incident (i.e., service ticket) using a saved template; the appropriate template is selected based on the selected categorization. In short, all of the standard features of the service ticket are available when managing incidents in the IT help desk scenario. These individual features were covered in detail in Chapter 6, IC Service.

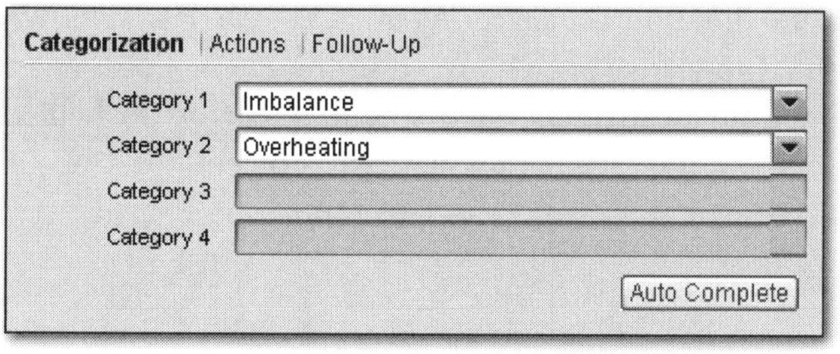

Figure 10.3 Usage of Service Ticket to Represent ITIL Incident

Problem Management

According to the parlance of ITIL, a *problem* is the unknown underlying root cause of an incident. While incident management focuses on resolving the customer's immediate issue, such as providing a short-term fix or workaround solution, problem management focuses on examining the cause of the incident in order to resolve the issue. Let's return to our previous example of an *incident* involving an "i" button on your BlackBerry that stops working. If only one or two customers report this issue, the manufacturer of the product that is, Research In Motion (RIM), might tell the customers that they need to buy a new device (or purchase an extended service contract). In this case, no problem needs to be logged because no follow-up investigation is necessary. On the other hand, if hundreds of customers report the same issue with a faulty "i" button, then the manufacturer would likely log a problem to investigate the underlying cause. In this scenario, hundreds of separate incidents would be logged (one for each customer issue) while only one problem would be logged.

Typically, a problem is logged in response to multiple incidents. However, in theory, a problem could certainly be logged for a single incident as well. In the IT help desk scenario using the SAP CRM Interaction Center, a problem can either be logged using the *service ticket* transaction (as with an incident) or using the *case* transaction. The case, as you may recall from Chapter 6, IC Service, allows you to link various related documents (such as individual service tickets) to a single case. In this manner, you are easily able to see which incidents (i.e., service tickets) are associated with each problem (i.e., case).

Regardless of whether you use the service ticket or case problems, once a solution or repair is identified for a problem, a new document called a *known error* is created. In the SAP CRM Interaction Center, a known error could be modeled using a solution document from the Solution Database. Agents can search for known errors (i.e., solutions) via the Knowledge Search screen in the Interaction Center (Figure 10.4). In addition, automatically suggested solutions can be pushed to agents via alert messages based on the categorization of the problem.

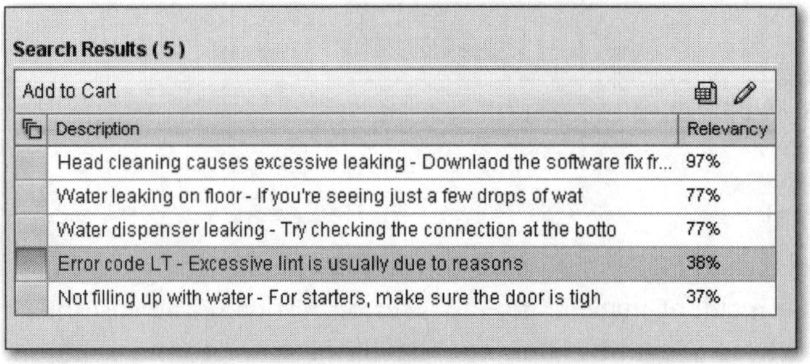

Search Results (5)

Add to Cart

	Description	Relevancy
	Head cleaning causes excessive leaking - Downlaod the software fix fr...	97%
	Water leaking on floor - If you're seeing just a few drops of wat	77%
	Water dispenser leaking - Try checking the connection at the botto	77%
	Error code LT - Excessive lint is usually due to reasons	38%
	Not filling up with water - For starters, make sure the door is tigh	37%

Figure 10.4 Usage of Solutions to Represent ITIL Known Errors

Change Management

The IT help desk scenario provided by the Interaction Center can be used to facilitate the ITIL change management process. Essentially, change management provides a method of managing changes to components of the IT infrastructure (hardware, software, accessories, etc.) in a controlled manner in order to minimize any disruption of IT services provided to users. The change management process controls how changes should be initiated, assessed, planned, scheduled, and implemented. The central aspect of the change management process is a concept known as a *request for change* (RFC), which is created to correct any faults in the IT infrastructure detected in the problem management process. In the SAP CRM Interaction Center, an RFC is represented using a service order (Figure 10.5).

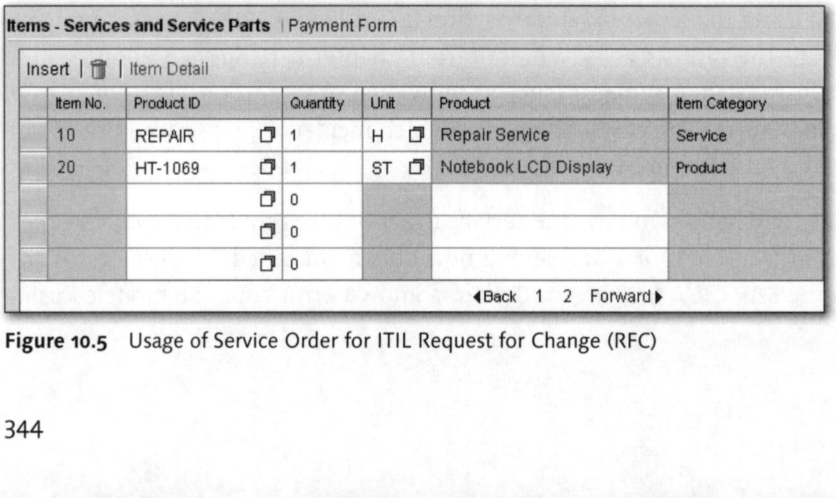

Items - Services and Service Parts | Payment Form

Insert | | Item Detail

Item No.	Product ID		Quantity	Unit		Product	Item Category
10	REPAIR		1	H		Repair Service	Service
20	HT-1069		1	ST		Notebook LCD Display	Product
			0				
			0				
			0				

◄Back   1   2   Forward►

Figure 10.5 Usage of Service Order for ITIL Request for Change (RFC)

After a RFC has been created by the Interaction Center agent (or by an engineer or other back-office IT user), the RFC is routed to a manager who prioritizes, categorizes, and evaluates the RFC (Figure 10.6). The manager may then route the RFC forward to another manager for final authorization and approval. If approved, engineers would then implement the change and then update the configuration management database (CMDB), which is used to keep track of all changes made to all IT assets. During this entire process, agents are able to monitor the status of RFCs by viewing the relevant RFC from the Agent Inbox.

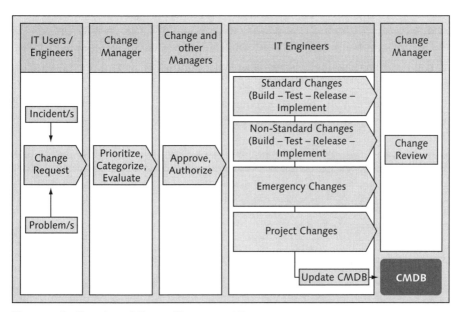

Figure 10.6 Overview of Change Management Process

IBase Management

A critical part of any IT help desk is keeping track of all of your IT assets (PCs, notebooks, servers, operating systems, software, etc.) so that you always know where each asset is located and to whom it is currently assigned. This process is known as IT asset management (ITAM). ITIL extends the traditional ITAM concept with an expanded process known as configuration management. Traditional ITAM mainly focuses on keeping up-to-date records about the location of assets across the organization. This approach is geared around the location and accounting aspects of IT assets. The ITIL configuration management process takes the ITAM approach a step further by also looking at the nature and importance of the relationships between assets. Note that ITIL uses the term configuration items (CI) rather than assets, and similarly uses the related term configuration management database (CMDB) rather than other terms like *asset management system,* which some readers might be familiar with.

SAP supports the traditional concept of IT asset management (ITAM) very well. In SAP, asset management is handled using either the CRM IBase or the IObject as seen in Figure 10.7. To some extent, this same approach can also be extended to support ITIL configuration management by mapping configuration items such as IBases or IObjects. Problems (i.e., service tickets) and RFC (i.e., service orders) are each fully integrated with both objects. Additionally, native integration to SAP ERP Enterprise Asset Management is available with both IObjects and IBases. You can integrate open interfaces to auto discovery and system management tools. This is important, because if you are a large company with millions of assets, you could easily end up spending all of your time just trying to keep up with your assets.

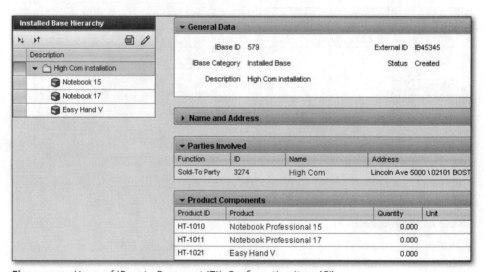

Figure 10.7 Usage of IBase to Represent ITIL Configuration Item (CI)

10.1.2   Employee Interaction Center

Now that you are familiar with the IT help desk, which helps you provide technical support to your employees for their IT-related issues, let's look at another type of back-office shared service center that is geared toward helping your employees with other types of non-IT issues. Employees often run into many other types of work issues that are not necessarily related to IT. They have questions about their benefits, compensation, pay checks, and other human resources–related topics. For example, see Figure 10.8, which illustrates an example of the percentage of different types of issues reported by employees at a particular company.

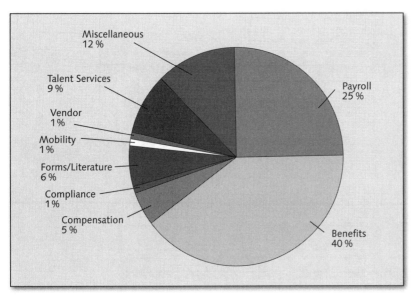

Figure 10.8   Example of Types of HR Issues Reported by Employees

To provide HR departments with a cost-effective HR service desk application to support their human capital management (HCM) efforts, SAP delivers the *employee interaction center* (EIC) scenario standard with the CRM Interaction Center. The EIC allows back-office HR generalists and specialist to process telephone calls, emails, or other types of communications from employees who require assistance with an HR issue (Figure 10.9). The EIC agent is able to search for and locate the employee's record in the back-end HR system directly from the front-end CRM system. The EIC agent can also view the employee's complete interaction history, including any currently open or unresolved HR issues. When necessary, the agent can also access the appropriate HR transactions from the back-office HCM system using the transaction launcher from the EIC.

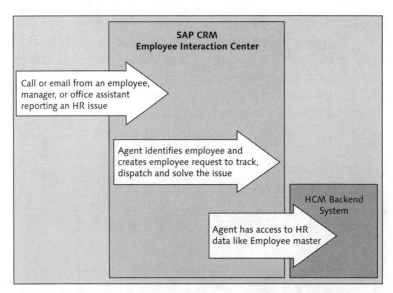

Figure 10.9 Overview of SAP CRM Employee Interaction Center

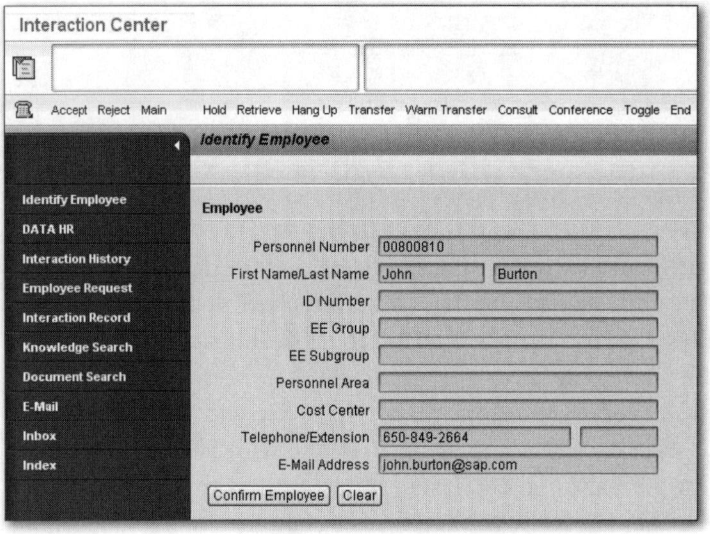

Figure 10.10 CRM Business Role IC_SSC_AGENT for EIC Scenario

SAP delivers a default CRM business role called IC_SSC_AGENT that provides the appropriate navigation bar, PFCG authorization profile, and function profiles necessary for running the EIC (Figure 10.10). Included in this business role is the function profile BPIDENT_EMPLOYEE (with value EMPLOYEE) rather than the standard function profile BPIDENT. This is necessary because we want to search for employees using employee specific criteria such as employee ID and cost center, rather than searching via the standard customer search criteria (Figure 10.11).

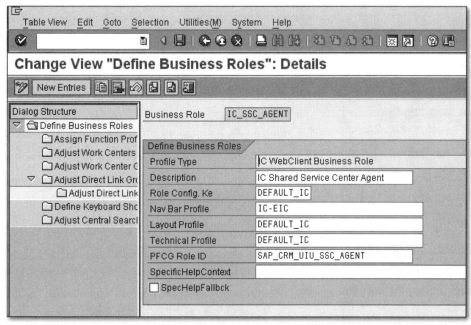

Figure 10.11 Function Profile BPIDENT_EMPLOYEE for Employee Search

The EIC provides built-in integration to the back-office SAP HCM system. EIC agents can directly access HR data from the employee interaction center in CRM without needing to separately log in to the HCM system. When the EIC agent clicks on an appropriate link in the navigation bar of the Interaction Center, the relevant HR transaction is retrieved from the back-office HCM system and displayed directly inside the CRM employee interaction center (Figure 10.12). Using the EIC, agents can perform a variety of HR-related tasks such as:

▶ Enroll new employees

▶ Update HR master data such as last name, address, bank details

▶ Execute other day-to-day processes such as handling of requests for vacation, sick leave, jury duty, etc.

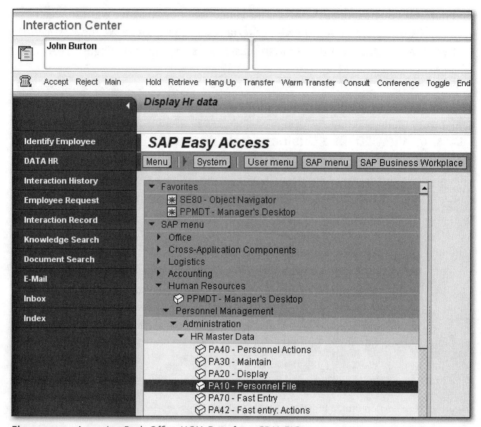

Figure 10.12 Accessing Back-Office HCM Data from CRM EIC

Let's look at an example featuring an international software company that was struggling to manage its North American employees. The HR department was having difficulty responding consistently to employee requests, which was resulting in costly multiple contacts for each employee issue. The HR department faced the challenge of dramatically increasing service quality, while also significantly decreasing costs and expenditures. Also, they wanted to improve service levels and maximize employee experience in order to help retain top talent in a competitive employee market. The HR department needed to provide the following key services:

▶ Pre-hire, new hire, rehire, and separation

▶ Employee changes, compensation, and payroll

▶ Health and welfare benefit plans (medical, dental, vision, prescription)

- Basic and supplemental life insurance, leave and disability programs
- Service awards and work-life benefit programs
- Defined benefit (DB)/defined contribution (DC) plans
- 401K, pension, and stock purchase plans

After implementing the employee interaction center scenario with the SAP CRM Interaction Center, the company can immediately see positive results. Many issues can now be resolved on the first contact, because EIC agents now had access to all required systems and information directly from the employee interaction center. For example, using the transaction launcher, agents can branch out to external knowledge repositories for forms and documents, access the employee self service application to update data on behalf of the employee, or launch back-end ERP and HCM transactions inside the interaction center. Agents also have full access to the employee's complete history in order to instantly pull up any unresolved or open issues while the employee was still on the telephone. These improvements were immediately felt by employees. Not only did employee satisfaction, engagement, and referral rates improve considerably, but the costs of providing employee service decreased dramatically, resulting in lower costs per hire and increased productivity and revenue per employee (Figure 10.13).

	Year 0	Year 1	Year 2	Improvement
Employee Referral Rate	20%	32%	45%	25 pts.
Employee Engagement	68%	76%	78%	10 pts.
Customer Satisfaction (1-10 scale)	7.0	7.8	7.8	.8
Cost per hire	$22,500	$11,400	$10,500	-53%
Sales Productivity (per employee)	$2.1M	$2.9M	$3M	43%
Revenue (per employee)	$473,000	$534,000	$593,000	25%

Figure 10.13 Benefits Achieved with Employee Interaction Center

10.1.3 Accounting Interaction Center (Consulting Solution)

As of CRM 2006s/CRM 2007, two shared services scenarios are provided by SAP out of the box — the IT help desk and the employee interaction center (both of these scenarios are also available in earlier releases like CRM 2005 as well). In addition to these two out of the box shared service centers, a third shared services scenario, the accounting interaction center (AIC), is available on a project basis as a consulting solution (Figure 10.14).

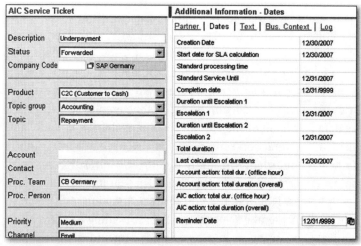

Figure 10.14 Accounting Interaction Center (AIC) Consulting Solution

The AIC is a shared services help desk that allows accountants or Interaction Center accounting specialists to handle accounting-related questions from customers, vendors, or employee users. The AIC integrates with the back-office ERP system connecting to accounts receivable or accounts payable – or both. AIC agents are able to access the financial accounts of customers or vendors and retrieve financial documents, such as invoices.

The following functionality is available for handling requests from customers:

▸ Changes in address data and partner information

▸ Update of payment card or bank data for automatic debit

▸ Account balance – open items information

▸ Dunning information

▸ Sales order related information like delivery and invoicing date

▸ Dispute case for a specific invoice

▸ Copy of invoice

The following functionality is available for handling request from vendors (suppliers):

- Changes in bank data
- Changes in address data and contact partner
- Payment status of a specific invoice
- Invoice receipt/verification information
- Payment plan regarding overdue items
- Clarification of payments
- Incorrect purchase order data (price of purchased item)

The following back-office transactions are available for handling request from employees (internal users):

- Create new profit center (transaction KE51)
- Change profit center – person responsible (transaction KE52)
- Create new cost center (transaction KS01)
- Change cost center – person responsible (transaction KS02)
- Create new general ledger (GL) account (transaction FS00)
- Change or block general ledger (GL) account (transaction FS00)
- Update credit limit of customer account (transaction FD32)
- Create new customer master (transaction XD01)
- Change customer master (transaction XD02)
- Block customer master (transaction XD05)
- Create supplier/vendor master (transaction XK01)
- Change supplier/vendor master (transaction XK02)
- Block supplier/vendor master (transaction XK05)
- Create asset for purchasing (transaction AS01)

> **Note**
>
> SAP is considering making the Accounting Interaction Center available as a standard solution in a release after CRM 2007.

10.2   Industry Solutions

The SAP CRM Interaction Center provides a flexible and powerful framework that can be used to support a variety of business processes across most vertical industries. For example, in the help desk scenario SAP provides service tickets for logging service requests and a solution database and knowledge search tool for creating and locating solutions. Similarly, for the lead qualification process, SAP provides interactive scripts with built-in surveys that can automatically create and qualify leads. These out of the box scenarios and processes satisfy the needs of most companies and a variety of industry verticals including high-tech, public sector (government), consumer packaged goods, fabricated metals, chemicals, pharmaceutical, life sciences, insurance, banking, and financial services. However, some industries have unique business processes that require additional out of the box functionality beyond what is provided by default with the SAP CRM Interaction Center. For example, in the utilities industry, agents need to perform specialized procedures such as entering meter readings for a premise, or processing move-ins and move-outs. Similarly, the telecommunications (Telco) industry requires support for what are known as MACDs (requests for move, add, change, delete), as well as other specialized requirements including integration of SAP credit management for conducting consumer credit checks. The automotive industry also has its own unique requirements, such as the ability to search for vehicles using VIN number or license plate number. To address the specific needs of these particular industries, SAP has developed additional, industry-specific versions of the Interaction Center geared toward each industry vertical.

10.2.1   Interaction Center for Utilities

Utilities companies generate and distribute services such as energy (e.g., electricity, natural gas, propane), water, or waste and recycling. Historically, most utility companies around the world were either government-owned or government-regulated monopolies. One designated company was solely responsible for providing services to a particular geographic region. In more recent years, starting with the privatization of the British electricity industry in the U.K. in the late 1980s, there has been a world-wide trend toward government deregulation and liberalization of utility markets.

Deregulation has dramatically changed the playing field for utilities companies. One effect of deregulated markets is that smaller players have been able to enter the market by focusing on a specific segment of the market, such as power generation, distribution, or trading and reselling. In the past, the complete process from energy distribution through retail supply was controlled by big companies with exclusive monopolies. Deregulated markets also mean that (at least in theory) a customer has a choice between different utilities providers. In the past, utilities companies could afford to be somewhat cavalier in their attitudes toward customer service and somewhat relaxed in their marketing efforts, as subscribers had no alternative but to do business with them. Now, however, with increased competition and additional players entering the market, utilities companies are turning to CRM to retain and expand their customer base.

As part of the transition from regulated to deregulated markets, utilities companies have shifted their mindsets to thinking of their *subscribers* as *customers*. In the past, where an energy company may have offered a single product (e.g., electricity) at a single rate, companies are now offering a plethora of product packages and product bundles with promotions geared toward specific target markets. For example, a company may offer a "Family Plan" product geared toward high-use households, and another product marketed toward smaller households.

> **Note**
>
> Telecommunications (Telco) is occasionally still considered part of the overall utilities industry. Although because it is generally is regarded as its own industry vertical, we will address the Telco Interaction Center separately in Section 10.1.3.

From R/3 IS-U to CRM Interaction Center WebClient for Utilities

Before we begin our discussion of the CRM Interaction Center WebClient version of the utilities solution, it is worth spending a minute to discuss the history and evolution of the utilities Interaction Center. The first utilities solution available from SAP was an R/3 offering called IS-U that was based on the R/3 Customer Interaction Center front office application (often referred to simply as the "front office"). The IS-U solution (Industry Solutions – Utilities), has been a highly successful product with over 500 live customers still running it today. Using the IS-U solution, utilities companies could perform a variety of front-office processes such as managing installations and premises, entering meter readings, conducting billing and invoicing, and resolving customer billing disputes and late payments.

The IS-U solution worked well and provided the necessary features to adequately handle the customer service processes of a utilities company. However, being an

ERP-based product, the IS-U obviously didn't have access to any CRM scenarios, such as marketing. As utilities companies recognized the need to embrace CRM, especially with increasing industry deregulation, it became clear that SAP needed to develop a utilities solution in CRM. The first utilities solution available in CRM was built on top of the IC WinClient. Later, with CRM release 4.0 Add-on for Service Industries, a version of the utilities solution was also offered for the IC WebClient. As of CRM 2006s/CRM 2007, only the IC WebClient (or to be more precise, the CRM WebClient Interaction Center version) is supported (Figure 10.15).

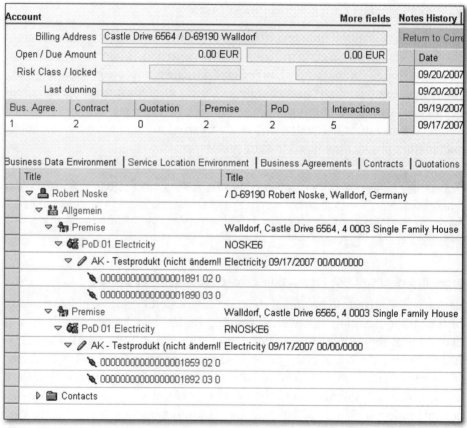

Figure 10.15 Utilities Interaction Center in CRM WebClient

Currently, SAP still offers both the ERP-based IS-U solution and the CRM-based Interaction Center solution for utilities. However, SAP's recommended strategy is that new customers should implement the CRM version, and existing ERP customers should migrate from ERP to CRM. There is no need to run both solutions in parallel; the CRM version can be run completely independent of the ERP version. However, it is technically possible to integrate the CRM version to the ERP IS-U version if required.

Interaction Center WebClient for Utilities

The CRM WebClient Utilities solution delivers about 40 different utilities front-office processes (e.g., move-in/move-out, outage notification, service request, and financials); additional templates for front-office processes are available via a consulting solution. Out of the box, the solution provides two business roles that Interaction Center agents can use to perform utility related tasks — the UTIL_IC role for regulated utilities and the UTIL_IC_LEAN for regulated utilities. Both roles include access to tools for providing customer service and conducting retail sales of utilities. However, the UTIL_IC role, designed for deregulated markets, provides additional capabilities for, for example, selling service contracts.

▶ The UTIL_IC role is designed for deregulated industries where, due to competition, energy providers need to leverage functionality like product proposals, real-time offer management, and agent guidance in order to generate additional revenue and provide higher-quality service.

▶ The UTIL_IC_LEAN business role is intended for regulated industries where there is no price competition.

Regardless of the two roles, the core business processes can be divided into two main processes: consumption and revenue collection. The consumption process involves collecting information, such as creating and printing meter-reading orders, and then uploading the results into the system. A partial list of consumption processes include:

▶ Move-in, move-out and move-in/out processes

▶ Meter reading entry

Revenue collection processes involve things like billing the customer, invoicing, and printing the bill. A partial list of some of the revenue collection processes include:

▶ Identification of business partner/contract account/premise

▶ Changes to business partner/contract account

- Changes to bank data
- Budget billing changes
- Bill information/bill correction
- Payment installation plan, deferral

> **Note**
>
> Additional consulting solutions are also available from SAP partners for locations with regional requirements, such as the Danish market.

10.2.2 Telco Interaction Center

The telecommunications (Telco) industry has often been considered part of the larger utilities industry, because telecommunications services such as telephone access have long been viewed as a public service/utility just like water or electricity. However, as telecommunications shift from land-line telephone service to mobile networks and Internet-based streaming of voice and data, telecommunications is generally now considered its own distinct industry.

The telecommunications (Telco) Interaction Center scenario is designed for companies who provide (i.e., carry) telephone and communications services including telephone, television, and Internet access, whether via traditional terrestrial-based wire networks or newer satellite-based networks. Using the Telco Interaction Center, telecommunications carriers can handle all of the needs of their subscribers, including sales order management and customer service, as well as collections management, dispute resolution, and financial customer care.

In the Telco industry, product and service are typically bundled in packages rather than sold as standalone products. For example, when purchasing a new mobile phone, a subscriber would not purchase just an actual telephone; rather, they would purchase a package including the telephone, a service contract (typically multi-year), a particular voice (or voice and data) plan such as basic or premium, and additional features such as ring tones and accessories. This is supported by the SAP in the Telco Interaction Center with the use of product packages in the sales order. When a product package is added to an order, the package is exploded into the individual items inside the order (Figure 10.16).

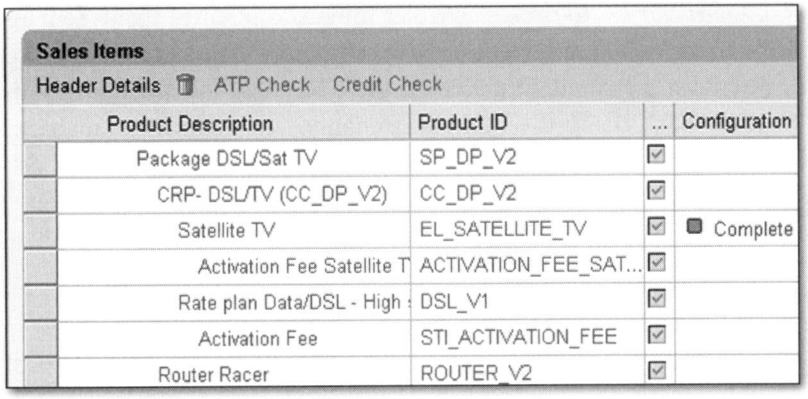

Sales Items

Header Details | ATP Check | Credit Check

Product Description	Product ID	...	Configuration
Package DSL/Sat TV	SP_DP_V2	☑	
CRP- DSL/TV (CC_DP_V2)	CC_DP_V2	☑	
Satellite TV	EL_SATELLITE_TV	☑	Complete
Activation Fee Satellite T	ACTIVATION_FEE_SAT...	☑	
Rate plan Data/DSL - High	DSL_V1	☑	
Activation Fee	STI_ACTIVATION_FEE	☑	
Router Racer	ROUTER_V2	☑	

Figure 10.16 Product Package Exploded in Sales Order as Multiple Items

The sales order process in the Telco Interaction Center also supports the separation of a one-time fee from the recurring (e.g., monthly charges). An agent is able to accept different payment types for the device and the rate plan in case the customer wants to, for example, use different payment cards for a phone and a calling plan. SAP Credit Management in fully integrated with the order process, and is executed before an order is saved. Agents are able to manually search within the product catalog when creating an order; additionally, built-in suggestions for cross-selling and up-selling are available.

In addition to enabling the sales order entry process, the Telco Interaction Center also provides support for customer financial customer care, billing disputes, and collections management. These processes help Telco Interaction Center agents provide answers about account balances and invoices, resolve billing disputes, and collect payments (or payment promises) from overdue accounts. Using the Telco Interaction Center, agents can see, for example, an overview of the business agreements and contacts for an account, including the open amount (Figure 10.17).

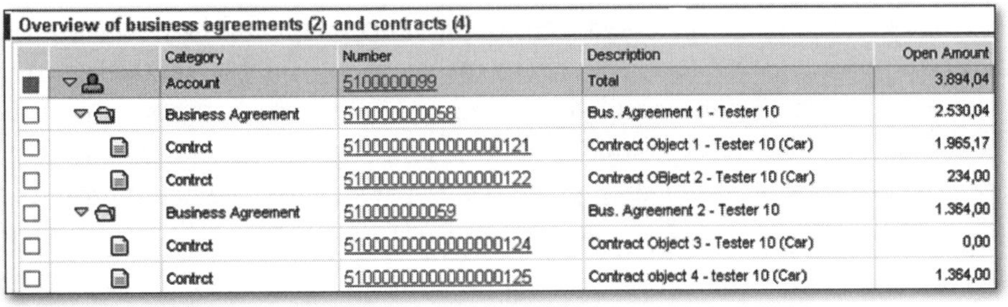

Overview of business agreements (2) and contracts (4)

Category	Number	Description	Open Amount
Account	5100000099	Total	3.894,04
Business Agreement	510000000058	Bus. Agreement 1 - Tester 10	2.530,04
Contrct	5100000000000000121	Contract Object 1 - Tester 10 (Car)	1.965,17
Contrct	5100000000000000122	Contract OBject 2 - Tester 10 (Car)	234,00
Business Agreement	510000000059	Bus. Agreement 2 - Tester 10	1.364,00
Contrct	5100000000000000124	Contract Object 3 - Tester 10 (Car)	0,00
Contrct	5100000000000000125	Contract object 4 - tester 10 (Car)	1.364,00

Figure 10.17 Overview of Telco Business Agreements and Contracts

The *financial customer care* (FCC) process enables Interaction Center agents to handle all types of finance-related interactions with customers. Agents can access the FCC functionality with the standard delivered CRM business role (or IC WebClient profile) TELCO_FCC. Using the FCC functionality, you can access, manage, and amend master data and contract account data. For example, you can check account balances, display invoices, remove locks, resolve disputes, reverse dunning notices, accept payments, and so on. A complete list of financial customer care (FCC) functionality includes:

- ▶ Check account balances and invoices
- ▶ Set and remove locks that prevent unwanted processing of certain items or accounts, such as payment locks and dunning locks
- ▶ Apply credit notes to resolve disputes
- ▶ Create or change installment plans
- ▶ Defer open items
- ▶ Reverse dunning notices
- ▶ Accept payments (via credit card or bank transfer, for example) and reactivate or reconnect service, where appropriate
- ▶ Initiate a dispute case and view previous ones

The billing dispute management process helps you resolve customer billing disputes quickly and effectively. Using the billing dispute functionality of the Telco Interaction Center you can load and display invoices from, for example, external, third-party, legacy billing systems, including the invoice line details. Interaction Center agents are empowered to resolve low-value disputes, by, for example, applying a credit memo to the subscriber's account. Agents can also create adjustment requests for higher-value disputes, either for the complete invoice or for individual line-items of the invoice.

The collections management process re-uses the functionality of the financial customer care process. At its core, collections management is about contacting customers with past due balances and getting either an actual payment or a promise to pay. Based on back-office dunning notices, calls lists are generated and then processed by the agent – who attempts to secure payment or a payment promise.

10.2.3   Insurance Interaction Center (Consulting Solution)

The insurance industry has some unique challenges from other industries. For example, people aren't calling in to report technical problems with their laptop or printer; rather, the majority of calls to an insurance help desk involve claim inquiries. Yet, the insurance industry also faces many of the same issues and challenges as the Telco industry does, particularly in the area of sales order management. Like many other industries including Telco and financial services, products in the insurance industry are increasingly more complex and personalized.

In today's ultra-competitive insurance industry, it's not enough to provide high-quality products. Insurers also need to deliver superior sales and services to the customers, while simultaneously reducing costs and ensuring greater profitability for the shareholders. The SAP Customer Service Management for Insurance — Consulting Package, addresses these challenges with software that enables efficient and customer-oriented processes between the front desk and the back office. The package, a preconfigured system, is based on the Interaction Center environment and supports core processes like complaint management and quick claim handling with straight-through processing (Figure 10.18). The package, including sales materials, implementation accelerators, and demo has been available since November 2007.

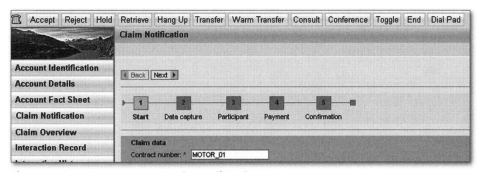

Figure 10.18   Insurance Interaction Center Claim Process

10.2.4   Automotive Interaction Center

The automotive Interaction Center solution supports automobile (auto) importers (i.e., distributors) as well as original equipment manufacturers (OEMs) (i.e., brand manufacturers like Toyota, Porsche, Volkswagen, Audi, and Yutong Bus). Using the automotive Interaction Center, as an OEM or importer, you can interact with both end customers and dealerships via a variety of communication channels, including telephone, email, and SMS, as well as telematics (i.e., embedded automated diagnostic software in the vehicle).

For OEMs and importers/distributors, it is crucial to have customer and vehicle information instantly available for efficient, customer-facing activities. Having this information at hand enables you to react quickly and deliver reliable, personal responses to customer complaint management or satisfaction surveys. The automotive Interaction Center also allows you to efficiently respond to requests for information from customers or dealers, for both simple and technical issues. Using the automotive Interaction Center, companies can effectively manage marketing campaigns, customer satisfaction surveys, complaints, service requests, appraisals, accessory sales, call backs, and roadside assistance.

The automotive Interaction Center is unique from the other industry solutions discussed in this chapter in that it does not generally involve any special back-office processes or integration. Rather, the main difference between the standard Interaction Center and the automotive Interaction Center is that the automotive version uses the vehicle as the main object for searches, while the standard solution uses the IBase or IObject. Agents can access the automotive Interaction Center via the standard CRM business role (or IC WebClient profile) AUTOMOTIVE. This will enable the vehicle search screen instead of the default IBase/IObject search screen. In the vehicle search screen, agents can search by a variety of vehicle-related criteria, including license plate number or vehicle identification number (VIN) as shown in Figure 10.19.

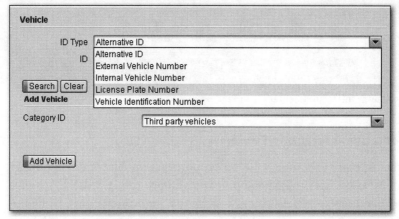

Figure 10.19 IC Automotive Vehicle Search Screen

After conducting a vehicle search, the appropriate vehicle record is located and displayed on the screen (Figure 10.20). Based on the confirmed vehicle, the current owner can automatically be retrieved by using the maintained relationship types of the driver. This allows the agent to automatically identify the customer without needing to do a manual search. Also, if desired, the agent can click the Details button to navigate to the full vehicle details page that shows additional data such as the vehicle manufacturer, owner, odometer reading, and so on.

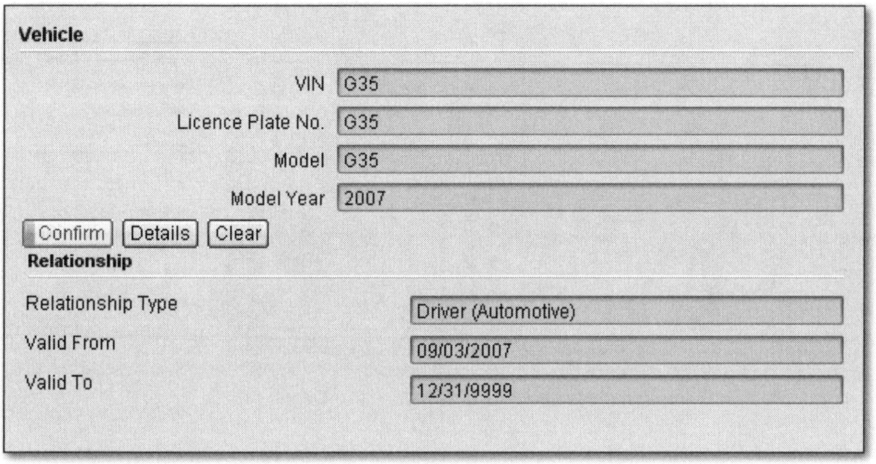

Figure 10.20 IC Automotive Vehicle Search Results

In addition, the IC Automotive Interaction Center supports integration of vehicle telematics (i.e., the user of embedded GPS and/or diagnostic devices in the vehicle that automatically communicate with external software). For example, let's consider the following scenario. An owner is driving their vehicle on a road trip when the vehicle's diagnostic system detects a problem and automatically sends a message to the vehicle manufacturer's service organization. The service organization telephones the driver via the hands-free phone system built into the car. The service technician creates a service order in the Interaction Center for an inspection/repair at the nearest authorized service center to the customer. Using the embedded mapping software in the Interaction Center, the agent can even provide the driver with directions to the service center (Figure 10.21).

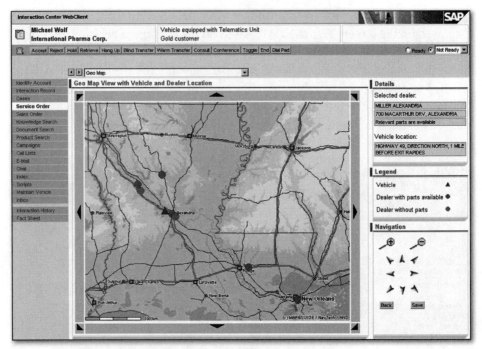

Figure 10.21 Map Showing Vehicle Location and Directions to Dealer

10.3 Summary

In this chapter, we explored how the Interaction Center can serve as a front office for your back-office IT, HR, and accounting operations in a shared services environment. We also looked at some industry verticals such as utilities, telecommunications (Telco), and insurance that heavily rely on back-office processes inside their front-office Interaction Center.

Some of the most important points to remember are:

▸ Shared services involve consolidating internal back-office processes such as IT, HR, or accounting across your company into a global shared service center.

▸ Vertical industries like utilities, telecommunications, and insurance often have unique industry-specific requirements that necessitate integration back-office ERP functionality into the front-office Interaction Center.

▸ SAP delivers two shared service center scenarios out of the box — the employee interaction center and the IT help desk. A third shared service center scenario

— the accounting interaction center — is currently available as a consulting solution.

▶ The IT help desk supports ITIL processes by mapping SAP business transactions and objects, such as the service ticket, service order, solution, and IBase, against the ITIL incident, problem, known error, request for change, and CMDB configuration items (CIs).

▶ The employee interaction center allows your agents to access back-office HR functionality from the back-end HCM system, directly from the front-office Interaction Center.

▶ The utilities Interaction Center provides two default business roles — one for utilities markets that are still regulated, and another for deregulated markets.

▶ The Telco Interaction Center includes a financial customer care (FCC) process as well as full support for billing dispute resolution and collections management.

In the next chapter, we will examine the SAP partner infrastructure around the Interaction Center. We will look at leading partner companies in the areas of contact-center infrastructure/business communications management, workforce management (and more broadly, workforce optimization), as well as systems integrators and consulting firms. If you are considering a new project, upgrade, or just some fine-tuning, we can help you find the right partner to talk with.

Choose your partners as carefully as your words. Mark Twain — master wordsmith — once noted, "The difference between the almost right word and the right word is really a large matter — 'tis the difference between the lightning bug and the lightning."

11   Partnerships and Certifications

SAP is the world's leading business software company, offering a complete suite of enterprise-grade applications. For each product, SAP has teams of product managers, developers, and consultants creating new and improved solutions to help you run your business. Even so, SAP can't do it alone. That's why SAP teams up with complementary software and service providers who offer best-of-breed products and services that integrate with SAP's solutions. To ensure that these partner solutions properly integrate with SAP applications in a high-quality manner, SAP offers a thorough testing and certification process.

In this chapter, we will examine the SAP partner infrastructure around the CRM Interaction Center. We will introduce you to leading software solution partners in the areas of contact-center infrastructure and contact-center workforce management and optimization.

> **Note**
>
> The term *contact-center* refers to software that is not part of the SAP CRM Interaction Center solution, but rather is part of the underlying communication management software infrastructure.

In addition, we will look at top SAP service partners — systems integrators and consulting companies — who have significant Interaction Center project experience and expertise. Whether you are considering a new implementation, upgrade, project-based enhancement or extension, or just fine-tuning of your SAP CRM Interaction Center, we can help you find the right partners.

11.1   Types of SAP Partnerships and Certifications

Before we introduce you to the top partners in the Interaction Center area, let's first discuss the SAP partnership program and certification process in general. SAP groups its partners into nine different partner categories including business processing outsourcing (BPO) providers, channel partners, content partners, education partners, hosting partners, services partners, software solution partner, support partners, and technology partners. The two categories that are most relevant for the Interaction Center are software solution partners and services partners.

SAP *software solution partners* are third-party companies who develop products that integrate with SAP solutions and add additional value by extending the native capabilities of the SAP solutions. The products of these companies have passed rigorous certification and validation tests administered by SAP. SAP *services partners*, on the other hand, are third-party companies who provide professional services. These consulting firms and systems integrators help SAP customers to design, implement, and integrate SAP solutions; optimize business processes; and provide strategic business consultation. Let's look closely at each.

> **Note**
>
> More details about the vital role that partners play in the SAP ecosystem can be found at: *http://www.sap.com/ecosystem/partners/index.epx*.

11.1.1   SAP Software Solution Partners

SAP software solution partners are third-party software companies who develop complementary software applications that integrate with SAP to extend the power of SAP across business processes and industries. For example, companies like Genesys, Avaya, and Siemens provide so-called contact-center infrastructure software that can be used to integrate telephony and additional communication channels into the Interaction Center. Similarly, companies like Verint offer contact-center workforce management (WFM) and workforce optimization (WFO) capabilities to help Interaction Center managers with agent scheduling, monitoring, and training. SAP offers three designations for products of software solution partners including SAP certification, SAP endorsed business solution, and SAP solution extension. In addition, SAP offers a program called SAP Partner Edge for premium partners.

Note

You can search for partners using the SAP Ecosystem and Partner Catalog available at *http://sspcatalog.sap.com/catalog/index.jsp*. The search features allow you to search by a combination of keywords, enterprise application (like CRM), and type of partnership, such as certification type (e.g., SAP Certification — Integration with SAP Applications) or solution type (e.g., SAP-endorsed business solution or SAP solution extension).

Certifications

Of the three types of product-related partnerships offered by SAP, *certification* represents the first tier — and the most common type of SAP partnership. A product that is designated as certified means that SAP has tested and confirmed only that the product *integrates* with SAP. SAP has not tested the complete product functionality and does not make any statements about the quality of the product. As such, certification should not be seen as an *endorsement* or recommendation by SAP. Rather, a certification is merely an acknowledgement that the third-party partner product correctly integrates with a defined SAP interface. Most of the partnerships in the Interaction Center area, such as contact center infrastructure providers or WFO suites, involve first-tier *certifications* rather than second-tier–endorsed business solutions or third-tier solution extensions.

SAP® Certified
Integration with SAP Applications

An application that has SAP-certified integration with SAP applications has proven to interoperate with one or more SAP applications using integration technologies such as a BAPI® programming interface, remote function call (RFC), or intermediate document (IDoc) technology.

Figure 11.1 SAP Certified — Integration with SAP Applications Logo

SAP offers three different types of "SAP Certified" certifications for software solution partners including: *Integration with SAP Applications*, *Integration with SAP NetWeaver*, and *Powered by SAP NetWeaver*. Most of the SAP software solution partners we will discuss in this chapter hold the Integration with SAP Applications certification (Figure 11.1). The actual certification process is conducted by an SAP organization known as the SAP Integration and Certification Center (SAP ICC). The SAP ICC has established testing and certification centers in three areas around the world, located in Walldorf, Germany; Palo Alto, California; and Bangalore, India. The benefit to SAP customers of working with certified partner products is that you can reduce integration time and costs, safeguard your existing IT investment, and ensure the integrity of your data via stable interfaces.

SAP-Endorsed Business Solution

The SAP-*endorsed business solution* (EBS) is an agreement between SAP and an SAP software solution partner to jointly co-market and sell the partner's product. As such, the EBS can be seen as a positive recommendation (or *endorsement*) by SAP on behalf of the partner's product. Due to the elevated status of the EBS, there are fewer EBS partnerships compared to the large number of partnerships via certifications. The EBS partnership process is much more involved and lengthy. It's not just a matter of spending a few days or weeks to test and certify the integration of the product with SAP. Rather, months of detailed analysis and evaluations are performed to make sure the partner and the partner's product are worthy of being recommended by SAP to customers. In the area of the Interaction Center, there are not many relevant EBS partnerships The Questra Remote Service Composite Application, which allows remote device monitoring for customer service processes, is an example of an EBS partnership that might have some relevance to the Interaction Center.

SAP Solution Extension

The SAP solution extension is the third, and most rare, type of partnership between SAP and third-party software solution partners. An SAP *solution extension* can be seen as a type of OEM reseller agreement where SAP bundles the software from the third-party partner into the standard SAP offering. Due to the nature of the solution extension partnership, these products need to be rock-solid. Examples of SAP solution extensions that might be relevant in the Interaction Center (or least in CRM) include Adobe Interactive Forms or SAP Price and Performance Management by Vendavo.

SAP Partner Edge for Software Solution Partners

The SAP Partner Edge program for software solution partners has been specifically designed for organizations that design and build complementary software solutions based on SAP technologies (Figure 11.2). Initially, the Partner Edge program was developed specifically for value-added resellers within the SAP partner ecosystem. However, the focus of the program has expanded to include partners who develop complementary software solutions based on SAP technologies. Membership in the SAP Partner Edge is not open to everyone and there are numerous guidelines and requirements designed to include only those partners whose software is not only certified by SAP but also actively used in production by SAP customers.

Figure 11.2 SAP Partner Edge — SAP Software Partner Logo

11.1.2 SAP Service Partners

Now that you have learned how the SAP software solution partnerships process works, let's look at the other type of partnership process that is relevant for the SAP CRM Interaction Center — the SAP services partnership process. SAP *service partners* focus on business solutions and typically provide consulting services and/or systems integration services, as well as support for evaluation, implementation, and continuous improvement efforts. Examples of SAP service partners who are frequently involved in Interaction Center projects include companies like Accenture, Axon, BearingPoint, Cap Gemini, Cognizant, Deloitte, ecenta, EoZen, Fujitsu, IBM, Knack, MindTree, Sparta, and TPC.

SAP Partner — Services

SAP service partners are actually classified into one of three different service partner categories: SAP partner, SAP alliance partner, and SAP global partner. The

SAP partner classification usually refers to smaller- or medium-sized companies (as well as local subsidiaries of larger international companies) who focus on local markets, specific industries, or specific SAP products. For example, many of the small- and medium-sized boutique consulting companies and system integrators who specialize in SAP CRM and the Interaction Center projects hold this type of certification. There are quite literally thousands of SAP service partner companies with the SAP partner designation, including companies such as Axon, ecenta AG, EoZen, Fujitsu, and MindTree.

SAP Alliance Partner — Services

The second type of SAP partner classification, the *SAP alliance partner*, designated consulting companies that offer comprehensive services to key SAP accounts in particular geographic markets. Alliance partners work closely with SAP to develop local markets and to deliver services. Participation at this level is by invitation only and requires a sufficient number of certified consultants. There are several hundred SAP service partner companies with the SAP alliance partner designation.

SAP Global Partner — Services

The third type of SAP partner classification, the *SAP global partner*, designates large international companies that deliver comprehensive services that cover at least two regions, including Europe and North America. There are only a few dozen SAP service partner companies who are classified as SAP global partners. These include big-name global consulting companies like Accenture, BearingPoint, Cap Gemini, Deloitte, HP, IBM, Siemens, TCS, and WiPro.

> **Note**
>
> You can search for partners by a variety of criteria including partner name, country, partner category (e.g., software partner, service partner), and partner membership level (i.e., partner, alliance partner, global partner) via the Partner Information Center Search page, which is located at the following URL: *http://www.sap.com/ecosystem/customers/directories/SearchPartner.epx*

This concludes our general discussion about the SAP partner infrastructure and the types of partnerships and certifications available. Now let's look specifically at some of the areas where partner solutions are heavily utilized by SAP customers in their Interaction Center projects. We will focus on two of the most prominent areas including contact center infrastructure (i.e., CTI and communication management software) including workforce optimization.

11.2   Contact Center Infrastructure Partners

The SAP CRM Interaction Center provides a framework that enables your Interaction Center agents to handle all the business needs of your customers across marketing, sales, and customer service. The Interaction Center also offers built-in hooks (i.e., certified interfaces) that allow you to plug in CTI and multi-channel functionality. Though the Interaction Center itself does not deliver any out-of-the-box CTI or multi-channel capabilities, additional products that provide CTI and multi-channel functionality are available from SAP, as well as from numerous SAP partner companies.

The software that enables integration of real-time telephony, email, Web chat, and other channels in the Interaction Center is referred to by SAP as Communication Management Software. However, this term is generally not recognized outside SAP in the contact-center industry where the term *contact center infrastructure* is preferred by analysts, customers, and other vendors. A large number of contact center infrastructure products are available for use with the Interaction Center, including products from SAP partners like Genesys, Avaya, Cisco, Siemens, Nortel, Aspect, Ericsson, and, Cycos — as well as SAP's own product, SAP Business Communication Management (BCM).

As explained in Chapter 2, SAP has a certification process that focuses on the vendor-specific *adapters* that connect individual contact center infrastructure products to the SAP interface. That is, SAP does not certify either the contact center infrastructure product or the vendor; rather, SAP certifies an additional piece of software that *translates* the communication (RFC or XML/SOAP messages) between the vendor's contact-center infrastructure products and the SAP interface. For a full list of certified adapters, you can visit the SAP Partner Information Center Search at *http://www.sap.com/partners/directories/SearchSolution.epx*. See Section 2.5 of Chapter 2 for full details on how to search for certified contact center infrastructure partners. Let's take a look at a few of the contact center infrastructure providers who work most closely with SAP.

11.2.1 Genesys Telecommunications Laboratories

Genesys Telecommunications Laboratories, an Alcatel-Lucent company head-quartered in San Francisco, is a market leader in the contact center infrastructure industry. Focusing exclusively on contact center software, Genesys provides award-wining contact center products geared toward medium to large businesses — and contact centers of all sizes. Genesys provides high-end type systems. Genesys products, such as the Genesys Gplus Adapter for SAP, support most major telephone switch vendors in the world. Genesys also provides extremely high scalability, with up to 50,000 users running on the same system in some cases. Together, Genesys and SAP have dozens of joint customers running the SAP CRM Interaction Center with Genesys integration.

Genesys and SAP have actually been working together for decades, dating back to the late 1990s. Genesys was one of the first companies to provide a third-party product that interfaced to the SAP Interaction Center. Even today, Genesys and SAP still continue their long-standing development and support partnership, where the two companies jointly develop and support each other's products. Collaboration between SAP and Genesys takes place on many different levels within both organizations. The product management and development organizations from both companies routinely meet to discuss requirements. The development and quality management teams also work closely together to deliver high-quality, integrated products. Whenever new contact-center relevant functionality is introduced in the SAP CRM Interaction Center, Genesys is often one of the first vendors to support the new feature.

For more information on Genesys integration with SAP, visit the website: *http://www.genesyslab.com/products/gplus_for_sap.asp.*

11.2.2 Avaya Inc.

Avaya Inc., a privately held U.S.-based telecommunications company, is a market leader in the contact center infrastructure industry. Avaya specializes in designing and implementing business communications systems that allow companies to deliver an optimal blend of customer access, convenience, and personalization to help nurture customer relationships and build repeat business. Avaya and SAP have been working together closely for several years, providing multi-channel integration for dozens of SAP CRM Interaction Center customers. Customers often describe Avaya as providing an optimal blend of features, performance, and value.

Avaya recognizes that in today's business market, success is determined less by what you sell but rather by the level of customer service that you provide to your customers. Increasingly, customers demand to be able to reach your organization anytime, anywhere, and by any communication channel. Avaya is one of the very few contact center software companies whose products and services are currently certified by SAP against both the SAPphone and ICI interfaces, and whose products are supported for all available communication channels, including telephony, email, and chat. Avaya provides a robust contact management platform — the Avaya Interaction Center — that manages interactions across multiple communication channels, including voice, email, web, and SMS. Additionally, Avaya is also one of the few contact center software companies that also provides its own connector to SAP, allowing Avaya and SAP applications to communicate directly without the need for any third-party adapters or middleware.

For more information on Avaya integration with SAP, visit the website: *http://www. avaya.com*. Also see Appendix A, which provides more detailed information about selected SAP partners such as Avaya.

11.2.3 SAP Business Communications Management (BCM) Software

The new kid on the block is SAP Business Communications Management (BCM) software. In 2007, SAP acquired a Finnish company called Wicom Communications, a leading, privately held provider of all-IP contact center and enterprise communications software based in Espoo, Finland. Wicom was rebranded as SAP Business Communications Management and positioned as a platform for a communications-enabled business process within SAP CRM, and across other products in the SAP Business Suite. Due to customer demand, SAP agreed to make SAP BCM available (along with other SAP partner solutions) as contact center infrastructure tool for enabling CTI and multi-channel integration in the Interaction Center.

SAP BCM is an Internet protocol (IP)–based multi-channel, enterprise communications platform. With SAP BCM, organizations can deploy IP telephony for everyone who needs it, including telemarketing experts, customer service agents, switchboard operators, office workers, mobile experts, and their managers. SAP BCM offers a range of contact channels and provides routing and queuing with integration to the Interaction Center. Wicom already had over 200 customers in

18 different countries prior to being acquired by SAP. Today, even more SAP customers look at how they can leverage SAP BCM to more effectively service their own customers.

It is important to note that SAP BCM is not intended to replace existing SAP partners, or to displace any active partner installations at customer sites. Rather, SAP BCM is an additional option for customers who are considering adding CTI or multi-channel integration (e.g., email, chat) to their SAP CRM Interaction Center. SAP BCM integrates with the Interaction Center in the same manner as other partner solutions via a certified SAP interface (i.e., the ICI interface). SAP BCM has also undergone the same rigorous testing and certification process as other partners and has a certification listing in the partner directory under Wicom Communications.

For more information on SAP BCM, visit *http://www.sap.com*.

11.3 Workforce Optimization Partners

Let's look at another area where partner solutions are heavily utilized in the interaction center — workforce optimization. Any company that runs an interaction center needs to be able to accurately forecast call volumes and schedule agents. Products that support forecasting, scheduling, and adherence to schedules are known as workforce management (WFM) applications. However, standalone WFM products are increasingly replaced by broader product suites known as *workforce optimization* (WFO) that include additional capabilities such as audio and screen recording, quality monitoring, contact center performance management, e-learning, coaching, and reporting. Essentially, WFO solutions help track and measure a company's return on investment in people and resources.

The single largest cost associated with running an interaction center is not the telephone system, computer hardware, CTI and CRM software, furniture, or real estate; rather, 60% of the costs of running an interaction center are directly related to agent salaries and compensation. Hence, as much as reasonably possible, you want your agents to actually work on customer issues whenever the agents are on the clock rather than sitting around idle. Even just a few minutes of lost productivity per day can result in millions of wasted dollars per year in a large, high-volume interaction center.

The thing that makes staffing the interaction center tricky is the uneven (and sometimes unpredictable) volume of calls that arrive throughout each day during the week. For example, call volumes may be very high during the morning when the interaction center first opens, then dip down in the late morning, and then spike again during lunch hours. If you overstaff your interaction center during slow periods, you are throwing money away. On the other hand, if you understaffed during busy periods you could be throwing customers away (by making them wait an unacceptable length of time before speaking to an agent). The challenge is to accurately forecast the spikes and lulls in call volume, and then schedule and staff your interaction center appropriately.

WFO software is a vital part of any large interaction center but is an extremely useful investment for small- and medium-sized interaction centers as well. With smaller interaction centers, it is possible to handle rudimentary agent scheduling using spreadsheet-based tools. However, once the number of agents exceeds 60 and starts to approach 100, a proper WFO solution becomes indispensable. WFO is valuable in both front-office and back-office interaction centers, including shared service centers for IT help desks, HR employee interaction centers, or accounting interaction centers. WFO can even be useful in any type of operation where you have a group of knowledge workers who need to handle customer communications, such as branch office of a bank or insurance company.

SAP does not provide a WFO solution itself but rather partners with industry leaders in the WFO market. In CRM releases 3.0 and 4.0, SAP offered a rudimentary workforce management (WMF) solution that provided basic agent scheduling capabilities for the Interaction Center. SAP's WFM solution was based on a product acquired in 1999 from Chicago-based Campbell Software that was geared toward the U.S. retail industry. However, as of CRM 2005, SAP discontinued its own WFM solution for the Interaction Center, removing it from the price list. The SAP WFM solution is now only available within the retail industry solution. Rather than trying to build up its WFM product to keep pace with the rapidly growing WFO market, SAP's strategy is to focus its efforts on core Interaction Center functionality, and to partner with industry leaders in the newly emerging WFO market. To that end, SAP is working closely with a WFO market leader, Verint Systems.

11.3.1 Verint Systems

There are a number of companies in the market who provide WFO capabilities including the leaders Verint Systems, Nice Systems, and Aspect. SAP has a partnership with *Verint Systems*, who is generally acknowledged as the industry leader by analysts and customers. In the past few years, there has been a great deal of consolidation in the WFO market. For example, Nice Systems purchased a couple of other companies, including EIX and Performix, and Verint Systems purchased Witness Systems, who had previously purchased Blue Pumpkin.

Verint Systems is a global company with thousands of customers around the world in all major industries, including banking, insurance, finance, telecommunications, high-tech, retail, hospitality, automotive, and general business. Verint is a certified, SAP software solution partner holding a Powered by SAP NetWeaver certification. Verint offers a complete suite of workforce optimization (WFO) applications that nicely complements the capabilities of the SAP CRM Interaction Center.

Technically, Verint actually offers two different workforce optimization solutions designed to fit the needs of SAP CRM Interaction Center customers. These two solutions, Impact 360 and Impact 360 Express, are available as part of the Verint Witness Actionable Solutions portfolio of products. Impact 360 is designed for large, multi-site, multi-channel interaction centers. Impact 360 Express is tailored toward smaller interaction centers. For more information, visit *http://www.verint. com*.

11.4   Systems Integration/Consulting Partners

Let's shift the conversation from SAP software solution partners to SAP *service partners*. As discussed in Section 11.1.2, SAP service partners include consulting companies, professional services organizations, and systems integrators who work with SAP customers to implement, customize, and enhance the SAP CRM Interaction Center. Let's look at some of the companies who are frequently involved in SAP CRM Interaction Center projects, and who work closely with SAP and SAP's customers.

11.4.1   ecenta

ecenta is a premium provider of SAP consulting services focused on SAP CRM and NetWeaver, with a long and successful track record of SAP CRM Interaction Center projects. Headquartered in Walldorf, Germany, ecenta has over 200 employees in subsidiaries located in the United States, Singapore, Malaysia, Sweden, China, Australia, and Chile. ecenta has many years of experience in the Interaction Center (both IC WebClient and IC WinClient), including Help Desk processes, CRM

Service, and CRM Sales. ecenta also specializes in the integration of external non-SAP systems with SAP CRM and the Interaction Center. ecenta's highly qualified, techno-functional consultants have delivered more than 60 successful CRM and Interaction Center implementations in various industries and regions of the world including companies like Intel, Adobe, HP, Varian Medical Systems, Bentley Systems, T-Mobile, Carl Zeiss Meditec, Data Domain, Network Appliances, Mayo Clinic, and Charles Machine Works. Additionally, ecenta is an SAP development partner and routinely works with SAP to develop new features for CRM and the Interaction Center. For more information on ecenta, see Appendix A or visit *http:// www.ecenta.com*. Also, see the two case studies in Chapter 13, featuring projects that were implemented by ecenta.

11.4.2   Axon Consulting

Axon is one of the largest global systems integrators who focus solely on SAP projects. As an organization, it employs over 2,000 experienced, SAP implementation professionals across North America, Europe, and Asia Pacific. Axon has been involved in numerous CRM Interaction Center projects across a wide range of industry sectors, including utilities, public sector, consumer packaged goods (CPG), and wholesale distribution. Projects implemented by Axon support over 7,500 agents in over 50 call center locations globally. Many of these projects involved computer telephony integration (CTI) and fully integrated interactive voice response (IVR) solutions. Regardless of the complexity of the system, Axon believes that *usability* is the key to any Interaction Center project. As such, Axon consultants are experts in the design and delivery of projects using SAP's latest, user-friendly, CRM WebClient user interface. For more information on Axon Consulting, see Appendix A or visit *http://www.AxonGlobal.com*.

11.4.3   The Principal Consulting (TPC)

The Principal Consulting (TPC) is an expert SAP consulting services organization. Based out of South Plainfield, New Jersey, TPC provides services nationally in the United States with offices in strategic cities and in the United States and India. With over 100 SAP specialists, TPC offers a range of services — from strategic planning to post-implementation support. TPC has a track record of successful SAP CRM Interaction Center implementations across a variety of industries, including utilities, consumer goods, high tech, and life sciences. One of the areas that TPC specializes in is helping companies implement SAP CRM 2007, either as an upgrade or new installation. TPC offers workshops and upgrade evaluations for customers considering moving to CRM 2007. For more information about The Principal Consulting, visit *http://www.TPCus.com*.

11.4.4 Sparta Consulting

Sparta Consulting, based out of Folsom, California, is a newly organized SAP consulting company, consisting of SAP veterans who previously worked in other "Big 5" consulting firms. Several members of the company's top management were high-level executives at Rapadigm Consulting, which was acquired by Fujitsu Consulting in 2006. One of Sparta Consulting's goals is to provide customers the most comprehensive SAP solutions at the most cost effective prices. Sparta Consulting strives to combine onshore and offshore staffing with an optimal mix of project management to provide flexible pricing options. To complement its on-site resources, Sparta also offers a 60,000-square-foot, 24/7-development facility in India with state-of-the-art infrastructure. Sparta Consulting also prides itself on customer service, offering a no questions asked, 30-day money back guarantee on their services. For more information about Sparta Consulting, visit *http://www. SpartaConsulting.com*.

11.4.5 iServiceGlobe

iServiceGlobe is a business solutions company dedicated and focused on SAP software, including CRM and ERP. iServiceGlobe provides end-to-end business and IT solutions with a focus on business process management, design, development, testing, QA, and support. iServiceGlobe is based out of the United States with offices in California and New Jersey, as well as the United Kingdom and India. iServiceGlobe's CRM client list includes industry leaders such as Hewlett-Packard, Varian Medical, Synopsys, and Konami Digital Entertainment. iServiceGlobe's own CEO, Srini Katta, recently published a book from SAP Press entitled, *Discover SAP CRM* (with technical development editor John Burton). For more information on iServiceGlobe, visit *http://www.iServiceGlobe.com*.

11.4.6 MindTree Consulting

MindTree Consulting is a global IT and R&D services company co-headquartered in the United States and India with offices in Somerset, New Jersey, and Bangalore, India. The SAP Practice is one of MindTree's fastest growing practices and includes expertise in CRM and the Interaction Center. MindTree was founded in 1999 by ten industry professionals from Cambridge Technology Partners, Lucent Technologies, and Wipro, who came together to create an international IT consulting company that delivers business and technology solutions through global software development. MindTree develops applications to help companies enhance their enterprise operations. The company also delivers product-development services and designs reusable building blocks for high-tech companies. MindTree practices a concept called Oneshore™ Consulting, which is designed to achieve a balance of quality, cost savings, and localization. MindTree is an SAP Global Services Partner, SAP Global Technology Partner, and a development partner. For more information about MindTree, see Appendix A or visit *http://www.MindTree.com*. Also, see the case study in Chapter 13 featuring a project at ICICI Prudential AMC that was implemented by MindTree.

11.4.7 EoZen

EoZen is a leading European SAP consulting firm, with a strong focus on customer satisfaction and innovation. EoZen has been involved in numerous SAP CRM Interaction Center projects in both the private and public sector, including projects with sophisticated CTI integration. Within the public sector, EoZen has significant experience in helping governments and municipalities meet the needs of their citizens to register complaints as well as handle requests for documents such as birth certificates, proof of residency, and marriage certificates. EoZen also has experience in the private sector, helping companies implement solutions for sales order management and customer service. With over 150 experienced consultants and offices in Belgium, Netherlands, Luxemburg, France, and Singapore, EoZen provides service to worldwide companies such as Glaverbel, Ashi Glass, Janssen Pharmaceutical, Philips, Carrefour, Bekaert, InBev, and Coca-Cola. EoZen has received various SAP awards including the prestigious "SAP Highest Customer Satisfaction" trophy, based on a comprehensive and independent customer satisfaction survey across SAP customers. For more information about EoZen, visit *http://www.EoZen.com*.

11.4.8 enapsys

enapsys is a young company founded by experienced SAP veterans, who after more than eight years as SAP employees in Mexico and Argentina, decided to start a consulting company. enapsys focuses on SAP CRM and SAP technology, and provides the highest quality and customer service standards. The core values of the company include a passion for quality and a long-term commitment to their customers. Through continuous investments in training and certifications, coupled with extensive project experience, enapsys is perhaps the top SAP CRM consulting company in Mexico, and one of the strongest in Latin America. enapsys provides a broad range of services, including CRM strategy and roadmap definition and project implementation of just spot consulting. enapsys has successfully implemented the SAP CRM Interaction Center in several projects. They provide consulting services across a wide variety of industries, including the public sector and the chemical industry. For more information on enapsys, see Appendix A or visit *http://www.enapsys.com*.

11.4.9 SAP Consulting

In addition to the various partner consulting companies, SAP also has its own professional services organization — SAP Consulting. With more than 30 years of experience in over 100,000 installations in more than 25 industries, SAP Consulting drives results from your SAP investment. No partner is more committed to seeing your SAP implementation succeed. SAP's constant life cycle engagement and dedication is illustrated by the fact that SAP consulting has never walked away from a customer. With direct access to SAP developers and product managers, SAP Consulting offers knowledge and resources unavailable elsewhere. For more information about SAP Consulting, visit *http://www.sap.com/services/bysubject/consulting/index.epx*.

11.4.10 The "Big 5"

All of the major global service providers, consulting firms, and systems integrators have their own SAP practices. Sometimes still referred to as the "Big 5" or the "Big 4," these include companies like Accenture, Bearing Point, Capgemini, Deloitte, Fujitsu Consulting, HP Services, IBM, Tata Consultancy Services (TCS), and Wipro Ltd. These large, full-service consulting companies may not necessarily all have the same detailed level of Interaction Center knowledge and experience as smaller, purely SAP-focused consulting firms. However, these large global consulting firms are heavily invested resources into the new SAP CRM 2007 product, impressed by the warm reception of the market to SAP's new and improved CRM offering. Several of the biggest players, including BearingPoint and Deloitte, already have significant experience with both the Interaction Center and SAP's new CRM WebClient.

11.5 Summary

In this chapter, you learned about the SAP partnership program and certification process, and examined the SAP partner infrastructure around the CRM Interaction Center. We highlighted leading SAP *software solution partners* in the areas of contact-center infrastructure and contact-center workforce optimization; we also highlighted top SAP *service partners* with significant Interaction Center project experience and expertise.

Some important points to remember are:

▶ SAP has various categories of partners, including software solution partners and service partners. Software solution partners develop applications that integrate with SAP. Service partners implement and extend SAP solutions.

▶ SAP offers three designations for products of software solution partners including: SAP certification, SAP endorsed business solution, and SAP solution extension. Most partners for the Interaction Center area fall into the first designation — SAP certification.

▶ Two types of software solution partners integrated most commonly in the Interaction Center include contact center software intrastructure providers and workforce optimization vendors.

▶ The three contact center software providers who work most closely with SAP in the Interaction Center area include Genesys, Avaya, and SAP BCM. However, other vendors like Cisco, Siemens, Nortel, Aspect, Ericcson, and Cycos are frequently also used in customer projects.

▶ SAP partners with Verint Systems for integration of workforce management (WFM) and workforce optimization capabilities inside the SAP CRM Interaction Center. As of CRM 2005, SAP no longer offers its own WFM product for use with the Interaction Center.

▶ SAP customers work closely with a number of service partners who specialize in SAP CRM and Interaction Center including ecenta, Axon Consulting, The Principal Consulting (TPC), Sparta Consulting, iServiceGlobe, MindTree Consulting, EoZen, enapsys, and SAP Consulting – as well as large global consulting firms like Accenture, BearingPoint, Deloitte, and Capgemini.

In the next chapter, we will look at some of the most commonly asked questions involving the Interaction Center. We will also strive to provide straightforward, helpful answers that succinctly address issues.

"Knowledge is a process of piling up facts; wisdom lies in their simplification."
— Martin Henry Fischer

12 Frequently Asked Questions

The goal of this book is to help you get the most out of your SAP CRM Interaction Center. On the one hand, we provide you with a high-level understanding of the Interaction Center to help formulate and guide your project strategy. On the other hand, we also deliver the relevant, in-depth details that you require to optimize your actual Interaction Center implementation and maximize the benefits. While the high-level theories and in-depth configuration details are great for explaining complicated concepts or configuration tasks, sometimes you just need an answer to a simple question. In this chapter, we will provide straight-forward, no-nonsense answers to some of the most commonly asked questions involving the Interaction Center.

The questions are divided into various sections, including technical topics such as user interface and framework-related questions, upgrade/migration questions, and questions about system performance. We'll also address questions regarding support of external products and standards such as computer telephony integration (CTI), Workforce Management (WFM), and the IT Infrastructure Library (ITIL). The answers provided in this chapter will be given in an honest, straight-forward, plain-spoken manner. Finally, we will wrap up with a list of 20 of the most helpful SAP notes for the Interaction Center.

12.1 User Interface and Framework Questions

As with any software application, the first questions that people usually ask about the Interaction Center have to do with the user interface and underlying technical framework. It's only natural for people to want to know more about their new enterprise software application. This natural curiosity is probably strengthened by the fact that SAP offers several different user interface options and has a reputation for rolling out new user interface technologies every couple of years. So, let's take a look at some of the most common questions people ask about the Interaction Center user interface and framework.

12.1.1 Browsers That are Supported

Which Web browser products and releases are supported? Will the Interaction Center run with Microsoft Internet Explorer 7.0? What about Mozilla Firefox or Apple Safari?

Microsoft Internet Explorer 7.0 and Mozilla Firefox 2.0 are both supported, depending on your CRM version, support package level, and operating system. See SAP note *1114557* (SAP CRM 2007 Internet Browser Releases), *981710* (Microsoft Internet Explorer Version 7.0 for end users) and *1152983* (IC Web Client Framework UI Web Browser Release Info). Support for Apple Safari is being investigated for a future release.

12.1.2 Windows Vista Support

Can users run the Interaction Center on computers using Microsoft Windows Vista operating system?

Yes, as described in SAP note *1159283*, the CRM WebClient (and hence the Interaction Center) support Windows Vista, but only in conjunction with Microsoft Internet Explorer (IE) 7.0, and currently for CRM 2006s/CRM 2007. Support for Windows Vista for CRM 2005 is planned for late 2008.

12.1.3 Interaction Center Requirement for a J2EE Server

Does the Interaction Center require a Java 2 Enterprise Edition (J2EE) server or J2EE components?

No, J2EE is no longer required to run the Interaction Center as of CRM 4.0 Add-On for Service Industries. In CRM 3.1 and 4.0, it was necessary to install a J2EE server and three J2EE components — IC Server, Software Agent Framework (SAF) Server, and Broadcast Messaging Server — in order to run the IC WebClient. In CRM 4.0 Add-On for Service Industries, an option was available to replace the J2EE functionality with a fully ABAP-based solution. In CRM 2005 and above (including CRM 2006s/CRM 2007), only the ABAP version is offered. No J2EE server or J2EE components are required for the Interaction Center itself. However, a J2EE server is required for SAP TREX.

12.1.4   JRE Requirements

Does the Interaction Center rely on any Java applets? If so, is any specific version of Sun Java Runtime Environment (JRE) required?

Yes, Sun JRE is required to use certain functionality. In CRM 2006s/CRM 2007, the Interactive Script Editor — accessible from the IC Manager role — still contains a server-side applet and requires Sun JRE. In addition, depending on your CRM release, you may also require JRE to run the Interaction Center. For example, in CRM 4.0 and prior release, Broadcast Messaging and server polling both contained Java applets and required JRE. However, as of CRM 2005 these applets were replaced with standard ABAP functionality. See SAP note *717921* (Required JRE version for IC WebClient, BMS, and ISE) and SAP note *1105843* (Scripting Editor JRE1.5 or later support) for more details. If you use the Free Seating feature of the Interaction Center, an applet is downloaded onto each agent's computer.

12.1.5   ActiveX Browser Plug-Ins

Does the Interaction Center require any ActiveX Web browser plug-ins or extensions?

Yes, various ActiveX controls are used in both SAP CRM and the Interaction Center for integration with various Microsoft Office applications. For example, an ActiveX control is required to access a user's personal Microsoft Outlook address book from within the Interaction Center E-Mail Editor screen. Similarly, integration of Fax and Letter using Microsoft Word as the text editor for the faxes and letters also requires an ActiveX control. See SAP notes *1018674* and *1047783* for details.

Mozilla Firefox and Apple Safari Web browser do not support the Microsoft ActiveX architecture. Hence, any Interaction Center functionality that relies on ActiveX will obviously not be available if running the Interaction Center in Mozilla Firefox or Apple Safari. See SAP note *1047783* for details.

12.1.6   Extranets, VPNs, and Firewalls

Is it possible to access the IC WebClient remotely from outside of a company's corporate network? Are there any concerns or restrictions regarding extranets, virtual private networks, firewalls, proxy servers, reverse proxy servers, or secure-sockets layer?

Yes, the Interaction Center WebClient (and the CRM WebClient) can be accessed remotely from outside the company's network by tunneling into the corporate extranet via a virtual private network (VPN). As described in SAP note *844929*, the WebClient architecture requires a direct connection between the CRM application server and client browser, which precludes the use of a firewall. Therefore, in order to provide adequate security in absence of a firewall, it is recommended to connect via VPN.

12.1.7 WinClient or WebClient

Should customers implement IC WinClient or IC WebClient?

Customers should implement the IC WebClient, which is SAP's chosen user interface for the Interaction Center application going forward. In CRM 2005, many new features are only available for the IC WebClient and are not available in the IC WinClient. After CRM 2005, the IC WinClient is no longer supported or available for use. If you are implementing a new Interaction Center project in CRM 2005, choose the IC WebClient unless there is a compelling reason not to do so (e.g., corporate restrictions against running Internet/Intranet-based applications).

12.1.8 WebDynpro Usage or Future Plans

Does the Interaction Center use WebDynpro based technology? Is SAP CRM or the Interaction Center planning to move to WebDynpro?

No, neither CRM nor the Interaction Center utilizes WebDynpro technology. Rather, the IC WebClient architecture relies on Business Server Pages (BSP), an SAP-proprietary extension of Java Server Pages (JSP). With CRM 2006s/CRM 2007, the other applications in CRM online have also adopted the WebClient architecture. There are no plans in CRM to adopt WebDynpro (used across other business applications powered by SAP NetWeaver) in the Interaction Center or in any other areas of SAP CRM.

12.1.9 Spell-Check Integration

Does SAP CRM or the Interaction Center provide out of the box spell-check functionality?

No, SAP does not provide an out of the box spell-checker in CRM or the Interaction Center. However, various options are available for integrating third-party spell-check tools into the Interaction Center, including both server-side and browser client-side solutions. You can implement a server-side solution such as Sentry Spelling Checker Engine for Windows from Wintertree-Software as described in SAP note *1083520*. You can also implement various third-party browser client-side solutions on each agent's computer, using products such as ieSpell, IE7Pro, Google Toolbar, etc. In addition, some web browsers such as Mozilla Firefox 2.0 have built-in spell-checkers. See SAP note *1169540* if you plan to use a third-party spell checker with Microsoft Internet Explorer, as you will likely need to enable the right-click context menu feature of Internet Explorer to properly leverage the spell-checker.

12.2 Migration/Upgrade Questions

If your organization is like most other companies, you are torn between wanting to continue leveraging your existing applications (in which you have invested significant effort and are hopefully now running smoothly), or dreaming about being able to take advantage of the new features and enhanced usability offered in updated versions of CRM. Naturally, then, some of the most frequently asked questions by existing Interaction Center customers have to do with migration and upgrade strategies.

12.2.1 Effort Required to Migrate from WinClient to WebClient

What is the upgrade effort to move from the IC WinClient (in CRM 4.0 or CRM 2005) to the IC WebClient in CRM 2005 or CRM 2006s/CRM 2007?

Migrating from the IC WinClient to the IC WebClient, even if just migrating from one user interface to the other *within the same CRM release,* should be viewed as a complete reimplementation exercise. Almost all of the configuration and administration activities will need to be redone, as the underlying architecture of the IC WebClient relies on the BOL/GenIL concept and is quite different from the architecture of the IC WinClient. Accordingly, you should plan adequate time for reconfiguration as well as recreation of related objects like interactive scripts, action box calls, and so on.

12.2.2 WinClient Availability in CRM 2006s/CRM 2007

Is the IC WinClient available in CRM 2006s/CRM 2007, even on a limited basis, to facilitate a phased migration of users from IC WinClient to IC WebClient?

No, the IC WinClient is not available after CRM 2005 and cannot be used. All of the IMG configuration activities and SAP Menu entries related to the Interaction Center have been removed. While the underlying IC WinClient coding, transaction codes, and infotypes still exist in the system, the code base has not been updated with SAP notes and support packages for IC WinClient–related corrections applied to lower releases such as CRM 2005.

Existing IC WinClient customers in CRM 4.0 and CRM 2005 will of course be allowed to continue using the IC WinClient until the end of the supported maintenance periods for their particular CRM release.

12.2.3 PC-UI Availability in CRM 2006s/CRM 2007

Is PC-UI still supported in CRM 2006s/CRM 2007 and above, or is it still at least technically possible to integrate PC-UI screens into the new CRM WebClient framework?

No, PC-UI is no longer supported in CRM 2006s/CRM 2007 and above, as mentioned in SAP note *1118231* that states that, "The People-centric User Interface (PC-UI) is not supported." Furthermore, it is no longer even technically possible to call PC-UI transactions from the Interaction Center using the Transaction Launcher in CRM 2006s/CRM 2007. Due to changes to the CRM UI Framework and the Transaction Launcher, there is no longer an option in the launch transaction wizard to generate PC-UI–based launch transactions.

12.2.4 Effort Required to Upgrade from CRM 2005 to CRM 2006s/CRM 2007

What is the upgrade effort to move from the IC WebClient in CRM 2005 to the new CRM WebClient?

Although SAP provides an upgrade path from earlier releases of CRM to new CRM 2006s/CRM 2007, there is no upgrade path for the Interaction Center. Even if you are already using the IC WebClient in CRM 2005, much of your IMG configuration settings and related customizing and objects will need to be reimplemented.

This is partially due to technical changes that were introduced to allow the rest of CRM to run on the IC WebClient architecture. Some examples of affected areas include:

▶ Interactive Scripting (scripts must be manually recreated in the Interactive Script Editor due to incompatibilities)

▶ Navigation Bar configuration (a new configuration concept was introduced and customizing for the navigation bar needs to be redone in transaction CRMC_UI_NBLINKS)

▶ Launch Transactions (a new configuration concept was introduced and launch transactions must be regenerated in transaction CRMC_UI_ACTIONWZ)

▶ Alerts (alerts must be recreated using the new Alert Editor tool available in the IC Manager CRM business role)

▶ Mail Forms (mail forms must be recreated in new HTML-based Mail Form tool available in the IC Manager CRM business role)

▶ Activity Clipboard (customizing for the activity clipboard needs to be maintained in the new view cluster CRMC_UI_CLIP)

▶ IC WebClient Profiles (the IC WebClient Profile concept was replaced by the CRM business role concept and is now maintained in transaction CRMC_UI_PROFILE)

12.2.5 Automated Tool for Converting PC-UI Screens to BSP

Are there any automated tools for converting custom PC-UI screens to BSP screens provided with the new CRM WebClient in CRM 2006s/CRM 2007 and above?

No, there are no such tools available to automatically translate custom PC-UI screens into CRM WebClient screens. However, one of the advantages of the new CRM WebClient UI is that any CRM screen can be integrated into the Interaction Center because both the Interaction Center and CRM online now run on the same CRM WebClient platform. In addition, new administrative tools are available such as the UI Config Tool and the Design Layer that make it much easier to make UI changes such as adding new fields, moving fields on the UI, and renaming field labels. In many cases, old your custom PC-UI screens may no longer be necessary at all.

12.2.6 Problem/Solution Maintenance in WebClient

There used to be a PC-UI screen for creating symptoms and solutions (in the Solution Database) directly from the IC Manager role in the Enterprise Portal. Is there a corresponding CRM WebClient screen available in CRM 2006s/CRM 2007 and above? If not, how should knowledge administrators maintain symptoms and solutions, without using SAP GUI transaction IS01?

No, there is no alternative screen available other than IS01 SAP GUI transaction code for creating problems and solutions in the Solution Database. However, it is possible to call a SAP GUI transaction code such as IS01 from the CRM WebClient using the Transaction Launcher. In such cases, the SAP GUI transaction will be rendered as HTML via the Internet Transaction Server (ITS) technology and embedded inside the work area of the CRM WebClient screen. The user does not need to separately log in to SAP GUI.

12.2.7 Call List Maintenance in WebClient

There used to be a PC-UI screen for monitoring and managing call lists directly from the IC Manager role in the Enterprise Portal. Is there a corresponding CRM WebClient screen available in CRM 2006s/CRM 2007 and above? If not, how should call center managers monitor and manage call lists, without using SAP GUI transaction CRMD_TM_CLDIST?

No, there is no alternative screen available other than CRMD_TM_CLDIST SAP GUI transaction code for monitoring and managing call lists. Additionally, it is not possible to access transaction CRMD_TM_CLDIST from the IC Manager role using the transaction launcher, as this particular transaction is not enabled for SAPGUI for HTML (as indicated in transaction SE93). The only option is for interaction center managers to directly access transaction CRMD_TM_CLDIST by logging into SAP GUI.

12.3 Performance and Benchmarking Questions

The next set of questions usually center on speed and performance once people are certain that a software application will run in their favorite browsers. In the Interaction Center, where agents are often still paid based on the number of calls that they process or the number of customer issues they resolve, performance is absolutely critical. Even just a one-second delay on the part of the application, can translate into a million dollars of lost revenue over the course of a year for companies running large interaction centers with 10,000 or more agents.

Performance is also an especially interesting topic for existing IC WinClient customers who are considering migrating to IC WebClient as part of an upgrade to a more recent CRM release. Users who are accustomed to the exceptionally fast response time and system performance afforded by the SAP GUI-based application are naturally suspicious of a thin-client browser-based application because web browsers tend to add an additional layer of latency by their very nature, due to the increased number of required server communication roundtrips between the browser and the CRM server. So, let's take a look at some of the most commonly asked questions related to system performance.

12.3.1 High-Volume IC Customers

Does SAP have any high-volume Interaction Center customers with ten thousand (10K) or more users?

Yes, SAP has several customers who have thousands and thousands of users, including customers with over ten thousand (10K) concurrent users.

Does SAP have high-volume Interaction Center customers with taking millions of telephone calls and emails per year?

Yes, SAP has numerous customers who receive millions of telephone calls and/ or emails per year, including some customers who receive millions of calls per month.

Does SAP have high-volume Interaction Center customers processing one hundred thousand (100K) orders or more per day?

Yes, SAP has several customers processing over one hundred thousand (100K) orders per day, including customers processing sales orders, customers processing service tickets, and customers processing a blend of both sales and service transactions.

Does SAP have high-volume Interaction Center customers with millions of customer master records?

Yes, SAP has customers with several million customer and registered product records, including customers with over 75 million customer records.

12.3.2 System Performance of IC WebClient Compared to IC WinClient

How does the system performance of the IC WebClient compare to the system performance of the older SAP GUI-based IC WinClient?

Benchmark tests have been conducted that show the performance of the IC Web-Client to be similar to (i.e., almost as fast as) the IC WinClient.

Obviously, thin-client Web-based applications introduce additional latency due to the increased amount of network traffic between the web browser client and the CRM application server. However, this can actually be an advantage in environments with limited bandwidth availability, because the more frequent (but smaller) server requests of the thin-client browser application can travel through the system faster than the less-frequent (but much larger) server requests made by a thick-client application.

12.3.3 Performance Benchmark Tests

Are any performance benchmark tests available for the Interaction Center?

Yes, performance benchmark tests have been conducted and are available for both the IC WinClient and IC WebClient for CRM release 3.0, 4.0, and 2005. No performance benchmarks were available for CRM 2006s/CRM 2007 at the time this book was written. The most recent benchmarks for the IC WebClient in CRM 2005 are available online. These tests were conducted using regular off-the-shelf hardware (Dell PowerEdge Model 6850) and resulted in sub-second average online response time (0.83 seconds). For full details, go to: *http://www.sap.com/solutions/benchmark/ic_results.htm*.

12.4 CTI Questions

Now that we have answered some of the most common questions about technical topics like the user interface, migration/upgrade strategy, and system performance, let's take a look at some frequently asked questions about the features and functionality supported by the Interaction Center. We'll start with computer telephony integration (CTI), which is a topic that goes hand in hand when talking about call centers or contact centers in general, or when talking about the SAP CRM Interaction Center in particular.

12.4.1 Certified CTI Hardware (PBX/ACD) and Software

What telephone switches (PBXs/ACDs) and hardware does the SAP CRM Interaction Center support? Which contact center software products work with the Interaction Center?

SAP does not directly certify or recommend specific hardware such as private branch exchanges (PBXs) or automated call distributors (ACDs). Rather, SAP offers certification for the communication management software (also known as contact center infrastructure software) that runs on top of the PBX/ACD. To be more precise, SAP does not actually certify the communication management software directly but rather provides certification for a small piece of software called an *adapter* that connects the communication management software to the SAP interface. The most commonly used vendors and products for which certified adapters are available include Genesys, Avaya, and SAP Business Communications Management (BCM). However, the full list includes many other vendors such as Cisco, Siemens, Nortel, Aspect, Ericsson, and Cycos. For more details on certified partners, see Section 11.2.

12.4.2 How to Configure CTI

What configuration steps are necessary to enable CTI (or multi-channel integration) by integrating an external communication management software application like Genesys, Avaya, SAP BCM, or other product with the SAP CRM Interaction Center?

The majority of work involved in configuring CTI or multi-channel integration is actually performed on the external software providing the CTI or multi-channel integration (e.g., Genesys, Avaya, SAP BCM). This configuration is specific to the chosen CTI vendor and is typically performed by an experienced consultant who is certified by the external vendor; hence, this configuration will not be discussed here. However, there are some SAP specific configuration tasks that also need to be carried out by a consultant on the SAP side of the project. The basic steps include:

1. In SAP GUI transaction SM59, *Configuration of RFC Connections*, define a new RFC destination in the folder *HTTP Connections to External Server* that points to your CTI server.

2. In the IMG activity *Define Communication Management Software Profiles,* enter an ID and description of your communication management software profile.

3. Assign the communication management software function profile created in Step 2 to your CRM business role (formerly IC WebClient profile).

4. In SAP GUI transaction CRMM_BCB_ADM, *Communication Management Software Connections,* create a new communication management software system ID and assign the RFC destination that you created in Step 1.

5. In SAP GUI transaction CRMM_IC_MCM_CCADM, *Maintain System Settings,* select the communication management software system ID that you created in Step 4. Then choose the desired communication channel (e.g., telephony) and open the *Queues* folder and enter the ID of your communication management software queue ID.

6. In SAP GUI transaction CRMM_IC_MCM_CCLNK, *IC MCM Com Mgt Software Link Profile and System,* assign the communication management software profile that you created in Step 2 to the communication management software connection that you created in Step 4.

12.4.3 How to Identify Account via Call Attached Data (CAD)

Is the Interaction Center able to identify a customer via account number contained in call attached data (CAD) rather the via automatic number identification (ANI) service?

Yes, it is possible to identify a customer by extracting the customer's account ID from the call attached data (CAD). This can be configured in the IMG activity Define Account Identification Profiles (transaction CRMC_IC_BPPROF) in the fields under *Contact-Attached Data Extraction.* In the *CAD Application ID* field, enter the value that appears in the application ID tag that appears in the XML code of the Interactive Voice Response (IVR) system that collects the customer's account number (e.g., "Genesys-CAD"). In the XSLT file field, enter the name of the XSLT program that is responsible for extracting the account ID from the contact attached data. You are responsible for creating this XSLT file. However, SAP delivers a sample XSLT file that you can reference, named CRM_IC_BPIDENT_EXT_IAD_TO_ABAP. SAP also provides a sample program showing how to extract CAD data from, for example, Genesys named CRM_IC_BPIDENT_EXT_IAD_GENESYS. See SAP note *707104* for additional information.

12.4.4 How to Configure the CCSUI Tool

What steps are necessary to configure the Contact Center Simulator User Interface (CCSUI) tool?

The CCSUI is a rudimentary tool provided by SAP that allows you to simulate basic telephone, email, and chat functionality to test CTI and multi-channel integration in the Interaction Center without having an actual communication management software system installed. Note that the CCSUI does not provide actual CTI or multi-channel integration and cannot be used to route and process actual live telephone calls, chats, or emails. Rather, it is only a simulation tool to enable you to test relevant features in the Interaction Center such as the multi-channel toolbar, context area, email editor, and chat editor. Full details on how to configure the CCSUI for test purposes is provided by Stephen Johannes of Bunge North America in a Blog entry on the SAP Community Network — Business Process Expert (BPX) website at: *https://www.sdn.sap.com/irj/sdn/weblogs?blog=/pub/wlg/9774.*

12.4.5 SAPphone or ICI

Should I use SAPphone or Integrated Communication Interface (ICI)?

One of the first questions that people often ask once they have decided to implement CTI or multi-channel integration is which of the two SAP multi-channel interfaces should they use — ICI or SAPphone? The short answer is ICI. The longer answer is that ICI is recommended for any project using the WebClient version of the Interaction Center, as well as for IC WinClient projects that require multi-channel integration.

SAPphone is an older interface based on remote function call (RFC) technology and only supports telephony integration — not email or chat. Historically, SAPphone was mainly used in the IC WinClient, although customers can also continue to use SAPphone on a temporary basis after migrating to IC WebClient until they are able to roll out ICI.

ICI is a newer XML/SOAP-based interface that supports full multi-channel integration including telephony email, chat, SMS, fax, postal letter, etc. Historically, ICI was the default interface for the IC WebClient and was not available for IC WinClient customers. However, as of CRM 2005 (SP08 and beyond) and CRM 4.0 Add-on for Service Industries (SP07 and beyond), it is now possible to also use ICI in the IC WinClient. See SAP notes *1038519* and *1001703* for details.

For more information on the difference between SAPphone and ICI, see the Blog on the SAP Customer Network — Business Process Expert website at: *https://www. sdn.sap.com/irj/sdn/weblogs?blog=/pub/wlg/7653*.

12.5 ITIL and IT Service Desk Questions

ITIL (IT Infrastructure Library) is a globally accepted set of best practices and standards for managing information technology (IT) published by the United Kingdom's Office of Government Commerce (OGC). Companies around the world, including the majority of SAP customers, use ITIL to some extent, often as part of their internal IT help desk process. SAP customers who run service desks, whether internally facing or customer facing, often have questions regarding how SAP supports ITIL processes. Let's look at some of the most commonly asked questions.

12.5.1 ITIL Certification

Is SAP ITIL "certified"?

One of the most commonly asked questions is whether SAP is "ITIL certified." This is actually a bit of a trick question, because the U.K. OCG who owns ITIL does not actually offer any ITIL certification for software products, nor does it recognize any so-called "certifications" offered by external companies such as Pink Elephant. For these reasons, SAP has not pursued any of these non-accredited certifications. However, SAP does endorse ITIL, and the SAP CRM and the Interaction Center do support ITIL processes. For example, the Service Ticket business transaction in the Interaction Center can be used as part of the ITIL Incident Management process. SAP is considering strengthening its support for ITIL in future releases by introducing new business transactions in CRM and the Interaction Center that better map with the ITIL concepts of Incident, Problem, and Request for Change.

12.5.2 Interaction Center or Solution Manager

Should customers use the Interaction Center IT Help Desk scenario or the SAP Solution Manager for internal IT issues?

The CRM Interaction Center is designed for handling general IT issues such as problems with computers, networks, related peripheral devices, and so on. The Solution Manager, on the other hand, is useful for handling your company's SAP-related issues such as errors in an SAP software application. The Solution Manager has built-in integration with the SAP Support Portal and Online Support System (OSS). So, both tools should be used. The Interaction Center can be used as the front-office tool for handling initial request. If the issue is a general non-SAP topic, it can stay in the Interaction Center as a service ticket or service order. On the other hand, if it is an SAP-related issue it should be passed on to the Solution Manager for resolution.

12.5.3 Business Process Outsourcing

Does the Interaction Center support business process outsourcing (BPO) for IT help desks? Does SAP have any BPO customers?

Yes, the SAP CRM Interaction Center enables and supports business process outsourcing. Key features such as *CRM client switching* allow outsourcers to maintain data from different corporate customers in separate CRM clients (within the same CRM instance) and to allow agents to seamlessly switch between clients at runtime depending on the company that each caller represents. Yes, several large, global outsourcing companies are using the SAP CRM Interaction Center as the platform for their BPO activities. Many of these companies provide IT help desk services and other shared services such as HR help desk or accounting/finance help desk.

12.6 Workforce Management (WFM) Questions

Workforce Management (WFM) tools help companies to accurately forecast work volumes for their contact centers, and to appropriately schedule the right number of agents at the right times. Typically, WFM tools provide support for forecasting, scheduling, and agent schedule adherence. As mentioned in Section 11.3, WFM is increasingly being rolled into a broader concept called Workforce Optimization (WFO) that provides a suite of tools for managing employees. WFO products typically include WFM as well as tools for audio recording and screen recording, quality monitoring, coaching, online training and e-learning, and performance management and reporting. Let's look at a couple of the most frequently asked questions about workforce management (WFM) and workforce optimization (WFO).

12.6.1 SAP and Workforce Management (WFM) Functionality

Does SAP offer its own Workforce Management product for the Interaction Center? If not, does SAP recommend a particular partner solution?

No, SAP no longer offers its own workforce management application for the Interaction Center. At one time, SAP offered an Interaction Center Workforce Management application as part of CRM 4.0. However, due to the rapid industry evolution of contact center WFM products toward holistic WFO suites, SAP discontinued its own Interaction Center Workforce Management product. As of CRM 2005, SAP removed its own IC WFM product from the price list as described in SAP note *1007837*. Instead, SAP partnered with industry leader Verint Systems, who previously acquired two other former industry leaders, Witness Systems and Blue Pumpkin. Currently, Verint Systems is a certified SAP software solution partner, holding a Powered by SAP NetWeaver certification.

12.6.2 The Size of an Interaction Center That Needs WFM

How big does a contact center have to be in order to benefit from workforce management? What are the typical cut-off points in terms of number of agents where a WFM solution becomes necessary?

Any size contact center can benefit from workforce management. Even a small operation with just a handful of users may require workforce management, depending on the importance of the contact center, and the nature of the call distribution. However, as a general rule, contact centers with less than 30 agents can often get by with using a spreadsheet for scheduling. As the operation grows from 30 to 60 users, the company should consider migrating to a proper workforce management solution. Once a company reaches from 60 to 100 users or more, spreadsheets become ineffective and workforce management is absolutely critical.

12.6.3 Call/Screen Recording or Quality Monitoring Functionality

Does SAP offer screen recording and call (voice) recording capabilities and/or other quality monitoring capabilities for the Interaction Center?

No, the SAP CRM Interaction Center product does not directly provide capabilities for listening in on an agent's telephone calls, nor for recording telephone calls or screen captures. However, an add-on product, SAP Business Communications Management (BCM), does indeed provide many of these features, such as the ability to listen in on an agent's telephone call and to silently "whisper" to the agent in coach mode so that the caller cannot hear the supervisor's voice. SAP BCM also provides the ability to record the voice stream of a call. Currently, SAP BCM does not provide the ability to link the voice stream recoding to the interaction record in the Interaction Center. Nor does SAP BCM provide any screen recording capabilities. However, SAP's partners such as Verint do provide certain call recording capabilities, which could be integrated with the Interaction Center on a project basis.

12.7   "Which One Should We Choose" Questions

SAP is known both for providing industry best business practices that specify the optimal way of doing some tasks, as well as for providing a myriad of configuration options to allow companies to tweak the best practices to fit their needs. Due to the flexibility of SAP, companies often discover that there are multiple options available for achieving the same, or similar, results. Hence, companies often find themselves asking, which option should we choose? In this section, we will try to answer the most frequently asked questions.

12.7.1   Employee Interaction Center: CRM or HCM

Which option should companies use for running an employee interaction center, the SAP CRM Interaction Center or SAP ERP Human Capital Management (HCM)?

The CRM Employee Interaction Center is usually the right choice for companies who have already deployed (or are planning to deploy) SAP CRM. There are a number of advantages to using the SAP CRM Employee Interaction Center rather than the HCM Employee Interaction Center. For example, having your agents work in CRM and access HR data in a limited and tightly controlled fashion provides strong data separation and greater piece of mind and security than having agents working directly in the same system where HR data is stored. Also, decoupling of the front-end CRM and back-end ERP HCM system can also be beneficial in terms of system maintenance, performance, load balancing, and so on. And, most importantly, while the generic Interaction Center framework is available in both CRM and HCM, the actual CRM functionality itself is of course only available in the CRM system.

Features that are only available in the CRM Employee Interaction Center and not in the HCM Employee Interaction Center include features like:

▸ Marketing campaign functionality for internal and personnel marketing

▸ E-Mail Response Management System (ERMS) for automated handling and routing of mass inbound emails

▸ Case management for linking multiple related documents to a single case

▸ Service level agreements (SLAs)

▸ Billable services

On the other hand, the HCM Employee Interaction Center provides an alternative solution for companies who are already using SAP ERP but have no immediate plans to implement CRM. Using the ERP HCM Employee Interaction Center, companies can leverage basic HR help desk functionality such as updating employee data, payroll information, benefits, vacation time, and so on.

12.7.2 CRM Billing or ERP Billing

Should companies conduct billing in CRM or in ERP?

Companies who use SAP CRM and the Interaction Center often wonder what the best strategy for conducting billing and invoicing is, whether for sales order management and/or service order management. In the most typical scenario, an existing SAP customer is already conducting billing in their SAP ERP system and now wants to evaluate whether any additional value would be gained by migrating the billing process from ERP to CRM.

The decision of whether to conduct billing in the front-office CRM system or in the back-office ERP system should be decided based on the specific billing requirements of your organization. Key decision criteria might include, for example, whether you need separate billing units (aside from sales organizations) and/or whether you want to use specific billing item categories to more flexibly determine how the system behaves during input processing and billing. To guide you in this decision process, let's summarize the key differences in functionality between CRM billing and ERP billing:

- **CRM billing**
  - Convergent billing based on collected items
  - Import of external billing relevant data
  - Multi-level inter-company billing (spare-parts scenario)
  - Supplementary invoicing (via partner based derivation)
  - Condition split
  - Flexible billing application generation to streamline performance
- **ERP billing**
  - Editable header conditions
  - Display of archived billing documents
  - Standard payment card support
  - Enhanced revenue recognition support
  - Down payment support

12.7.3 Interaction Record, Service Ticket, Service Order, Complaint, Case

What is the difference between the various service-related transactions available in the Interaction Center including the interaction record, service ticket, service order, complaint, and case? Which option should companies use?

It is important to note that the various available service-related transactions are not mutually exclusive. Rather, they work together, with each one tailored to a specific purpose. The *interaction record* is the leading business transaction used for logging every customer interaction; every call results in a new interaction record. Optionally, one or more service-related *follow-up transactions* can be created as necessary including service tickets, service orders, complaints, and cases. The various follow-up transactions each have their own purpose, as well as their own specific set of features and function (Table 12.1).

- The *service ticket* is typically used to report product defects. Using the service ticket, agents can perform technical analysis of problems (with multi-level categorization) and provide solutions within defined SLA periods.
- The *service order* is ideal for facilitating repairs, installations, or field service appointments. Using the service order, agents can perform technical analysis of problems and assign correct spare parts and service products.

403

▶ The *complaint* is appropriate when a customer has a problem or issue with delivery shipment or billing invoice. Agents can create complaints from reference documents such as sales orders or invoices. Agents can also then generate appropriate follow-on tasks such as a credit/debit memo, QM notification, free-of-charge shipment, or return.

▶ The *case* is a follow-up document that allows you to group together multiple documents or objects related to a single root cause or issue. For example, a company might create a case for linking together all of the service tickets related to a particular product recall, service outage, insurance claim, criminal investigation, etc.

	Ticket	Order	Complaint	Case
Partner determination	x	x	x	x
Status management	x	x	x	x
Multilevel categorization	x	x	x	x
Rule-based routing	x	x	x	x
Reference product	x	x	x	x
Actions	x	x	x	
Follow-up	x	x	x	
Notes	x	x	x	x
Business context	x	x	x	
SLA	x	x		
Time recording	x			
Document flow	x	x	x	
Change history	x	x	x	

Table 12.1 Matrix of Functionality for Follow-Up Service Transactions

12.7.4 Creation or Suppression of the Interaction Record

Is there a possibility to suppress the creation of interaction records in order to just use service tickets and avoid using this bizarre "interaction record" thing?

Yes and no — but mostly "no." There is indeed a BADI that allows companies to suppress the creation of the Interaction Record as described in SAP note *828402*. However, SAP strongly recommends against doing this as the interaction record is critical to normal functioning of both the Interaction Center itself as well as the related Interaction Center reports. Without the interaction record (and the activity clipboard feature of the interaction record), there is no automatic linking of all the objects that were touched during an interaction, aside from the document flow links maintained in the business context of any created business transaction such as the service ticket. Also, the interaction record is necessary for the creation of follow-up transactions; without the interaction record, the creation of any follow-up transactions will fail.

12.7.5 Sales Order, Sales Ticket, ERP Sales Order, R/3 Sales Order

Which sales order entry and processing strategy should be used for processing sales orders from the Interaction Center?

The Interaction Center offers various possibilities for capturing and processing sales orders including several options for entering the order against the CRM system, as well as a couple of options for entering the order directly into the backend ERP system (Table 12.2). Your decision of which option to select will depend on several factors including whether or not you have already configured your sales processes in ERP and to what extent you leverage custom user statuses, pricing conditions, and variant configuration. Your decision may also depend on whether you want to be able to leverage integrated CRM product proposal functionality or not. To guide you in this decision process, let's summarize the key differences in functionality between the various order entry options. See Section 5.3 for full details on each option.

▶ The user interface of the IC *sales order* is ideal for B2B scenarios involving professional buyers. For example, the sales order screen provides minimal header information by default, saving as much of the screen as possible for entering line items, because B2B orders typically involve far more items than, for example, consumer orders. In addition, the sales order provides pricing information on both the order header and the product line item, which is well suited for B2B scenarios where pricing and discounts are usually tied to purchasing agreements and contracts.

▶ The *sales ticket* was designed more for B2C scenarios, in which a consumer wants to purchase just a few items. The user interface of the sales ticket attempts to make all necessary information available on the screen, enabling faster order entry by eliminating the need for the agent to navigate to other screens. This saves time and helps prevent errors.

	CRM		R/3 and ERP	
	Sales Order	Sales ticket	R/3 sales order	ERP Sales Order
Scenario	B2B	B2C	B2B	B2B
Customer	Professional buyer	Consumer	Professional buyer	Professional buyer
Line Items	Many	Fewer	Many	Many
CRM Marketing Product Proposal Integration	Out-of-the-box integration	Out-of-the-box integration	Integration not supported	Out-of-the-box integration
Required release	SAP CRM 4.0 +	SAP CRM 2005 +	CRM 4.0 and R/3 4.6C +	CRM 2005 and ECC 6.0 +
Pricing	IPC	IPC	R/3 or ERP	ERP
Variant pricing & configuration	IPC	IPC	R/3 or ERP	Not supported
ATP	APO, R/3 or ERP	APO, R/3 or ERP	APO, R/3 or ERP	APO, R/3 or ERP
Order replication	To R/3 or ERP	To R/3 or ERP	To SAP CRM	None required

Table 12.2 Matrix of Features for Various IC Sales Entry Options

▶ The *R/3 sales order* option uses the transaction launcher, which relies on Internet Transaction Server (ITS) technology, to directly embed backend R/3 or ERP transactions (such as VA01) into the Interaction Center. This option is ideal for companies who have already configured their sales processes in R/3 or ERP and make heavy use of custom user statuses, pricing conditions, and variants. Despite its name, the R/3 sales order also works with newer versions of ERP including ECC 5.0 and ECC 6.0.

▶ The *ERP sales order* attempts to provide the best of both worlds, allowing you to leverage your backend custom ERP order entry functionality while also providing access to frontend CRM marketing and product proposal functionality.

However, due to the various restrictions of early versions, it could be argued that the ERP sales order doesn't yet provide the best of either world but rather provides a compromise solution that might only be suitable for certain types of companies. Some of the restrictions include a reliance on ECC 6.0 or higher, which precludes customers with older backends such as ECC 5.0, ERP 4.7, or R/3 4.6C from leveraging this solution. Additionally, the API is still enhanced by SAP and the earliest versions, providing the most basic features with no support for advanced topics like user statuses and variant configuration and pricing.

12.7.6 Alerts, System Messages, Broadcast Messages

What is the difference between Alerts, System Messages, and Broadcast Messages in the Interaction Center?

Alerts, system messages, and broadcast messages are similar in that they are all ways of delivering pertinent information to agents in real time. However, each of these three tools each serve a different purpose. Additionally, alerts, system messages, and broadcast messages each appear in different areas of the screen and each deliver different types of information to the agent.

▶ Alerts appear in the context area at the top of the screen. *Alerts* display information about the current customers and are usually triggered in response to a specific action executed by the agent. For example, when the agent confirms that customer's information, the system might trigger an alert informing the agent that the customer has two open service tickets, or that the customer's warranty or service contract is expiring within the next 30 days.

▶ System messages are at the top of the main application area or workspace where the agents do most of their work. *System messages* provide information, warnings, and error messages related to the specific object or task on which the agent is currently working. For example, if the agent forgets to confirm the account, a system message will warn the agent to "Please confirm the account."

▶ Broadcast messages appear at the bottom of the screen in a scrolling ticker. *Broadcast messages* contain general information sent by a supervisor to one or more agents. These messages are usually not related to the current customer interaction but rather provide general announcements, updates, and instructions. For example, a supervisor might inform the agents that the company is currently experiencing a spike in call volumes and to keep calls as short as possible. Or, a supervisor might instruct an agent to go on break after wrapping up the current customer interaction.

12.7.7 JavaScript or ABAP for Multi-Level Categorization

Rumor has it that there is a secret option to use browser-side JavaScript to enable faster performance for multi-level categorization of business transactions (e.g., service tickets) instead of using the standard server-side ABAP option that executes a separate round-trip every time the user selects a new category. Is this true? If so, how do we enable this feature?

Yes, in CRM 2005, there was indeed an option to either use JavaScript or ABAP for multi-level categorization. However, this option is no longer available in CRM 2006s/CRM 2007 and above. The idea behind the JavaScript option was to buffer all of your categories into memory of the web browser sessions. This provided the advantage that each time you selected a category in one level of the multi-level categorization; all of the dependent levels were immediately updated, without the need for a roundtrip between the browser and the SAP Web application server. Thus, an agent could immediately select the next category instead of waiting for a system to execute a roundtrip. However, this technique was only effective if you are using a few hundred (or fewer) categories. For companies with several hundred to a thousand (or more) categories, the response time is unfavorable; faster performance could be achieved via a server roundtrip using the regular ABAP configuration.

12.7.8 IC Knowledge Search or SAP NetWeaver Knowledge Management

Can the Interaction Center Knowledge Search integrate the SAP NetWeaver Knowledge Management?

Yes, SAP NetWeaver Knowledge Management (KM), which supports the integration and management of unstructured information from different sources, can be integrated into the Interaction Center Knowledge Search *on a project basis* in lieu of (or in addition to) using the standard Solution Database (SDB). This project-based work would need to be done by a skilled consultant familiar with the Interaction Center Software Agent Framework. The basic procedure involves registering KM as a knowledge base in the Software Agent Framework (SAF) IMG configuration and then creating a BADI implementation for the KM that implements the various compilation-related methods of the SAF. Of course, you would finally need to set up and compile the new knowledge base via the standard tools available in the IC Manager role.

12.8 Bonus: Top 20 SAP Notes for the Interaction Center

Whenever several SAP customers ask the same questions about the same issue, it is a pretty good signal to SAP that some action needs to be taken. Either the online documentation needs to be updated, the product needs to be simplified or improved, or a new SAP note needs to be produced. Quite often, an FAQ consulting note can solve the problem by providing clarity or guidance to answer a frequently asked question or resolve a frequently encountered issue. Here is a list of the top 20 most useful SAP notes for the Interaction Center, as ranked by the author of this book. Using a slight twist on the well-known 80/20 principle, these 20 notes might be able solve up to 80 percent of the basic questions and issues that you will encounter during any Interaction Center project. Without further ado, here they are:

- *759923* – IC WebClient: FAQ Note
- *882653* – Frequently Asked Questions (FAQs) about the Agent Inbox
- *894493* – Frequently Asked Questions about Fax and Letter
- *940882* – ERMS FAQ Note
- *1118231* – Supported user interfaces for SAP CRM
- *1114557* – SAP CRM 2007 Internet Browser Releases
- *1152983* – IC WebClient UI (Web Browser) Release Information
- *981710* – Microsoft Internet Explorer Version 7.0 for end users
- *455140* – Configuration of e-mail, fax, paging or SMS using SMTP
- *904711* – SAPoffice: Where are documents physically stored?
- *717921* – Required JRE version for IC WebClient, BMS, and ISE
- *864439* – Category modeler: Transporting categories
- *707104* – Account identification from attached data
- *1083520* – Wintertree spell checker integration for IC WebClient
- *1169540* – Enable third-party spell check in WebClient with MSIE

- *664382* – Report: Import and maintenance of the "Do Not Call" list
- *1007837* – Interaction Center Workforce Management Discontinued
- *1001703* – How to use ICI in IC WinClient
- *828402* – How to suppress the creation of the Interaction Record
- *1160252* – Auto-suggested solutions not shown in knowledge search

12.9 Summary

In this chapter, we addressed some of the most commonly asked questions involving the Interaction Center. We provided straightforward, no-nonsense responses that either answered the question directly, or at least gave you the relevant information and resources to enable you to arrive at the correct decision. We also provided a list of the 20 the most useful SAP FAQ consulting notes related to the Interaction Center.

Some important points to remember are:

- Various operating systems and web browsers combinations are supported for the Interaction Center, depending on your specific release of SAP CRM, including Microsoft Vista, Microsoft Internet Explorer 7.0, and Mozilla Firefox 2.0. Support for Microsoft Internet Explorer 8.0 and Apple Safari are planned for the future.

- Several performance benchmark studies have been conducted for the Interaction Center and are available online from SAP. In general, the performance of the IC WinClient and IC WebClient are comparable.

- Two different applications are available for processing internal IT help desk issues. The SAP Solution Manager is designed for logging issues related to SAP software. The Interaction Center IT Help Desk scenario is appropriate for all other, non-SAP IT-related issues.

- Two options are available for enabling an HR employee interaction center. Companies who are already running SAP CRM should use the Interaction Center option; ERP customers who have no immediate plans to implement CRM can leverage the ERP HCM version.

- In addition to the interaction record that serves as the leading business transaction for documenting all customer interactions, various service-related follow-up transactions are also available, including the service ticket, service order, complaint, and case.

▶ The interaction record plays a critical role in the Interaction Center framework, linking objects, and enabling reporting. A BAdI is available to suppress the creation of interaction records, but SAP strongly recommends against using this approach.

▶ The SAP CRM Interaction Center provides several different sales order entry options to suit your sales order processing needs, whether you want to process orders in CRM or ERP.

▶ Various FAQ notes are available to help answer many of the most commonly encountered questions surrounding the Interaction Center.

In the next chapter, we will wrap up by sharing some customer success stories and discussing SAP's long-term vision and product roadmap strategy for the Interaction Center.

"If we don't change the direction we are going, we are likely to end up where we are heading."
— Anonymous

13 Conclusion

At this point, you should now have a great understanding of the strengths and capabilities of the SAP CRM Interaction Center, including how to get the most out of the system via optimal set-up and configuration. If you are still in the early planning stages of your project (or evaluating the system), you at least now know what is capable, and what it will take to get where you want to go. If you are an existing customer who is considering rolling out additional functionality or upgrading to a newer release such as CRM 2007, you should hopefully now have a clear overview of the benefits of extending or upgrading your project.

You have all the tools you need to start — or continue — your Interaction Center project. Certainly, you are going to run into issues along the way. No project goes completely smoothly. However, some projects definitely go smoother than others; the goal of this book is to give you the tools and insight to make your project one of the smoothest ones. To that end, we want to provide you with two additional resources to help guide you and ensure the success of your project. First, we will provide five real-life short stories from Interaction Center customers who succeeded in devising innovative solutions to maximize their Interaction Center. Then, we will look at a somewhat longer case study involving a company who is actually its own customer. Finally, we will wrap up by sharing SAP's long-term vision for the future of the Interaction Center in order to help you best *plan* for the future, while executing today.

13.1 Real Customers, Real (Short) Stories

In the following sections, five succinct stories involve customer projects that highlight different ways in which the Interaction Center can be used to solve real business challenges. What you are about to read are not dramatizations; these are real customer stories involving actual Interaction Center projects. In most cases, you will hear directly from the people involved in the implementation of the project. These are uncensored accounts, described by the consultants and business analysts working in the trenches. These stories are definitely not your typically polished marketing collaterals, crafted by folks from corporate marketing who don't work in the system and don't know the difference between a BAPI and an RFC. These are real stories from real people. In some cases, we changed the names of companies in order to respect the privacy of individuals.

13.1.1 ICICI Prudential AMC, Presented by MindTree

In this true customer story, ICICI Prudential AMC puts customers at the heart of its business using the Interaction Center and SAP E-Mail Response Management System (ERMS). This story is brought to us by Shridhar Deshpande of MindTree, the global IT and RD services company involved in the project.

The Company

ICICI Prudential Asset Management Company (AMC) is a pre-eminent player in the Indian mutual fund industry and one of the largest asset management companies in India, managing 40 different funds. ICICI Prudential is the offspring of U.K.-based Prudential plc, and Indian based ICICI Bank.

The Challenge

ICICI Prudential's customer service executives (CSEs) were in need of a powerful tool to address thousands of queries, complaints, and service requests received across various channels from the investors and provide timely resolution. One of the primary channels of communication with customers is email; however, the impersonal, uninformative nature of the email response often left investors unsatisfied and disgruntled.

Given the fact that mutual fund companies have to manage multiple customer hierarchies, it's a challenge to consistently maintain relationships and visibility with the end investor. A significant percentage of the revenue comes from intermediaries — distributors, channel partners, and individual financial analysts — who are the primary customers of a mutual fund company. Hence, it is critical to manage these important relationships. But, what about investor relationships? Across all industries, intermediaries act as the middlemen between suppliers and the end investor. This reduced interaction between principals and end investors leads to reduced visibility of the relationship. This has become difficult to do in the digital age, because consumers have grown to expect Internet interaction with their suppliers, at a minimum.

The Solution

MindTree implemented the SAP CRM Interaction Center for ICICI Prudential AMC, including the E-Mail Response Management System (ERMS) to allow CSEs to efficiently handle customer query management, service request management, and crisis management. In order to cope with a mature, hyper-competitive industry and a volatile saturated market — in which it is more difficult and costly to find and acquire new customers than to retain existing customers — ICIC Prudential recognized the need to focus on personalized customer relationships. The Interaction Center was configured to help CSEs treat customers with special care and appreciation, by reminding the CSE to wish the customer happiness on their birthday, or to notify the CSE if the customer is a premiere investor.

The Results

Using real-time information provided by the Interaction Center, ICICI Prudential now delivers better customer service and added value. The Interaction Center helps minimize any barriers between ICICI Prudential and the investor, enabling effective and personalized customer service. Though ICICI Prudential agents do not know the identity of their customers sold through certain brokers and fund supermarkets, the effective and faster customer service strengthened the intermediary's relationship with the customer. CSEs also have more control over service delivery thanks to automated service level agreements that make commitments to customers transparent and manageable. Even the back office staff can now view customer interaction history from the comfort of their offices in order to keep track of the customer service.

The new E-mail Response Management System (ERMS) capabilities enable ICICI Prudential to effectively manage high-volume email traffic as well as improvised inbound and outbound customer email communications while providing cost-efficient, personalized customer service. The benefits ICICI reaped from ERMS include the ability to route and organize incoming emails, automatically generate service confirmations, and track and respond to high volumes of incoming customer emails. In this way, email responses to customers contain greater depth and provide customers with a more personal relationship with the organization.

13.1.2 Sloan Valve Company, presented by Sloan Valve Company

This is an amazing but true story about Sloan Valve Company, a privately held family business that carried out a sophisticated Interaction Center project, including CTI, ERMS, and several project based enhancements, using *in-house resources*, with almost no use of external consultants. This story is brought to us directly by the internal project team, including the lead Business Analyst, Glenn Michaels, and the CIO/Chief Process Officer, Tom Coleman.

The Company

Sloan Valve Company is a 102-year-old privately held U.S. company that manufactures specialized, commercial-grade plumbing products and systems used in office buildings, hotels, airports, hospitals, schools, and sports stadiums around the world. Sloan sells directly to dealers and distributors (both domestically and internationally) who resell and distribute the company's products along the customer chain. Customers of Sloan's products include architects, building owners, contractors, plumbing engineers, dealers, distributors, third-party sales reps, and even end users.

The Challenge

Sloan had already implemented SAP ERP and CRM Internet Sales to replace a legacy e-commerce application that was previously used by sales representatives to enter orders on behalf of dealers. Sloan was faced with the challenge of getting warranty costs back under control, which were growing at an unexpected rate. Sloan needed to gain a better understanding of who were returning products, and whether the system was being abused in order to return non-defective products.

The Solution

An initial project was undertaken in 2006, which went live in October of that year. The project involved replacing a Microsoft Access database system with the Interaction Center for collecting data on incoming calls and callers. After the success of the first project, a follow-up project was undertaken in early 2007 to expand the IC implementation to include support for sales as well as service by combining sales and support into a single organization. ERMS was included in the project to provide email support, and Cisco VoIP system was added to provide CTI capabilities.

The Results

The updated project went live in 2008 using in-house resources with minimal external consulting support (less than 200 hours over a 1-year period). The new system allows agents to capture information about who calls are coming from (end customers or from dealers/distributors), and to easily view the history of repeat callers. This has allowed Sloan to eliminate the practice of users abusing the system for free warranty parts, while still providing prompt warranty replacement products to valued end customers. By integrating service ticket data with SAP NetWeaver BI, Sloan is able to provide the quality management organization with data about which product lines are receiving the most technical questions or support calls. Sloan is also able to identify areas where additional training or support for sales reps is required.

13.1.3   "CAD-CAM Systems," Presented by ecenta

In this customer example, an Interaction Center implementation is provided for a customer, who we shall refer to as "CAD-CAM Systems" in order to protect the identities of those involved. The story is told by Amit Venugopal of ecenta, the SAP-certified consulting partner involved in the implementation. ecenta provided custom, project-based enhancements to the Interaction Center and ERMS in order to help the customer, CAD-CAM Systems, keep better track of incidents reported by their customers.

The Company

CAD-CAM Systems provides comprehensive software solutions for the infrastructure life cycle: from buildings to bridges, transit to utilities, clean energy to clean water. CAD-CAM Systems' software helps engineers, architects, contractors, governments, institutions, utilities, and owner-operators design, build and operate, collaborate and deliver infrastructure assets. In over 50 offices worldwide, CAD-CAM Systems employs more than 2,800 staff and had annual revenues surpassing $450 million (USD) in 2007.

The Challenge

CAD-CAM Systems needed a solution for their software support processes for their customers. The solution had to meet the following requirements:

- Ability to create and track incidents reported by clients over telephone and email
- Ability to monitor and enforce the timely resolution of incidents
- Ability to hand-over incident reports to other organizational units within the company for follow-up activities

At the time that CAD-CAM Systems was searching for an IT solution in this area, there was no well-structured incident handling process in place. In fact, the company was in constant danger of losing track of reported customer incidents inside the organization, or not being able to answer them in a timely fashion. Likewise, additional sales opportunities were not followed-up on in a structured way.

The Solution

The solution proposed by ecenta was a service ticket implementation involving: ticket categorization, service level agreements, a back-office process with follow-up activities, and ERMS. Several enhancements were implemented in order to fill various gaps between the available SAP standard functionality (in release CRM 4.0 Add-on for Service Industries) and specific requirements of CAD-CAM Systems Inc. In particular, these enhancements related to the automatic creation of *interaction records*, the use of the *Agent Inbox* in the back-office process, the account search, and several ERMS email-related functions. Some of these project-based enhancements have subsequently been implemented by SAP in the standard product (CRM 2005 and above).

The solution was designed and built by three ecenta consultants over a time span of four months. After cut-over, an ad hoc support period of another two months was established. It was possible to partly deliver the solution in an off-site model because CAD-CAM Systems' business analysts in the area were well-anchored with the company's business and had a thorough understanding of SAP CRM.

The Results

The business users of the company were very happy with the intuitive usability of the solution as well as the solution's alignment with the way CAD-CAM Systems is running their customer service business. There was very little user training needed (only a session of a few hours per team). The richness of the enhanced functionality and the feeling that no tickets were lost contributed to the success of the solution. In addition, management now has a clearer picture about the performance of the service organization, and in particular the service levels reached.

13.1.4 Data Domain Presented by ecenta

This next true customer story is told by Amit Venugopal of ecenta, the SAP-certified consulting partner involved in the project. The client involved, Data Domain was looking for ways to improve their quotation to order process to support their growing sales force.

The Company

Founded in 2001, Data Domain is a pioneer in the data deduplication market. Its Global Compression technology performs inline deduplication at high speed, requiring very few disk drives. Achieving 10x-30x data reduction rates, Data Domain systems easily store several months of backup and/or archival data. Because the volume of the data is significantly reduced, disk-based backup becomes cost efficient and the data also becomes highly mobile, enabling secure replication via customers' existing network infrastructure for disaster recovery purposes. Data Domain is a mid-size company of about 600 employees worldwide. It posted revenue of $123 million USD in 2007.

The Challenge

As part of its projected sales growth, the sales force at Data Domain has been increasing its headcount very rapidly. It was determined that the legacy solution of creating quotations and sales orders via macro-driven Microsoft Excel spreadsheets was no longer a viable option. The distributed nature of the spreadsheet tool made it difficult to ensure that sales reps were creating quotes for the most recent product line and using up-to-date product configuration and pricing. Also, difficulty in enforcing the inputting of correct data placed the burden of customer master data validation, quotation creation verification, etc. on the back-office support team. Data Domain sought to create a more efficient tool that better represented their business and sales processes. The new solution should also facilitate the training of new sales employees.

The Solution

The solution proposed by ecenta was to use the SAP CRM Interaction Center Web-Client 2005 as a quoting tool. Quotations are configured in the WebClient and replicated to ERP where they are converted to orders by the back-office. The sales order with current status is downloaded back into CRM so that the sales reps have visibility as to the progress in shipping and invoicing. Several usability enhancements were made to the IC WebClient based on end user feedback which have helped drive user adoption. Data Domain is now upgrading the system to CRM 2007 to take advantage of out-of-the box features that come with the new user interface.

The Results

As the quoting tool has been rolled out to North American users, the feedback from the sales management team has been increasingly positive. The tool ensures that quotations are created using the latest configuration model and with the correct price list. Enhancements to the IC WebClient helped streamline the Data Domain sales business process while adhering to the standard SAP quoting scenario. For example, manual discounts can now be easily applied to line items in the "cart" view. In addition, new customers can now be created on-the-fly without sacrificing customer data integrity.

The quoting tool has also vastly improved the back-office support team business process. The rules-based solution drastically reduced the need for manual verification of the created quotation. The ability to move a quote from the system in which it was created to the ERP system (where the order is created) eliminates the need for duplicate and unnecessary data entry.

13.1.5 Eclipse Aviation, Presented by Eclipse Aviation

This last unbelievable but true story comes from Eclipse Aviation, manufacturers of very light business jets. This story is brought to us directly from Eclipse Senior Manager, Mike Burianek, who relates how Eclipse managed to upgrade their Interaction Center to SAP's newest CRM 2007 release *in only 8 weeks* in order to better support their sales force.

The Company

Eclipse Aviation is a privately held company based out of Albuquerque, New Mexico, who manufacturers very light jets such as the Eclipse 500 and Eclipse 400 that are marketed for business use. With all the troubles in the airline industry today, including rising costs and reduced flights, many companies are purchasing private jets for business use, such as those offered by Eclipse.

The Challenge

Eclipse was already an SAP CRM customer, running the IC WinClient as part of CRM 3.0. However, after seeing the usability improvements offered by the WebClient user interface available in CRM 2007, Eclipse knew they needed to upgrade. The goal was to increase user adoption in the sales department, where sales professionals demanded a highly usable Web-based tool to help them close high-value orders for the company's million-dollar aircraft. Mike Burianek explained that if they could increase usability to help sell one more aircraft, then the project would pay for itself.

The Solution

While a typical Interaction Center upgrade project usually takes between two to three months from blueprinting to go live, Eclipse went live in just eight weeks. The project team consisted of six people plus an SAP ramp-up coach who brought experience with the new CRM WebClient user interface and tools. Using the improved toolset provided with CRM 2007 such as the UI Config Tool, the project team was able to quickly make UI configuration changes in minutes, which would have taken hours or days of actual coding in older releases such as CRM 3.0.

The Results

Just eight short weeks after kicking off the project to upgrade from IC WinClient to IC WebClient, Eclipse was up and running smoothly. One of the main benefits was that the sales organization embraced the new Web-based interface. This increased level of user adoption has translated into fewer errors in sales orders, increased productivity, and reduced training of new hires, all of which reduce costs and increase productivity.

13.2 A Case Study: Portugal Telecom

In this case study, we will look at the shared services Interaction Center implementation at PT PRO, one of the largest shared services companies in Europe. PT PRO provide professional services for all of the various umbrella companies belonging to the parent company, Portugal Telecom Group, allowing the companies to focus on running their businesses rather than worrying about IT. This case study is presented by Bruno Garcia of PT SI, the IT systems and services arm of Portugal Telecom, who not only implemented the solution but who also continues to maintain the solution today.

The structure of PT PRO includes a department called Customer Service, which uses the Interaction Center to process the large volume of requests that arrive via traditional communication channels such as telephone, email, letter, and fax. This interaction center provides the connection between the organization and its customers. The *customers* are actually *employees* — from either the PT Group, from one of the group's companies, or from a supplier. In addition to the Interaction Center, PT PRO also has specialized back-office teams that support ticket resolution by providing provision of service such as logistics, HR, and communications.

This project began in January 2005 with a very limited scope. The main goal was to provide services to employees of the parent company Portugal Telecom (PT) Group. In the summer of 2006, there was a second phase of implementation where the services were extended to all umbrella companies of PT Group, as well as all of their suppliers.

13.2.1 Service Ticket Processing

The main process for resolving reported service issues in the PT PRO scenario can be represented in a six-step process (Figure 13.1). First, the customer must be identified. This is normally achieved by employee number or by e-mail address. After the employee is confirmed, the agent is automatically routed into the interaction record document. The agent fills in the interaction record information in Step 2, and then creates a service ticket as follow-up document in Step 3. This will be the document that represents any issue inserted into the system. If the Interaction Center agent cannot resolve it, the service ticket will be routed into a specialized area as shown in Step 4. This specialized area will be determined by reading the service ticket multi-level classification.

After the issue has been resolved, a response is provided to the customer as shown in Step 5. The response can be given by phone, or by a response email. Normally, an email response occurs if the ticket was transferred to a specialized area. Finally, after resolving the customer issue, the service ticket is closed in Step 6, and cannot be reopened. However, there are some situations where a resolved ticket requires further handling. In these cases, a new service ticket is created by issuing a follow-up service ticket from the original (the new service ticket will display a new field, indicating the previous resolved document).

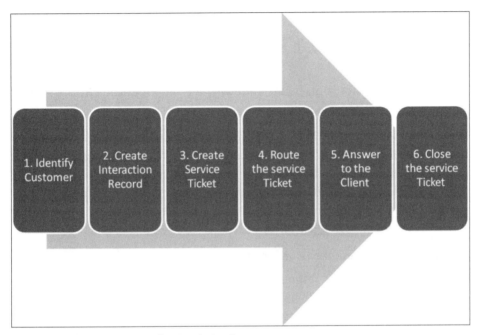

Figure 13.1 PT PRO Service Ticket Resolution Process

> **Note**
>
> Every contact established by a customer with the Interaction Center is represented by an *interaction record*. This document represents all interactions made with the Interaction Center. If PT PRO wants to know how many times in a month a customer contacted the Interaction Center, it is only necessary to simply count the interaction records created in that period. In each interaction record, the main information filled in by the agents includes the contact reason, the communication channel, and a short-text description of the issue. From there, a follow-up *service ticket* document is generated.

Service Ticket Creation and Categorization

This service ticket is generated whenever there is a new issue to be resolved. For other situations such as when a customer calls to request speeding up of the resolution of an existing service ticket or to give additional information, it is simply necessary to associate the new interaction record with an existing service ticket. Basically, three different service transaction types are available, depending on the customer:

▶ If an employee contacts the Interaction Center concerning an issue related to himself or to another employee, the document created is an *employee service ticket*.

▶ If someone is calling on behalf of a PT Group company, a *client service ticket* is created.

▶ Finally, if a supplier contacts the company, the output document is a *supplier service ticket*.

The information contained in each service ticket is the same for all situations. This information entered for each service ticket includes five levels of classification for each service ticket. The main role of this categorization is to route a service ticket or to determine the SLA expiration date. The company also has four text types configured in text management profile, to retain all relevant information about the service ticket. These text types include:

▶ Description — where the issue long text description is kept

▶ Response — where the response given to the customer is kept. The text contained in this text type will be automatically integrated into an email response when the user chooses an email standard response template.

▶ Observations — where the users can register internal notes about the ticket

▶ Information Log — a read-only text type where all changes made in other text types are stored, with timestamp information

Service Level Agreement (SLA) Determination

Instead of the traditional customer-contract relationship, the SLA calculation is based on document type, classification, communication channel, priority, and time of day. With this, we can set a predefined period during which the ticket should be resolved. If the user does not agree with the SLA period calculated, the agent is allowed to change it once, but a reason must be indicated for this in the text type Observations. To check if the SLA has been accomplished, the company has an algorithm that runs every time a service ticket is closed. It verifies from twelve rules if the SLA has been violated, and calculates which entity was responsible for the failure using business rules.

One rule is invoked if the service ticket SLA expired while the status was set at: "awaiting information from the customer." In this case, because the closed service ticket was on the customer side when it reached the SLA date, it is not considered as violated and the reason determined is "awaiting customer info" and the responsibility is set as belonging to the customer.

A second rule is invoked if the service ticket SLA did not expire but rather the application detects (by consulting user modifications on the SLA date from the history table) that this date was changed more than once. When the service ticket is closed, the SLA will be considered violated, and will determine the reason as "too many changes of SLA date," and the responsibility is set as belonging to the group responsible for making the additional changes.

Custom Service Ticket Change Log

The company implemented custom functionality to provide a service ticket change log in order to display all changes made in a service ticket including key fields such as changes made to: status, classification, SLA date, and partner functions. This log is represented in table format and easily identifies the changes made to a service ticket, dividing them into interactions.

Organizational Structure Management

If there is a tool that is indispensable for implementing and maintaining IC Web-Client applications, this tool is Organizational Structure Management. PT PRO makes use of it in two transactions:

► Transaction code PPOMW (Change Organization and Staffing) — To configure specific IC Webclient attributes, such as assigning IC Webclient profiles to positions.

► T-code PPOMA_CRM (Maintain Organizational Model) — To configure general organizational structure information, such as setting attributes of an organizational unit or assigning users (through business partner relationships) to positions.

In the organizational unit that represents the Interaction Center, there are predefined positions to provide front-office teams, back-office teams, and supervisor teams. In each of these teams, there is a specific IC WebClient profile (i.e., CRM business role) that provides the appropriate workplace to be displayed according to functions. The front-office profile provides CTI integration; the back-office profile provides utilizes the agent. A supervisor profile even provides tools that permit management of some information, such as configuration of the knowledge base problems and solutions repository.

Underneath each organizational unit, two positions are always maintained. Because there are some users that don't log into the system all day, the system sends them email notifications when a new service ticket arrives at their sub-department. So, one position is configured for users that want to receive email notifications and another position for users that do not want to receive email notifications.

Communication Channels

Two communication channels are integrated with the PT PRO application: telephone and email. Phone is used mainly used for receiving inbound calls. However, agents can also make outbound calls, perform blind and warm transfers, or request a wrap-up time to finish the interaction. CTI integration allows the agent to automatically identify the caller, without asking him any questions.

In this integration, instead of identifying the customers by phone number, the customer is identified via employee number. When the customer makes a phone call to the Interaction Center, an IVR system guides the customer to the desired service. There the caller is asked to insert their employee number or his supplier tax number using the phone keys, so that the application may identify the caller automatically. This was possible by making a development at the IVR side, where there is a table that maps all employee numbers and tax numbers, with partner identification (technical term: GUIDs). Then, the partner identification is passed on in the call attached data information to the CRM system, and it is automatically identified.

The email channel is used in both inbound and outbound email. Outbound interactions can be divided into two types: automatic and manual. Every time a service ticket is created, if the customer's email address is in the system, then an automatic notification is generated, indicating that a service ticket has been created on his behalf of the respective identification. Manual interactions involve emails that are sent by the Interaction Center agents to customers with responses to their requests, or requesting more information for further processing. Standard response email templates are used to ensure that all responses made by the Interaction Center have the same font, size, initial text, end text, and signature.

There are also email account addresses (or mailboxes) that are integrated with IC WebClient, whose purpose is to allow the receipt of inbound emails sent by customers. In the Call Center, a methodology is implemented where one person in the back-office team is responsible for forwarding the emails to his teammates. This person is normally a very experienced person who can identify the issue just by reading the subject, the sender, and the mailbox of the email. Because multi-selection was not supported in the Agent Inbox in CRM 4.0, the user had to forward the emails to other users one by one. This was very time-consuming. To speed up the process, a custom application was developed in the SAP GUI environment using an application that consists of an ALV list, allowing users to see all emails that are not finished, and forward them to another user.

ERMS

ERMS (E-Mail Response Management System) is, according to Bruno Garcia from PT SI who implemented the solution for PT PRO, "One of the most interesting tools that we have come across in the application." One of the most appreciated features of ERMS is the ability to create service tickets automatically by reading email attributes, without any action required from an Interaction Center agent. PT PRO leverages this feature for certain types of emails that require an urgent response from a specialized area of the PT-PRO structure.

To identify these emails, codes were distributed to employees or suppliers and are inserted alongside the subject of the email. Then, a new service in the ERMS repository will run for every email received, and check if the email subject has a code that indicates that a service ticket should be created. If so, and if the sender email is associated to a unique business partner, a new interaction record and a new service ticket is created, just as if it was created by a call center agent in a manual process. Depending on the code, some attributes are automatically filled in, such as the type of service ticket, the priority, the multi-level classification, the group responsible, or even the partner functions.

Another ERMS feature that PT PRO heavily relies upon is the ability to automatically route emails or service tickets to the appropriate organizational unit. With the aid of the Category Modeler and Rule Modeler, the company is able to determine the responsible group for each incoming email depending on the target mailbox, or alternatively depending on the various possible combinations of the classifications of the service tickets.

Key Figures

Here are some interesting key figures from the project:

► Over 1,000 active users

► 40 different companies in the PT Group use IC WebClient

► 150 organizational units in the PT-PRO business structure

► 11,000 active employees and 40,000 managed persons on the system (ALE migration from HR)

► 1,300 suppliers (custom development to get the suppliers from R3)

► 5,000 interaction records created per day

► 1,400 service tickets (employee, suppliers and customer) created per day

► 1,300 inbound emails received per day

► 8,500 outbound emails sent per day

13.3 SAP Future Roadmap and Strategy

In the last sections, we read some amazing stories about customers who overcame various challenges such as poor customer visibility, inability to track customer incidents, and cumbersome quote-to-order and order-entry processes within the Interaction Center. We also heard about the amazing results such as drastically increased customer visibility and engagement, reduced order entry errors, decreases in number of product returns, and increased user adoption. We heard about customers who managed to upgrade in weeks, rather than months. We even got an in-depth look into one of the most advanced shared service center implementations in the world. Hopefully, you are now motivated and excited — and ready to begin your new project or next upgrade.

Before you jump right in, however, it might make sense to already start thinking about the future, even while you are planning for today. For example, it's always important to keep your long-term plans in mind when making implementation decisions today. Also, it can be helpful to have a general idea about SAP's future strategy and plans for the Interaction Center, in order to ensure that any custom project-based work you undertake is not wasted and does not conflict with SAP future's plans. For example, you might be able to hold off (or at least scale down) a custom enhancement if you know that SAP is rolling out the same feature in the next release. Similarly, knowing SAP's roadmap and strategy can help you avoid heavy, time-consuming, and expensive enhancements to areas in which SAP might not continue to invest in the future.

Let's start off by first discussing some general advice around planning an upgrade strategy. Then, we will look specifically at SAP's roadmap and strategy — both for the next CRM release as well as for the future.

13.3.1 Upgrade Strategy

One of the most frequently asked questions by SAP CRM customers has to do with deciding which CRM release to implement or upgrade. If you are a new customer, the choice is pretty easy — you implement the most current release that is generally available (i.e., at the time of this writing, CRM 2007). However, things get more complicated if you are already an existing customer considering an upgrade. For example, do you upgrade right away to the most current generally available release? Do you wait a few months and apply to participate in the ramp-up program for the first customer shipment of the next release and risk being one of the first customers to go live on a new product? Do you wait an additional six months until the new products graduate from the Ramp-Up program and become generally available?

These kinds of decisions are obviously not easy. Some SAP customers might see a demo of the improved usability and features available in a new release and decide to take the software as soon as it comes out, even if it means being the very first customer to take possession and implement of the software. On the other hand, other SAP customers continually postpone their upgrade plans every time a new release is announced. Each time the company makes up their mind to upgrade to a particular release, they hear about some new great new feature that they can't live without, which will be available in an newer upcoming release — and suddenly the project gets postponed again.

As with almost everything else, timing is critical. If you have a pressing pain point that needs to be resolved immediately, you most likely will need to start a project and may not even have the option of waiting several months to a year for the arrival of the next release. Similarly, you might have a budget that needs to be spent immediately. Or, maybe your organization just finished a project and now you have resources that need to be deployed immediately. Or, perhaps you have a long-term project plan that is dependent on other projects, such as an SAP ECC upgrade, and your timelines aren't flexible and don't allow you to wait before upgrading. In such cases, your options might be limited, with no choice but to upgrade immediately to the currently available version.

If, on the other hand, you are lucky enough to have some flexibility in deciding whether to upgrade immediately to the currently generally available version, whether to apply for ramp-up of the next upcoming release, or whether to wait until the next upcoming release is generally available — you should consider the following criteria.

▶ Would you classify the culture of your organization and its top management as aggressive leading-edge visionaries who like to push the envelope, or would you characterize your organization as more conservative and risk aversive? Aggressive visionaries make better ramp-up candidates, while conservative risk avoiders often prefer to implement a new software version only after it has been on the market for a certain period of time and been successfully implemented by a certain number of other companies.

▶ Do you have world-renowned SAP CRM Interaction Center experts in your organization who regularly speak at SAP events (ASUG, SAPPHIRE, CRM Insider, CRM Elite Council, etc.), work closely with SAP product management, are active "top contributors" on the SAP Community Network website, and appear in the acknowledgments section of this book? If yes, you are probably very well positioned as a candidate for a ramp-up product or new release. On the other hand, if you lack in-house SAP Interaction Center experts and plan to primarily rely on external consultants, you might want to consider a more conservative strategy of implementing an already-proven, generally available product.

▶ Are you located in a geographic region and vertical industry with plenty of available Interaction Center experts with implementation experience in the new WebClient architecture? If so, this should give you more confidence in selecting a newer release or ramp-up product. On the other hand, if you observe that it is difficult to find qualified experts with real implementation experience in your industry or geographic location, you may be wise to wait a few months until such resources can be secured.

▶ Is there a specific feature or capability in a certain release that you absolutely require and don't want to implement on your own as a project-based solution in the current release? If so, this might be the deciding criteria in your decision of which release to select.

13.3.2 CRM 2007 Interaction Center New Features

SAP CRM 2007 (also sometimes referred to as CRM 6.0) was released for select ramp-up customers in December 2007. Just three months later, in March 2008, the product was released for general availability in the United States and Germany. Shortly afterwards, the product was made generally available for all countries. CRM 2007 includes everything that was introduced with the interim release, CRM 2006s (CRM 5.1 and CRM 5.2), as well as new functionality available exclusively in CRM 2007. Here is a summary of bullet points for the key features provided in CRM 2007 that were not available with the previous standard release, CRM 2005. Full descriptions of each feature can be found in the online documentation available at *http://help.sap.com*.

Customer Search, Details, and History

▶ Mixed B2B/B2C scenario for account identification that allows agents to search for either companies or consumers from the same search screen

▶ Support for additional business partner relationships besides contact person such as activity partner, shareholder, lawyer, family member, etc.

▶ Index-based business partner search for increased performance using commonly searched fields

▶ Address validation and duplicate check to prevent creation of duplicate records or faulty customer records

▶ Support for IObject in addition to IBase to allow creation of and search for registered serialized products

▶ Configurable account identification search options including IBase, IObject, contract, business agreements, vehicle, etc.

▶ Configurable account fact sheet allowing different customer overview screens with different type of information tailored to particular user groups such as sales professionals, service professionals, or marketing professionals

▶ Configurable pop-up dialogue boxes for contract determination, sales/service org determination, or business transaction type determination to allow agents to manually determine appropriate objects at runtime (rather than via a BAdI)

Product Search and Sales Order

▶ Add-to-cart feature for product search, and import-from-cart feature for sales order to allow selection of products without having already created an order

▶ Integrated product search result list and product preview that allow agents to compare the details of multiple selected products from the same screen without the need to navigate back and forth between search results page and product details page

▶ Product search by campaign or product catalog to help agents more easily locate a product being referenced by a customer

▶ Integration of SAP Real-Time Offer Management (RTOM) to provide intelligent real-time product proposal recommendations based on customer data and current transactional data

Email, Chat, and Telephony

▶ ERMS Push for pre-processing SAPconnect emails via ERMS for things like auto-acknowledge and auto-prepare, and then handing the emails over to the ICI interface for real-time routing via screen pop to an agent using external communication management software

▶ Support for agent signatures in email templates allowing all agents to use the same signature template, which is dynamically filled with the agent's information including name, title, telephone number, and email address

▶ Display and maintenance of call-attached data (CAD) from interactive voice response (IVR) system

▶ Integration of dual tone multi-frequency (DTMF) functionality (i.e., "touchtone" buttons) in the communication toolbar

▶ Support for multiple chat sessions (as of CRM 2007 SP02) allowing an agent to receive and work on up to six separate customer chat sessions in parallel from the same browser window

▶ Integration of SAP Business Communications Management (BCM) to enable real-time routing of telephone calls, emails, chats, SMS, fax, and letter without any third-party external software

▶ Integration of fax and letter functionality (which was previously available in CRM 2005 but not available in CRM 2006s) allowing agents to send and receive faxes and letters from the Interaction Center

IC Manager Functionality

▶ Intent-Driven Interaction (IDI) providing rule-based agent guidance using business rules to trigger alerts, scripts, and automatic navigation within the Interaction Center

▶ Alert Editor for creating re-usable alerts that can contain text variables and hyperlinks that navigate to other IC screens or objects

▶ OLTP-based Interactive Reporting that allow real-time BI style reporting and analytics (currently only for Service Tickets/Service Orders) directly using live CRM data without the need to install SAP NetWeaver BI

▶ "Is Like" wildcard operator for Rule Modeler which provides additional flexibility over the standard operators (i.e., equals, contains) when comparing text strings in business rules

13.3.3 SAP Roadmap for the Interaction Center

Now that we have reviewed the new features available in CRM 2007, let's turn our attention to the roadmap for the next planned release, CRM 7.0. Roadmap discussions are tricky. On one hand, readers are always interested to know about SAP's future strategy and direction in order to make the decisions today that are consistent with SAP's long-term plans. On the other hand, for legal reasons, companies today not able to provide a list of planned features and functions for a future release without having a room full of lawyers and legal disclaimers. For that reason, we won't be able to provide you with a list of exact features and functions that will appear in the next release of SAP CRM. However, we can at least try to provide some general guidance about SAP's strategy and direction. Please be advised that the information presented here is not subject to your license agreement or any other agreement with SAP. This information contained here only represents forward-looking statements and is not intended to be binding upon SAP to any particular course of business, product strategy, and/or development.

There are several areas where SAP would like to invest in around the Interaction Center. These areas include general improvements to the Interaction Center including enhancements to the Context Area, Agent Inbox, and Chat Editor. SAP would also like to provide enhanced support for sales processes in the Interaction Center, including deeper integration with sales-related functionality available in the CRM sales professional role. SAP would also like to invest further in areas like ITIL IT service management as well as shared service center scenarios like the employee interaction center (EIC) and accounting interaction center (AIC). Finally, SAP would like to strengthen the integration of communications-enabled business processes (CEBP) in the Interaction Center.

Core Interaction Center Improvements

Within the core Interaction Center functionality, SAP is considering a number of enhancements, including allowing SAP customers to configure the Interaction Center context area through IMG configuration in order to determine which items of the context area (e.g., account info, alerts, communication info) to show on the screen and in which order to display them. SAP would also like to provide configurable toolbar buttons that allows companies to use text and/or icons, including their own non-SAP icons. SAP is also considering allowing companies to configure the frequency of the SAM polling in order to optimize performance. Other improvements that are under consideration include incorporating standard search features into the Agent Inbox such as advanced search and saved searches, along with sorting of columns. Finally, SAP would also like to enhance the Intent-Driven Interaction functionality of the Rule Modeler with additional features and actions.

Integration of CRM Online Business Transactions in the Interaction Center

One of the things that SAP is considering as part of the roadmap for a future release such as CRM 7.0 is to allow CRM transactions from other business roles to run inside the Interaction Center in a fully integrated mode. This would allow the Interaction Center to leverage CRM business transactions that so far have not been available in the Interaction Center such as the CRM opportunity, quotations, sales contract, service quotation, service contract, and so on. It would also allow companies to replace their IC-specific transactions, such as the IC service ticket or IC sales order with standard CRM business transactions used in other roles such as the Sales Professional and Service Professional role. These transactions would of course integrate with the Interaction Center in the normal fashion, including automatically determining the correct partner functions after a business partner is confirmed, automatically showing up in the activity clipboard after creation, and automatically saving when the End button is pressed in the Interaction Center toolbar.

Improved Support for ITIL and Shared Service Centers

SAP is considering providing some investment in the areas of ITIL service management and shared service centers, including enhancements to the employee interaction center and new accounting interaction center functionality. The enhancements that are being considered for the employee interaction center would allow multiple business partners to be confirmed for an interaction, including, for example, a contact person and a manager. The ITIL service management functionality that is being considered would help bring SAP's service management solution more in line with the ITIL best practices. With the accounting interaction center, requests from customers, vendors/ suppliers, and employees could be tracked and resolved.

Increased Support of Communications-Enabled Business Processes

In order to make better use of SAP Business Communications Management (BCM) and other third-party communication management software systems, SAP is considering providing increased support of communications-enabled business processes. This could include the addition of features such as click to dial (or click to connect) where, for example, a telephone call could be automatically dialed just by clicking on the telephone number inside a customer's master record. Similarly, presence information could be integrated into business transactions, allowing a user to see whether, for example, the various salespeople assigned to the partner functions of a sales opportunity are currently online, available for a call to discuss the sales opportunity. SAP is also considering to allow the Rule Modeler to be used to route business transactions directly to CRM users via a real-time screen pop, much like is currently done with emails as part of ERMS Push functionality introduced in CRM 2006s/CRM 2007.

13.3.4 SAP Long-Term Future Strategy of the Interaction Center

In general, SAP's long-term roadmap strategy will likely focus in four broad areas including: enabling high-volume professional contact centers, shared service centers, communications-enabled business processes, and analytics.

Obviously, with the acquisition of Business Objects, SAP will likely look to leverage analytics more strongly throughout CRM, including in the Interaction Center. Most likely, SAP will also continue to look for ways to leverage the investment it made in SAP BCM, by more tightly integrating communications-enabled business processes inside the Interaction Center and across CRM. Other long-term strategic significances to the Interaction Center will likely include further investment in agent-guidance tools such as enhanced rule-modeling functionality and a move toward a task-based user interface and guided procedures.

13.4   Thank You!

Dear reader, thank you for taking the time to read this book. We hope that you have enjoyed our journey together, and that you are now an Interaction Center expert — or that you at least picked up a handful of helpful tips and tricks along the way. We trust that you found the book informative and helpful. Hopefully, this book will be of use to you in your work, and will assist you in helping maximize your SAP CRM Interaction Center project. If you have any questions or comments about this book, please feel free to contact the author at *john.burton@sap.com*.

Appendices

A   SAP Partners   439

B   The Author   443

A   SAP Partners

This appendix provides additional information on select SAP partners who work closely with SAP and who have significant Interaction Center project experience. The goal of this Appendix is to help you identify potential partners to work with, who might be a good fit with your organization and who might be able to contribute to the success of your Interaction Center project.

A.1   Avaya

http://www.avaya.com

A.1.1   Company Overview

Avaya delivers Intelligent Communications solutions that help companies transform their businesses to achieve marketplace advantage. More than one million businesses worldwide, including more than 90% of the FORTUNE 500®, use Avaya solutions for IP Telephony, Unified Communications, Contact Centers, and Communications-Enabled Business Processes. Avaya Global Services provides comprehensive service and support for companies, small to large.

SAP-certified adapters for Avaya's products are available directly from Avaya with no need to additional third-party middleware or connectors. Certified adapters are available for the following interfaces:

▶ SAPphone Telephony

▶ ICI Telephony

▶ ICI Email

▶ ICI Chat

Avaya actually holds two ICI telephony certifications, one for the Avaya AIC platform and one for the Avaya AES platform. In addition, Avaya also offers support for the SAP IC Statistics Interface via Avaya Global Services customization as well as support for the SAP IC Manager Dashboard based on additional professional services.

A.1.2   Value Proposition

Extraordinary customer service can be the difference between a one-time connection and a long-time relationship. Rethinking your organization in these terms can ultimately lead to customer loyalty and reduced costs. For businesses everywhere, keeping both customers and agents happy is the key to a successful contact center.

The Customer Experience

Avaya, a market leader in Contact Center solutions, provides SAP integration with both Avaya Interaction Center (AIC) and Avaya Enablement Services (AES). Contact Center features include, but are not limited to, the ability to merge customer contacts from multiple communication channels (voice, email, Web, chat, self-service) into a universal queue and route them to the best available agent. Using the Avaya advanced and patented routing algorithm, companies can optimize the match rate of their best customers to their best agents, improving the customer experience and sales results. Avaya Contact Center solutions enable customers to flatten, consolidate, and extend contact centers by utilizing IP Telephony to create a virtual contact center that spans multiple locations.

Avaya CRM Connector

The Avaya CRM Connector provides a single integrated agent desktop tool through the native integration of SAP Interaction Center and Avaya Contact Center Solutions. Contact center agents manage voice, email, and Web chat contacts in real time directly through the SAP interface. The result: a 360-degree view of the customer, improved customer loyalty, more opportunity to cross-sell/up-sell, and increased velocity of call handling — thereby increasing revenue and decreasing costs.

A.1.3   Core Areas of Expertise

Avaya Global Services provides the knowledge and skills needed to integrate the Avaya and SAP solution successfully. With a large and growing portfolio of service options to choose from, you can turn to Avaya for comprehensive support — or bring Avaya in only as needed to supplement your own in-house expertise.

Applying the solution to your business

The solution begins with an analysis of the customer's current or planned SAP and Avaya environments, including the number of contact center agents to be communication enabled, the channels to be included (voice, email, Web chat) and any specific integration, feature or interface requirements they may have.

In addition, Avaya Global Services offers a choice of support solutions to deliver the capabilities you need based on the integration option you have chosen. Avaya Global Services experts are backed by leading-edge technologies, including state-of-the-art infrastructure at their global support centers and more than 150 patented tools, such as the Avaya ExpertNet™ VoIP Assessment Tool, Avaya EXPERT SystemsSM Diagnostics Tools, and the Avaya Enterprise Services Platform. At the same time, Avaya Global Services delivers according to Service Level Agreements and within fixed cost frameworks — so, you get the fast, expert support you need, with no hidden costs.

Integration with SAP

The Avaya CRM Connector solution leverages published SAP interfaces to extract data from, and supply data to, the SAP environment, while presenting the customer's information via the SAP Interaction Center (SAP IC) agent desktop. The standard features provided via the integrated SAP desktop include:

▶ Customer Identification for inbound call based on Automatic Number Identification (ANI)

▶ Automatic Screen Pops when a call is delivered

▶ Easily accessible call features such as Answer Call, End Call, Conference & Transfer

▶ Direct dial phone numbers

▶ Sign on/Sign off to Avaya Call Center Application

▶ Agent states management

▶ AUX Work Codes with agent state handling

For a more complete list of Avaya Contact Center features and functionality, please visit avaya.com, and for insights on delivering extraordinary customer experience go to *http://www.avaya.com/cci*.

A.2   Axon Consulting

http://www.axonglobal.com

A.2.1   Company Overview

Axon is the largest global systems integrator committed solely to SAP-enabled business transformation. As an organization, it employs over 2,000 of the most experienced SAP implementation professionals across North America, Europe, and Asia Pacific. Axon's capability spans the full SAP life cycle from benefits case development and program planning, through systems implementation and business change to applications management, outsourcing, and benefits realization.

Axon has unparalleled experience in the design and implementation of integrated SAP Customer Contact and CRM solutions across a range of industry sectors, including utilities, CPG, public sector, and wholesale distribution — solutions that have allowed its clients to improve their call center and field force efficiency, reduce customer churn, increase market share, grow their customer base, and improve customer satisfaction.

As an organization, Axon has successfully delivered solutions that cover all of the major aspects of CRM in a consistent, integrated manner across all channels allowing customers to transact using the most appropriate channel at the particular time.

A.2.2   Value Proposition

Axon pioneered the use of SAP in customer call center environments, developing a packaged SAP contact center solution called Axon Telesales prior to the existence of SAP CRM, which was designed specifically to meet the needs of high-volume, scripted inbound and outbound call center environments. The solution was so well received that it was included as part of the standard SAP demonstration environments.

With the advent of SAP CRM, Axon leveraged this body of knowledge to work with clients to deliver world-class SAP-enabled customer contact center solutions such that they have now implemented solutions that support over 7,500 agents in over 50 call centers globally, in turn supporting over 9,000 field service personnel. Many of these call centers have included fully integrated IVR solutions. Axon understands that usability is the key to delivering step changes in contact center improvements and they are experts in the design and delivery of the latest SAP CRM WebClient technologies.

A.3   ecenta

http://www.ecenta.com

A.3.1   Company Overview

ecenta is a premium provider of SAP Consulting services focused on SAP CRM and NetWeaver. A valued Best Practice Development Partner and Consulting Partner since 2000, ecenta has successfully delivered 60+ CRM implementations in various industries and regions of the world. Headquartered in Walldorf, Germany, ecenta has subsidiaries in the United States, Singapore, Malaysia, Sweden, China, Australia, and Chile. Started with an initial strength of three people, the company has grown at over 50% per year and is now 200 people strong globally. Their services include Consulting Services, Application Management, Offshore Delivery, Solution Roadmaps, and Management Consulting. They are purely focused on SAP applications and are closely aligned with the product strategy and roadmap of SAP. Some of their customers in the North American market include Intel, Adobe, HP, Varian Medical Systems, Bentley Systems, T-Mobile, Carl Zeiss Meditec, Data Domain, Network Appliances, Mayo Clinic, and Charles Machine Works.

A.3.2   Value Proposition

ecenta has a unique place in the SAP Consulting Services Industry. Since 2000, they have been focusing on delivering value in the CRM Interaction Center space. ecenta executed the first Interaction Center WebClient Implementation at Tetra Pak in Sweden and since then has been a valued partner and advisor to SAP Product Development on the Best Practices in the industry for Interaction Centers. ecenta was named as the trusted advisor to Ericsson and Carl Zeiss in the SAP CRM and BI spaces. Some of their core values include:

▶ Providing premium consulting based on a strong understanding of the capabilities of SAP CRM

▶ Growing organically; no sub-contracting of work

▶ Aligning customer solution with core product development roadmap

▶ Always presenting Best Practices from SAP and from the Industry

▶ Continuing to participate in core product development and advise SAP on the best practices in the industry (ecenta has provided several features in the core SAP CRM product since 3.1, right up to CRM 2007). This allows ecenta to be ahead of the curve both in new features and functions of the new releases as well as the technology.

▶ Delivering projects on time and budget using PROPS Methodology (toll gate-based delivery model with strict milestones and acceptance criteria)

▶ Providing a one-stop shop for all services around CRM including related NetWeaver technologies like Business Intelligence, Business Objects frontend tools, Process Integration, Composite Environment (Adobe Forms, Visual Composer, etc.), SAP Portal, Duet, etc.

▶ Being a Trusted Advisor to help customers realize the benefits of a SAP CRM footprint

▶ Continuing to add to their portfolio of skills as demanded by their customers and the market

A.3.3 Core Areas of Expertise

Some of the many areas in which they have project expertise include:

▶ Interaction Center for Sales, Service, and Marketing (including IT Helpdesk, Financial Helpdesk, Employee Helpdesk and Utility Helpdesk)

▶ Business Communication Management — Multi-Channel Integration into the Interaction Center (Voice, Chat, E-mail, Fax, SMS, etc.)

▶ CTI Integration with third-party solutions like Avaya, Genesys and Cisco

▶ Core CRM Service Processes (In-House Repair, Complaints, Contracts, Service Orders, etc.)

▶ Core Marketing Processes (Campaigns, Marketing Calendar, Marketing Development Fund, TPM, etc.)

▶ Core Sales Process (Lead and Opportunity Management, Sales Planning and Forecasting, Quotations and Order Management, Variant Configuration and Pricing using IPC, etc.)

▶ SAP AFL (Asset Finance and Leasing)

- Case Management for Public Sector (Collections Management, Appeals, etc.)
- Partner Channel Management
- eCommerce (B2B and B2C for Sales and Service)
- Custom Development of unique functionality, which is closely aligned with SAP's product strategy and development guidelines

A.3.4 Core Industries

Some of the industries in which they have project experience include:

- High-tech
- Telecommunications
- Consumer products
- Public sector
- Financial services
- Software
- Manufacturing

A.4 enapsys

http://www.enapsys.com/

A.4.1 Company Overview

enapsys was created from the sum of the experience of its partners, who after more than eight years as SAP employees in Mexico and Argentina, decided to start a consulting company. The company is focused on providing SAP solutions implementation services with the highest quality and customer service standards. Through continuous investment in training and certifications, plus extensive project experience, their consulting force is the best prepared in SAP CRM in Mexico and one of the strongest in Latin America.

Customer Relationship Management

In the SAP CRM area, enapsys provides a broad range of services. These services span from a full CRM strategy and roadmap definition to a project implementation or just spot consulting. enapsys has broad experience in CRM project implementations, upgrades, and custom made solutions. Their SAP CRM service portfolio covers a wide range of modules, components, and industry scenarios. Additionally, enapsys offers custom made Web solutions based on the NetWeaver platform using tools such as BSP (Business Server Pages), WebDynpro, and JSP (Java Server Pages).

Business Intelligence

In the Business Intelligence area, enapsys offers a range of services from a full information analysis and reporting strategy to BW spot consulting. enapsys is also ramping up its dedicated Business Objects consulting team to cover all the information analysis and reporting needs.

A.4.2 Value Proposition

Their value proposition is built upon many aspects, each of them a key factor that enables us to assure a successful project execution or CRM strategy definition delivery. Aspects like their extensive experience and know-how, based on an adequate training and SAP certification program for their consulting force, enable them to be the reference for SAP CRM in the Mexican market and one of the key players in Latin America. Their solid experience in project management using ASAP and SAP PMM methodologies minimizes the inherent risks of any implementation process, allowing them to deliver on time and on budget. Theses core values and skills make enapsys the company of choice when implementing SAP solutions.

A.4.3 Core Industries

enapsys has an extensive experience in many industries and project types including:

- Financial services
- Logistics and transportation (railways)
- Chemicals

▸ Consumer products (paints and coatings)

▸ Pharmaceutical

▸ Manufacturing

▸ Retail

Some of their key customers include Volkswagen Bank México, Volkswagen Leasing México, Ferromex, Mexichem, Pochteca Materias Primas, Grupo Sayer, AstraZeneca México, Amanco México, El Palacio de Hierro, Liverpool.

In addition, enapsys has implemented the Interaction Center WebClient for two customers in the chemicals industry in Mexico: Mexichem and Pochteca Materias Primas.

A.5   EoZen

http://www.EoZen.com

A.5.1   Company Overview

EoZen is a leading European SAP consulting firm with a strong focus on customer satisfaction and innovation. With offices in the Benelux, France and Singapore, around 150 highly experienced consultants provide a unique blend of business and technology skills.

A.5.2   Value Proposition

Firmly established and recognized in the SAP community, EoZen has received many prestigious SAP awards. In particular, they are very proud on being awarded the prestigious "SAP Highest Customer Satisfaction" trophy, based on a comprehensive and independent customer satisfaction survey held with all SAP customers. They wish to thank their customers for the confidence in EoZen.

EoZen is Where Business Meets Technology

Technology is playing an ever increasing role in shaping the business world of today and tomorrow. More than ever, seamless integration of business and technology is a powerful asset that makes a difference. They have it deeply embedded in their solutions, their people, their know-how, their services, and their culture. It's what EoZen stands for.

EoZen is a Preferred Partner of SAP

EoZen firmly believes in technology as a foundation for business. With SAP, they have found a partner that shares this philosophy. Together, they want to be at the forefront to leverage the powerful combination of business and technology.

A.5.3 Core Areas of Expertise

EoZen has demonstrated a solid track record of success and profitability, consistently exceeding its annual objectives and serving leading companies in different industries both private and public. They service worldwide companies such as Glaverbel, Ashi Glass, Janssen Pharmaceutical, Philips, Carrefour, Bekaert, Inbev, and Coca-Cola. Their mission is to help their customers make effective use of (SAP) information technology to turn business opportunities into tangible results.

A.6   Genesys

http://www.genesyslab.com

A.6.1   Company Overview

Genesys Telecommunications Laboratories, an Alcatel-Lucent company headquartered in San Francisco, is a market leader in the contact center infrastructure industry. Focusing exclusively on contact center software, Genesys delivers provides award-winning contact center products geared toward medium to large businesses — and contact centers of all sizes.

A.6.2   Core Areas of Expertise

Genesys products, such as the Genesys Gplus Adapter for SAP, support most major telephone switch vendors in the world. Genesys also provides extremely high scalability, with up to 50,000 users running on the same system in some cases. Together, Genesys and SAP have dozens of joint customers running the SAP CRM Interaction Center with Genesys integration.

A.7 MindTree

http://www.MindTree.com/

A.7.1 Company Overview

Founded in 1999 by 10 industry professionals who came from Cambridge Technology Partners, Lucent Technologies and Wipro, MindTree Consulting is an international IT consulting company that delivers business and technology solutions through global software development. Co-headquartered in Somerset, New Jersey, and Bangalore, India, the company's seasoned management team and employees skilled in technology, business analysis, and project management approach technology initiatives in a business context. MindTree develops applications to help companies enhance their enterprise operations. The company also delivers product-development services and designs reusable building blocks for high-tech companies.

A.7.2 Value Proposition

At MindTree, they have forged a distinct business culture called "OneShore." It describes how they serve their clients and how they view their company. Oneshore™ represents their method for global development that achieves a balance of quality, cost savings, and localization. For every client, they build a unified team of software engineers and business consultants who collaborate from start to finish on all stages of a project. They do not have separate camps of frontend and backend specialists, and projects are always managed wherever their clients are located.

A.7.3 Core Areas of Expertise

The SAP Practice is one of MindTree's fastest growing practices. They have global expertise in addressing business issues using SAP solutions. MindTree's highly experienced SAP consultants and unique work environment allow delivery of SAP solutions with unmatched speed and quality. They have experience in executing large SAP engagements for global companies. They have a consistent track record of being on time and within budget on implementations and rollouts. They are an SAP Global Services Partner, SAP Global Technology Partner, and a development partner.

MindTree provides services in Financials and Human Capital Management/ HRMS, Logistics and operations, Supply Chain Management (SCM)/APO, Supplier Relationship Management (SRM), Customer Relationship Management (CRM), SAP NetWeaver - Enterprise Portal (EP), Exchange Infrastructure (XI), Mobile Infrastructure (MI), Business Intelligence (BIW), Master Data Management (MDM), Enterprise Service Architecture (eSOA).

IT Services

MindTree Consulting designs, develops, and maintains enterprise solutions, using a world-class methodology, for business-to-business and business-to-consumer applications. These applications are built to leverage emerging and classic communication channels. They offer services that range from defining business needs to building solutions using best-of-breed tools and technologies to maintaining applications.

The areas in which they offer services are:

- E-Business
- Supply Chain Management
- Data Warehousing/Business Intelligence
- Enterprise Application Integration (EAI)
- Enterprise Resource Planning (ERP)
- Web Services
- iSeries and Mainframe
- Testing Practice
- Product Engineering
- Infrastructure Management

R&D Services

MindTree offers R&D services to a wide range of industries with their extensive experience and knowledge in diverse domains. MindTree adds functionality and helps companies bring products to market faster, through product engineering expertise and reusable building blocks, known as MindTree Incubated New Technologies (MINTs). Specific focus areas include:

- VLSI/IC design

- Board design

- Embedded software development

- Datacom protocol development

- Element management and network management solutions

- Turnkey electronic product design

- Application development

- Testing and product Assurance

- Continuous engineering and support

- Technical support

A.7.4   Core Industries

MindTree offers the above-mentioned services with a strong focus on the following industries:

- Capital markets

- Insurance

- Manufacturing

- Retail

- Travel and transportation

MindTree's R&D services cater to the needs of the following industries:

- Automotive

- Communication systems

- Consumer appliances and computer peripherals

- Industrial system

- Storage and computing system

B   The Author

 **John Burton** (Palo Alto, CA) is currently the Director of Product Management at SAP Labs with global responsibility for the Interaction Center product. He has been involved with the SAP CRM Interaction Center since 1999. John served as the technical editor of the book, "Discover SAP CRM," published by Galileo Press in 2008. John has also published numerous articles for CRM Expert, and has presented at dozens of conferences and events for organizations such as ASUG, SAPPHIRE, SAP CRM Insider, and Silicon Valley Product Management Association (SVPMA). John is also an active blogger on the SAP CRM Business Process Expert (BPX) Community Website. Prior to joining SAP in 1999, John was a faculty member at Central Michigan University, teaching undergraduate courses in SAP and business software. John holds a B.A. degree from the University of Michigan, Ann Arbor and an MBA (concentration in Management Information Systems) from Central Michigan University. When he is not writing about CRM, John enjoys reading and writing poetry, ultra-marathon running, and martial arts.

Index

A

Accenture, 371, 382
Account Assignment, 281
Account ID
  Profile, 188
Account Identification
  Account ID, 186
  Account Name, 186
Account Indicator, 205
Accounting Interaction Center (AIC), 339, 351, 352, 353, 434
Account Product ID, 159
Action Box, 171
Active X, 82
Activity Clipboard, 172, 293, 391
Address Validation, 188, 431
Advanced Planning and Optimization (APO), 168
Agent dashboard, 92
Agent Inbox, 181, 213, 342, 409, 418, 427, 433, 434
Agents, 221
  Definition of, 24
Agent Signature, 244, 245, 432
Agent work mode, 59
Alert, 53, 250, 391, 407
Alert Editor → see Alert Modeler, 250, 320
Alert Editor, 222, 250, 251, 320
Alert Modeler → see Alert Editor, 250
Alert Modeler, 250, 320
Analytics, 221
Apple Safari, 386, 387
Appointments, 205
Aspect, 395
Asset Management Company (AMC), 414
Asset Management System, 346
Assign Work Center, 101
Attribute, 297
Authorization Group, 273
Auto Complete, 332, 342
Auto Dialing, 133

Automated Call Distributor (ACD), 50, 26, 395
Automated Dialer, 27
  Predictive dialing, 27, 45
  Preview dialing, 27, 45
  Progressive dialing, 45
  Progressive/power dialing, 27
Automated Dialing, 45
Automatic Number Identification (ANI), 52, 53, 55, 57, 396, 441
  ANI lookup, 52
Automotive Interaction Center, 361, 362
Auto Search, 193
Auto Suggest Solution, 331, 410
Available-to-Promise (ATP), 166, 168, 180
Avaya, 50, 58, 374, 395, 439
  CRM Connector, 440, 441
  ExpertNet, 441
  Global Services, 440
  Interaction Center, 375
Avaya Enablement Services (AES), 440
Avaya Interaction Center (AIC), 440
Average Lead Time, 255
Axon, 371, 379, 442

B

BearingPoint, 371, 382
Billing, 402
Billing Dispute, 360
Blended Analytics, 259
  Live Interactions (CTI), 259
Blue Pumpkin, 400
BOL, 389
BOL/GenIL, 109
Breadcrumb, 92
Broadcast Message, 407
Broadcast Messaging, 43, 93, 222, 240
  Distribution List, 240
  Server, 386
BSP, 110
BSP Component Workbench, 196

Business Add-In (BAdI), 96
Business Address Service (BAS), 53
Business Agreement, 359
  Search By, 193
Business Communication Management (BCM),
51, 69, 444
Business Communications Interface (BCI), 308
Business Data Display (BDD), 96
Business Object Layer (BOL), 108
Business Objects, 259
Business Process Outsourcing (BPO), 33, 368,
399
Business Role, 282
Business Role Assignment, 239
Business Rules Engines (BRE), 295
Business Rules Management (BRM), 295
Business Server Pages (BSP), 388, 446
Business Transaction, 328
Business Transaction Assignment (BTA), 224,
233

C

Call-Attached Data (CAD), 55, 57, 396, 432
Call Center
  Definition of, 22
Caller Line Identification (CLID), 52
Calling Line Identification (CLI), 52
Call List, 45, 120, 121, 123, 241
  Creation, 121
  Exporting, 124
  Generate, 125
  Generation, 241, 242
  Maintenance, 122, 124, 278, 392
  Merging, 124
  Rescheduling, 128
  Splitting, 124
Call Recording, 401
Call Treatment, 26, 50, 51
Campaign → see Marketing Campaign, 163
Campaign, 45, 116
Campaign Attributes, 118
Campaign Determination, 120
CapGemini, 371, 382
Case, 403
Case Management, 216

Catalog Profile, 162
Categorization Schema, 243, 326, 328
  Interaction Center Automation, 331
Category Modeler, 210, 212, 222, 243, 295,
304, 311, 324, 326, 327, 328, 333, 427
Cathode-ray tube, 83
CCSUI, 397
Certification, 369
Change Management, 344
  Process, 345
Chat, 60, 397
Chat Editor, 433
Chat Integration, 292
CIC, 44
CIC0 transaction code, 40
Cisco, 395, 417
Client Switching, 399
Cognizant, 371
Communication Management Software
(CMS), 59, 227, 258, 373
Communications Enabled Business Processes
(CEBP), 434
Communication Toolbar, 57, 86, 112, 432
Complaint, 403
Complaint Management, 212
Component, 111
  Runtime Repository, 111
  Window, 111
Computer Telephony Integration (CTI), 50,
52, 57
  Outbound Dialing, 132
Configurable Product, 176
Configurable Toolbar, 434
Configuration Management Database (CMDB),
345
Consumer Help Desk, 184
Consumer Packaged Goods (CPG), 379
Consumer Product Goods (CPG) → see
Consumer Products, 153
Consumer Products, 153
Consumption, 357
Contact Center
  Definition of, 23
Contact Center Infrastructure, 373
Contact Center Simulator User Interface
(CCSUI), 397
Contact Person, 194

Context Area, 53, 112, 433
  Account info, 84
  Alert, 85
  Communication Info, 85
Contract Determination, 431
Contracts, 193
Creating Scripts, 270
Credit Management → see SAP Credit
Management, 359
CRM 7.0, 433
CRM 2005, 388
CRM Business Role, 98, 99, 391
CRM Employee Interaction Center, 401
CRM Interactive Reports → see OLTP Reports,
256
CRM Interactive Reports, 254
CRM Opportunity, 434
CRM Survey Tool, 137
CRM Web Application Server, 82
CRM WebClient, 81, 173
  Sales Order, 175
  Upgrade, 111
  User interface, 43
Cross-Sellers, 116, 145
Cross-sell revenue, 29
CTI, 38, 395, 426
  Adapter, 373
CTI Integration, 444
Current Event, 317
Custom Development Project (CDP), 172
Customer Identification, 186
Customer Interaction Center (CIC), 40
Customer Lifetime Value (CLV), 30, 116
Customer Listing, 179
Customer save/Retention rate, 30
Customer Segment, 115
Customer Service Representatives (CSRs), 24
Cycos, 395

D

Dashboard, 259
Define Categorization Profiles, 328, 332
Define Object Profile, 192
Deloitte, 371, 382
Deregulated Market, 355

  Customer, 355
  Subscriber, 355
Design Layer, 391
Dialed Number Identification Service (DNIS),
53, 54, 56, 57
Direct Store Delivery, 125
Dispatching, 312
Distributor
  Automotive, 362
Document Templates, 244
Do-Not-Call List, 129, 410
  Fine, 129
Do Not Contact → see Do Not Call (DNC), 410
Down-Sellers, 145
Dual Tone Multi Frequency (DTMF), 432
Dual-Tone Multi-Frequency (DTMF), 54
Duplicate
  Checking, 188
  Records, 186

E

ECC 5.0, 406
ECC 6.0, 406, 407
ecenta, 371, 378, 379, 417, 419, 443
Eclipse Aviation, 420
eCommerce, 445
Email, 60, 397
E-Mail Editor, 204, 304
E-Mail Reports, 258
E-Mail Response Management System
(ERMS), 63, 224, 229, 281, 295, 296, 299,
313, 342, 402, 409, 414, 426
  Actions, 301
  Auto Acknowledgement, 300
  Auto Prepare, 303, 333
  Auto Respond, 301
  Business Rules, 231
  Category Schema, 302
  Factbase, 235
  Push, 310, 435
  Service Ticket Tracking ID, 307, 308
  Simulator, 236, 237
E-Mail Status Overview, 229, 230, 239
Email Template, 432
Email Threading, 305

E-Mail Volume, 229, 231
E-Mail Workbench, 234
Employee Interaction Center (EIC), 339, 347, 439
   Benefits, 351
   HR, 349
enapsys, 381, 445
Endorsed Business Solution (EBS), 370
Enterprise Portal (EP), 44
EoZen, 371, 381, 447
Erlang C, 32
ERP Sales Order, 173
Escalation, 312
Exclude Terms, 202
Extranets, 387

F

Fact Sheet, 431
   Configuration, 195
Fax, 60, 397, 409
Fax Integration, 432
Financial Customer Care (FCC), 360
Firewall, 387, 388
First Contact Resolution (FCR), 29
Front-Office, 337, 357
Fujitsu, 371, 382

G

Generate Business Transaction, 122, 123, 241, 277
Genesys, 58, 395, 448
   Gplus Adapter, 374, 448
Genesys Telecommunications Laboratories, 374
GenIL, 389
Global Trade Identification Number (GTIN), 158
Google, 202

H

Hardphone, 86
HCM, 401
Help Desk, 184
   Information, 184
High-Speed Business Partner Search, 186
High-volume, 393
Home-based agents, 35
HP Services, 382
HR Organizational Model, 107
Human Resources, 337

I

IBase, 431
IBM, 371, 382
IC Event, 282
   BPConfirmed, 283
   CurrentEvent, 283
ICI, 64, 397, 432
   External Dailers, 132
IC Keyboard Shortcuts, 89
IC Management, 221
IC Manager, 221
   Dashboard, 222, 226, 228, 439
   Standard Report, 254
IC Sales, 153
IC Sales Order, 166, 167, 173, 175, 180
   Pricing, 167
IC Sales Ticket, 168, 169, 175, 180
IC Sales Transactions, 166
IC Service Ticket, 208
IC WebClient, 41, 389
   Upgrade, 111
IC WinClient, 41, 42, 43, 44, 81, 389, 394, 397, 410, 421
Identification Account
   Transaction ID, 186
Identify Account, 191, 194
Implementation Guide (IMG), 196
Incident Management, 342
Index-Based Business Partner Search, 186
Individual Object (IObject), 190

Information Technology Infrastructure Library
(ITIL), 339, 398, 434, 435
  Certification, 398
  Configuration Item (CI), 346
  Incident, 342
  Known Errors, 344
  Problem, 343
Information Technology (IT), 337
  Asset Management (ITAM), 345
  Help Desk, 339
  Service Desk, 341
Installed Base (IBase), 190
Insurance Interaction Center, 361
Integrated Communication Interface, 227
Intent-Driven Interaction, 259, 281, 282, 295,
315, 324, 433
Intent-Driven Interaction (IDI), 315
  Launch Scripts, 320
  Navigate To, 323
  Navigation, 321
  Setting Up, 315
  Terminate Alert, 319
  Trigger Alert, 319
Interaction Center
  Agents, 24
  Architecture, 108
  Call List, 126
  Context Area, 84
  Definition of, 23
  Leads, 140
  Title Bar, 84
  User Interface, 81
  Workforce Management, 410
Interaction History, 181
Interaction Record, 81, 94, 95, 119, 122, 205,
212, 404, 410
  Activity Clipboard, 95, 96, 203
  Business transaction, 112
  Suppression, 404
Interactive Intelligent Agent (IIA), 200
Interactive Script, 45, 116, 252, 263, 275, 285
  Answer, 286
  Chapters, 272
  Customer Data, 288
  Question, 286
  Script ID Requirements, 272
  Starting Node, 272
  Validity Dates, 272

Interactive Script Editor, 222, 264, 265, 275,
287, 387
  Navigator, 267
  Properties, 269
  Script Repository, 266
  Search, 267
Interactive Scripting, 135, 391
  Download and Upload of Scripts, 275
  Evaluation, 252
  Upgrading to CRM 2006s/CRM 2007, 264
Interactive Voice Response (IVR), 50, 51, 53,
55, 57, 432
  IVR data, 57
Internet Communication Manager (ICM), 308
Internet Explorer, 389
Internet Pricing and Configurator (IPC), 168
Internet Protocol (IP), 375
Internet Sales, 172, 176
Internet Transaction Server (ITS), 171, 241,
392, 406
IObject, 431
IS01, 392
  Transaction Code, 198
iServiceGlobe, 380
IS-U, 355, 357
Item Detail, 205

J

Java 2 Enterprise Edition (J2EE), 42, 386
  Components, 386
  Server, 43
Java Applet, 42, 265, 387
JavaScript, 408
Java Server Page, 388

K

Knack, 371
Knowledge Administrator, 246
Knowledge Management, 242, 305
Knowledge Search, 197, 202, 211, 344
Known Error, 343

L

Launch transaction, 104
Lead, 155, 290
Lead Distribution, 281, 296
Lead Integration → see Lead Qualification, 138
Lead Integration, 136, 138
Lead Qualification, 138, 139, 290
Letter, 60
Letter Integration, 432
Live Interaction Report, 257
L-shape, 83

M

Mail Form, 244, 391
Mailform Template, 222
Managing Operations, 233
Manual Outbound Dialing, 116
Mapping, 323
Marketing, 115
Marketing Attributes, 284, 288
Marketing-Based Product Proposals
    Up-selling, 143
Marketing Bounce Management, 296
Marketing Campaign, 115, 163
Marketing Plan, 115
Marketing Product, 179
Marketing Product Proposals, 116
Marketing Professional, 195
Marketing Questionnaires → see Survey Integration, 136
Marketing Questionnaires, 136
    Integration, 137
Marketing Survey → see Questionnaire, 289
Microsoft Internet Explorer 7.0, 386, 409
Microsoft Windows
    ActiveX, 387
    Vista, 386
MindTree, 371, 380, 414, 449
Mobile Sales, 172
Monitoring Operations, 224
Mozilla Firefox 2.0, 386, 387, 389
Multi-Channel Integration, 50

Multi-Level Categorization, 408
Multiple Chat, 432

N

Navigational link, 106
Navigation bar, 89, 100, 112, 391
    Configuration, 101
    Profile, 101, 105
New Account, 187
Nortel, 395

O

Object Component, 193
Objection Script, 273, 287
Office of Government Commerce (OGC), 339
OLTP Reports, 256
Oneshore, 449
Open Service Ticket, 255
    History, 255
Operations
    Offshore, 339
Operator, 297
Opportunity
    CRM WebClient, 156
Opportunity Distribution, 281
Order History, 179
Order Management
    End-to-end Process, 154
Order Routing, 250, 295, 312, 313, 314
Original Equipment Manufacturers (OEMs)
    Automotive, 361
Outbound Dialing, 60, 116, 131
    Automated, 116
    Manual, 116
    Marketing Campaigns, 132
    Outbound dialer, 60
    Predictive dialing, 60
    Progressive dialing, 60
    Recordings, 132
Outbound Plug Mapping, 101, 323
Outsourcing, 21, 33, 34, 339

P

Parameter, 297
People-centric User Interface (PC-UI), 44, 390, 391
Performance Benchmark Test, 394
Personalized Products, 176
PFCG Role, 99
Pink Elephant, 398
Planned Activities, 120, 121, 124
  Agent Inbox, 125
Planned End Date, 164
Postal Letter, 397
Post Processing Framework (PPF)
  PPF Actions, 207, 218
Power Dialing, 134
PPOMA_CRM, 425
PPOMW, 425
Predictive Dialers, 134
Predictive Dialing, 134
Preview Dialing, 133
Pricing, 168, 180
Private Branch Exchange (PBX), 52, 395
Problem Management, 343
Problem Type, 203
Process Modeling, 250
Product Catalog, 157, 161
  Product Search, 161
Product ID, 205
Product Identification, 189
Product List Preview, 165
Product Modeling Environment, 177
Product Proposals, 142, 148, 172, 178
  Method Schema, 146
Product Search, 157, 158, 161
Product Service Letter (PSL), 207, 322
Product Workbench, 143
Progressive Dialing, 134
Prospect, 187
PT PRO, 421, 426, 427
PT SI, 422

Q

Quality Monitoring, 399
Quality Notification, 213

Questionnaire, 289
Questra, 370
Queue, 50
Queuing, 50, 51
Quotation, 434

R

R/3 Customer Interaction Center, 81
Real-Time Offer Management (RTOM), 179
Reference Object Hierarchy, 207
Reporting Framework, 187
Repository, 297
Request for Change (RFC), 340, 344
Research In Motion (RIM), 343
Retention Offer, 116
Return Material Authorization (RMA), 213, 215
Revenue Collection, 357
Reverse Proxy Servers, 387
Route E-Mail, 304
Routing, 51
  Skill-based routing, 51
Routing Action, 304
Rule Condition, 297
Rule Modeler, 155, 211, 222, 251, 252, 259, 295, 296, 314, 320, 326, 342, 427, 433, 434
  Action, 297
  Context, 298
  Policy, 296
  Rule, 296
  Value, 297
  Service Manager Profiles, 298
Runtime repository, 110

S

SAF Compilation Administration, 201
Sales Contract, 434
Sales Order, 194, 405
  Add to Cart, 165
  R/3, 406
Sales Revenue, 183
Sales Ticket, 405
SAP Polling, 434

SAP Alliance Partner, 372
SAP Business Communication Services (BCS), 308
SAP Business Communication Management (BCM) → see Wicom, 375
SAP Business Communications Management (BCM), 51, 55, 57, 375, 395, 400, 432, 435
SAP BW → see SAP NetWeaver BI, 232, 252, 253
SAPconnect, 308
   Interface, 310
SAP Consulting, 382
SAP Credit Management, 359
SAP Customer Relationship Management, 435
SAP Global Partner, 372
SAP GUI Transports Organizer, 274
SAP NetWeaver BI, 232, 252, 253, 417
SAPoffice, 409
SAP_ORDERROUTING, 314
SAP Partner Edge, 368
SAP People-Centric User Interface, 170
SAPphone, 397
   External Dialers, 132
SAPphone Telephony, 439
SAP Real-Time Offer Management (RTOM), 116, 149, 432
SAP Service Partner, 371, 378
SAP Software Agent Framework (SAF), 197
SAP Solution Database (SDB), 197, 198, 199, 249
   Detailed Feedback, 246, 248
   Usage Report, 248
Save/Retention rate, 29
Scratchpad, 59
Scratch Pad, 87
Screen pop, 52, 55
Script, 433
   Automatically Launching, 277
   Business Rule, 280
   Call List, 277
   IC Event, 279
   Manual Selection, 276
   Process Flow, 269
   Transferring, 292
Search and Classification, 197
Self Service, 219
Service Confirmations, 210

Service Contract, 340, 434
   Renewal, 289
Service Cost, 183
Service Desk, 184
Service Industry, 386, 397
Service Interaction Center (SIC), 41
Service Level, 340
Service Level Agreement (SLA), 340, 402, 424
Service Manager Profile, 297, 309
Service Order, 207, 403
   Valuation Type, 205
Service Parts, 143
Service Quotation, 434
Service Ticket, 332, 341, 403, 424, 426
   Reports, 255
   Tracking ID, 244
Session Initiation Protocol (SIP), 35
SetType, 192
Shared Service Center, 337, 338, 339
   Benefits, 338
Shared Services, 421
   Shared Service Center, 32
Shore Message Service (SMS), 60, 399, 409
Skill-based routing, 51
SLA, 423, 424
Sloan Valve Company, 416
SM59, 395
SO28
   Transaction Code, 308
Softphone, 52, 57, 86
Software Agent Framework → see Interactive Intelligent Agent (IIA), 200
Software Agent Framework (SAF), 43, 200, 248, 386, 408
Sold-to-Party, 187, 192
Solution Database, 344
Solution Manager, 398
Sparta, 371, 380
Spell-Check
   Integration, 388
Spell-Checker, 409
SRVO
   Transaction Type, 207
Subject Profile, 328
Sun Java Runtime Engine, 82
Sun Java Runtime Environment (JRE), 265, 387

Supervisors, 221
Survey Integration, 136
Survey Suite, 289
System Message, 85, 88, 407
System Performance, 394

T

Tata Consultancy Services (TCS), 382
Team Leaders, 221
Telco → see Telecommunications, 338, 355
Telco, 338, 355, 358, 445
Telco Interaction Center, 358
Telecommunications, 338, 355
Telemarketing, 184
Telematics, 363
Telephone Sales Representatives (TSRs), 24
Telephony, 50, 397
Tensegrity Software, 265
Thank You, 436
The Principal Consulting (TPC), 371, 379
Thin-client, 82
Ticket Dispatching, 312
Time Recording, 209, 210
Top N List, 178
Transaction Launcher, 103, 171, 390, 406
Transporting Categories, 330
Transporting Script, 274
TREX, 187, 200, 334
Trigger Alert, 433
Trigger Script, 284
TSRV, 209, 297, 301
TSVO, 297, 301
  Transaction Type, 207

U

UI Configuration Tool, 110, 169, 329, 391, 420, 421
UI Control, 111
Up-Sell, 116, 145
User Interface, 83
Utilities, 354, 355

V

VA01, 406
Vehicle
  Search By, 193
Vehicle identification number (VIN), 362
Vendavo, 370
Verint Systems, 377, 400
  Blue Pumpkin, 378
  Impact 360, 378
  Impact 360 Express, 378
  Witness Systems, 378
Vertical industry, 337
Virtual Private Network (VPN), 388
Voice over IP (VoIP) → see Internet Protocol (IP), 375
Voice portal, 55
Voice Response Unit (VRU), 54, 55, 57
VoIP, 35
VPN, 387

W

Web Channel E-Commerce, 176
WebDynpro, 388, 446
Web Form, 311
Wicom, 375
Wipro Ltd, 382
Work at Home Mothers (WAHMs), 36
Workforce Management (WFM), 32, 222, 368, 376, 377, 399
Workforce Optimization (WFO), 222, 368, 376, 377, 399
  Verint Systems, 378
Workspace, 112
Wrap-Up List, 324

X

Xcelsius, 260
XML, 396
XSLT, 396

Interested in reading more?

Please visit our Web site for all
new book releases from SAP PRESS.

www.sap-press.com